Early Alaska Aviator Harold Gillam, Sr.
Lucky or Legend?

BUSH PILOT

Arnold Griese

foreword by George Clayton

Since 1978

PO Box 221974 Anchorage, Alaska 99522-1974

ISBN 1-59433-026-3

Library of Congress Catalog Card Number: 2005928763

Copyright 2005 by Arnold Griese
—First Edition—

Manufactured in the United States of America.

Dedication

To the memory of:

Robert W. Stevens (May 22, 1918—July 23, 2003)

Bud Saltenrich (February 15, 1915—November 8, 1999)

Both dedicated their lives to Alaska's aviation.

ACKNOWLEDGMENTS

Making this biography both factual and interesting involved the expertise of many. More than that, it involved a genuine willingness to give of their time and effort. Also, in a very real sense, they gave more than could be expected.

There comes easily to mind Randy Acord who gave not only of his own knowledge but also made available the resources of the Alaskaland Pioneer Museum. Then the University of Alaska Fairbanks Archives; there Caroline and Rose, among others, never seemed to tire in their efforts to teach the author how to enter into the rich resources to be found there. Ron Inouye came to be an unexpected source of facts about Gillam. Ted Spenser, former head of the Alaska Aviation Heritage Museum, made the resources of that organization available. Robert Stevens' two volumes on Alaska aviation history provided essential facts while the author went out of his way to answer and fill in missing detail. Jean Potter in her, *The Flying North*, provided anecdotes gleaned from personal interviews with people alive and involved in Alaska aviation during Gillam's time. Then there were those individuals who had actual contact with Gillam. Through personal interviews, the author obtained insights into Gillam as a person and as a pilot. These included Bud Seltenreich, Robert Gleason, Bill Loftholm, Ray Peterson, Jess Bachner, Harold Starkey, Alaska Linck, Tim Eakstrom, Bob Hanson, Adena Knutson, Vernice Reid, James (Hutch) Hutchinson, Lillian Crosson, Lucy Brenwick, and the Gillam Children—Harold Jr, Don, Maurine and Winona. And for those who were inadvertently left out, a sincere thank you.

And special thanks to Jeri Croucher and Val Scullion, for bringing the pages and ideas of this book together.

Contents

Dedication 3
Foreword 6
Chapter 1 ..... WHEN IS A LIFE A LEGEND ? 8
Chapter 2 ..... A QUEST BEGINS 12
Chapter 3 ..... A WIDER WORLD 16
Chapter 4 ..... ALASKA 21
Chapter 5 ..... BEING HIS OWN BOSS 36
Chapter 6 ..... THE LAST CHANGE 50
Chapter 7 ..... AVIATION IN THE WESTERN WORLD; 57
Chapter 8 ..... A BEGINNING 67
Chapter 9 ..... WHEN THE GOING GETS TOUGH 75
Chapter 10 ... CHANGES 85
Chapter 11 ... THE CONTRACT 97
Chapter 12 ... THE SEARCH 112
Chapter 13 ... MOUNTAINS, GLACIERS AND WEATHER 133
Chapter 14 ... MEETING CHALLENGES 157
Chapter 15 ... CHANGES 170
Chapter 16 ... HOME AND FAMILY 190
Chapter 17 ... NEW PLACE, NEW START 213
Chapter 18 ... A SPECIAL CHALLENGE 224
Chapter 19 ... FLIGHT INTO THE ARCTIC NIGHT 235
Chapter 20 ... THE NEXT STEP 252
Chapter 21 ... FINAL FLIGHT 269
Chapter 22 ... THE RESCUE 282
Chapter 23 ... LEGEND OR LUCKY? 299
Chapter 24 ... AN UNFINISHED ENDING 323
Index 341

Foreword
by George C. Clayton

*Retired from Wein Air Alaska after 30 years,
and after 24,600 hours in airplane cockpits.*

I have never written a foreword before, so please forgive my taking the liberty to stray from conventional protocol.

Charles Harold Gillam was born in Kankakee, Illinois in 1903, the year the Wright brothers made the first successful heavier than air flight. Could it be possible the Gillam legend had its start on this truly remarkable day in aviation history?

When Arnold Griese asked me to prepare a foreword for this most interesting biography of Harold Gillam Senior's life and times, I was at first hesitant. I really didn't feel sufficiently qualified to recommend a book that dealt with this complicated airman's abilities, skills, and dreams. I had never met Gillam, but after giving the author's request considerable thought, I asked myself; who in my generation, a pilot who had followed Gillam's career closely and had actually flown Gillam's Kuskokwim mail run, who would be more qualified than myself? It is my hope that by accepting this request, I can bring into focus yet another ray of light on the life of pilot Harold Gillam.

During my efforts to prepare this foreword I have relived the Gillam years in my mind many times. I have made long distance calls and talked at length with former pilots that flew during Gillam's career. For the most part we were in agreement that Gillam was indeed a legend, one not easily diminished by the passage of time. We were also in agreement that Gillam was a gambler that played for very high stakes.

For 10 years Gillam had won every bet against the grim reaper. For all of those years he had never had an engine failure, but on January 5, 1943 he lost the highest bet of his life. I truly wish I could have "cut his deck" on that fateful day. Then, perhaps he might have lived to see his dream of safe, worldwide transportation by air come true.

All of this sad story is ancient history, now the author's research has uncovered in great detail the crash, search, and rescue of the survivors of this terribly tragic ordeal. I wish to extend my thanks to the author for his research and to all those who helped in the collection of more than 350 pages of hair-raising, heart-wrenching, and tearful misadventures contained within these pages.

I am sincere in my prediction that all who read this biography will be brought to a climax of emotions not easily explained. Once readers have started this book it will command their fascination and will compel them to absorb all it its contents from cover to cover. Then, and only then, can the reader come to an accurate assessment of this remarkable, caring, but often misunderstood man.

One final question confronts us all. Did the legend Gillam created perish with him on his final flight or does it live on somewhere out there in the twilight zone? I prefer to believe it lives in the hearts of all who loved him then and still love him dearly today.

In conclusion, let me convey my best wishes to Arnold Griese, and to all who will treasure this wonderful biography of Harold Gillam Sr.

George C Clayton

Chapter 1
WHEN IS A LIFE A LEGEND ?
The love of Flying is the love of beauty.
(Amelia Earhart)

The focus of this biography is a man. This man, Harold Gillam Sr., has in the eyes of some, both young and old, become a legend. Webster defines *legend* as "a story coming down from the past; especially one popularly regarded as historical (true) although not verifiable." A related definition states, "a person or something that inspires such stories." Robin Hood, grounded in the history of England, comes quickly to mind and satisfies both definitions. What about Gillam?

Although now dead, he is a part of history. Many feel that by his courage, his daring, and his exceptional skill, especially in flying safely through extreme weather, he has made himself a legend. Much has been written over the years since his untimely death to support this claim. Are these written accounts true? Can they be verified?

Gillam's Final Career? (Morrison - Knudsen Photo Courtesy of Pioneer Air Museum Fairbanks, Alaska)

Certainly with the information-gathering technology available in today's world, legends can and should be verified to a greater extent than was possible during the era when Robin Hood stories came into being.

In this regard, though, information gathering has it limits. Yes, it can effectively uncover recorded facts. However, a biography that presents only facts would be boring and would probably leave out what makes the subject an interesting human being. In most instances it would leave out the *why* behind actions and behind words both spoken and written.

Yet biography is not fiction; it is not a story. Thus the author's task is to first examine the subject's life for important actions, statements, even thoughts and then make reasonable interpretations of this information (*interpretations* being defined by Webster as explanations). An author of biography should make every effort to report the details as accurately as possible and to separate such detail from the author's interpretations. Important also is a check for consistency between and among different information sources.

Biographers face yet another problem. Their subjects are usually exceptional people who fulfill their potential by achieving exceptionally. That is, they perform exceptionally in what they set out to do. They are also admired, and not only admired but "talked about." Most people would agree we don't often talk about ordinary people who do ordinary things.

For some reason there is in most of us a tendency to exaggerate when we share an unusual happening. In other words, when we are telling something we become the center of attention and shift into a storytelling mode. This, in turn, justifies our exaggerations.

This happened when Harold Gillam Sr.'s life was researched. The incidents reported, for the most part, did happen. These incidents, however, when first encountered, were often submerged in words that distorted or exaggerated. This was usually done to create a dramatic effect which would better hold the reader's or listener's attention.

Newspapers, an important source because many of Gillam's activities were newsworthy, tended to discourage exaggeration or distortions. On the other hand, because of their interest in getting out news while it was still news, newspapers were sometimes guilty of reporting facts inaccurately.

In any case, exaggeration or distortion tended to create an image of Gillam that made him appear larger than life. Such storytelling, when blended with accurate detail, can easily lead to unjustified legend building.

The subject of a biography has presumably achieved prominence through his or her own competence. To include distortion or exaggeration may well destroy credibility in the minds of readers. To lose reader credibility may, in turn, deny legendary status to one who has rightfully earned it.

Reporting on the life of Gillam was especially difficult because he left no journal and but one letter to his father and one formal report which he was required to write on the Eielson-Borland search in the Siberian Arctic. Although his belongings were carefully packed and stored after his death, they were later tragically and accidentally destroyed. These would surely have contained information helpful to a biographer. Also, one cannot help but feel that had he taken time to do more writing, the Gillam legend might have blossomed more fully. Perhaps not. Action is the stuff of legends, not writing.

He also left little in the way of conversations pertaining to his views, not even views relating to aviation. This lack of everyday sharing with fellow pilots was best explained by Frank Barr, a well-known Alaska pilot who once flew for Gillam. He stated in Dermot Cole's biography of Barr:

> When bush pilots were weathered in at some remote roadhouse, sitting around a woodstove, each with a drink in his hand, they were prone to talk shop, recounting frightening or funny things that had happened in the air. Gillam, however, never was one for this type of hangar talk. At these times Harold would sit slightly in the background, grin at some of the humorous remarks, and once in a while interject one of his own, but never offer information about his experiences.

Barr's statement makes clear why pilots who knew him, knew little about his opinions and views. Nevertheless, his statement does suggest that Gillam felt comfortable in the company of fellow pilots.

One single and important source with whom Gillam did tend to open up and share his thoughts, opinions, and feelings was his life-long friend, Cecil Higgins. They became close friends during their growing-up years and kept up that friendship until Gillam's death. In both interviews and writings Higgins shared what he felt were some of Gillam's thoughts, motivations, and feelings.

Although Gillam talked and wrote little about himself, he was at the same time a talked—and written—about individual. This unusual situation gave rise to a body of information about him which, to a considerable extent, has been personalized and at times embellished.

Obviously the task of providing a firmer factual foundation for these highly personalized oral and written statements was a difficult one. Therefore the results, as set forth in this biography, certainly have their weaknesses. Nevertheless, this work is a genuine attempt to help the reader make a more reasoned interpretation of whether Harold Gillam Sr. deserves to be seen as a legendary figure.

This biography also has a broader purpose. Besides sharing with the reader the life of an unusual man, it also attempts to share the lives, places, and times in which this man lived and flew.

The main focus of place and time was the Territory of Alaska between June 1, 1923 and January 14, 1943. This time period allows comments on the beginning of Alaska aviation. It was an interesting period in which much was ventured by such pilots as Ben Eielson, Noel Wien, Joe Crosson, Harold Gillam and others. Much was gained that benefitted every individual living in that cold, forbidding Territory. Some of those who ventured paid with their lives, including Gillam.

Finally, this story of Gillam's life—that part where he played a significant role in the development of aviation in Alaska—cannot be told without reference to the growth of aviation in the Lower-48 states and the Western world. This broader portrayal of aviation may be a refresher to some and new to others. The hope is always to engage you, the reader, in the ever changing field of aviation and to touch on the lives of those men and women who dedicated themselves to helping it build a richer, better world.

Chapter 2
A QUEST BEGINS

If humans were meant to fly....
(Anonymous)

The meaning of Gillam's life—its passionate commitment—
was flying. This commitment did not take root and grow slowly as it
did in other young men, also mostly from the Midwest, who came to
Alaska in the 1920s and became respected bush pilots; men such as
Ben Eielson and Noel Wien.

Harold Gillam's passionate involvement in flying came suddenly on a summer day in 1927
at Fairbanks, Alaska. It came
while he leveled ground on
Weeks Field with his Holt crawling tractor (now known as a Caterpillar). He was twenty-four
years old. Gillam's lifelong friend,
Cecil Higgins, tells about their
growing up together in Chadron,

***A place in Chadron that influenced
Gillam's growing -up years. 2nd
and Main, Chadron, Nebraska***
(Dawes County-Chadron Museum Collection)

Nebraska. Higgins says, "His only hobby in those younger days was
sports. He never became interested in flying until after he was in this
country (meaning Alaska)."

Bob Stevens, a retired airline captain and author of books on Alaska
aviation history, gives this view of Gillam's sudden conversion. "Once
a pilot, beginning with an OX-5-powered aircraft, he never wanted
to be anything else."

Now back to Gillam's early years, weren't they important? The highlights were, but not the details. What were the highlights from those
early years of his life that suggest formation of character traits? Traits that
may have laid the foundation for his becoming an exceptional, unique,
and unforgettable figure in the early days of Alaska's commercial air
transportation. A brief overview of those early years will attempt to
shows a framework of events that may influenced his adult years.

Gillam was born in 1903 in Kankakee, Illinois, a fair-sized town south of Chicago. He had a sister, Elsie, and a younger brother, Earl, who died in infancy. His father was a car salesman and provider. His mother concerned herself with hearth and home. Gillam's family was somewhat different, though. They moved to Chadron, Nebraska, some distance to the west, when Harold was six. Moving away from where previous generations had put down roots was not common back then.

Highlights in those first formative years of Gillam's life leads to a search for the quality of family life; the values held and so forth. No information of this type is directly available except to note that this was a two-parent family and did remain one during Gillam's growing-up years. From this we might infer that both parents believed in the importance of family life. Thus we can further assume a sound foundation was laid early on for Harold's future growth and achievements.

Such an assumption is supported by our knowledge of Gillam's positive value traits as attested to by direct report of his close friend, Cecil Higgins. The two first met when Gillam moved to Chadron. For the next ten years they lived across the street from each other, went to the same public schools, and became close friends, being about the same age.

Chadron as it appeared during Gillam's youth. *(Dawes County-Chadron Museum Collection)*

Even considering the possibility of bias, Higgins' firsthand report gives a fair assessment of Gillam's activities, achievements, growth and personality for those ten years immediately before he left home to join the Navy. It also allows the making of moderate assumptions about Gillam's growth during his first six years of life when his family lived in Kankakee.

Here are Higgins' statements about Gillam. These are his exact words taken from a letter he had written giving an evaluation of his friend. He states, "In all the years I knew him I don't think he knew what fear was."

Higgins then justified and gave credibility to his statement by describing Gillam's fearless actions by stating, "he would fight any kid in town regardless of size, with one hand tied behind him, and he never lost."

At first glance the two statements made by Higgins portrayed Gillam at an early age as being courageous, fearless and, an exceptional fighter. Here one can indeed see the beginning of a legend, provided one views the situation in a positive light.

However, what happens if one looks negatively at what Higgins has said? Then reread his statement "fight any kid in town regardless of size" and one may doubt his truthfulness. Reading, "with one hand tied behind his back" and there is even more reason to doubt.

Here clarification is needed. These statements were written by a mature adult. Because of his accomplishments in Alaska over a long lifetime, Higgins has written a number of articles and has been interviewed at length. In none of these public statements has there ever been any suggestion that he was one to exaggerate or fabricate.

Even assuming the statements are true, one might still view them negatively. Instead of seeing Gillam's behavior as "courageous and fearless" why not see it as "foolhardy and reckless"? Why not? Isn't this a reasonable conclusion?

However, such a conclusion can be considered reasonable only if we ignore an important fact. Gillam was successful not just once, or perhaps twice. This might have occurred accidentally. No, he succeeded against great odds in every instance. The description of Gillam as courageous and fearless is now less in doubt.

How did he achieve such prowess? A complete answer is perhaps not possible. Apparent however, is a natural aptitude which can be broken down into agility, eye-hand coordination, and both manual and mental dexterity. Not to be overlooked is his obvious motivation and the high standards of excellence he set for himself. The latter, in turn, led naturally to disciplined practice.

Once Gillam made his passionate commitment to becoming a pilot; his aptitude, motivation, high expectation, disciplined study and practice help explain his possibly legendary competence in this newly chosen field.

The courthouse, a building that may well have helped develop Gillam's sense of values. (Dawes County-Chadron Museum Collection)

All this leads to a more serious question–a moral one. Is the aggressive behavior exhibited by young Gillam laudable and to be encouraged in our young people? The answer will depend on one's point of view.

Another of Higgins' statements moves toward an affirmative answer. He states, "Gillam did not like a show-off, or a bully, or a smart aleck.

This brief statement also says a great deal about the boy. He had, at an early age, developed a value system; a clear idea, in his own mind, of what constitutes right and wrong behavior.

In addition, he also seemed to take on crusader-like behavior in defense of what he believed in—a defense in which he was willing to endure possible physical harm.

His opposition to oppression, whether physical or psychological, is still a value held in our society. Also, his strong belief in himself is not only an accepted value but is considered basic to success in life.

So is Gillam's belief in himself, when opposing bullies, realistic or reckless? This is still a good question. The same one was asked later during Gillam's flying career. It was asked when he accomplished daring flying missions, especially flying through impossible weather conditions. He had his share of damaged airplanes because of off-airport operations, but never because of bad weather. Also, none of his accidents involved injuries or loss of life. This legendary record led a 3rd-grade Indian boy in Cordova, Alaska, when asked by the teacher to write about his favorite pilot, to compose the following:

High school; an institution that certainly influenced Gillam's adolescent years in significant ways. (Dawes County-Chadron Museum Collection)

> Thrillem
> Chillem
> Spillem
> But no killem
> Gillam

At the end of this biography mention will be made of those who refer to "luck" as a major factor in keeping Gillam out of danger. To these, Cecil Higgins replied, "In Gillam's mind he never took chances. He knew his business and worked hard to perfect it."

Those who observed Gillam honing his flying skills, studying the latest techniques, and acquiring the latest in equipment would agree with Higgins' statement.

Thus Gillam at age 20 with absolutely no interest in flying, was developing aptitudes, setting high standards and practicing disciplined behavior in whatever he set out to do. He was subconsciously preparing himself for a yet unknown destiny.

Chapter 3
A WIDER WORLD
Your Attitude Determines Your Altitude.
(Anonymous)

Certainly Gillam's joining the navy was a highlighting experience; an experience that allows further inferences about his character and motivations. Some writers have reported this event as, "He ran away from home and joined the navy." Such a statement carries a dramatic impact. Nearly all magazine articles about Gillam were written

Young Gillam begins to "find himself." (Gillam Family Collection)

ten long after his death and during the time the Gillam legend was very much alive. So it was quite possible that writers, and their readers, had an expectation that Gillam would also have done the unusual in his youth.

Since Gillam left little written correspondence, his reasons for joining the navy can never be fully known. However, it seems reasonable to assume that extending his world beyond that of Chadron, Nebraska had entered his mind.

The only source of information about that period of his life is the person who was there when it happened—Cecil Higgins. In a letter telling of their association, he matter-of-factly included this statement, "…until he left home and joined the Navy."

It was not unusual for boys back then, especially small-town boys, to leave home to find a better life, to find adventure, or perhaps to find independence. Gillam may well have had similar reasons for leaving.

One of his first acts after discharge from the Navy was to return to his folks' home, now in Seattle, Washington. This suggests no serious estrangement and discredits the suggestion that he had run away four years earlier rather than leaving with the family's blessing.

As a small-town boy with a possible desire to see the world outside Chadron, he may have found the navy's popular recruiting slogan, "Join the Navy and see the world," particularly appealing. So, possibly, were recruiting posters which appealed to both patriotism and manhood.

Because he had no direct experience of the world, it probably wasn't until he was sworn in and obligated that he discovered the truth about shipboard life in the navy. Then as now, navy ships sailed the seven seas. Men were, and still are, trained to carry out assigned duties. But in the 1920s the assigned duties of the sailor were, for the most part, simple and not particularly interesting.

The navy has had a tradition, on the limited space of ocean-going vessels, of keeping men busy. In achieving this goal it had a ready ally, the salt-water of the world's oceans. Ever since iron ships replaced the wooden sailing vessels in the late 1800s, the navy has fought the battle of rust on exposed iron surfaces. At least until recent times, lowly sailors were the navy's first line of defense. Their task? To scrape and repaint wherever rust appeared, or might appear. It takes little imagination to see this work as boring. Certainly the sailors found it so.

Gillam's first lessons in life. (Artist: James Montgomery "U. S. Navy" Nathan Miller)

Most adjusted to the shock that not all assigned duties in the navy were challenging adventures. They apparently carried out these boring duties without too much resistance; at least, U.S. naval history carries no record of mutiny stemming from boring duties at sea. Undoubtedly, many sailors reduced boredom by letting their imaginations run wild regarding what they would do when the ship made port and shore leaves were issued.

Gillam took another course of action. As Higgins mentioned, his main interest in school was sports. It is not clear whether his tendency to challenge bullies and smart-alecks informally in the streets led him into the school's formal boxing program. In any case, his reputation followed him into the navy, where he achieved amateur boxing status. All branches of the Service emphasized competitive sports. Not only did they actively recruit individuals with special athletic skills, they also provided them ample time to further hone their skills. This meant those individuals were excused from any routine, repetitive activities. Whether Gillam was one of those excused is not known. It is known, however, that boxing was, at that time, a particularly popular competitive sport and one suited to the cramped shipboard space.

Gillam also chose to use his time in the navy to explore a totally unknown world of work, work both challenging and dangerous. He volunteered as a deep-sea diver aboard a destroyer. The danger is obvious. It involved being placed on an iron platform and lowered over the side of a destroyer, in fair weather and foul, to the ocean floor. There the diver was to retrieve spent dummy torpedoes. These were then reused in practice battle maneuvers.

Gillam takes a dangerous task seriously.
(Hoyt's *Destroyers, Foxes of the Sea* - Title Page)

Back then, modern technology did not yet exist in deep-sea diving. The heavy, clumsy, hard-hat suits used then were made of canvas or rubber with rounded, airtight metal head pieces, complete with viewing windows and attached air hoses. The air hoses reached up to the ocean's surface where pumps on the destroyer provided needed oxygen as well as air pressure comparable to that at the surface.

Old- fashioned diving gear. (http://www.westsea.com/ts937/itemlocker/10pixlocker/10-14.jpc)

Any failure of men or equipment, either above or below, meant instant death, either by suffocation or by the painful bends. Escape was made impossible by the weight of the lead-loaded boots needed to keep the diver on the ocean floor while he slowly moved and searched for spent torpedoes. No quick-release device existed which would automatically shed the heavy suit and allow the diver to pop to the surface. Such a procedure would also have required a then nonexistent independent, compressed-air cylinder with a regulator that would maintain steady air pressure as the diver's body rose to the surface, thus preventing the dreaded bends.

It is obvious why the navy required volunteers for this work. Gillam was especially successful in the dangerous task. He not only stayed alive but continued in this work until discharged at the end of his four-year obligation. Also, since he voluntarily accepted this challenge and then met its requirements, he had unknowingly prepared himself to meet future challenges.

Gillam seemed to possess a need to reach out and test himself. Perhaps searching for a life's vocation, one that would continuously provide challenges and, to some degree, satisfy a restless yearning.

At this point mention needs to be made of several coincidences which had a profound influence on Gillam's future. They involved reunion with his longtime friend, Cecil Higgins. Higgins' own words, taped during a formal interview, told what happened:

> I made a trip to the West Coast-the first time I'd ever left home. I was 19 years old and went to the West Coast, and when I got to Los Angeles I ran across a friend of mine who used to live in the same town, and he asked me if I'd seen Harold, and I said, "No, I didn't know he was in town," and he told me Gillam had just gotten out of the Navy day before yesterday. So he gave me the name of his hotel and I called Harold up (this happened in the spring of 1923).

By Higgins' own admission, his decision to go to Los Angeles at the exact time that Gillam was there and newly discharged from the navy, had not been planned. In a second coincidence, Higgins accidentally ran across a friend from Chadron in the large city of Los Angeles.

These two happenings were significant. They brought Gillam and Higgins back together. After that, they kept in close contact until Gillam's death. This would probably not have happened if Higgins had not come to Los Angeles at that particular time and had not, coincidentally, been put in touch with Gillam through this friend. By this time, Gillam's parents had moved to Seattle and there would have been no urgent reason for Gillam to return to Chadron. The fact that the two had made no particular effort to keep in touch during their four-year separation suggests that there had been a natural drifting apart. This probably would have continued had it not been for these coincidences.

All of this brings to mind the passage "two ships that pass in the night" with its suggestion that chance plays a role in human lives. Later, when Gillam achieved special competence in flying safely through extreme weather, some attributed it to luck or chance. Others suggested a mystical quality. *Mystical* being defined by Webster as; "unknowable, remote, or beyond human comprehension."

At this point in time young Gillam, newly discharged from the navy, made an unexpected decision. A decision that not only gave direction to his future but also seemed to fly in the face of common sense. He chose not to make deep-sea diving his life's work—this in spite of years of experience, which made him highly qualified, and in spite of employment offers which probably involved high pay because of his experience and the nature of the work. Also, he had no qualifications for any other type of work. A prudent man would have settled for the sure thing. Yet this decision could also portray Gillam as one who takes a long range view of what his life might become.

In the previously cited interview, Higgins had this to say on the matter:

> He was offered several jobs in San Diego to work for companies, salvage companies, but he never did go to work for them. He didn't like it. He didn't care for it, although he had done a lot of it, but he simply didn't care for it. He wanted something higher up, and he got higher up.

At this point Gillam may not have known what his life's work would be. However, he knew clearly what he did not want it to be— deep-sea diving. And so his search continued.

Referring back to the interview, Higgins said,

Seattle (Beacon Hill) in the early 1900s.
(http://www.northweststuff.com/jj/seattle/beaconhill1900.jpg)

I went up to see him, and we decided to go up to Harold's folks who had moved to Seattle while he was in the Navy. So after seeing a bit of each other and discussing this further, we decided to do just that.

In any work Gillam consciously chose, he stayed long enough to know he wasn't a quitter, and, second, to know enough about that work to allow him to make a fair judgment as to whether or not it was satisfying to him. This may not have been a conscious concern but his actions seemed to imply it.

Higgins' statement did not suggest that either he or Gillam had any sort of conscious plan to begin a search for their life's work. The year was 1923. Gillam was twenty-one and Higgins nineteen. It seems that for Gillam the immediate goal was to visit his parents. For Higgins it seemed more a matter of tagging along and renewing a long-neglected friendship. Seattle was chosen for no other reason than that Gillam's parents had moved there. If they had stayed in Chadron, Nebraska, that would undoubtedly have been their destination. Yet Seattle rather than Chadron, a choice made for them by circumstances, would turn out to be a significant one for both.

Chapter 4

ALASKA

Send me the best of your breeding, lend me your chosen ones;
Them will I take to my bosom, them will I call my sons.
(*Robert Service*)

The trip from Los Angeles to Seattle went as planned, except that the number went up to three. A man Gillam knew, Sode Thomas, got out of the army the same day Gillam got paid off by the navy. Being also without plans, Gillam and Higgins invited him to join them. So they took off for Seattle.

With the Gillam family reunited, the three wanderers got day-labor jobs as house painters. This gave them money for living expenses and a reason for staying in Seattle where Gillam could continue visiting his folks. At the same time it gave all three a chance to think about long-range plans.

Gillam's train at the Chitina depot. (UAF Archives)

Once again, an accidental happening gave firm direction to their lives. This time it involved Thomas. Because he was only slightly acquainted with Gillam and had just recently met Higgins, it would have been natural for Thomas to leave the two close buddies and go off on his own. It didn't happen that way. In fact, it was Thomas who brought about the change in their lives. It was he who joined the American Legion. It was he who visited the Legion's social hall after work and casually looked at the bulletin board. There he saw a notice that the Alaska Road Commission was hiring laborers to do road maintenance and construction in Alaska. All three signed up and the number going increased still more when Gillam's father signed up also.

This turn of events would not have happened if Gillam's parents had stayed in Chadron, Nebraska, and the three wanderers had gone there to visit. Only in Seattle, Washington—then known as "the gateway to Alaska"— would the Alaska Road Commission have posted its notice of job openings. And so chance, or whatever it might have been, was leading Gillam toward his destiny. Higgins gave this account of what happened:

> We came to Alaska on a government contract to work for the Alaska Road Commission. All we had was an agreement to come up here for at least 100 days for $150 a month (plus room and board), beginning from the day we left Seattle until we returned or stayed and there was work to do. But we had to stay 100 days to get return passage paid.

Higgins didn't mention the working hours—an eight-hour day, seven days a week. The only time off was the 4th of July. On that day the foreman of the road crew found some form of transportation to get everybody, including the cook, to the nearest settlement. There a celebration always awaited them.

A Pleasure cruise for certain.
(Alaska Line Photo)

Probably no one paid any attention to the contract's fine print. After all, it was only a 100-day obligation, and the Alaska Road Commission pampered them with a first-class, six-day passage on an Alaska Steamship vessel. During those first days of their contract they lived in style: free passage, free staterooms, free food, also free time to walk the deck and enjoy the fresh air and the beautiful scenery of the Inside Passage.

Not all passengers found the voyage so pleasant. Emil Goulet who, like the Gillam group made the water voyage to Cordova but did so a few years later, gave this account in his book *Rugged Years on the Alaska Frontier:*

> There were two types of passage available: first class and steerage. Like over a hundred other rainbow-chasers, I took steerage primarily because of the forty dollars difference in price.... There were between forty and fifty more steerage passengers than bunks, and some mighty hard-looking characters in that lot. By noon the air was heavy with the odor of liquor. Some of the men became belligerent inebriates while others, whose stupor overcame them sooner, fell asleep wherever they chanced to fall. A venture in any direction would have necessitated hurdling a body or participating in a fist fight.

If the Gillam group did explore down in the hold where the steerage passengers were housed, they would have had an even greater appreciation for the conditions of their 100-day contract.

The six-day steamship voyage ended on June 1, 1923. The last part of the trip, the 131 miles from Cordova to the small village of Chitina, regional headquarters of the Alaska Road Commission, would be by train.

The Copper River and Northwestern Railroad was owned and operated by the Kennecott Copper Company. Its roadbed started at Cordova, ran northward through scenic snowcapped mountains; across snowfields, around melting glaciers and over ever changing glacial streams. After 170 miles of winding and wandering, and after passing through the small villages of Chitina and McCarthy, the roadbed ended at the Kennecott mine. The mine's buildings were perched on a mountainside tinted with green outcroppings of almost pure copper ore. All of this was overshadowed by peaks

The area in which Gillam worked for the road commission and later flew over. (The Alaska Line Photo)

of the Wrangell Mountain Range. These peaks towered to 17,000 feet. It was in this rugged region that Gillam would, some day, set up his own air service.

The railroad was built in 1910 to carry copper ore from the mine to the seaport at Cordova. However, just because the railroad was built to carry ore doesn't mean it didn't haul other items, including people. The Kennecott Copper Company spent many millions of dollars building the railroad and millions more keeping it open. Springtime brought

Human effort gives way to the forces of nature. (Adena Knudsen Photo)

the force of raging rivers and moving ice which caused much damage. This is how Goulet, in his book, described the yearly bridge destruction:

> Spring came early that year. With a rush the ice in the Copper River started to move, shearing off the bridge piling (the railroad bridge at Chitina) as if they were match sticks.

Given the expense of running the railroad, the Kennecott Copper Company saw that hauling empty ore cars back from the seaport didn't make money or sense. So on this first day of June 1923, sacks of copper ore stored on the Cordova dock, were waiting to be loaded on the next steamship going south. Meanwhile, the northbound ship, which the Gillam group had just left, would be unloading freight that

the empty ore cars would carry north to the various small mines, to the villages of Chitina and McCarthy, and finally to the Kennecott mine itself. A passenger car or two had been added to carry people such as Gillam's group.

Without enough freight and passengers to justify a daily train, the group was put up in a hotel for at least a night, waiting for the train to start its northward journey. The

Gillam will be visiting Cordova often. (The Alaska Line Photo)

magazines in the lobby of that hotel were doubtlessly not current but the daily *Cordova Times* gave them timely news on what was happening in Alaska, the Lower-48, and in the world. It was summer and it was not surprising that visiting bureaucrats from Washington (Alaska was still a Territory and governed directly from the nation's capital) could be found there on fact-finding tours. Neither was it surprising

EMPRESS

TONIGHT AT 8 SHARP

Tom Mix
—In—
"Chasing The Moon"
A romance that travels with the speed of light

PATHE NEWS — COMEDY

(Courtesy Cordova Times)

that locals gave them an earful. All this found its way onto the front page of the *Times*. The prohibition amendment to the U.S. Constitution was still in force. According to the front page, it was being strongly opposed in various states. The editorial page criticized the town's failure to display the flag at half-mast during the Memorial Day ceremony on the previous day.

Tom Mix in *chasing the moon* was then showing at the Empress Theater. This was a silent film; talkies were to appear in the near future.

According to an account given by Tom Appleton, who later became Gillam's chief aircraft mechanic, Gillam was actively preparing himself for challenging work with the Alaska Road Commission. And he was doing this even before landing at the Cordova docks. This is how it happened. The Road Commission was switching over from the use of horses for its pulling power, mainly to tractors. Tractors were obviously more efficient in moving earth, grading, and so forth. Also, they were more economical, because tractors, unlike horses, were not required to be fed and cared for during the long winters when road construction and maintenance stopped. However, conventional tractors had certain drawbacks. They tended to get stuck in muddy, unfinished roadbeds and to tip over when moving across steep hillsides or through deep ditches.

The "crawling tractor" was not yet a bulldozer. (Caterpillar Inc. Bulletin/courtesy Pioneer Air Museum, Fairbanks)

These drawbacks were resolved when the U.S. Army (the Alaska Road Commission was under the Army) gave the Commission a large number of surplus World War I crawling tractors. Some of these had armor plating still in place. During the war, these vehicles had been used to haul ammunition and other material to the fighting fronts. They were to prove especially effective for the Road Commission's task of building and repairing roadbeds.

As the Commission moved more and more into replacing horsepower with mechanical power, the need arose for skilled operators of the new vehicles. This was especially true of the crawling tractors. These were versatile machines but their versatility depended greatly on the skill of the operators.

The decision by the Alaska Road commission to use crawling tractors benefitted Gillam richly. (Caterpillar Inc. Bulletin/courtesy Pioneer Air Museum, Fairbanks)

Meanwhile, the Commission's recruiting was simply for strong men who could use a shovel, handle horses or, at most, drive the primitive trucks coming into use. From this pool of recruited laborers, supervisors searched for men with some level of skill, experience, or aptitude, and trained them to operate the more complex mechanical equipment.

Gillam must have sensed this need for skilled labor. Or he might have simply overheard, while on board ship, someone who had worked for the Commission before. As Frank Barr reported, Gillam didn't talk much but was a good listener when a topic interested him.

In any case, the Alaska Road Commission's annual reports from 1913 through 1925 not only provided the information given above but also indicated that, because the crawling tractors were proving so effective, an inventory of new ones called the *Holt* was being built up.

According to Tom Appleton 's account, a Holt tractor was on board the ship carrying Gillam and he, exploring in the ship's hold, came across it. He then proceeded to study the machine and its operating manual.

Continuing with Appleton's account, Gillam evidently hung around the dock at Cordova where the Holt would be driven off the ship. Here he made known to the Road Commission personnel, who were waiting their turn to unload and who were a bit uncertain about operating the tractor, that he had a basic familiarity with the new machine (which he did). At this point Tom remembered being told, supposedly

"Town Lake " at Chitna. (Author Photo)

by Gillam since they worked together some thirteen years as pilot and mechanic, that his future boss was permitted to start the tractor and drive it out of the hold onto the railroad siding.

So, based on the above information obtained from credible sources (Tom Appleton and the Alaska Road Commission Reports), it appears Gillam believed in preparing for whatever the future might offer. Before the Gillam group left Cordova, one person dropped out. Sode Thomas, who was mainly responsible for this adventure, stayed on the ship. He got off at Valdez and worked for the Road Commission there. So it was Gillam, his father, and Cecil Higgins who finally arrived at the Commission's divisional headquarters in Chitina.

During this summer of 1923, while Gillam gave all his energy and attention to his new career of heavy equipment operator, he had no way of knowing he would be making one more career change—his last. Nor could he have known that the lake which he saw directly in front of him as he stepped off the train at the Chitina depot would some day be the focus of his newly created Gillam Airways, the airline that would be the first to bring reliable air transportation to the Copper River region.

Meanwhile, busy days working for the Road Commission lay ahead.

Some attention was given to regular road work. Soon, however, Gillam and Higgins were assigned to the Nazina River bridge project. The project was located ten miles from McCarthy and seventy miles southeast of Chitina. Gillam began immediately working a crawler tractor and the primitive power shovels used at the project.

It's unclear where his father was assigned. It is known that he returned to Seattle but not before he had worked the 100 days of his contract. He was an adventurous type who moved about to find work. However, he was also a man who took seriously the obligation to support his wife, who by this time was determined to have her permanent home in Seattle.

Alaska in its early days had few roads, mainly because of its small population, great distance between populated areas, and inhospitable terrain. Maintaining the roads that did exist, as well as attempting to construct new ones, was the responsibility of the Alaska Road Commission. The most expensive and time-consuming of all this roadwork involved the building and rebuilding of bridges.

This was true throughout the Territory but was especially true of the Copper River region where Gillam was to work for the next three years. In this region, towering mountains joined with the warm Japanese ocean current off the coast to produce heavy

Mountains and Glaciers. *(Author Photo)*

snowfall. This in turn, over thousands of years produced massive glaciers—rivers of ice—that inched their way from mountaintops toward the coast.

A relationship exists between glaciers and bridge building and repair, work that Gillam was about to engage in. Most of us think of glaciers as large bodies of frozen, hard-packed snow which aren't going anywhere except to move an inch or so downward each year. This is true, but not for the lower part, where most of the melting occurs.

In the Copper River region the problem was aggravated by Alaska's midnight sun. These twenty-four hours of sunlight caused excessive melting which, in turn, brought streams of water falling off in many directions. The power of falling water is shown in the hydroelectric plants of the West where it produces electricity for even its largest cities.

Emil Goulet described earlier how the power of glacier-fed waters of the Copper River destroyed the railroad bridge at Chitina during the spring breakup. Goulet spent a year, in 1931, working in the Kennecott mine. While there, he observed how the continuous sun of summer gave additional destructive power to the waters of the Nizina River. Here are his observations:

To the north, east, and south of the camp (part of the Kennecott Mine site) high mountain peaks of the Wrangell Mountain Range, topped by volcanic Mt. Wrangell and Mt. Blackburn, 17,000 feet high, stood like sentries at attention. As the season wore on the sun gained more power, staying with us longer each day until midsummer, when we had no darkness whatever. As the snow melted, torrents of water rushed down from the castle peaks. Cutting their course over the glacier on which our camp was located, then under the Kennicott Glacier a stone's throw to the westward, they emerged to combine with numerous small streams to form a main tributary of the Nizina River. The bed of the Nizina had been originally the path of the Kennicott Glacier. Huge boulders which, no doubt, had been carried hundreds of miles by the glacier were clearly visible high above the racing waters.

A paradox: the mine's railroad created a need for Gillam airlines. (UAF Archives)

It was across this Nizina River that the Road Commission waged its continuous and in the end, unsuccessful, battle to build a permanent bridge. Gillam, in the three years he worked for the Commission, was part of that battle.

Gillam spent much time and effort on both road building and bridge building. (Bridging Alaska; Ralph Soberg)

Pressure for the Nizina bridge construction came from gold miners in the Nizina Mining District. This district lay some twenty miles southeast of McCarthy and was separated from it by the Nizina River. Need for the bridge arose only after the Copper River and Northwest Railroad began operating in 1911 and made stops going to and from Kennecott and Cordova. Building a wagon road from McCarthy, which the railroad served, to the Nizina and a bridge across it would give the miners a practical supply point and encourage further development. Both projects were worked on at the same time but the bridge building proved the most difficult.

The first plans for the Nizina Bridge were drawn up and approved in 1912. Materials were shipped in but even before construction began the site location was changed "because changes in the river since the original site was selected made this necessary." The bridge was completed in 1914 but was washed away before any vehicle passed over it.

Efforts to rebuild the bridge proceeded slowly, but a new structure was in place by 1918. Unfortunately, before that year ended the bridge was declared impassable, part of the structure having been washed away.

Another beginning on the Nizina Bridge. *(Bridging Alaska; Ralph Soberg)*

Although plans for reconstruction were again being considered, there seems to have been a general lack of enthusiasm in following through. It was not until the early 1920s that firm action was taken. Spude, in his *Historic Structures Inventory* reported the reason for firm action. He stated:

> In the early 1920s, with renewed speculation and corporate investment in the Nizina Mining District, the Alaska Road Commission proceeded to redesign and reconstruct the derelict bridge.

Spude then detailed the design aimed at creating a stronger bridge.

> ARC engineers planned a steel structure with concrete foundations that theoretically could withstand the breaking ice in the spring as well as the Nizina River's notorious shifting channels.

As Gillam and Higgins moved to the Road Commission's camp on the Nizina River in the summer of 1923 the construction phase of this attempt was already in motion.

The Road Commission had a standard plan for the workers' food and housing. Camps were set up, always near a water source, and

The Alaska Road Commission made a serious effort to help the miner. (Bridging Alaska; Ralph Soberg)

the men were housed in tents. A separate tent allowed the cook to give special attention to the quality of the meals in the hope that a combination of long hours, hard work, and good food would help overcome the extreme isolation and the boredom that went with it.

The camps were moved to a new location as soon as a job was finished. In the case of the Nizina bridge project, because of the focus repeatedly given to it, the camp took on the appearance of a permanent site.

It is generally known that Gillam, and Higgins worked on the Nizina bridge project during much of their three years with the Road Commission. This included building roads from McCarthy to the bridge site

The McCarthy-Nizina bridge road become more than just a trail. (Valdez Museum Collection)

and from there to the two mines on Chititu and Dan Creeks.

From the very beginning Gillam worked as operator of the Holt crawling tractor. Although he and the Holt were kept busy that first season, his busiest time came when the Road Commission closed down its summer work. Then, when the rivers froze over, he moved needed bridge construction materials from the railroad supply point in McCarthy to the bridge site. Large sleds, hooked to the Holt, moved the smaller, lighter items. Clumsy materials such as logs were simply chained to the tractor's drawbar. In all cases, Gillam maneuvered the Holt and its load down the Kennicott River, which ran through McCarthy, to the Nizina, a distance of about seven miles. Then he turned east down this river about another seven miles, to the bridge site.

The main bridge building was to be finished during the summer of 1924. Since the road to the bridge site was still far from finished, all construction materials would need to be moved in during the winter of 1923-24, using the river route.

This seemed like an easy task. Just head the Holt down the Kennicott, take a left at the Nazina, drop the load at the bridge site, then head back. No chance of getting lost, just follow the rivers.

It wasn't quite that easy. Gillam earned his pay that winter and also learned a lot about driving the Holt. He learned even more about running engine-driven machines in the unfriendly winter weather of Alaska. Whether he was aware of it or not, his work that winter prepared him for his future winter flying.

One of the problems Gillam faced, one that loomed above all others, was time. Supervisors had observed his handling of the Holt that first summer. They also saw how he handled work generally and especially how he handled tough jobs that required thinking and staying with it. These supervisors were convinced he was the one to get the construction materials moved that coming winter. However, they told him the river ice wouldn't hold heavy loads until perhaps the beginning of November; depending on the weather. They also told him that spring with its increasingly longer days would bring thaws in April. These would also make river-hauling hazardous. Knowing all this, what he was up against, he took the job anyway. It wasn't any wonder that time was on his mind and that he worked hard on ways to make it up.

There were other things that made the job difficult. When the rivers first froze over, getting started as early as possible was important. This meant that on his first trips, besides finding the smoothest ice to travel on, he had to test the ice. It meant making quick and sound judgements and hauling lighter loads.

Then there was always the weather. As winter set in, days got shorter, temperatures dropped, and blizzards blew up more often. The Nizina River at the bridge site was about one mile wide and had many channels. In the darkness of a winter day with a full blizzard blowing, it was hard to tell which channel led to the bridge site. Losing his way was always a strong possibility.

Cold weather caused other problems. There were no enclosed cabs or heaters. So it was hard to keep warm on a minus 45 degree day, especially with the wind chill factor added to that temperature. Also it was hard to keep the engine running during the coldest days.

With such problems on his mind, Gillam took off on his first trip to the bridge site as soon as he felt the ice was safe. Getting started early put him at the site while it was still light. This gave him a chance to look over the unloading area so everything would be where it should be when construction started in the spring. It was already dark, though, when he pulled up off the river ice back at McCarthy.

Gillam became an all-around expert in handling a crawling tractor. (Alaska Road Commission Annual Report 1913-1925)

Yet there was still work to do. A load had to be readied for the next morning. The Road Commission had leased the Anderson Garage in McCarthy, where the Holt could be stored overnight out of the cold. The garage also served as a warm place to do maintenance. Keeping the tractor running was not just a life or death matter. It also involved Gillam's concern about getting all construction material to the site before the thawing ice became unsafe.

As winter progressed, he could better estimate what still needed to be done. If he felt himself behind schedule, he would make trips on days when blowing snow cut visibility almost to zero. By this time he knew the route and was aware of his keen eyesight and his inborn sense of direction and location, so he always made it back. However, poor visibility slowed things down and made the trip both longer and more difficult. Then there were those minus 60 degree days. It would have made sense to cancel the trip. Still, when he felt a need to gain time, he'd leave the heated garage, hook up his load, and take off. People wondered about his good sense in such instances but soon came to recognize this was no ordinary man. Needless to say, he finished the hauling before the ice became unsafe.

The reader probably assumes that Gillam's friend, Cecil Higgins, gave all this detailed information. He too had been assigned to the Nizina Bridge project. No, Higgins had taken off at the end of his 100 day contract to visit his folks in Chadron, Nebraska. Most of the information about this period was provided by a then ten-year old boy, Bud Seltenreich, who demonstrated exceptional traits at an early age. Of these traits, the ones that made him a competent observer of Gillam's activities and character were curiosity and memory.

Bud's parents were also not ordinary people with ordinary dreams. It was the two of them who heard of the gold strike of 1915 in the Chisana area, some 100 miles north and east of McCarthy. Like a few other adventurous souls, they gathered up a few belongings and their three boys, Bud was the youngest and still a baby, and headed north. Their route and mode of transportation was the same that Gillam took some ten years later: by steamship from Seattle to Cordova and by railroad to McCarthy. Here Bud's parents changed their original plan. While other gold seekers traveled on foot or by horses or dog team to the mining area at Chisana, Bud's parents were struck by the beauty of a valley lying at the foot of the towering Wrangell Mountains. This valley contained flat land suitable for farming and had just then been opened for homesteading. So they traded the

Nizina Bridge Construction; Nearing Completion. *(Bridging Alaska; Ralph Soberg)*

hard work and hardships of mining, which promised uncertain riches in gold, for a life that also involved hard work and hardships but promised a possible rich, rewarding life for themselves and their three boys.

In hindsight, the choice proved to be a good one. The riches of gold did not materialize for those who traveled the last 100 miles to the mining area. The homestead on the other hand, although it did test the perseverance of all, proved to be an ideal environment in which to bring up three boys. It even taught the boys to help their daughterless mother with the housework. Today the homestead remains in the family.

Bud, now in his mid-eighties (note: Bud died recently), had retired after a satisfying career in Alaska aviation. This career had its beginning when he first worked as Gillam's helper and then as mechanic for Gillam Airways.

However, Bud's first sight of Gillam had nothing to do with aviation. It came about because the homestead his parents had chosen lay a few miles south of McCarthy and bordered the Nizina River at a point where the bridge was being rebuilt in the summer of 1923.

Perhaps because he was the youngest, not yet ten, and had fewer responsibilities than the two older boys; or perhaps his curiosity about all the activity at the bridge got the best of him. He often sat some way off and watched the activities at the bridge, especially the crawling tractor which was new to him. A man in town owned a small tractor that moved on its own tracks but it looked more like a toy and couldn't do most of the things this big one was doing. The big one could hook onto two or three long logs that were chained together and pull them up and down banks till they lay lined up at the saw-

Gillam's future mechanic. (Bud Sultan-rich Photo)

mill. Here they were rolled by hand onto a platform and fed into a revolving saw blade. This monster could spin around in its tracks, go up and down steep banks, and along the sides of hills where it looked like it would have to roll over. He even saw it drop down the bank of the Nizina pulling a thick sheet of steel through pretty deep water to where the chain on the steam-driven pile driver hooked onto it, lifted one end up, and then pounded it into the ground like a stake. Bud watched all this and wondered, first about the crawling tractor and then about the guy who could make it do all those things. That summer Gillam was just a man running a machine. Bud didn't get up close and he couldn't hang around too much because he had work to do too.

The winter Bud started first grade, the Seltenreich family moved into McCarthy so the boys wouldn't have to commute to school by dog team. Bud remembered especially the winter Gillam hauled construction equipment and materials out to the Nizina bridge site. He wasn't always up in the morning to watch Gillam pull out of the garage in the dark, hook up to his load, and drop down the bank of the Kennicott River. After school, though, he got through with his chores early so he could take off when the snarl of the Holt's engine was still a long way off. It was almost always dark when Gillam pulled up off the River. The tiny light out front made the hulk of the Holt seem even bigger. Bud watched from a little way off while Gillam got the next day's load ready. He kept watching while somebody opened the garage door and Gillam rolled the tractor inside, then shut down the engine. After that the town went back to being quiet enough that the bark of a dog seemed loud.

This was the winter Bud got to know Gillam. He had time after school and always liked being around the tractor. So it wasn't long before he made himself useful at the garage.

At first he just hung around and watched. He really wanted to know more about that machine but was too shy to ask questions. Then one time Gillam said something to him and that started things going. Bud asked questions and Gillam took time to answer, explain, and show.

On the homestead there weren't many machines, just the ones they used to cut grass, plow, and things like that. These were all pulled by horses. In winter dog teams pulled sleds for trips into town or to haul wood. Most of the work, though, that Bud grew up with was done by hand, such as pitching hay, feeding animals, chopping wood, and milking cows. Still, the three boys always found time to invent machines of some sort. Some worked, some didn't. Being around Gillam was different. His Holt was a strange new machine. Gillam knew everything about it and seemed to enjoy helping Bud learn all he could.

In the summer that followed (1924), reconstruction of the Nizina Bridge was the focus of the Road Commission's efforts for that region. The road between McCarthy and the bridge was part of that effort so Gillam and his Holt were kept busy. Although Bud saw him from time to time that summer, there was no chance for quiet interaction as happened that first winter. During the next winter Gillam had no rush jobs. He did spend some time at the Anderson Garage but also worked in the regional headquarters at Chitina. Bud remembered friendly talks when they did meet. However, gradually Gillam was moved to other jobs in the Chitina region. Bud didn't expect to see him again but that wasn't the way things worked out.

Still, in that short time and with such few contacts, Gillam made a strong positive impression on this young boy; an impression that did not dim or dull with the passage of years. In fact, this positive impression was made even stronger when Gillam returned to that same Copper River region, established Gillam Airways, and hired Bud as a mechanic.

Chapter 5
BEING HIS OWN BOSS

Just that small still voice that says,
"This might work and I'll try it"
(Diane Mariechild)

In late fall 1925 Gillam, Higgins, and Herb Larison—the man who had come up with Higgins from Chadron the year before—moved to Fairbanks and rented a cabin. This may have been a temporary move because all three could have signed up for another 100-day contract that following spring. A job would have been waiting since the Road Commission favored previously employed workers.

A horse-drawn stage; Alaska surface (winter) transportation. (UAF Archives)

Gillam, however, had in mind a permanent change. The previous winter (1924-1925) he had made a visit to Fairbanks. It may have been a way to kill time between contracts or to get a change of scenery. However, if this had been the case, other, more attractive possibilities would have presented themselves. A winter trip from Chitina to Fairbanks and back was anything but pleasant in those days.

The trip involved enduring cold weather on an open sled drawn by a team of slow-moving horses. And, once there, the cost of living was higher simply because of the town's isolated location. A far better solution, if change of scenery were the motive, would have been to make a comfortable train trip from Chitina to Cordova and remain there for the winter. There, living costs were lower and sufficient social activities could be anticipated. If this arrangement proved unsatisfactory, he could simply have taken an Alaska Steamship vessel to Seattle. There he could, among other things, have stayed and visited his parents. No, Gillam had a more serious reason for visiting Fairbanks.

As later events would bear out, Gillam had in mind a change in his work situation. Yet he had no intention of discarding his years of experience operating heavy equipment in the hostile environment of Alaska. This experience had provided both challenge and satisfaction but now Gillam wanted to be his own boss.

And so the winter trip to Fairbanks was an exploratory one. In Alaska, gold mining was the main economic activity. It required freighters to move equipment, materials, and newly mined gold-bearing ore from railroad stopping points to and from isolated mines. Such freighting could be done over rugged and isolated terrain but only in winter, when rivers were frozen over and the land somewhat frozen underfoot. These were perfect working conditions for a crawler tractor, provided it had an experienced operator making quick decisions. Gillam saw himself as such an operator.

A miner needing equipment moved, could easily lease a crawling tractor. What he really needed was an operator with enough confidence in himself to sign a contract guaranteeing delivery. No delivery, no pay. Paying an operator by the hour left open a possibility that the equipment and material would not be at the mine before spring breakup. In that case, mining would be delayed another whole year.

Gillam knew this. And confidence, based on his actual work with heavy equipment during Alaska's winters, made him willing to guarantee delivery. Also, signing such contracts would build his reputation as to reliability, while at the same time earning money to buy a crawling tractor.

In planning for his own freighting business, one more question needed to be answered. What part of Alaska had the greatest gold mining potential? Gillam had two years to observe firsthand the mining operations in the Copper River region. He must not have been impressed. True, opening of the Kennecott Copper Mine in 1911 and construction of a railroad through potential mining properties had increased prospecting and some small mine openings, such as those at Dan and Chichichu Creeks. However, the collapse of the purported gold find at Chisana was discouraging. Also to be considered was the remote possibility of the Kennecott mine's closing. Even a rich source could eventually become exhausted. A more immediate danger would be a reduction in the price of copper due to a glut caused by worldwide production. If the mine closed, so would the railroad. This would be a disaster to both current and future small gold-mining ventures in the Copper River region.

On the other hand, what did Fairbanks have to offer in terms of gold-mining prospects— that Gillam could tap into for his freighting venture? On the surface, very little. Fairbanks had its "gold rush" of the early 1900s. Felix Pedro's discovery had spread throughout the rivers of the Interior and given particularly rich results in the area surrounding Fairbanks. The output shrank slowly, though, as the initial discoveries simply played out. Much gold still remained underground but greater effort and heavy equipment would be required to retrieve it. Yet, the price of gold had not increased to encourage such extra expense.

When Gillam arrived on his winter visit, Fairbanks had become a ghost town, its population down to 1500 people. If he listened to the old-timers who came in from their "summer diggins" to crowd the

Fairbanks Mid- 1920s. (Candy Waugaman Collection)

lobbies of the hotels and talk, he probably heard about the "poor prospects" for the years to come. These men had mostly one-man operations, out on the creeks panning for gold in the surface sands. They were right. The gold they were after had pretty well played out. But these weren't the men who were thinking big. Gillam was after the guys who would hire him to bring in heavy equipment to remove the overburden (surface dirt) and get to the "pay dirt" underneath.

He probably talked to the top men who had just begun the Fairbanks Exploration Company in 1922. It was a subsidiary of the large U.S. Smelting and Refining Company with headquarters in Boston. Like Kennecott Copper, the F.E. Company had money to back its efforts. It was after gold but only in large quantities. This would naturally require large investments for heavy equipment and for freighting this equipment to mine sites.

Gillam may also have run into people who wanted to go into dredge

Gold Dredge; Gillam planned to serve these mines. (Candy Waugaman Collection)

mining. This method had been introduced in the Nome and Kuskokwim areas of the Territory but had only been talked about in the Fairbanks Mining District. The dredging method was described in the *Fairbanks Daily News Miner* as: "A complete mining and treatment plant involving digging, sluicing, and concentration—using a floating plant with an emphasis on water, large quantities of it." This method would also require large investments

for heavy equipment and the freighting of that equipment.

There is little doubt that Gillam returned from Fairbanks impressed. Certainly an important factor in his decision was the just-completed federally built and operated Alaska Railroad. It began at Seward, a terminal for the Alaska Steamship Company's vessels coming in from Seattle. From Seward it ran through Anchorage, then on to the important Tanana River port at Nenana, ending at Fairbanks. The map on page 25 shows its routing. Unlike the Northwestern and Copper River Railroad, it was there to stay and to serve all the people of the Territory. Gillam knew what this railroad meant to the mining interests using Fairbanks as their shipping point.

So it was that in late fall 1925 Gillam made his move to Fairbanks. Once there, he wasted no time getting established in the freighting business.

By the beginning of 1926 he had signed a contract to move equipment for a well-known miner, Sam Godfrey. Godfrey signed him up for a hauling job many freighters thought couldn't be done.

The job, in the beginning, didn't seem too difficult. Godfrey and his five partners set out to build the first gold dredge in Fairbanks. They would then move it to Nome Creek some forty miles north and east of that town. There they would begin dredging operation in early summer of 1926. Since the heavy dredge had to be moved in midwinter, before the spring thaw set in, construction began in spring of the previous year, 1925. Thanks to the Alaska Railroad's weekly schedule, the needed materials were in place in Fairbanks on schedule.

From then on problems arose which affected the completion date scheduled for late fall, 1925. As in most construction projects, unexpected delays occurred. If there are enough of them, they need not be big to result in a missed completion date. So, as work continued into winter, severe cold slowed construction even more.

As 1925 ended and the calender moved toward spring, experienced freighters withdrew their bids. It couldn't be done. Finally, only Gillam stayed. For Godfrey and his partners the situation became desperate. They had invested a total of $300,000 in the project— a lot of money at that time. Some of the money had been borrowed with a promise that repayment would come out of gold mined during the approaching summer. Miners tend to be gamblers and it appeared Godfrey's group was about to lose on this throw of the dice.

What if Gillam also withdrew? He had a right to, but he didn't. Certainly he demanded higher payment if he succeeded in what had now become a doubtful venture. The investors must have been somewhat relieved by his confidence and even more so when Gillam did what he could while the delay continued. He personally laid out the route, carefully noting possible problem areas and solutions. He made a rough winter trail and moved all supplies and equipment to the mine site except the bare dredge itself. Every possible piece of equipment he might need for the final move stood ready.

Finally, during those first days of April, when some snowmelt already showed on the hillsides exposed to the sun, the dredge was finished. Gillam went into action.

Ignoring a few minor errors of fact, Jean Potter, in her book *The Flying North* best conveyed a feeling for what happened, for what Gillam did, and how the oldtime freighters reacted to what he did. She recorded the event in 1944, when some of those men were still alive and able to express what they saw and felt. Potter stated:

> Sourdoughs shook their heads when the newcomer signed a contract to move forty tons of supplies from Fairbanks to the Nome Creek dredge site. It was a rough job and a rush job. Spring break was near, and the trip needed to be made before it came. Part of the trail must be cut through virgin wilderness.

Gillam and cat; his first contract - on his way toward becoming his own boss. (Dot Franklin Photo/ courtesy Dirk Tordoff)

> Gillam succeeded. When a formidable crag blocked his route he did not take time to detour but put a big block shive (an arrangement of pulleys that gave a mechanical advantage) on top. He then linked tractors to sleds by cable and hauled the load up as the cats plunged down the other side.

> "Gillam liked tough work," pioneer freighting men said, "and he always found a way to do it."

It is interesting to note that even during that brief period when Gillam was involved in the freighting field, he had made a name for himself, and he had done this within a fraternity of men who prided themselves on a willingness to take on difficult jobs. Men who then stayed to do what they promised. Also, they evidenced no shame that he, not they, had done the seemingly impossible.

With the dredge and supplies in place, Gillam looked for other opportunities and quickly discovered one. Some would say that Gillam's encounter with his next opportunity was an accident; a chance happening. That he happened to be in the right place at the right time. Others see such encounters differently. Albert Szent-Gyorgyi stated, "A discovery is said to be an accident meeting a prepared mind." Louis Pasteur stated the same matter in a slightly different way. He said, "Did you ever observe to whom the accidents happen? Chance favors only the prepared mind."

Gillam had been "preparing his mind" way back while studying the crawling tractor in the hold of the steamship on its way to Cordova. His response to this next chance opportunity supports the position that, "Chance favors only the prepared mind."

Gillam's next opportunity came in the spring of 1926 when the Fairbanks Exploration Company (F.E. Company) made a total commitment to the dredge method of mining. Land had been purchased—along with mineral rights—at Goldstream, Cleary, Gilmore, and Esther Creeks—enough area to float up to seven dredges. The material needed to build the first two dredges had been ordered and was being delivered via the Alaska Railroad. The engineering plans providing for an adequate water supply had been completed. Completion of a tremendous earth-moving task still lay ahead. This task, when completed, would guarantee seven gold dredges an adequate water supply for the entire summer mining season.

The plan was to dam two creeks, Faith and McManus, located some seventy-five miles up in the rugged mountains north of Fairbanks. From the dam site the water would move mostly by gravity flow along man-made open ditches to Chatanika, near Fairbanks. Here it would be diverted, as needed, to float the various dredges.

Carrying out the complicated engineering plan resulted in *The Davidson Ditch;* named after the man who drew up the plan—J.M.

Using pipe; only part of the way. (UAF Archives)

Davidson. The building of this ditch through the work of the men involved (including Gillam), and the machines they used, was an unbelievable accomplishment. The drawings called for open ditches to carry the water 65 percent of the way. To accomplish this, the earth itself needed to be rearranged over the entire seventy-five miles the water would travel.

Not only would the earth have to be rearranged but, because much of the route passed over permafrost, the top layer along these stretches had to be stripped in advance in order that the sun could thaw the layer directly beneath it. *Permafrost* is defined as a section of the earth in the northern latitudes where the surface layer is normal, that is, it freezes in winter and thaws in summer. However, unlike normal earth, in permafrost the earth directly beneath the surface layer remains frozen year round. It is essentially an ice formation and remains so unless its surface layer is removed. It then thaws.

In addition to all this, siphons made of 48-inch diameter pipe had to be built. These were positioned over various creeks that lay in the path of the ditch, as well as over certain low spots. Otherwise the water would simply follow the flow of gravity. That is, it would leave the ditch and become part of the creek's flow or disappear into the surrounding lower land. The final challenge occurred when a mountain top between Vault Creek and Fox Gulch rose too high to allow siphoning. At that point a 4,000-foot- tunnel with an opening of 7 feet by 7 feet had to be dug.

It is no wonder that the Davidson Ditch was considered, back then and even today, an engineering and construction marvel. Also adding to the problem, the F.E. Company and its parent, the American Smelting and Refining Company of Boston, were naturally interested in getting the dredges operating and mining gold as soon as possible.

By the spring of 1926, the F.E. Company stood ready to put all

Gillam's Cat is also hired by the F.E. Company *(UAF Archives)*

its resources into getting the Davidson Ditch dug. Gillam, with his special preparedness and expertise, stood ready to fit into this rushed and difficult earth-moving project. The F.E. Company's management, aware of his ability, experience, and reliability, hired him immediately.

At about that time Gillam found a used Holt tractor for sale, managed to obtain the money needed, and bought it.

Meanwhile the company, in its organization for the rushed project, had scheduled all earth-moving equipment to work two daily ten hour shifts. Gillam's Holt was leased and put on the same schedule. He operated it himself on one of those ten hour shifts; someone else did the other. At this point Gillam was well on his way to becoming his own boss in the freighting business.

Although the F.E. Company was also investing money and resources into getting the first two dredges built, its main focus had to be on the Davidson Ditch. Without its water the dredges could not operate and, in turn, no gold could be retrieved.

The main work in building the ditch, the one requiring the most time and money, was obviously earth moving. And this work could only be done on unfrozen ground. Thus the summer months were precious. During those few months, with men and machines working on a twenty-four hour daily schedule, the right-of-way had to be cleared and the ditch dug.

During the fall, winter and early spring of 1925-26 the F.E. Company organized its resources. Chatanika, located near Fairbanks, was to be the headquarters directing the total operation. Warehouses were built. Temporary rail lines were laid to move supplies and equipment from the Alaska Railroad terminal at Fairbanks. Winter trails were laid out by crawling tractors to haul men and materials needed to build twenty two camps along the proposed seventy five-mile ditch. At each camp, bunkhouses and mess halls were built and stood ready for the labor-

The Davidson Ditch- a view from above. (Candy Waugaman Collection)

ers who would work on and alongside the machines. In spite of the heavy machines brought in to move so much earth, manual laborers and specialists such as carpenters, mechanics, welders, and others were also needed. For example, when rocks proved too big for a power shovel or caterpillar to move, men specialized in the use of dynamite were called in. The need for manual labor was so great that at one time 1,400 men were spread out along the route.

Yet, in spite of the many men working on the ditch, the heavy equipment did the work men could not do economically: clear trees, brush, and rocks; strip off the top layer of earth on top of permafrost so the frozen layer below could thaw;

Chatanika Mid 1920s; a boom town. (UAF Archives)

and finally, haul dirt out of the way or to where it could be used to build banks along the ditch.

Much of the smaller equipment needed, such as scrapers, graders, and small tractors were available locally and could be leased or bought. The most modern heavy equipment was purchased outside and brought in during the winter of 1925-26. These items included five 10-ton caterpillar tractors and five self-propelled power shovels. These vital pieces of equipment were teamed up (power shovel with caterpillar) and spaced out along the proposed right-of-way. Each team had the same task for its section: clear vegetation, scrape, dig, and haul dirt.

Gillam moved around and operated both the new big machines and his own. We can assume he felt at home on the new caterpillars because they were direct descendants of his own World War I Holt. In 1925 the Holt and the Best machines were merged into the new Caterpillar Company.

Gillam's versatility was also demonstrated and appreciated on those rare occasions when he was called on to operate the new power shovel. These were not too different from those he had at times operated during his three summer seasons with the Alaska Road Commission.

An explanation needs to be made as to why the caterpillar tractors were teamed with the power shovels. Today we think of caterpillars as bulldozers—vehicles with movable blades up front that can topple and clear anything in their paths except lumber-sized trees. The immense power of the modern caterpillar or bulldozer was clearly demonstrated in its use as a destructive weapon during the Gulf War. *Time Magazine's* book, *Desert Storm* stated,

The Davidson Ditch today. Inoperative but still standing. (Author Photo)

As the February deadline approached, Allied tanks equipped with bulldozer blades cut openings through the sand berms that Iraqi troops had built as their first defense wall. The Saudis for their part, used bulldozers and tanks fitted with earth-moving blades to collapse the trenches and fill them with dirt. Within hours, Allied forces had burst through these supposedly impregnable defenses, sweeping past heavy concentrations of enemy troops and armor...

The above account of the bulldozer's destructive force supports Webster's definition of the word *bulldoze. It* gives this definition: "to intimidate by the use of a bullwhip."

Yet the caterpillar manufactured in 1925 was a relatively harmless creation. It had no formidable, adjustable blade up front. Benjamin Holt, the inventor of the "crawler tractor" before World War I, envisioned it as a machine that could pull agricultural implements over the rich but wet delta lands of northern California, and do this without becoming mired in the mud. During World War I the Holt (now designated a "caterpillar" by Holt himself), was used not as a destructive vehicle of war, but as a vehicle that could pull loads of ammunition and supplies over the impossible terrain of the front lines. Its status was still that of a pulling vehicle, especially over difficult or treacherous terrain. After World War I the Holt tractor returned to serving agricultural needs, especially in the West, which now included the logging industry.

Henry Ford's mass production of the Model T (daily production increased to 11,000 by 1913) led to a need for roads. In turn, road building led to a need for machines that could clear rights-of-way and move earth. However, the first earth-moving machines used in road building were the simple scrapers and graders often pulled by horses (see photo p.27).

Older Alaska Road Commission Cat and Power shovel working as a team. (1913-1925/ Courtesy Fairbanks Pioneer Air Museum)

It was not until the U.S. Government gave its World War I caterpillars to state highway departments (and to the Road Commission in Alaska) that the idea of attaching a blade to the front end of caterpillars and turning them into bulldozers was taken seriously. The Federal Highway Act of 1921, which subsidized road building, also promoted interest in making earth-moving equipment more efficient. The idea of attaching blades to caterpillars was difficult to implement and the first results were not always practical. Serious attempts to manufacture blades for existing caterpillars by large construction machinery manufacturers such as LeTourneau and Bucyrus Erie did not come until after 1925.

The five new ten-ton caterpillars bought by the F.E. Company were not bulldozers. But by buying the five new self-propelled power shovels they put together the caterpillar-power shovel team. This teaming improved the caterpillar's performance. The power shovel could uproot objects and clear a right-of-way but it was not a true earth mover. It could do no more than lift the uprooted objects and earth in its bucket and drop it off to the side. Power shovels were first used in building The Panama Canal (1903-14) and were extremely clumsy. They were not self-propelled and, being powered

45

with steam engines, were extremely heavy. They were effective in canal building, though, because water was available to float a barge from which the shovel could operate and be moved about.

The power shovel, since it was specifically designed to excavate dirt, was continuously improved upon. First, the gasoline engine was

used to produce power, which made it lighter and more manageable. Then it became self-propelled, when the unit was placed on tracks similar to those on a caterpillar. The modern shovels purchased by the F.E. Company were both gasoline powered and self-propelled. These

Modern Equipment. (Caterpillar Co./Courtesy Fairbanks Pioneer Air Museum)

features were most important because the shovel needed to move forward often as it uprooted and excavated. The ditch was shallow, narrow (10 feet wide), but had a length of seventy five mile.

As part of the team arrangement, the caterpillar kept especially built wagons abreast of the shovel which could then dump loads directly into them. When full, the loaded wagons were moved to a designated area by the cats.

A problem arose with regard to keeping the wagons alongside the

shovel, a problem which required a skilled cat operator like Gillam. The Davidson Ditch, to insure the best gravity flow of the water and to insure using the 48 inch siphoning pipe as little as possible, was routed along hillsides. Some of these hillsides sloped steeply and presented a particular danger. The shovels were safe. They used their buckets to level a

Danger digging ditch on a steep hillside.
(Candy Waugaman Collection)

path directly in front of them. This space always gave them a safe base from which to operate.

The cats and wagons, however, had to move along beside the shovel on sloping ground and often stood in danger of rolling over. Fortunately, the cat was known for its ability to move over uneven ground without tumbling because its main weight was located next to the ground. Yet the safety of both cat and wagon lay with the operator.

It was the operator who had to constantly look ahead and make judgments. Where the slope seemed too steep, he would stop and signal the shovel operator to dump a few bucketfuls in front of the cat. Although the dumped earth would be uneven and not packed, it still provided a safe surface. In extreme cases, the cat operator might require additional work before proceeding with his equipment. Gillam did well in these situations. He was not too cautious, thus slowing down the work of the shovel. Yet, he never did roll a cat or its wagon.

Because the cat was a versatile vehicle, it did other tasks during the ditch digging. For example, on parts of the right-of-way without trees or heavy vegetation, it pulled a wheeled scraper which could excavate a shallow ditch and deposit the earth alongside to form a ditch bank. Another example: After the shovel had passed through, the cat moved in, pulling a grading device. This leveled loose dirt and packed it down for efficient water flow. During the winter, cats pulled heavy sleds to haul siphon pipe to where it would be needed.

A special feeling for Gillam and his work during that hectic time of ditch digging was given by Jo Anne Wold in her article, *"No Kill Em Gillam."*

> The following summer when the Fairbanks Exploration Company (F.E. Company) hired a crew to build the Davidson Ditch, a 90-mile open canal to carry water to the dredges near Fairbanks, Gillam was on the payroll. He hung off the sides of mountains clearing brush, moving dirt, pulling loads. Safety equipment did not exist; a man had to take care of himself. Harold tied a rock on the end of a string and suspended it inside the cab of his tractor. When the rock leaned too far one way or the other he knew it was time to get level or jump.

The earth-moving phase of the project was shut down at the end of October (1926) because of frozen ground. However, Gillam and his Holt stayed on to move siphon pipes from Chatanika headquarters to the various sites. He also installed some of the pipes that winter. This gave

Gillam moving pipe into position for welding. (Crosson Collection/ R.W. Stevens)

further evidence that his skill and ingenuity were valued.

By Christmas 1926 his work was completed. It would be a good five months before the Ditch project would start up again. He decided to keep his Holt working by putting an ad in the Fairbanks *News Miner.* This he did on January 26, 1927. It was an unlikely time to be putting in a "job wanted" ad. It was cold, dark and everything seemed to be closed up for the winter. Gillam, though, never did much negative thinking. He knew that the F.E. Company's going into mining in a big way would put others to thinking about getting involved in mining with heavy equipment. From experience he knew that heavy equipment needed to be moved during the cold winter months. So this is how his ad read:

LET MY CAT DO YOUR FREIGHTING
PROMPT AND RELIABLE SERVICE
C. H. Gillam
ALASKA HOTEL

On March 2, 1927, with the approaching spring breakup closing out freighting work, the wording of his ad changed as follows:

CATERPILLAR MAKES IT SURE
SEE C. H. Gillam, CHATANIKA
FOR MOVING MACHINERY, HAULING ORE, STRIPPING
GROUND, DITCH BUILDING, CLEARING GROUND,
PULLING STUMPS, SITE LEVELING, EXCAVATION OR
FOR ANYTHING ELSE REQUIRING POWER

Gillam was not a person to state he could do something that he couldn't, but it was amazing how many things he could do with his Holt caterpillar—a caterpillar which was not a bulldozer as we think of it today. This same ingenuity Gillam used to get a caterpillar to do what it was not specifically built to do, he later applied to the airplane.

During the summer of 1927 Gillam and his Holt were hired to work on a major improvement of the Fairbanks Airport. It was a project that would go right into fall so he cancelled his *News Miner* ad on June 2, 1927.

The following excerpt from the October 13, 1927 issue of the *Fairbanks News Miner* describes in glowing terms the work done on the airport during that previous summer,

...the finest airplane field in Alaska, the Fairbanks municipal airport. This airport, built during the past summer by the town of Fairbanks and the Territorial board of road commissioners cooperating, makes the aviator independent of the wind. The two bi-

48

secting rectangles make it possible for him to land or takeoff in any favorable direction.

Gillam's success as a heavy equipment operator during his first four years in Alaska, and considering his more recent success at being his own boss, seemed to predict that his future life's work would continue in the direction it had taken. But this was not the case.

The Davidson Ditch. A part of Alaska's mining history. (Author Photo)

Chapter 6
THE LAST CHANGE
We were flying for no better reason then that we
needed flying for our souls.
(Wolfgang Langewiesche)

Harold Gillam's interest in, and commitment to, flying came suddenly one summer day in 1927 in Fairbanks, Alaska, when he had turned twenty-four. Jean Potter, in her book, *The Flying North*, reported the event from the viewpoint of someone who was there—Joe Crosson, a young pilot who at that time flew for the Fairbanks Airplane Company and who was still living when Potter did research for her book back in 1944. She wrote:

> Joe Crosson's first recollection of Gillam is of a husky kid bumping along on a tractor, smoothing the surface of the old Fairbanks field. After the job Gillam used to hang around the airport, dourly watching the planes. He asked Crosson questions. One day he told him he believed he would learn to fly.

Dog team on Weeks Field; mixture of old and new. (UAF Archives)

What caused him to make this sudden and drastic change in his life's work? It is clear that up to that point, he'd taken seriously anything he'd gone into, whether it was challenging bullies, boxing, deep-sea diving, or operating heavy equipment. Also, he stayed with what he started until it was clear to him, as well as to others, that he was one of the best in that particular work. However, when that time came he seemed prone to ask himself, "Do I want to do this the rest of my life?"

In the case of deep-sea diving the answer was obviously, no. He stayed with heavy equipment operating even after he became one of the best. But he added another goal: to be is own boss. By the summer of 1927 his caterpillar business was well established financially, having been hired into a number of long-term projects. Further evidence of this financial success was suggested by his ability to purchase his own tractor.

So why would he give up his financially established business, a business in which his competence insured continued success? True, this new aviation endeavor would allow him to buy a plane and continue to be his own boss, but only if operating his own plane would provide a steady source of income. This was questionable. Commercial aviation had just begun in Interior Alaska two years earlier, in the spring of 1925. During those two years it had proven anything but a sound financial venture. In 1926 Jimmy Rodebaugh, one of the first entrepreneurs to invest monies in commercial aviation, in an interview with Jean Potter made the following evaluation of his success:

Rodeburgh aviation entrepreneur filling the radiator of a Hisso Engine. (Crosson Collection/ Courtesy R.W. Stevens)

> "Crack! Crack! Crack," Rodebaugh began, ruefully shaking his head. "Some aviation sucker had to put up the money." His brand-new Wacos were wrecked in six weeks. One smashed onto a sandbar in the Koyukuk region. Another "slid off like a dart" and crashed by the Fairbanks field. The third nosed over in the Kantishna. He and Bennett (his partner) had not one flyable plane left.

In the summer of 1926 Gillam was still working his Holt caterpillar on the Davidson Ditch project, not in the least interested in flying. However, in a small town like Fairbanks with a population between 1,500 and 2,000, he certainly couldn't have missed hearing about the misfortunes of this newly established aviation venture.

So there had to be some other reason for giving up a secure financial future in his established business. A response to challenge had always been a part of Gillam's life and was undoubtedly a factor in this decision. Joe Crosson mentioned Gillam's hanging around the field and watching the planes. Planes were a novelty in Fairbanks and held a curiosity for all who saw or heard them, probably including Gillam. Yet Gillam's was not an idle curiosity, for he immediately began asking questions. Perhaps he saw himself as mastering the skills needed to operate this machine as he had the "crawling tractor." This seems reasonable, since soon after the questions came his decision to fly, which he then communicated to Crosson.

Did his decision to become a pilot lead to immediate action? His ads in the *Fairbanks News Miner*, began again January 25, 1927. With

The Hazards of river ice in late fall. (Crosson Collection/ Courtesy R.W. Stevens)

his longtime involvement in the Davidson Ditch project over, these daily ads indicated a need to generally publicize his business and let the community know he was now available for short-term jobs. The ads ended on June 2, 1927. This coincided with his obtaining the summer-long contract for the improving of Weeks Field. An article in the October 13, 1927 issue of the *News Miner* reported on the successful completion of the airport project.

The ad offering his Cat service did not reappear, but it didn't it mean he was closing out his business and giving full attention to his new aviation career. The ads began again in May 1928. He evidently had

Gillam using cat in aviation related work. (Mills and Phillips/ Courtesy Sourdough Sky p. 55)

not sold his Holt and intended to use it as a source of income while learning to fly. Being a practical man, he knew there would be no money coming in while he learned to fly. Also, knowing there would be no local jobs during the long winter, he probably turned to freighting heavy equipment and supplies for miners. Here his reputation made formal advertising for jobs unnecessary.

This winter work did not interfere with making long-range plans for his move into flying. Needed support and information came quickly from a small group of pilots in the Fairbanks area. They formed a close fraternity of sorts but it was not a closed group. Flying was a hazardous occupation and ideas that might increase chances of staying alive, both while in the air and when returning unexpectedly to earth, were generally shared. This group met informally at Crosson's cabin. It was located off Cushman Street, which was then on the edge of town and next to Weeks Field. Usually on Sunday afternoon pilots who happened to be in town stopped by and often brought with them anyone with a serious interest in flying. Crosson, who was the first to know of Gillam's interest, made it a point to invite him to the gatherings. He soon became known among the pilots as a good listener anytime talk turned to flying.

Gillam brought with him into aviation certain personal attitudes that would serve him well—a desire to become the best in what he set out to do, and the discipline needed to achieve that goal. His later actions demonstrated that, to him, being a pilot involved a never ending process of learning and honing skills, and a never ending commitment to search out advances in equipment and techniques which he could incorporate into his flying.

It probably didn't take Gillam long to discover, through his interactions with the group, that pilot training in Fairbanks would not be easily attained. The long, cold, dark winters would make learning to fly in open-cockpit planes uncomfortable. More important was the simple fact that organized flight training simply did not exist either in Fairbanks or Anchorage. Pilots then flying out of Fairbanks, such as Noel Wien and Joe Crosson, got their training in the lower forty-eight. They were then hired and brought up north to fly.

The reason for the lack of organized flight training lay mainly with entrepreneurs such as Rodebaugh. They saw that Alaskans sorely needed fast transportation and, in many cases, to areas that could be reached only by walking. The entrepreneurs also knew these Alaskans would pay well to obtain such transportation. The risks were great. The entrepreneur risked his money, the pilot his life. With regard to flight training, the entrepreneur did not want to increase the risk of his already risky venture by putting his expensive and hard-to-get aircraft into the hands of learners. They would, more than likely, make the plane unflyable temporarily, or permanently. Also, from the investor's viewpoint, training pilots would only indirectly contribute to commercial air transportation. No, these Alaskan entrepreneurs would hire experienced pilots in the lower forty-eight. Pilots who had done most of their disabling of airplanes at some other commercial operator's expense.

Gillam was undoubtedly aware of these risks but this firsthand knowledge did nothing to change his mind.

Soon after joining the pilot group something happened that helped Gillam with his long-range planning. Crosson, as pilot for the Fairbanks Airplane Company, decided he and his open-cockpit, two-passenger, water-cooled Spano Huiza engine couldn't compete against the Bennett-Rodebaugh Air Service. This company owned, among other planes, an enclosed five-passenger Swallow with a more reliable Wright J4A air-cooled engine. Crosson finally convinced the company's management and they authorized him to go outside to look for another plane. He left in August, 1927 and returned in October, not with an airplane, but with a sister.

Marvel, his sister, was also a licensed pilot and, since she was staying with Joe in his cabin, naturally joined the informal Sunday gatherings.

Marvel Crosson; she and her brother Joe started building and flying airplanes early. (Kay Kennedy Collection/ Courtesy UAF Archives)

Considering that Alaska had a low ratio of women to men and had no women pilots, much less one who had logged considerable hours, her appearance in the group should have created a stir. It didn't. Flying was still the focus of the conversations. Yes, Marvel was attractive, but her femininity only added a richness which the men valued. In a wilderness land where feminine contact was rare, especially among unmarried men, the mere presence of a woman added a dimension that went beyond sexual desire. In today's world, with its emphasis on immediate gratification in all areas of life, such thinking about the relationship of men and women may seem unbelievably naive. However, it did exist seventy five years ago.

Gillam of course, as a member of that gathering, responded to Marvel Crosson's presence in the same appreciative manner as did the others.

At the time this biography was researched and written, none of the participants in that informal gathering, including Marvel Crosson, were still living. The details of Marvel's influence on the all-male group and how she influence Gillam's approach to becoming a flyer came quite by accident from a young student, Lillian Osborne, who was attending the college at Fairbanks.

She met Marvel and they became close friends. When Marvel's brother took a job flying for an air service in Canada shortly after bringing his sister to Fairbanks, the two women made an important decision. Lillian would spend her weekends at the cabin. This would give her a break from college dorm living and the two of them could enjoy each other's company. And so it happened that for the better part of a year Lillian Osborne was present at the Sunday afternoon gatherings.

Because matters of the heart moved slowly and cautiously back in that long-ago time, it wasn't until some years later that Lillian Osborne became Mrs. Joe Crosson and raised a family in Fairbanks. When interviewed she was a widow and had reached her ninety-first birthday. Except for loss of eyesight she retained her physical health, mental faculties and lived independently in her Seattle home—surrounded, of course, by her immediate family.

It was this gracious lady who agreed to talk about her associations with Alaska's aviation and the people responsible for its growth during that early period, including the wives of the pilots.

With regard to the Sunday meetings at the cabin, she was quick to say that hers was not the role of a participant but rather that of a lis-

Lillian and Marvel equipped for an Alaska Winter. (Crosson Collection/ Courtesy R.W. Stevens)

tener. As a listener she not only gained an interest in aviation but also, as an observer of those first sessions where Marvel participated, gained an insight into the reaction of the men to this new member of the group.

As to Gillam's plans for flight instruction, there seemed to be no ready answer on how to proceed. According to the then Miss Osborne, it was Marvel who presented a practical plan that he accepted, with some modifications. She suggested he leave Alaska that very winter and go to San Diego. There, in the center for aviation activities on the west coast and with a favorable climate he would find opportunity to take systematic flight instruction. Perhaps he could even get in enough hours to obtain a license and still get back to Alaska before the busy summer began.

This plan fit Gillam's strong need to be his own boss by starting his own flying service. And it was this strong motivation that led him to modify Marvel's suggested plan. He decided to purchase a plane in San Diego, where planes were plentiful, while at the same time using that plane to build up hours. Then he would crate and ship the plane to Fairbanks and continue building up hours during the long daylight of the Alaska summer.

And so it was that, after finishing his freight hauling, he left Fairbanks on January 1, 1928 and proceeded by train and steamship to San Diego.

Chapter 7
AVIATION IN THE WESTERN WORLD;
A BRIEF LOOK

A life without risk is not worth living.
(*Charles A. Lindbergh*)

Harold Gillam left Fairbanks for San Diego in January 1928, to begin his new life as a pilot. The history of aviation to that point was short. Flight as we know it was born in December 1903 when the Wright brothers first successfully flew a powered and controlled heavier-than-air machine. This event happened to coincide with the year Gillam was born.

The broader picture of aviation in our Western world suggests that progress was significantly influenced by the distances which separated people and by attitudes of people toward accepting new ideas that might reduce such distances.

Thus, in Alaska, where great distances created an urgent need to reduce them, the individuals with the monies needed to do this, lacked the vision to do so. Not until 1924 was the airplane seen as a vehicle through which this need might be met.

In the lower forty-eight, immense distances were also

Lindbergh's 1927 flight gave a boost to aviation in the Western World - even Alaska. (Taylor and Munson, *History of Aviation* p.149)

a factor, but these had been shrunk by the coast-to-coast railroad systems laid before the Wright brothers' successful flight and by the automobile soon thereafter. Thus the early efforts of Orville and Wilbur Wright to demonstrate the future potential of their airplane were largely ignored. Even when World War I demonstrated the destructive potential of the airplane, an Army trainer, the Curtiss JN-4D or Jenny, was at that time the only lasting contribution to American aviation. The production of this plane ended with the armistice. The surplus planes were sold to adventurous spirits who became the "barn-stormers."

These men did not shrink distances between people and places but they did bring the airplane to the attention of the American people. Yet, by the early 1920s use of the airplane had slowly declined.

Scheduled passenger travel by air did not appear in the United States until well into the 1920s whereas the idea of the airplane carrying the mail took shape immediately after World War I. Using a systematic mail service to bind together the people of a vast land had its beginning back in pre-Revolutionary times. Now, with the advent of the airplane, men with vision saw how it could enhance that mail delivery. The United States government, using army planes, began airmail service in 1919. By 1925, when the Kelly Bill turned the service over to private companies, a transcontinental route along with short "feeder lines" were firmly in place. Over the years the well-established tradition of getting the mails through had become a reasonable goal using ground transportation. Achieving this goal using the airplane, however, would prove more difficult. The government did establish navigational aids along the mail routes to reduce the danger. Nevertheless, weather usually meant reduced visibility and continued to produce a major hazard.

Government support of airmail led to Ben Eielson's pioneering of airmail in Interior Alaska.
(Roger Bilstein, *Flight in America*)

Charles Lindbergh's solo flight across the Atlantic on May 20 and 21, 1927, although it apparently had no influence on Gillam's decision to become a pilot, did place a renewed emphasis on aviation in America. Before the flight, except for the airmail service and a few local passenger flights using the newly established airways, the airplane had done little to reduce distances between people and places.

In Europe there existed no vast distances between people and places that needed to be overcome. Also, trains and autos were already in place to transport people, mail, and cargo. The well-organized rail systems, since they needed only to cover short distances, proved particularly effective in moving people and mail rapidly and often. In Europe it was more an attitude of openness to new ideas—as pertains to aviation— that made the airplane flourish, at least in the more prominent nations. It is interesting to note that the Wrights' first offer to demonstrate their plane's potential went to England. There, during the pre-World War I era (1908), it was rejected. This suggests a lack of openness to a new approach to transportation.

The offer was next made to France, where the Wrights' machine was genuinely welcomed. This nation prided itself on the prestige it had attained in the fields of fashion design and in quality automotive design and production. The airplane lent itself to the same creativity. Also, it carried the same aura of prestige.

France's greatest push for the creative development of the airplane, however, came from its competition with Germany. Both nations saw, early on, how the airplane could serve as a weapon of destruction. Thus, the resources of both nations focused on aircraft design and production, especially as the possibility of war increased.

France's readiness on the aviation front was apparent when war finally broke out. Taylor and Munson, in their *History of Aviation,* stated;

What must never be forgotten, however, is the debt that the British aircraft industry, like that of the other early Allies, owed

The British Aircraft Industries belated entry into WWI airplane production resulted in the familiar Sopwith Camel Fighter. (Taylor and Munson, *History of Aviation* p 105)

to its French counterpart. Only the French had a large and well-organized industry when the war started. (p.134)

As it turned out, the airplane did prove itself effective in war, and France's early readiness undoubtedly helped bring victory to the Allies. This victory came in spite of Germany's edge in the air for much of the war. This edge was partly due to the genius of aircraft designer Tony Fokker, a Dutchman who had established himself in German aviation before the war. Germany, as a defeated nation, had problems that did not permit its striving for leadership in aviation. Such problems as the Treaty of Versailles which forbade Germany building or owning military aircraft.

France, on the other hand, had more than expertise in aircraft design and production. It also had, as the war ended, thousands of aircraft, many of them suited for transport of passengers and mail. Along with these, it also had thousands of well-trained pilots. These pilots, having survived the dangers of aerial combat, were equipped with courage enough to fly inadequate planes with unreliable engines, to accomplish impossible missions.

It seems appropriate to point out a similarity between early French pilots and early Alaska bush pilots. The latter, although having no combat experience to prove and develop their courage, amply demonstrated it by also flying inadequate planes with unreliable engines to successfully accomplish seemingly impossible tasks. And Harold Gillam proved himself one of the best in accomplishing these tasks.

With an ample supply of pilots and planes, it was France's intention immediately after World War I to maintain its prestige through its leadership in developing civil aviation. Its first focus was on providing scheduled passenger service.

Fokker, a Dutchman, gave Germany an edge in WWI aviation, his influence moved on to commercial aviation and his planes were found even in Alaska. (Taylor and Munson, *History of Aviation* p105)

Other European nations set out to do the same. However unlike Alaska, where vast distances cried out for air travel, the close proximity of these nations and their populations to each other gave little justification for travel by air. Quite likely, this lack of urgent need led in turn to a lack of assurance that seats would be occupied once the schedule was set and planes and pilots secured.

There were, of course, other reasons why people did not fly. For example, weather gave little assurance that airlines would deliver on schedule. Add to this the unreliability of aircraft engines and the related danger of forced landings. Forced landings also added to the likelihood of passengers' not arriving on schedule.

Perhaps the single most important reason why people hesitated to travel by air was fear. The experience of flying held many unknowns and encouraged the imagination to enlarge on them.

Early airline travel. (Taylor and Mucson/ *History of Aviation* p145)

When the war ended, those who inaugurated scheduled passenger services immediately resorted to the use of open-cockpit planes, where being uncomfortably strapped in with seatbelts was an absolute necessity. In those situations there was neither time nor need for the imagination to function. The fear was clearly present. Marcel Migeo, in his biography of Antoine de Saint-Exupery, vividly describes the fate awaiting the air traveler of that early period.

> At these airfields one also met men and women making their first trip by air to Prague or Paris or Bucharest. And in what a plane! An old Salmson biplane, used during the war for reconnaissance and artillery-range practice. The pilot sat in front of the wings, near the engine. Behind, and separated from him by the fuel tanks, the passenger sat in what had once been the gun turret— two passengers at most, and these had to be lightweights! Wearing helmets and goggles, muffled up in greatcoats, their bags between their feet, their faces whipped by the wind or pelted by the rain, these travelers were admirably stoical. Accidents were numerous, a horrifying percentage which today would soon ruin the airline. Newspapers did not feature them; accidents were a forbidden subject. (p.33)

Fokker FII. (Henri Hegener, *Fokker-the Man and the Aircraft* p.36)

Changes aimed at passenger welfare and comfort obviously needed to be made. The first was to discontinue use of the open-cockpit planes. This was done by again using war surplus planes but larger ones, usually bombers, that had enclosed areas where benches or wicker chairs could be put in to accommodate passengers. This moved the passengers out of the elements but wasn't a practical solution. The larger surplus planes cost more and, most important, were expensive to operate. At that beginning stage of airline operation the lack of confidence and comfort kept potential passengers from filling the extra seats. All this tended to make scheduled airline operations unprofitable.

By 1919 individuals with vision regarding the airplane's potential as people movers, who had the financial means needed to carry out their vision, set out to manufacture airplanes specifically designed for scheduled airline travel. Two men pioneered in this manufacturing of airliners back then. Anthony Fokker, a young man without formal training in aircraft design became a key figure in designing and producing advanced biplanes and monoplanes for the German air force. Hugo Junkers, an elderly German college professor, designed and built the first all-metal low-wing monoplane during the war. His design, however, did not gain favor with the military. These two men, with totally different airplanes, were united in their vision of using the airplane to bring Europeans closer together. In 1919, they practiced the same entrepreneurship that James Rodebaugh in Fairbanks, Alaska practiced in 1924. And all three had a significant influence on the growth of air travel in their respective parts of the world.

Fokker and Junkers, with modifications in their aircraft, provided leadership in the production of airliners in the Western world until the early thirties. At that time the United States, after a late start, brought in its technology and took over leadership in all aspects of airline service. Meanwhile, each European nation consolidated its failing airlines into a single company. Then, with special governmental subsidies, the large national airlines of today emerged, Such as Lufthansa, British Overseas Airways, Air France, and KLM of the Netherlands.

Junker F 13; sturdy and practical but did not catch on in Alaska. Used in Canada where it served as a rugged float plane. (Taylor and Munson, History of Aviation p138)

An interesting development occurred when open-cockpit airliners gave way to passenger travel in enclosed cabins. With this change came the attitude that, within the security of the enclosed cabin, being strapped down into a seat with seatbelts was no longer necessary. The focus of the airlines was now on furthering a sense of security. Strapping people down with seatbelts would work against such a goal. It would strongly remind passengers of possible danger. Taylor and Munson, in their *History of Aviation,* reported "...few aircraft had carpets and for many years the various Junkers types were the only transports with seatbelts." (p.257)

A quote of an Englishman's enthusiastic report on the interior of a KLM 1927 Fokker F VIII (as taken from Hegner's *Fokker-the Man and the Aircraft)* gives an indication of that airline's focus on security.

> The cabin is the finest thing of the kind yet seen. The effect is that of being in a comfortable room rather than being made to sit in a corridor, which is the effect in most machines. Comfortable and roomy armchairs rather like the old Alhambra stalls are fitted, and

the whole effect is one of Dutch roominess and solidity which cannot fail to inspire its occupants with a feeling of safety (p.81).

Being strapped into one of those roomy armchairs would undoubtedly dissipate the occupants' "feeling of safety."

This feeling would also have been quickly destroyed when potential air travelers of that era were confronted with headlines telling of an airliner crash, usually due to weather, with fifteen to twenty passengers on board and no survivors.

As noted, France desired to retain its prestige by becoming the leader in European civil aviation immediately following World War I. It must have been quickly apparent that a focus on the establishment of scheduled passenger air-

The French used rugged, uncomfortable WWI plane to take the leadership in mail flights. (Taylor and Munson, History of Aviation p.206)

lines in those early years would not result in heightened prestige for the passengers, the airline, or the nation. Thus, although France did its share in laying a foundation for future airline passenger service, its real effort was toward establishing a scheduled airmail service that would be surpassed by no other nation. Its specific goal was to be a practical and much needed one: to achieve quicker communication between France and her North African possessions. Obviously, this goal held a greater urgency for the French people than that of bringing the people of Europe into a closer relationship.

Getting mail through regularly and reliably has long been important to all nations in Western Civilization. However, it was in America, with its vastness and its scattered population, that such a goal created a challenge. And it was perhaps in America that the motto, "Neither rain, nor snow, nor heat, nor gloom of night will keep these carriers from swift delivery of the mail" was first coined. Yet it was in France, immediately at war's end, that a successful attempt was

St. Exupery; a daring pilot but he is known more for his writing in which he paid tributes to the early French airmail pilots. He was one of them. (Taylor and Munson, History of Aviation p.205)

made to apply this motto to mail carried on airplanes. And this was to be delivery, not within France itself, but to its far-off possessions in Africa. To provide regular flights over vast distances regardless of weather was to be a first in the history of aviation. Even then it was known, as it is still known today, that to fly regular schedules without regard to weather is a most dangerous task. France would be the first to take on this task and would use its hardened veteran wartime pilots to do it.

This emphasis on airmail flights was basically the decision of a single man, Pierre Latecoere; an industrialist who, during World War I, produced munitions and aircraft and who immediately following the war established the Latecoere Airplane Company. His purpose was to connect France with its African possessions through regular airmail routes from Toulouse in the south of France to Casa Blanca in northern Africa, then south as far as Dakar.

By the time Gillam was on his way to San Diego to begin his flying career in 1928, the French pilots were already flying established routes along the African coast as far as Dakar. At the same time "The Line" (as the company came to be informally called) was making plans to extend its airmail routes into South America by crossing the South Atlantic. This was to be done with sea planes between St. Louis (just above Dakar) and Natal in Brazil. At that point the official name of The Line was changed to Compagnie Generale Aeropostale.

This pioneering air work of Latecoere brought the French government in closer contact with its possessions and also enhanced both the country's prestige and its economic benefits. The government, in turn, amply subsidized the company's efforts.

However, money alone did not bring the desired results. Pilots were the key element. Their courage was beyond question. However, more than courage was needed to achieve the company's stated goal, "The mail must get through." Discipline had to be joined with courage. This was achieved by one of those same veteran wartime pilots who became manager. Didier Duarat was chosen manager because, like the company's owner, he firmly believed the impossible vision could be achieved. Duarat chose his pilots carefully. He had a large pool to select from. Then, in a sense, he molded the character of each pilot to where delivering the mail and not failing either Duarat or his fellow pilots became a point of honor. Neither storms, fog, the unbearable heat of the Sahara, nor the danger of being beheaded by hostile Arabs should a forced landing place him at their mercy could deter the pilot from carrying out his duty.

The strategy was successful. By 1931 planes of The Line were flying mail across the South Atlantic. Soon after, mail routes were established in Argentina and Chile, where the French were held in high regard. These successes were not achieved without sacrifices, however. During the beginning fifteen months of The Line, 125 lives were lost, almost all pilots, a few were innocent passengers.

An intimate knowledge of the feelings and accomplishments of those French pilots-both living and dead-was chronicled by one of their own, Antoine De Saint-Exupery, himself a pilot of The Line for eight years and a national literary figure. He wrote poignantly of these pilots in his, *Wind Sand and Stars*. He, at the same time, immortalized the achievements of The Line.

In the following passage from that book, Saint-Exupery speaks of the special fellowship of the French pilots. But these same words could apply as well to the thoughts of the early bush pilots of Alaska who gathered for fellowship in Joe Crosson's cabin in Fairbanks on Sunday afternoons. Saint-Exupery writes,

> This is the earth at once a desert and a paradise, rich in secret hidden gardens, gardens inaccessible, but to which the craft leads us ever back, one day or another, life may scatter us and keep us apart; it may prevent us from thinking very often of one another; but we know that our comrades are somewhere "out here"- where one can hardly say— silent, forgotten, but deeply faithful. And when our path crosses theirs, they greet us with such manifest joy, shake us so gaily by the shoulders! Indeed we are accustomed to waiting (pp29-30).

Now, leaving this general, brief history of aviation and going back to January 1928 when Gillam was making his way to San Diego to begin his new career, it can be seen that much has already been achieved since aviation's birth and Gillam's birth in 1903. And that much more remained to be achieved.

In this brief history, it should also be noted that greater achievements had been made in providing scheduled airmail flights than in scheduled passenger flights. In this, risk was an important factor. In airmail flights the only life endangered was the pilot's who could be expected to accept higher risk situations than would passengers.

It should also be noted that Gillam was entering aviation at a time when the United States was taking leadership in scheduled airline passenger travel by dramatically reducing the risk for passengers as well as for pilots. This was done by improving the airplanes and their engines and by providing the auxiliary facilities needed for safe flight. These included adequate airports, radio communications, weather reporting, and using navigational systems with instruments both in the plane and on the ground. All these permitted safer air travel on take-off, while enroute, and on landing even when darkness or weather obscured the ground from the naked eye.

In Alaska, where Gillam would be flying passengers, the situation would differ somewhat. Here the planes would be smaller but safe and the engines reliable. However, modern instruments such as air-to-ground radio or ground-based navigational aids which would facilitate night flights or flights when weather obscured sight of the ground were, for the most part, unavailable. The decision to fly or not to fly was mainly in the hands of the individual bush pilot who always had to weigh reliability of a travel schedule against the safety of the passengers. Gillam paid particular attention to the balancing of these two factors and in the process, this biography will attempt to show, he became respected within the pilot fraternity and among his passengers. This may well have been the foundation of a legend.

Chapter 8
A BEGINNING

*Once a pilot, beginning with an OX-5 powered
aircraft, he never wanted to be anything else.*
(Robert W. Stevens. Alaska Aviation Historian)

The Alaska winter was past the halfway mark when Gillam
boarded the train in early January 1928. Work obligation must have
kept him from leaving sooner—sense of duty, perhaps. Yet money,
too, must have entered in. Not just money for the San Diego trip.
Knowing his thoroughness following a commitment, the decision to
have his own plane must have come dearly. Since he did not sell his
Cat, money was needed to buy the plane.

Curtis Jenny, OX5 powered, Gillam's first Aircraft. *(San Diego Aerospace Museum)*

Finances were undoubtedly also a reason for his early return on May
7, 1928. His "Caterpillar for Hire" ad appeared in the *Fairbanks News
Miner* on May 9. Although construction and earth-moving projects did
not start early in the frozen north, planning for them did. Gillam made
certain that individuals concerned knew he was available.

So a need for cash reserves limited the time he could spend in San
Diego. He had only four months to build his foundation in the world
of flight, and travel used up part of that time. Today, by air, a round
trip from Fairbanks to San Diego would take less than two days.

Back then, over seventy years ago, Gillam traveled by train and steamship and the round trip took slightly more than three weeks.

Help, which allowed him to get much done during that brief stay, came from the Crosson family. Joe and Marvel had grown up in San Diego. Here their minds and hearts had been shaped by aviation and people involved in it. The feeling for flight was contagious and infected these two teenagers early. With their parents' obvious approval they used the family garage and backyard to shape a flying machine, a machine built out of parts they bought with hard-earned money, or begged off owners of junked Jenny's.

This fascination moved them to encourage others. Although Gillam was already enthused, he benefited from their enthusiasm. They insisted, again with parental approval, that Gillam stay at their folks'

Joe and Marvel Crosson at their parents home in San Diego, 1929.
(George "Ed" Young Collection/ Courtesy UAF Archives)

house. He did. This saved both time and money. Gillam was helped in yet another way by the Crosson family. A young pilot was already staying with the elder Crossons, again thanks to the encouragement of Joe and Marvel. Twenty-two year-old Marcel Leroy (Danny) Danforth had learned to fly at Pensacola, Florida while in the navy. Upon discharge he came to the mecca of west coast aviation, San Diego, to begin his career. He had been staying with the Crossons for some time before Gillam's arrival. During that time he'd acquired an instructor's rating and a firsthand knowledge of aviation activities in the area.

The sequence of coincidences mentioned earlier, which had a profound influence on Gillam's future, was somewhat like those that happened to him on his arrival in San Diego. There was, however, one obvious difference. Here, helping hands were at work with chance playing only a minor role.

In any case, circumstances brought the two together. This led to Danforth's expediting Gillam's journey into flying. Getting an airplane came first, so it could be used for Gillam's instruction. Given the circumstances, Danforth quite naturally became his instructor. Mutual trust and respect grew gradually so that the relationship did not end when Gillam left for Alaska. A partnership of sorts developed. The basic arrangement was that Gillam provided the airplane, a Jenny, for the opening of a flight school. Danforth would move to Fairbanks and become the instructor. He would be free to make flights for the flying services there when the need arose. However, his first obligation was to provide flight instruction for Gillam and for whatever other students signed up.

So it was agreed and Gillam now felt free to leave early to line up work for his cat. Before leaving, Gillam arranged a shipping schedule that would bring the crated Jenny to Fairbanks on July 22.

Meanwhile Danforth, after settling his affairs, was responsible for disassembling the Jenny and accompanying it up north. He did get the plane to its destination on schedule and the business relationship was off to a good start.

The crucial information as to the number of air hours Gillam logged in San Diego is not available. It never will be because his log could not be found. Evidently after his death, Gillam Airways employees carefully packed it along with other personal items, and shipped these to his parents' home in Seattle. There the boxes were stored by his sister, Elsie, in an outbuilding on her farm. After her death, the boxes were inadvertently disposed of.

Besides the log, Danforth was the only one who could have estimated the number of hours Gillam flew in San Diego. Unfortunately, his death shortly after his arrival in Fairbanks closed off that source.

One can make a reasonable guess that Gillam did

Navy Douglas SBD Dive bomber; sank three Japanese ships in the Battle of Midway, one of many military aircraft manufactured at San Diego. (Roger Bilstein/ courtesy *Flight in Americs* p. 86)

not fly many hours before leaving for Fairbanks. This is supported by the fact that in the fall of 1929, more than a year after his return from San Diego, he was reported as having less than the forty hours needed to be eligible for a pilot's license.

One might wonder why he had not built up more hours in San Diego. Knowing what we do about his commitment to a goal, it seems unlikely that he simply "took a vacation" in the agreeable climate of southern California. It seems more likely that the three months flew by swiftly as he attended to the immediate tasks of checking out suitable airplanes for sale. Then, once the purchase was made, he probably started serious flight instruction. Certainly any remaining days and hours were devoted to his total immersion in the exciting aviation environment that surrounded him at the time.

The Navy's Pacific fleet, well known to Gillam at an earlier time, had its home anchorage in San Diego. And of growing importance to that fleet was its aviation arm. Civilian planes were also being manufactured there. However, more important were the men whose ideas focused on the limitless possibilities of future flying. Most of these possibilities were still dreams. Even where those dreams did take shape, there was no mass production as one found fifteen years later when large factories covered acres of land and produced thousands of planes used in World War II.

No, the city of San Diego of 1928 was still a sleepy town. Here the

Ryan Aircraft Company, which produced Lindbergh's *Spirit of St. Louis* only a little over a year previously, was housed in a modest building when compared to today's factories. It employed but a dozen or so workers. It was the unseen talent of its

Harbor view of San Diego in 1920s. (ubterbet htp:/ /www.sandiegohistory.org/collections/cityscape/imaged/ 22301.jpg

few designers and engineers along with dedicated workers who, in a matter of months created an airplane which met the exact specifications of the pilot, Lindbergh. This exceptional aircraft, with its reliable air-cooled Wright Whirlwind J-5 engine, joined forces with the skill and courage of the pilot to make the first nonstop crossing of the harsh North Atlantic.

Gillam's ability to listen when talk turned to aviation, especially when new ideas were being considered, leaves no doubt that he spent every extra waking moment looking and listening to everything going on in this frontier of flying. He probably saw this as his one chance to live among, and listen to, people whose whole lives were committed to flight, building planes for the present while dreaming and designing new ones for the future. As it turned out, it was Gillam's only chance to participate in this feast of flight. This participation was undoubtedly, in part, responsible for his inexhaustible desire to take in and possess new ideas and devices. Ideas and devices that would make the airplane a safe and reliable vehicle of transportation, especially where such a vehicle was so urgently needed, as in Alaska, his new homeland.

Gillam had also apparently taken time to cement a relationship with the elder Crossons. Evidence of this came when he returned to Fairbanks accompanied by Joe and Marvel's dad. This first visit was followed by many more after Joe married Lillian Osborne who had become close friends with daughter Marvel.

Not surprising, what Gillam did during his brief stay in San Diego produced nothing newsworthy. At least Ray Wagner, archivist at the San Diego Aerospace Museum, found no mention of Harold Gillam in the newspapers of the period, January-May 1928. This should not suggest that his activities there did not lay a foundation for a possible future legend.

The beginning of May in Fairbanks and much of Interior Alaska is special even to those who have not experienced the rigors of the long, dark, cold winters. No one can miss the sense of spring with its continuous light and warmth, which so quickly restores life once more to a frozen land. And so it must have seemed to those waiting for the train to pull in on that Tuesday evening of May 7, 1928. The sun was still well above the horizon as Marvel Crosson stood waiting for her father. Yet there was a coolness in the evening air; and its stillness let the far-off sound of the approaching train be heard. All this encourages the mind to create images that are personal but also speak of this haunting land that is Alaska.

Fairbanks R. R. Depot in late 1920s when Gillam arrived in Fairbanks, 1928. (Naske and Rowinski/Courtesy of Fairbanks, A Pictorial History)

The elder Crosson planned to spend the summer in Fairbanks and so moved in with Marvel into Joe's cabin. Joe was, and would remain, absent until the fall of 1929. This, as will be pointed out, was unfortunate from the standpoint of Gillam's attempt to set up a new flying school.

Gillam moved into the Alaska Hotel. He gave it as headquarters for his caterpillar operation in the *Fairbanks News Miner* ad which appeared the next day. He seemed to be giving his full attention once more to his old line of work. The *News Miner* in its "Local Happenings" section took note of his arrival.

> C.H. Gillam returned to Fairbanks last evening from San Diego, where he had been living since January. On arrival in San Diego he purchased an airplane and spent a good deal of his time flying...

Nowhere in the interview did Gillam mention any future flying plans.

Looking back, we know that, on his arrival in Fairbanks, he was already formulating plans for a flying school. However, he also intended spending his first months making money.

At this point, the prospects for flying as a business venture were good. The need for air transportation was stated in vivid detail by Naske and Rowinski in their book, *Fairbanks, a Pictorial History.*

For Alaskans, "The Aviation" as they called it, was a natural. A vast wilderness separated the small settlements and movement between these settlements was slow. In the summer stern-wheeled steamers, launches, and poling boats floated along the many rivers, but after the fall freeze-up each settlement dug in for a long, cold, and dark winter alone. Dog teams and their drivers struggled along the trails with mail and freight. There was only one railroad of any length in this vast territory, reaching 470 miles from the port of Seward to the interior town of Fairbanks. In the winter, snow slides often closed the

Wilkins and Eielson with their Lockheed Vega before taking off for Barrow on a flight across the Arctic Ocean to Spitsbergen, Norway, 1928. *(Lockheed Aircraft Corp.)*

route. And in all of Alaska there was only one long road, the Richardson Highway. It was narrow and crooked, and also reached inland to Fairbanks from the Port of Valdez on Prince William Sound. In the summer, cars, with luck, navigated the 360 miles in three days. In the winter, deep snow drifts blocked the road. So it was not long before everybody in Alaska traveled by air, including fishermen and miners, trappers, congressmen, engineers, prostitutes, and salesmen; Indians, Aleuts, Eskimos, and whites all crowded together aloft in the narrow cabins of the airplanes. (p.59)

Also by that summer, Fairbanks had taken the lead in meeting this need. Indication of leadership and its results was given in a report, dated October 30, 1928, by Howard Rough, Supervisor for the U.S. Department of Commerce's Aviation Inspection Division. He found there were eight licensed pilots in all of Alaska, six of them in Fairbanks. Also, of the twelve licensed "mechanicans" (as they were then called) in all of Alaska, nine were in Fairbanks. The first steps toward aviation activity in the Fairbanks area took place in the summer of 1923. At that time the Farthest North Airplane Company brought in a Jenny with Carl Ben Eielson as pilot. Previous to that time there had been only two aviation events in the city. In 1913 James Martin and his wife Lily brought the first airplane to Fairbanks by boat and made exhibition flights. In 1920 the Army Air Service's Black Wolf Squadron, during its New York-to-Nome flight, made stopovers at Fairbanks.

Both of these events used what was then called "Exposition Park" for their landings and takeoffs. Over time, this flat piece of ground came to be known as "the race track" and then "the baseball field" as its uses changed. It was not until serious aviation activities came to Fairbanks that the Fairbanks Town Council officially designated this plot of ground as an airfield and named it "Weeks Field" in honor of then Secretary of War, John Weeks.

At this same time, a strip of farm land owned by Paul Rickerts, which connected with Week's Field, came into existence and came to be known as Rickerts Field. It had a longer runway—1,500 feet as compared to Weeks' roll-out distance of 900 feet. Also, the first hangar in Fairbanks was built on Rickerts Field in 1924. This was done in connection with issuance of the first airmail contract for the Interior of Alaska. This hangar was built where the two fields met and it was convenient for planes to be stored and repaired there. However, Weeks was a bit closer to the town's center, and since pilots of that time felt little need for a longer runway, almost all flying activity centered at Weeks. The only exceptions were the special flights, such as the Detroit Arctic Expedition. These involved larger, more heavily loaded planes.

Weeks Field expanded as aviation activity increased. Not even counting the Fairbanks Airplane Company's hangar and Swallow aircraft on the adjoining Rickerts Field, Weeks housed five hangars and four active aircraft. Bennett-Rodebaugh was the major air service out of Fairbanks with three pilots— Bennett, Gerard, and Young—hardly able to keep up with the demand for flights. Noel Wien, although Wien Alaska Airways was officially located at Nome, flew in and out of Fairbanks and other parts of the Interior regularly. These flights included Territorial air mail subsidies which were awarded to Wien in early 1928.

Ben Eielson and George Hubert Wilkins had just completed (April 17, 1928) the first flight across the polar regions from Barrow to Spitsbergen, Norway. Preparations for the flight, in a Lockheed Vega, were made in Fairbanks. Another flight activity with significance outside Alaska was the decision by Fox Film Corporation of Los Angeles to film Eskimo lifestyle as well as arctic birds and animals, especially whales. The contract to fly the crew, equipment and supplies was awarded to Wien Alaska Airways in April 1928 and the staging area for the expedition was Fairbanks.

This exceptional amount of aviation activity in Fairbanks as well as in Anchorage (which had a much later start) can be attributed in great part to the development of the reliable, air-cooled, radial Wright Whirlwind engine (basically the one used by Lindbergh in crossing the Atlantic). The OX-5 and Hispano Suiza, the common engines used in Alaska, were water cooled. Unreliability of these engines stemmed mainly from their water cooling system. Their performance in the extreme cold of Alaska made flying hazardous, to say the least.

Passenger confidence was also a factor in the stirring of aviation activity. This confidence stemmed from reliable service and absence of fatal crashes. Until September 1928 there had been no fatality in Interior Alaska aviation except for the death of Palmer Hutchinson, a correspondent for the Detroit Arctic Expedition of 1926. He walked into the propeller of a Fokker aircraft being readied for the Expedition. This safety record was achieved in spite of unreliable engines, which resulted in frequent forced landings. The lack of fatalities can be attributed mainly to the skill and judgment of those early pilots. Slow aircraft speeds of that period were undoubtedly also a factor. Here it should be noted that photographs of that early period frequently showed pilots wearing high-topped laced boots. This had little to do with handsome attire. These boots were an essential part of the pilot's survival gear. When forced down far from human habitation, pilots had to walk out. Cautious pilots took, whenever possible, a less direct route that more or less followed mail trails. A forced landing near one of these insured a reasonable walking surface and a sure knowledge that a roadhouse would be not too far ahead or back. With reliability and confidence fueling the need for more pilots and planes, Gillam had the additional assurance that his plan for a flight school would be successful.

Chapter 9
WHEN THE GOING GETS TOUGH

Cowards die many times before their deaths;
the valiant taste of death but once.
(Shakespeare; Julius Caesar)

Danny Danforth and Gillam's crated Jenny arrived on the evening train, July 22, 1928. By this date the darkness of fall had again appeared on the Fairbanks scene. Yet only a deep dusk met Danny as his train pulled into the station.

Weeks after improvement. Upper center photo shows 2nd runway and attached to it an outline of the old race track. (Courtesy UAF Archives)

Three people knew the young pilot when he arrived; the elder Crosson, his daughter Marvel, and Gillam. As anyone who travels knows, it is always comforting to see familiar faces at journey's end. Certainly this was true of young Danforth as he arrived in Fairbanks after weeks of travel.

Gillam could, of course, have gotten Danny a room at the Alaska Hotel. Yet, the Crosson family, both young and old, with its inborn capacity for gracious hospitality, probably led Marvel and her dad to insist he share with them Joe's two-bedroom cabin. Certainly they were convinced that his introduction into a new flying venture in a wholly different land would be softened by living under the same roof with people he had known and lived with before. Yet, there is no clear evidence where he did stay.

In any case, a warm welcome met him at the train station. That welcome was quickly extended by the pilot community during his short, interrupted stay.

Gillam's resolve to continue with his caterpillar work was undoubtedly weakened with the arrival of his Jenny and his instructor. Some sort of priority had to be given to assembling the Jenny and getting it in the air. It also became Gillam's responsibility to introduce the new pilot-instructor to the aviation establishment.

The face-to-face meetings with pilots led him naturally into learning what he, as an Alaskan pilot, would be called on to do. The just completed search for Noel Wien and Russ Merrill was a good example. Hauling the Hollywood Fox film crew and its equipment from Fairbanks to Barrow, although not a routine flight, had been made before, most recently during the two Detroit-Wilkins transpolar expeditions.

The conditions for the Fox film crew flights were ideal. The month of May saw spring moving into summer. And with summer came long hours of daylight and reasonable temperatures. Finally, there was the reassurance of two planes flying in sight of each other.

Yet, there were also factors that made this flight between Fairbanks and Barrow an adventure. Some of these factors remained when, ten years later, Gillam specialized in trips to Barrow during all seasons of the year.

The considerable distance (555 miles) was one such factor. This, combined with the slow airspeeds of planes, and even with an intermediate fueling stop at Wiseman, left only a limited reserve when reaching Barrow. Weather added to the fuel problem. No facilities existed for reporting weather in this isolated arctic region, where fog and low clouds often cling to Barrow's Arctic Ocean shoreline.

Penetrating such weather conditions to land is always hazardous. It is made more so at Barrow, where flat land covered with a blanket of snow during most of the year makes it difficult to tell where earth and sky meet. This condition is referred to as "whiteout."

The Wien-Merrill flight encountered ideal weather until they were some hundred miles from their destination. There, in the distance, they saw a typical low cloud layer covering the Barrow coastline. A low fuel reserve prompted Wien to make a precautionary landing on one of the many lakes. Both planes made it down without incident. However, Merrill's plane, having smaller wheels, sank through the snow and would need to be emptied and shoveled out before taking off. The decision was made to put the equipment and one passenger in Wien's plane, take it to Barrow when the weather lifted, unload, and come back with shovels and so forth.

By morning the low clouds had disappeared and Wien took off in his Stinson Detroiter, as planned; leaving Merrill, the two passengers, and the open-cockpit Travelaire behind. The weather cooperated and that same day Wien was back in the air with the needed items.

Normally, he would have contacted Fairbanks before taking off again. However, since radio contact did not exist in these parts, he quickly made his way back toward the stranded party. At this point there still would have been no problem. They would simply have shoveled to where Merrill could

Fox film crew to Barrow suffered because of the weather. (Millie Dodson Collection/ courtesy R.W. Stevens)

get the empty plane in the air and then Wien would follow, carrying the two passengers. With planes, people, and equipment safe at Barrow; refueling would have been followed by a quick return to Wiseman. There, radio contact could be made with Fairbanks.

This didn't happen. Wien, getting a general orientation from the shoreline and the sun found himself looking out on a flat landscape filled with hundreds of identical lakes. With no specific charts to help, he simply was unable to locate the lake he had taken off from. Wien had considerable flying hours in Alaska but all of these had been in the Interior. There were definite landmarks. He always made a habit of fixing these in his mind while flying in good weather so he could find his way in bad, when forced to fly low, where locating landmarks became more difficult. Also, in the Interior there were villages and mail trails between them. Wien as well as other pilots, whenever possible, flew with these trails in sight. Here, the flat barren land, a land with which he was completely unfamiliar, put him at a disadvantage. Without navigational aids except the compass, which was unreliable due to the North Pole's proximity; pilotage could mean the difference between life and death.

Flying until low on fuel, he returned to Barrow. Then followed days of bad weather. When it cleared, Wien joined dog teams in the search but without results.

A routine cautionary landing resulted in unexpected problems. (Crosson Collection/ Courtesy R.W. Stevens)

Now lack of communication did become a problem. When the planes did not return to Fairbanks and were not heard from, a plane, also a Travelaire, was sent out to search. Then another complication. The special radio it carried to report back to Fairbanks from Barrow, failed. The mood in Fairbanks became even more anxious. They now assumed something might have happened to their search plane.

Unknown to those in Fairbanks, their plane had arrived in Barrow and had joined the search, along with Wien and the dog teams. At last all, including Merrill's plane, were brought in to Barrow. With the search ended, a plane took off immediately for Kotzebue where radio relayed the happy ending to Fairbanks. This welcome news was received exactly 25 days after the two planes had left Fairbanks on May 13.

Wiley Post also became disoriented as his flight approached Barrow. (Mills and Phillips Photo/courtesy Sourdough Sky p. 141)

Today the details of this expedition might suggest a debacle resulting from ineptness. Such a conclusion could only result from a failure to grasp the vastness of that part of Alaska with its lack of adequate charts and radio facilities. Also important was its missing signs of human habitation. Signs that give a pilot not only physical orientation, but the promise of safety, comfort, and hope of survival. In the 1920s and 30s aviation was indeed in its infancy. Pilots as well as passengers were at the mercy of a harsh environment. Advances in technology today make it difficult to imagine what it was like back then.

To visualize arctic flying as it was then, there is no better illustration than the tragic ending of Wiley Post and Will Rogers' flight from Fairbanks to Barrow. It took place some five years after the Fox Film expedition. Post also became disoriented by the lack of landmarks as he approached Barrow. Countless lakes, now having a water surface rather than ice because it was August, swept by as the fast plane passed over them at a low altitude. He too was plagued by weather. An ADF in the plane combined with a simple broadcast band from Barrow would have allowed him to home directly to that tiny spit of land. With his eyes trying to locate his destination, a tiny human habitation appeared—an Eskimo fish camp. He landed, got the needed information, and took off for what should have been a routine landing at Barrow. Instead, during takeoff and while in a turn, the engine failed and the plane dove into the water. A simple navigational aid would have made all the difference.

It was also in this arctic location and some ten years after the Fox Film expedition that Gillam, during a winter night flight to Barrow, became disoriented. By this time he had gained the reputation of having an infallible sense of his geographical location. Yet, in that situation he had to admit "being unsure" of his position and actually

Lindbergh made a late arrival at Mexico City due to disorientation. (Brendan Gill/Courtesy Lindbergh Alone p181)

used the word "lost." There is no record of his ever having used that word again in this connection. The details of that situation follow in a later chapter.

In the matter of possessing an uncanny sense of place, Gillam can be numbered in the company of another aviator, Charles A. Lindbergh. Lindbergh is also reported to have used the word "lost" with regard to his location during a flight. Of course it was not during his solo across the Atlantic. It happened afterward when he made a nonstop goodwill flight in the *SPIRIT OF SAINT LOUIS* from Washington D.C. to Mexico City. Having flown through storms and darkness across the eastern United States and across the Gulf of Mexico, he suddenly found himself in clear skies over the land mass of Mexico and close to his destination. However, before him in all directions lay mountain ranges. He passed over tiny villages nestled on hillsides but found no indications of any large city. He flew along uncomfortably knowing that, according to his time and distance calculations, he could be traveling past his destination. Fuel was not a problem but a matter of some importance was troubling him. He had given his hour of arrival and his watch told him that the time had passed. He also knew that at that particular moment his future father-in-law, the ambassador to Mexico, the president of Mexico, and thousands of people were waiting to greet him. Suddenly, in desperation, he put the plane into a steep climb and spiraled upward. At last, passing through 13,000 feet his scan revealed a large city some distance off his original course and well to his rear. He immediately dove toward it. Landing approximately two hours late, he received a hero's welcome. At one point in the festivities he sheepishly, but honestly, confessed to being lost. In his case also there is no record of his ever having used that word again with regard to his location in flight. (Walter S. Ross, *The Last Hero,* pp.164-167)

One other episode that relates to the Fox film expedition was also much talked about and surely made an impression on young Danforth. Noel Wien was to have returned from his Barrow flight in time to complete his airmail contract. It involved a round-trip flight to Nome with intermediate stops enroute. It was to begin on May 22. When that date approached and there was no word from Noel Wien, his younger brother, Ralph, decided to fulfill the contract using an open-cockpit Waco. Although Noel Wien had pioneered flights to Nome on the Bering Sea only a few years earlier, by this time flying there and to intermediate stops was somewhat routine. What made Ralph's decision worthy of comment was the fact that he had only ten hours of solo with no cross-country experience. This meant no experience landing at strange airfields, no opportunity to practice pilotage skills, and no brushes with weather enroute.

Ralph's decision to make the mail contract flight certainly spoke to his courage. That he satisfactorily completed it—having brushes with weather, landing at strange and marginal fields, and even bringing in a sick man to medical facilities—speaks to determination, judgment, and skills that would ordinarily not be found in a pilot with so little experience.

Gillam returned to Fairbanks in time to have received first-hand knowledge of the waiting and worrying connected with the Fox film expedition and to hear about the courage and skill required of Ralph Wien. These also must have been his first encounters with actual dramatic events in Alaska aviation. As such, they must have influenced him. That such influence tended to be positive is evidenced by his continued determination to make flying his lifetime work.

Danny Danforth may well have been intimidated. Certainly hearing of these experiences made him aware of possible challenges his future flying in Alaska would bring. However, both of these incidents dealt with cross-country flying. Thus he could have taken comfort knowing that his flying, especially in the beginning, would essentially involve flight instruction, an area in which he had developed confidence.

As it happened, matters turned out differently. Almost immediately the Fairbanks Airplane Company's management asked Danny to make a freight flight to Brooks—a mining community some seventy air miles to the west. The flight was to be made in an open-cockpit, three-passenger Super Swallow with a 180 hp Hispano Suiza, water-cooled engine. Crosson had flown it extensively.

Since Gillam and young Danforth were still thinking through arrangements for the flight school, the trip to Brooks was agreed to and scheduled for July 25, just three days after the young pilot's arrival. When Gillam found there would be room for him, and since it would only be a short afternoon flight, he decided to go along. Although just a passenger, it would give him time in the air along with cross-country experience.

Gillam, as a passenger, began his first Alaska cross-country flight from this hangar. *(Grosson collection/ Courtesy R.W. Stevens)*

It turned out the flight would be anything but short and uneventful. After rolling the plane out of the hangar that morning and checking himself out in it, Danny loaded Gillam in with the freight in the front cockpit and took off that afternoon. While climbing out to the west, the water-cooled Hisso engine overheated. Before losing power altogether and possibly damaging the engine, Danforth managed to set the plane down on a sandbar on the Chatanika River without damage. One cannot help but admire the versatility and skill shown by this young pilot. A pilot accustomed to landing on normal runways with more than adequate length, where no danger existed from unexpected obstacles. Yet, in an emergency situation he had the presence of mind to choose a sandbar long enough and relatively free of debris and rocks, and to land without incident. Even experienced bush pilots attempting such a landing have been known to put a plane on its nose and damaging a propeller, or perhaps catching a wing on an overlooked piece of driftwood and having to walk out.

After temporary repairs on the engine were made, they took off and headed back to Fairbanks. Then another problem arose during climb-out. The engine-driven fuel pump acted up and the engine faltered intermittently. Using an emergency hand pump smoothed the engine out somewhat. Danforth climbed the plane as rapidly as the engine permitted in order to have height in case it shut down completely. At 5,000 feet, and almost close enough to make the field, the engine did quit. He made no attempt to stretch the glide. Instead, searching the tree-covered, hilly terrain, he located a partially cleared field. There he brought the plane in a tad too fast and touched down beyond the intended spot. One wing hit a tree stump and swung the plane around before stopping. Both Gillam and Danforth got out without a scratch. The plane was damaged but repairable locally except for the lower wing. A cautionary and a forced landing over inhospitable terrain all in one day, all without injury to pilot or passenger, spoke well for a pilot new to Alaska aviation. It also spoke well for the firmness of Gillam's commitment to flying.

Two other aviation misfortunes occurred during those last days of July while Gillam was taking steps to start up his own flying service.

Owen Meals' crash, and other incidents, convey a negative view of aviation. (Crosson collection/ Courtesy R.W. Stevens)

Both involved individuals who, like Gillam, were trying to establish an independent business using the airplane. Cecil Crawford, as part-owner of the Arctic Prospecting and Development Company, had recently purchased a Stearman C-2B. This plane was to be used hauling freight from the village of Alatna to the company's mining claim near Walker Lake in the Brooks Range. On July 22 Crawford made a hard landing on an improvised airstrip at Walker Lake. No injuries, but the plane was damaged extensively. This ended the company's resolve to fly freight with its own plane.

Another misfortune happened to Owen Meals, a Ford dealer at Valdez, who also made a decision to enter aviation. He ordered an Alexander Eaglerock biplane from the factory in Denver, Colorado in November 1927, then spent the rest of that winter taking instruction from the chief pilot at the factory. He returned with his new plane and license to Valdez on March 30, 1928. There he flew passengers frequently but did not make any extensive cross-country trips. On July 27 he took off for Fairbanks with two passengers. On his return to Valdez on July 29 weather caused him to turn back. This, in turn, caused him to run out of gas and crash-land on a gravel bar in the Copper River at Gakona. Both passengers were severely injured but survived.

These incidents might have combined to deter an individual less determined than Gillam. Instead, he continued with his plans. On August 10 he withdrew his "Caterpillar for hire" ad from the Fairbanks *News Miner*. Now the die was cast. Future income would have to come from aviation-related activities.

On August 15, 1928 Gillam announced through the *News Miner* the opening of his flight school with an enrollment of four students. For those formally enrolled, the school would provide ten hours of instruction in what today would be considered "ground school" subjects. The school was formally to begin the following week.

The date for the formal opening may have been somewhat delayed because of Gillam's decision to replace the OX-5 engine (90 hp) in his Jenny with a 150 hp Hispano Suiza. An identical conversion had been accomplished by Joe Crosson, Ed Young, and George King in the spring of 1927 on the Fairbanks Airplane Company's Jenny. This conversion had involved a considerable number of changes. Since none of the three men were at that time in Fairbanks to give help by answering questions, more time was needed to complete the work. The ground school would have proceeded since the plane was available to serve as a training aid and a general introduction to aircraft controls, their operations, and so forth.

In any case, nothing newsworthy occurred until September 10, when Gillam and Danny Danforth went up for an instructional flight. The *News Miner* headline for that day read, "Spinning Biplane falls to the Ground Here—Gillam and Danforth Are Hurt." The article went on,

> The accident was witnessed by several persons on Weeks Field. They saw the airplane take off, circle over the Fairbanks Airplane Corporation field and then head west. It had attained an altitude of 1,000 feet or more when the motor was shut off and the two pilots could be heard talking. Then the plane suddenly went into a tailspin and plunged toward earth.

In this same article Gillam gave his account of the accident.

> In his room at the hospital this afternoon Gillam said he was flying the plane and Danforth was acting as instructor. Gillam had just made a turn and Danforth was instructing him as to the proper method of turning when the plane stalled and began to spin. Danforth took hold of the controls but could not level the ship off.

The *News Miner's* account of that same day described the words and actions of those involved in the accident that indicated the concern that each had for the other. It states that rescuers at the scene of the crash reported, "Gillam was already out of his cockpit and supporting Danforth's head." The article then went on, "…He (Danforth) asked how Gillam was and the latter's first query in the hospital was directed toward the condition of his comrade."

On the day following the crash the *News Miner* reported Young Danforth's condition as follows,

Conscious from shortly after the time of the crash until he was in the hospital, Danforth had a clear idea of what was going on but sank into a coma without realizing that his hurts were so grievous that he would never awaken again.

The young pilot died the following day, just twenty-four hours follow-

A serious blow to Gillam's plans. (Ray Hoyt Photo/ Courtesy R.W. Stevens)

ing the crash. His death marks the first flight-related fatality in Interior Alaska.

So, within a brief twenty-four hour period, with the destruction of his plane and the death of his instructor, Gillam's dream had been dealt a deadly blow. Yet, his concern was not for the death of his dream but for the life of Danny Danforth. As the *News Miner* mentioned, "At the scene of the crash he gave little attention to his own injuries as he attempted to ease the pain of his instructor." And as the *News Miner* also reported, "In the hospital Gillam's first query was directed toward the condition of his comrade." This deep caring for the welfare of others would be repeated in future situations when Gillam encountered people who were hurting physically, mentally, or emotionally.

Chapter 10
CHANGES
What doesn't kill me makes me stronger.
(Albert Camus)

Danny Danforth's stay in Alaska was brief; less then two months. Yet, in that short period he had become known to Fairbanks even beyond the pilot community. The *News Miner* for Friday, September 14, 1928 referred to the impressive funeral held under the auspices of the American Legion which, in the words of the reporter "was attended by a large number of people."

Still, it was the pilot fraternity that was most deeply moved by the young man's death. That same Friday's paper carried a detailed coverage of the gesture of farewell given by his fellow pilots.

> Hail and farewell was bid to M.L. Danforth today by his comrades of the skies, who dropped wreaths on the train which was to bear the body toward its last resting place and who accompanied the train a short distance out of Fairbanks.

In formation three airplanes piloted by Ed Young, Noel Wien and A.A. Bennett rose into the air a short time before the train was to leave. They circled the depot several times and then, one by one,

Rodebaugh plane line up. *(Crosson Collection/Courtesy R.W. Stevens)*

coming down until they were only a few feet above the train, roared past in a last salute of farewell. Taking up formation once again the planes pivoted and returned to drop wreaths.

St. Joseph's Hospital, located directly across from the train depot, must have given Gillam a close-up view of this aerial salute. And he may have felt satisfaction knowing this young pilot he had brought into the country had been quickly accepted into its flying fraternity. In our modern world some may feel this symbolic gesture no longer has heartfelt meaning, but one might do well to remember that the "missing man formation" as a tribute to a fallen comrade is still very much alive and treasured.

Finally an emotion-laden letter from Danny's parents to the people of Fairbanks, published in the October 18, 1928 issue of the *News Miner*, communicated so well how that community took a relative stranger into their homes and their hearts.

> Mr. E.E. Crosson, father of the young aviator now on his way with Wilkins to the South Pole, brought us the first word of the funeral, and until then we had thought Marcell had died among the utmost strangers.

> When the casket was lowered from the decks of the *SS Yukon*, great quantities of withered, but once beautiful flowers that covered it, carried a message that no words could have conveyed—of many kind hearts and loving hands.

> Our sincere and heartfelt thanks go to the officers of the American Legion and all those who assisted in any way to comfort our son in his last hours and who paid their respects at his funeral.

> And to those brave young aviators who circled the funeral coach, dropping flowers from above as their final salute to their departed comrade and our son—we will always wish them Godspeed over the mountain passes and hope for their safe return.

> And to Mr. Gillam, who so fortunately escaped death—we hope for his speedy recovery and that his spirit will be undaunted by that fatal plunge and that he will continue on and win for himself laurels in the aviation field that might have come to our own son.

As Gillam's life unfolds it will show that he did live up to the Danforth family's hopes.

Gillam's injuries were not minor. In addition to general shock and a sprained ankle, his back was hurt and bones in his left hand broken. Nevertheless, he was out of the hospital in a matter of days with new plans in mind.

Unlike today, there was no National Transportation Safety Board to study the wrecked airplane and attempt to determine specific causes for the crash. Although it involved Interior Alaska's first fatality, the aviation community simply shrugged it off as a stall/spin accident. If "Pilot error" crossed the mind of any pilot back then it was not voiced. It was not until many years later that James (Hutch) Hutchison, well-known Alaska mechanic, confided to Gillam's oldest son, Harold Jr. (who then recorded it in his journal) that it was not Danny Danforth's lack of flying skills that kept him from stall recovery. Rather it was the basic instability of the aircraft caused by the installation of the heavier 150 hp Hispano Suiza engine.

Weight and balance calculations were always a concern to aircraft manufacturers. However, early bush pilots flew mostly two-cockpit planes where the hauling space was both limited and fixed. Thus, careful consideration of "weight and balance" became a concern only as passenger cockpits were enclosed and made larger to carry greater loads.

Approximately a year and a half before the fatal crash Joe Crosson, helped by two other pilot-mechanics, had made the exact same conversion Gillam made. Crosson's conversion

Crosson beside Jenny in which he switched to a heavier engine causing numerous in-flight problems. *(Crosson Collection/Courtesy R.W. Stevens)*

was common knowledge and is probably what prompted Gillam to do the same. What was little known, and what gives support to Hutchison's observation on the possible cause of the Gillam-Danforth crash, were the difficulties Crosson encountered. These involved a nose-heavy condition, which Crosson resolved by using his practical engineering knowledge to substantially rerig the plane.

Unfortunately, Crosson was away with Wilkins on the Antarctic expedition when Gillam made his conversion. Had Crosson been there, he would certainly have advised his friend on the problems and, more important, shared his solution. Had this happened, there is a good chance a life would have been spared and Gillam's plan for a flight school would not have ended so abruptly.

Courtney, in chapter four of his book, *The Eighth Sea*, discusses British pilot training immediately preceding World War I. He made the following remark about student reaction to dangers encountered during training in a vocation which, at that point, was considered a particularly dangerous one: "Often the student's first crash was his last flight, in one way or the other."

This comment, although intended to be humorous, contained a deadly truth.

Aviation, by 1928 when Gillam entered pilot training, had lost much of its deadly nature. However, given his two recent forced landings (as a passenger) during his first cross country, his more recent brush with death in the Danforth crash and, finally, the abrupt ending of his dream for a flight instruction school, one might be sympathetic if he had chosen to make his second crash his last flight. But he didn't. What did have to change was how he would achieve his goal of becoming a pilot and becoming his own boss in the flying world.

Without an instructor and his own plane, the flying school idea had to be dropped. It was dropped. However, Gillam's open and creative mind allowed him to change misfortune into a different, perhaps better way to achieve his original goal: that of becoming, at one and the same time, a pilot and his own boss.

The increased aviation activity at Weeks Field resulted in an increased need for planes, pilots, and mechanics. Bennett-Rodebaugh, with its increased number of planes in the air, was the first to feel this need and by 1928 began hiring apprentice mechanics. Back then, few qualified mechanics had ever received formal schooling. Individuals with a mechanical aptitude and interest naturally gravitated toward informal repair work. Then, in Alaska at least, they signed on as a mechanic under a more experienced man who had come up the same way. Gillam, for example, had gained experience in heavy equipment repair and maintenance since 1923. First, working for the Alaska Road Commission and later, by maintaining his own Cat.

Airplane Service

Fairbanks, Alaska   Chas. L. Thompson, Mgr.

PASSENGER AND EXPRESS RATES--1928

Fairbanks to and from	One Pass.	Two or More Pass. Each	Express Per Lb.
Livengood	$ 50.00	$ 37.50	$ .15
Chena Hot Springs	50.00	40.00	.15
Nenana	50.00	40.00	.15
Palmer Creek	75.00	65.00	.20
Manley Hot Springs	100.00	80.00	.25
Circle Hot Springs	100.00	80.00	.25
Circle City	125.00	100.00	.30
Beaver	125.00	100.00	.30
Kantishna	125.00	100.00	.30
Minchumina	125.00	100.00	.30
American Creek	125.00	100.00	.30
Tanana	125.00	100.00	.30
Rampart	150.00	125.00	.40
Fort. Yukon	150.00	125.00	.40
Bettles	175.00	137.50	.40
Wiseman	200.00	150.00	.40
Ruby	225.00	175.00	.50
Chandalar	225.00	175.00	.50
Eagle	225.00	175.00	.50
Tetlin Lake	250.00	200.00	.50
McGrath	250.00	200.00	.50
Tacotna	265.00	212.50	.50
Ophir	265.00	212.50	.50
Flat	300.00	250.00	.50
Iditarod	300.00	250.00	.50
Nixmut	350.00	275.00	.75
Anulato	350.00	275.00	.75
Bethel	750.00	500.00	1.00
Nome	750.00	500.00	1.00
	750.00	500.00	1.00

BAGGAGE ALLOWANCE 20 Lbs. PER PASSENGER.

Bennett and Rodeburgh published fares and destinations. Shows increased commercial aviation activity at Weeks Field. (Jack Peck Collection/ Courtesy R.W. Stevens)

Gillam, seeing the opportunity to supplement his income while learning to fly, immediately applied for the position. He had another strong motivation: developing his skills as an aircraft mechanic. At that time it was not unusual for mechanics to accompany flights in order to make emergency repairs and thus make air travel more reliable. Being his own mechanic could insure this more reliable service without reducing the amount of freight and passengers carried. Because of his strong background and motivation, he was hired.

At that same time Gillam made another commitment to his goal of becoming a pilot. At the end of September, shortly after leaving the hospital, he bought a Swallow biplane; *The Arctic Prospector*.

Gillam planned to have Noel Wien instruct him but Wien's heavy flying schedule made this unlikely. Again, Gillam's lost log makes it difficult to determine who did give him instruction. It appears most likely that Ed

Gillam purchased this plane after the crash of his Jenny. *(Crosson Collection/Courtesy R.W. Stevens)*

Young and Tom Gerard, both flying for Bennett-Rodebaugh, gave him instruction as they were able to fit it into their flight schedules.

From the standpoint of availability it would appear Tom Gerard was the main instructor. He flew continuously for Bennett-Rodebaugh beginning in March 1927. Also, he got to know Gillam on a more personal basis since they both attended the Sunday afternoon gatherings at Joe Crosson's cabin. Gerard found even more time to instruct when he resigned from Bennett-Rodebaugh in August 1928. At that time he ordered a plane with the intention of beginning his own flying service. The plane did not arrive until October. After it arrived and was put together, the plane was damaged in November and considerable time was spent waiting for parts.

On the other hand, although Ed Young was hired by Bennett-Rodebaugh back in August 1926, he went outside that winter. On returning in March 1927, he hired on with Anchorage Air Transport and did not return to Fairbanks until January 1928.

Thus it was Gerard's availability and his personal association with Gillam that resulted in his doing more of the instruction. It was also Gerard who, at one point, told Gillam, "There is nothing else I can teach you. So if you want to do any more flying you'll have to do it alone" (from Jo Anne Wold's "No Kill'em Gillam" article in the *Alaska Journal*).

The above comment brings to light an interesting insight into Gillam's attitude toward learning to fly. Earlier, when entering the new field of heavy equipment operator, he took the initiative and learned on his own. He even relied on the reading of an operating manual as the sole source of instruction before starting the engine of a "crawling tractor," setting himself in the driver's seat, and moving the numerous levers which set the clumsy machine in motion.

This was so different from his attitude toward learning to fly. At the time he entered into aviation there were individuals who engaged in a certain amount of "self-instruction." Not so Gillam. He started out with an attitude that stayed with him throughout his flying days. He would learn all he could and leave little to chance. Put in his friend Higgins' words, "Gillam didn't take chances." In a sense, Gillam's desire for more dual instruction, and Gerard's response, were not unlike the exchange between student and instructor of today when the moment for the first solo flight arrives. With Gillam the attitude of always learning and applying what he learned did much to make flying, especially his own flying, safer and more reliable.

In spite of having no pilot log to provide the day-to-day activities of Gillam's student pilot days, there were special events, usually reported in the local paper, which told of his progress in aviation-related activities. One of these dealt with his getting into the air even if just as an observer. For example, the *News Miner* reported,

> On Friday, October 26, Ed Young, with Gillam as observer, was searching the Tanana (River) for C.I. "Tom" Driscoll, missing since the twenty-third. Searching every place he might possibly have reached, the men flew for more than two hours. They expected to go out again that same afternoon.

The desire to use the airplane on searches and to bring in people in need of medical aid appeared early in Gillam's life as a pilot, and grew with time. Certainly Alaska, with its rugged terrain and lack of roads, gave him many opportunities to put his desire into practice.

Although it may not have been a conscious motive, the careful study of terrain on these aerial searches undoubtedly helped him build his reputation for having an infallible sense of location. This, in turn, helped him to fly through weather where sight of terrain was obscured.

Gillam's progress as a beginner was noted with reference to his first cross country. It involved a Saturday flight to Nenana on February 2, 1929 to pick up his friend, Cecil Higgins, and returning Higgins to Nenana on the following Monday. This being his first cross country, he was obviously unlicensed. In today's aviation world, publicizing an unlicensed pilot carrying a passenger would be duly noted by the authorities and action taken. The newspaper article ends with: "More will be heard of the young pilot before the year is out."

Little did the reporter then know how true his prediction would be, and under what unusual circumstances.

Not long after, on April 25, 1929, Gillam again became the subject of a news article. It reported:

> C.H. Gillam in his Swallow, *Arctic Prospector,* had started out on a short flight and had not returned. Anxiety over his absence was relieved when Tom Gerard reported finding him near Chena. While landing, with Charles Showers aboard, the aircraft had nosed over in soft snow, breaking the propeller. Gillam remained with Showers until Tom Gerard brought him another propeller.

Since the town of Chena had no airstrip, it suggests Gillam had begun early practicing the all-important skill of off-airport landings. The fact that he stayed with his passenger also points to a practice that never left him, concern for the safety and comfort of his passengers.

Gillam provides special skis to get travelers on their way. *(Sylvia "Tapu" Ross Collection/Courtesy R.W. Stevens)*

Gillam's decision to give his full attention and energy to aviation, rather than supplement his income through Cat work, turned out to be a sound one. Not only was he becoming an experienced mechanic and pilot, but his motivation and curiosity resulted in his obtaining a broader knowledge of aviation. As fellow pilot Frank Barr said of him, "He was a great listener." At the same time he became known for his helpfulness. It was not unexpected that his *Arctic Prospector* appeared in a picture showing a January 1929 lineup of planes serving the Fairbanks community.

With Gillam's constant and serious immersion in aviation it was also not unexpected that he was able to give specialized help to Parker D. Cramer and Willard S. Gamble. These two men passed through Fairbanks in early spring 1929 during their Chicago-to-Siberia flight in a stock Cessna AW (forerunner of the Cessna 195). Landing at Weeks Field on their return trip, melting snow made the takeoff impossible. Gillam loaned them a more suitable pair of skis which allowed them to get off early the next morning to complete the journey.

On May 13, 1929 Gillam again volunteered for a search. This time he went with Noel Wien in a search for his brother, Ralph, who was reported missing in the Stearman biplane # NC5415. This plane had been damaged at Walker Lake and the Wien brothers had bought and repaired it. In the near future this plane would change hands once more and figure importantly in Gillam's flying life. On this particular search he was listed as "relief pilot" rather than "observer." This suggests that, as he accrued flying hours, he was looked on more and more as a pilot.

It was shortly after the search for Ralph Wien was successfully completed that Marvel Crosson again touched the lives of the pilots in the Fairbanks area. The first time it was good news through the nationally published report that she had set a new altitude record of 23,996 feet over Los Angeles on May 28, 1929. Shortly thereafter, on August 19, came the tragic news of her death in the crash of her plane during the first Women's Air Derby between Santa Monica and Cleveland. During her year's stay in Fairbanks she had brightened the lives of all she met, especially those of the young, single pilots, including Gillam.

Marvel Crosson enjoying her visit to Fairbanks. (Sylvia "Tapu" Ross Collection/Courtesy R.W. Stevens)

The sorrow over her death went beyond the Fairbanks community. The newspaper headlines nationwide on August 24, referring to the final activities of the Air Race, read, "A period of silence was held for the aviatrix and a vacant seat at the celebration banquet was accorded her."

Arthur Brisbane's eulogy for Marvel showed respect for all women. Some today might view his remarks as patronizing but back then it was an expression of sincerity. He stated:

> A courageous and admirable young woman. For the present such races should be confined to men. Their deaths are less important. When a woman such as Miss Crosson is killed there is no knowing what brilliantly useful men and women may, in her death, have been deprived of the chance of life.

Will Rogers' eulogy, although less direct, carries an unmistakable tone of respect. He stated,

> We met and had a long chat with Marvel Crosson that was killed. We both talked at the time of what a fine wholesome type of girl she was. No riding boots or riding breeches or spurs or anything but just a neat gray suit. She had a great record as a flyer.

August 29, 1929, just a week after Marvel Crosson's tragic death, marked an important event in the history of aviation for Interior Alaska. On that day all air services within that wide area, including Anchorage on the Cook Inlet and as far as Nome on the shores of the Bering Sea, were consolidated into one and became known as Alaska Airways. This consolidation was brought about through the efforts of the well-known Alaska aviator, Carl Ben Eielson. He obtained the financial backing of the holding company which had invested capital in well-known airlines on the East Coast, such as American Airlines and Pan American.

Fairbanks Aviation Mechanics-as part of newly created Alaska Airways. (Courtesy T.M. Spencer)

Alaska Airways then owned ten planes plus two more which were being shipped from the factory. Ben Eielson became the general manager. His pilots included familiar names: Ed Young, Noel Wien, A.A. Bennett, Ralph Wien, Russ Merrill, Frank Dorbandt, and Tom Gerard. The latter also served as chief mechanic. Six of his mechanics were located in Fairbanks. These included Gillam and his friend, Cecil Higgins.

The new company was to have a role in creating the beginning of a possible Gillam legend. This happened when the new manager signed a particularly challenging and lucrative contract which led to the Eielson-Borland search.

Meanwhile, the new company was focusing on getting diverse people and their planes, spread over a large area, to work as a team. During this time, the master mechanic, James (Hutch) Hutchison, chose Gillam to work on what had become a problem providing Weeks Field with a wind indicator. Previously, few planes used the runways, and the pilots knew the hard way of telling wind direction: smoke, wind on water, and blowing sand off river bars. However, with less-experienced pilots, trained to rely on windsocks, a greater likelihood arose of a damaged plane.

The problem could have been solved somewhat quickly had the

master mechanic and his apprentice settled for what is known today as a simple windsock. Instead they decided on a tetrahedron, and not an ordinary one but a full-sized airplane which would attract the attention of pilots and nonpilots alike. Their creativity and hard work resulted in a hybrid plane, part Swallow and part Curtis Robin. It was mounted on a pipe-and-bushing arrangement which kept the nose of the plane pointed into winds of any consequence. This wind indicator was placed on the roof of a hangar in early 1929. It almost suffered an early death when that hangar burned on December 22, 1929. After Eielson consolidated all air services of the interior it was immediately decided that this unique wind indicator should rest atop the highest han-

Master Mechanic Hutch and his apprentice Harold Gillam who designed and built a unique wind-indicator. (Courtesy T.M. Spencer)

gar on the field which, fortunately, was not the one that burned. This

Wind-direction indicator (plane shaped) blends creativity with utility. (UAF Archives)

change to another hangar turned out to be merely a reprieve. In 1931, the home of that handsome work of art also burned to the ground and took the indicator with it.

No other effort of this type was recorded until a full-sized DC-3, formerly part of the Canadian Pacific Airline, was donated by Great Northern Airways to the Yukon Flying Club in Whitehorse, Canada. In 1977 the club began restoration and in 1981 mounted it on a pivot pedestal. There, except when undergoing major renovations, it remains today, a graceful monument to aviation for locals and travelers on the Alaska Highway, to admire.

Both of these wind indicators suggest a creative bent in the minds of the men involved (including Gillam) who felt that a piece of equipment could be both useful and a work of art.

A more recent, and more sophisticated version of Hutch and Gillam's idea. (Studio North Ltd. Photo)

On October 3, 1929 Gillam was again mentioned in the *News Miner*. It stated that he accompanied A.A. Bennett on a flight to McCarthy and then on to the Chisana mine to pick up an injured miner. Gillam was taken along because he "knew the area," having previously worked there—the Copper River region—for the Alaska Road Commission.

An incident occurred during that flight, where Gillam was supposed to be merely a passenger, but where, to an observer, he was assumed to be the pilot. Bennett and Gillam landed at Copper Center to refuel (they carried their own gas). Mrs. Lucy Brenwick, now an elderly lady, was there on that occasion and was interviewed for her impressions of the event. She was then a young woman, born in Copper Center and had lived there her entire life. To her it had been an important happening and she stated, "Gillam was the first pilot to land in Copper Center." She then shared a photo taken at that time. It showed her and Mrs. Barnes, the roadhouse owner, watching Gillam refueling the plane. She shared additional information about Gillam which supported her belief that

The beginning of a special relationship between Gillam, Copper Center and Ma Barnes. (Mrs. Lucy Brenwick Photo)

he was the pilot on that trip. Bennett was hardly mentioned. Since she had been there watching the preparations for the takeoff and the takeoff itself, it is likely that Gillam was actually flying the plane.

On November 22, 1929 Gillam made the front page of the *News*

Miner where it stated, "Gillam Will Fly For His New Company." The article went on to explain that the McCarthy-Chitina residents backed his air transport. This was to be the first air service for their region. The article also stated that Gillam would fly there in December to begin service. An unexpected event caused a delay until summer of the following year.

This unexpected event, the stock market crash of 1929, had a tremendous influence on Gillam's flying career. The *SS Nanuk* lay trapped in the ice at North Cape in Russian Siberia and had a cargo of valuable furs on board. The trader, Olaf Swenson, fearing a drop in fur prices, contracted with Ben Eielson's Alaska Airways for fifteen round trips to transport the furs and passengers from the vessel. To obtain an idea of the importance of the contract, the cost of each of the fifteen trips was estimated to be $4,000. A large sum considering the value of the dollar back then.

Chapter 11

THE CONTRACT

The best laid schemes of mice and men
(gang aft agley) often go astray.
(Robert Burns, To a Mouse)

The *Fairbanks* News Miner, in its October 25, 1929 issue, reported on what appeared to be a routine, and hardly newsworthy event. It read, in part,

> Contract made for fifteen trips into Arctic - to bring out passengers and furs...Ben Eielson (general manager of Alaska Airways) will fly one of the two planes to be used.

As it turned out, fulfilling the terms of this seemingly routine obligation became complicated in terms of time and resources required. Even more serious, and emotion-laden, was the unexpected loss of two lives. This heart-rending aspect, in turn, brought out the courageous and tenacious behavior (under extreme, almost hopeless, conditions) of the men involved, both pilots and nonpilots. Thus it became more than just a local event. It stirred national interest and, finally, involved partici-

The SS Nanuk at North Cape. (Sylvia "Tapu" Ross Collection/Courtesy R.W. Stevens)

pants from three different nations. In a very real sense the search for an unreported plane and its occupants set the stage for an unfolding drama in which Gillam was to play a leading role.

Stuart Morris, writing in the December 29, 1929 issue of the *Seattle Washington Times*, gave a dramatic but accurate description of the setting and characters involved in this search. Under the title, "The Convoy of Courage" he stated,

> Into the frozen gloom of the long arctic night a score of heroic aviators from three nations will wing their way in search of Carl Ben Eielson and Earl Borland, with the phantom of death riding close by. American, Canadian and Russian flyers will join in the quest over the arctic ice.

How it came to be that Gillam, still an inexperienced student pilot, became a central figure in the search will be explained later. First comes the need to examine in detail the single most important factor which changed a routine event into a dramatic one. This factor not only led to the tragic deaths but also seriously challenged the airplane's ability to provide safe, reliable transportation. The factor, simply stated, is weather. And even today weather challenges the airplane's ability to provide the traveler with both safety and reliability.

Severe Arctic winds. *(Russian Photo/ Courtesy Sylvia Ross)*

Early bush pilots viewed weather basically as a danger stemming from obscuration of vision and accompanied often by turbulent winds which served as an additional barrier to safety and reliability. This simple definition was sound but tended to overlook that the degree of danger found in "flying weather" varied with the degree of visual impairment. This, in turn, changed constantly as the plane moved through the air. As a result, pilots were making constant decisions where error could lead to unexpected encounters with terrain and sudden death. Such risks could be avoided by only flying in "good" weather which, of course, further reduced reliability. With today's radio and instrumentation, commercial flights have accrued a high level of reliability. However, in the late 1920s weather figured as the major reason for lack of reliability in air transportation. In Alaska, with its great distances and lack of roads and railroads, this unreliability was especially felt.

To improve reliability yet safeguard the lives of those aboard a plane, including their own, bush pilots made careful preparation for flights into obscured visibility. Every flight in good visibility became a practice lesson. In these, height was obtained which gave a panoramic view of significant landmarks. Early bush pilots had little in the way of maps. This led them to make their own; either on paper or in their minds. On the other hand, pilots back then were aided by slow airspeed, which gave time to observe and note; by the relative short distances of most flights; by the fact that pilots, whenever possible, followed trails and waterways which gave ongoing geographic orientation as well as assurance of human habitation should a forced landing occur; and finally, they were aided in their primitive map making by the fact that most routes were often repeated.

Bush pilots did not stop there, however. Satisfied that landmarks were properly imprinted, they then flew those same routes, again during good visibility, but now at extremely low altitudes. Altitudes that would normally be flown if weather actually did obscure terrain. Here they could actually see what the terrain looked like at that height and note where turns needed to be made to follow landmarks such as creeks and trails or to avoid higher terrain. Such simulated training was essential before encountering the real thing.

Because of the need for visibility in order to keep planes and terrain apart, night flying was not considered. This presented a particular problem in Alaska, especially in the north above the Arctic Circle (the frigid zone, 26 degrees below the North pole). Here, the summers provide an abundance of daylight, twenty-four hours. On the other hand, the opposite prevails in winter. No sunlight or—at most—a few hours of shadowless light as the sun touches the horizon and then drops quickly back down. Obviously, flight in the northern arctic during the winter months is extremely limited. Therefore, weather and pilot preparation to safely "fly weather" were seen as the only way to achieve more reliable air transportation. Gillam seemed to understand this need to prepare for flying weather. From the very beginning, he possessed an unusual ability to fly safely through extreme weather. Some saw this as a special capacity. This appeared to be true. However, from the start of his training he was always preparing himself to fly weather. He did this by paying attention to terrain and special landmarks whenever he was in the air, whether as pilot or observer.

Still, pilot preparation for penetration of weather has its limitations. Constant changes in degrees of visual obscuration can impose stressful decision-making. Other weather-related factors also endanger safe flight. Mountainous terrain while flying weather increases stress even more since it involves abrupt changes in terrain height and a need for immediate response to these changes. Here the possibility of human error is even greater and, consequently, further impairs flight safety.

As was suggested earlier, Alaska suffers even greater unreliability in air travel during its arctic winter with its limited daylight and its severe storms caused by intrusion of cold polar air currents. Here yet another special hazard, involving weather and terrain, prevails. The terrain may be perfectly level but is totally snow covered. Combined with partial obscuration of the sky, a whiteout results. It then becomes impossible to tell where earth and sky meet. Without modern instrumentation, there is no escape from this total loss of orientation.

In view of the ways in which weather and related factors influence air safety and reliability, especially in Alaska, it seems odd that a contract was signed requiring an airplane to prove itself both reliable and safe while performing during an arctic winter when weather is at its worst and daylight is limited to some three hours when skies are clear and considerably less when skies are obscured.

Swenson and Daughter. *(Lomen Brothers Photo/ /Courtesy R.W. Stevens)*

Certain factors relating to the October 24 contract were fixed. The need for air transportation arose at that moment. The motor vessel, *SS Nanuk*, with a valuable load of furs and its crew on board, was locked in the Siberian ice pack. It would remain there until May or June of the following year. The trader, Olaf Swenson, was especially anxious to get the furs to market. His anxiety was enhanced, as was his willingness to pay additionally for air transportation, by erratic behavior of the U.S. stock market. This instability could drastically reduce the value of his million dollar's worth of furs. The stock market did indeed crash on October 29 which added to the urgency of the need for air transportation.

And how was the matter viewed by Ben Eielson, general manager of the newly created Alaskan Airways? To him it would be an opportunity to convince the Eastern parent corporation that their financial investment in the newly formed company was a sound one. Yes, the expected $50,000 revenue was certainly a factor. Perhaps more important was Eielson's dream of the important role aviation would play in Alaska's future. Like Gillam, he saw that the airplane must prove itself both safe and reliable in meeting Alaska's transportation needs. Although the obstacles were great, to not accept the challenge would send the wrong message to those looking to aviation as an answer to their unique transportation problems.

Eielson's knowledge of these obstacles came from experience. He had been chief pilot on George Hubert Wilkins' two arctic expeditions in 1926 and 1927. During one of these, while on an exploration flight over the Arctic Ocean near the North Pole, strong adverse winds and engine problems led to fuel exhaustion and a forced landing on moving polar ice. Knowledge, endurance, hope, and a sixteen-day struggle over rough pressure ridges finally brought them to land at a nearby trading post. Other than utter exhaustion, the only damage was the amputation of a frozen finger on Eielson's right hand.

Just the previous year, 1928, Wilkins, with Eielson as pilot, had flown across the Arctic Ocean from Barrow in Alaska to Spitsbergen in Norway in a single-engine Lockheed Vega. This flight was not without an incident involving weather and survival. It happened but a short distance from their destination. A storm lay across their path and required a difficult landing into blowing snow. Safely down, and with everything secured, they waited five days inside the plane while constantly being buffeted by the wind. Finally the storm lifted and with great difficulty they got the plane airborne. Shortly thereafter, Spits-

Eielson's' planned route from Teller, Alaska to North Cape and the Nanuk. *(reprinted from "Mercy Pilot"" courtesy of Epicenter Press)*

bergen came into view. Since leaving Barrow, they had spent approximately twenty-two hours in the air. Even more recently, Eielson had again served as Wilkins' pilot in an exploration of the Antarctic.

Yes, Eielson knew the hazards of arctic flying through personal experience. Yet in these instances, he and Wilkins chose the time in which to do that flying. In the north they chose March and April which would provide approximately twelve hours of daylight as well as milder weather. His contract did not allow him the liberty of choice. To offset this disadvantage, he carefully planned a route that crossed the Bering Strait soon after leaving Teller, then following the Siberian coast until reaching North Cape where the *SS Nanuk* lay marooned. Along this shore lay a number of Chukchi (Siberian Eskimo) settlements. In the winter numerous hard-frozen stretches of ice, cleared of snow by the wind, provided safe landing locations. These settlements and the landing locations would provide a safe haven should a pilot encounter darkness or weather-obscured skies.

Radio communication also figured in Eielson's decision to accept the challenges of the contract. Radio communication existed between the *SS Nanuk* and the roadhouse at Teller. A fixed schedule was arranged to exchange current weather information and relay messages. There was, of course, no air-to-ground radio. Nor were there radios in any of the Siberian villages which could communicate a plane's safe landing to wait out weather.

In spite of the careful planning, the wild weather of the arctic winter remained to be dealt with. On the 500 mile-route, the worst weather lay across the Bering Strait. Here, frequent winds funneled through the Strait, either from the Bering Sea on the south or from the Arctic Ocean on the north. These winds resulted in turbulence along with obscured visibility from blowing snow. In addition to the winds at work, open water leads frequented the Strait, which created a dense fog. This happened as the warmer water came in contact with the colder Polar air.

Also, except for the short distance from Teller to the Bering Strait, firsthand knowledge of the route which early bush pilots depended on for safe flight in bad weather was completely lacking. At that time the United States did not formally recognize the Soviet government so few commercial contacts were made. Noel Wien had made the only known round-trip flight from Teller to the Siberian coast. It also involved retrieving furs from a vessel marooned in the ice at North Cape. Since this was to be a single flight made in March during long hours of daylight in relatively warm weather with clear skies, no attempt was made to fly low and observe landmarks at that height.

In spite of these difficulties, Eielson signed the contract on October 24. In doing so he was evidently putting his trust in the courage, skill, and judgment of his pilots. To set an example, as well as study firsthand the landmarks and general terrain along the route, Eielson decided to make the first flights himself. As the busy manager of a newly formed corporation he could easily have assigned the task of these first flights to any of his qualified pilots, but he didn't.

So, on October 29, 1929 the first round-trip was begun. The plan called for two planes. The larger, faster Hamilton monoplane was to be flown by Eielson, and the smaller, slower Stinson Detroiter biplane by Frank Dorbandt. Both planes had enclosed cabins and were well suited for cold-weather flying. The plan also called for the planes to fly as a team. This would add an element of security. If one plane encountered difficulties while in the air, the other might provide immediate assistance or note the plane's location and nature of the problem before flying on to seek help.

The French, on their early airmail routes into their African possessions, solved the problem of additional safety by carrying a radio operator on each flight. These operators used code transmission to communicate progress of the flight to monitoring ground stations. Later, Pan American used this system on its long-distance routes which included Alaska. Gillam initiated his own primitive voice radio system of communication during his flying in the Copper River region. This was in the early 1930s and he used roadhouse owners, or others, at given villages who could monitor the radio and communicate weather or emergency information.

In the case of Alaskan Airways' contract, using two planes would also reduce the number of fifteen round-trips by one half. This was an important decision, given the short hours of daylight and the urgent need to get people and furs out quickly.

On the initial flight to the *SS Nanuk* the team arrangement was not used because Eielson was delayed

Eielson lands at the SS Nanuk. *(Eddie Bowman Collection//Courtesy R.W. Stevens)*

at Nome with a damaged landing gear. Dorbandt took off on October 29 from Teller alone. He did this on schedule, flying nonstop to the *SS Nanuk* (at North Cape) in six hours and twenty minutes. Because he crossed the international date line, he lost a day and landed October 30. Eielson, after making quick repairs, took off from Nome on October 30. He was also favored with good weather, but being faster, flew nonstop from Nome (a longer distance) in four hours and twenty minutes. Having also crossed the international date line, he lost a day and landed on the ice next to the *SS Nanuk*, October 31.

Everything had gone well to that point, mainly because the weather had cooperated. Furs were loaded and people assigned to each plane on the afternoon of October 31 (*SS Nanuk* time). That evening the people living on board the *SS Nanuk*, having been isolated geographically and living in cramped quarters, enjoyed their evening with the visitors. Their positive response was conveyed in a simple statement by Bob Gleason who, as radio operator on the *SS Nanuk*, was present. In his book, *Icebound In The Siberian Arctic*, he states, "We had a great evening with these men," and added, "We anticipated many more pleasant evenings together, realizing not at all that tragedy lay ahead."

Yet, a seed of disenchantment had already been planted by one of the pilots, Frank Dorbandt. His behavior, on arrival the previous day, had an influence not just on those then marooned on the *SS Nanuk* but on others involved in the drama that was soon to unfold. Some even placed blame on Dorbandt as contributing to the tragedy. Gleason first told what actually happened when Dorbandt landed, then added a brief observation.

> As big Frank Dorbandt cut the engine and opened the door, we cheered. It was a great and happy occasion for all. Then he filed one message with me, to be sent to the Associated Press in New York something like "Pioneer Alaska aviator pilot Frank Dorbandt completed a hazardous 6 hour 20 minute flight from Teller to North Cape in a Stinson Detroiter to rescue *SS Nanuk's* crew. (At this point Gleason inserts his observation.) In later years I was to learn more about Dorbandt's braggadocio, but on this night we loved him.

Dorbandt's message, sent from within the confines of the *SS Nanuk's* cramped quarters, could not help but become known and discussed. However, it is doubtful that in the beginning anyone felt negative, especially since Dorbandt was the first to reach the *SS Nanuk*. This made him a hero. It was not until much later that his actions gave reason for resentment. After all, he had been chosen by Eielson to become a member of the two-plane team to haul furs and to take the people to civilization.

Yet, with all this expectation, Dorbandt never returned to the *SS Nanuk*. Nor did he ever cross the Bering Strait again. He made attempts but these attempts failed; most, but not all, failures stemmed from the demon, weather. Damage to landing gear during takeoff; extreme cold that would not allow the engine to produce normal power; all of these were also reasons. However, the people on the *SS Nanuk*, waiting for Dorbandt to rescue them, or at least make an appearance, made judgments not based entirely on reason. It was little wonder then that Gillam and Joe Crosson, being the next arrivals and braving the shorter days and bitter cold in open-cockpit airplanes, were viewed as special people by those waiting on the *SS Nanuk*.

More criticism of Dorbandt will be mentioned later. However, in this entire episode it should be remembered that the criticisms dealt not with his competence as a pilot. Rather, it involved his abrasive manner, a manner ill-suited to situations involving extreme pressures and confined quarters.

The return to Teller on that first trip on November 1 (*SS Nanuk* time) began on schedule. Weather, as always, was a prime concern to the pilots. Although clear skies prevailed at the *SS Nanuk*, there were heavy clouds to the east, their direction of flight. Also, Gleason's radioed weather report from Teller read, "Not very good."

As it turned out, weather did give Eielson a chance to use his plan for a weather-related landing on the ice near a Chukchi settlement.

Gleason obtained the details of that flight, and the precautionary landing, from Clark Crichton Jr., who was a passenger on Dorbandt's plane that morning. Although Eielson had the faster plane, he returned and landed back at the *SS Nanuk* to shut off the plane's heater, fearing the high temperatures would damage the furs which were his main

Chukchi yarang (skin hut). (Crosson Collection/Courtesy R.W. Stevens)

cargo. Meanwhile, Dorbandt was in the lead when he encountered heavy snow not far from the Bering crossing. After fighting the snow for some time, he spotted a Chukchi settlement and landed near it on smooth sea ice. Eielson, following a few minutes later, saw the Stinson and landed next to it. The Chukchi heard the planes, located them on the ice, led the passengers to their huts and cared for them.

The planes were held up for three days. Then, on the fourth day, the weather cleared. After heating the engines with firepots, fueled with gasoline, the flight continued. Both planes landed at Nome on November 4 (Nome time) with Dorbandt making a fuel stop at Teller. Having unloaded passengers and furs, both planes flew to Teller that same day. There they loaded extra gasoline, badly needed at the *SS Nanuk*, and special foods which might make the enforced stay of those on the *SS Nanuk* more bearable

The next morning, November 5, with planes, pilots and mechanics ready, weather moved in at Teller and completely closed in at North Cape with snow and dense fog. Planes and crews remained storm-bound for the following four days. Quite naturally, at this point tensions arose. These tensions obviously contributed to what was soon to follow. In 1944, Jean Potter interviewed the various people involved in the 1929-1930 search. Jack Warren, manager of the roadhouse at Teller, was one of those interviewed. In her book, *The Flying North*, Potter gave his firsthand feelings and observations,

> Jack Warren, the roadhouse manager, who was host to the Eielson Relief Expedition at Teller, experienced such strain that he cannot discuss the search calmly even today (some fourteen years after the event). "These pilots," he says, "were a bunch of nerves." As time passed, Dorbandt was reported to be verging on a breakdown. Crowded together in the bleak frame building, the men looked out past high snowbanks to whirling gloom. Weather at North Cape was reported no better. "Ceiling and visibility nil," the *SS Nanuk* flashed day after day. "High winds." The universal edginess of weather-bound airmen was sharpened by a driving sense of hopelessness.

Jean Potter's book is also the source detailing the specific interactions between Eielson and Dorbandt on that fateful November 9.

> On the gloomy morning of November 9th Eielson and Dorbandt, according to an eyewitness account, waited together after breakfast in the Teller roadhouse. Eielson sat with his feet propped on the counter reading a magazine. Dorbandt restlessly paced the floor. The two men were temperamentally opposites and had clashed on several occasions since Eielson had returned to Alaska with his new title and power. Dorbandt, an Anchorage pioneer, was big of heart, hot of temper, and loud of mouth. He was one of the ablest pilots in the North but also one of the most reckless and impulsive. A few weeks earlier, when Eielson had postponed a local trip because of bad weather, Dorbandt had accused his new boss of cowardice.

> "When are we going to take off?" Dorbandt asked on that fateful morning.

> "We'll wait for the next weather report from the *SS Nanuk*," Eielson tersely told him.

> Dorbandt tore a piece of wrapping paper from the counter and scrawled a rough diagram of Bering Strait and the two continents.

"You know," he shouted, "all we have to do is hit right across here!"

Eielson did not reply.

"Well," Dorbandt told him, "You can sit here if you want, I'm leaving."

At 10:45 people in the roadhouse heard the roar of the Stinson's engine and saw Dorbandt's ship lift into the air, heading toward Asia.

Eielson went silently upstairs and returned with his parka. He and Borland walked to their ship. At 11:15 the Hamilton bumped off the sea ice and disappeared into the unsettled sky to the west. Some time later, Dorbandt and Bassett (the mechanic), foiled by dense fog in Bering Strait, returned.

Teller, Alaska. (Crosson Collection/Courtesy R.W. Stevens)

Eielson and Borland did not return.

Here it is interesting to note that Dorbandt, seen as an able pilot but an impulsive one, returned that day after encountering dense fog at the Bering Strait, and Eielson, an experienced and careful pilot, flew through that same weather at approximately the same time and, as later information would prove, arrived safely on the Siberian side.

At the end of that short but remembered day, Eielson and Borland had not returned to Teller nor had they landed at the *SS Nanuk*. Disappointment rather than anxiety ruled for the moment. It was assumed that weather had necessitated a landing on the ice and, hopefully, next to a Chukchi settlement. When a week went by, with a day or so of good weather, a hopeful mood still prevailed. Eielson himself had said that an unreported plane should not be a cause for concern or lead to an organized search until two weeks or more had passed. Given the carefully laid-out plan for this series of flights to the *SS Nanuk*, this was not an unreasonable view; especially since the route passed over numerous settlements with landing sites and the planes would be flying as a team.

Here, an important deviation from the plan occurred. On that second flight the planes took off into questionable weather but not as a team. Dorbandt had taken off first and there was no report that the planes had made visual contact while in the air. This deviation from the plan complicated any search that might become necessary. Dorbandt, not having had visual contact, was in no position to report where and when he had last seen Eielson's plane. These circumstances put an even heavier burden on him to break through to the *SS Nanuk*. By so doing, he and his mechanic as an observer, would be flying directly over the route Eielson had taken. He would then be making an organized search while at the same time his arrival at the *SS Nanuk* would allow him to bring out another load of furs and repeat the search procedure on his return to Teller. However, Dorbandt did not return, to search or to haul out cargo.

Meanwhile, with no means of communication along the five hundred miles between Teller and the *SS Nanuk*, the people on the icebound vessel and at Alaskan Airways home office in Fairbanks took a wait-and-see attitude. This seemed a prudent approach since the Airways had other, far-flung flight obligations to fulfill. The company assumed, of course, that Dorbandt would use the remaining plane assigned to the *SS Nanuk* contract to haul, and now also, to search. As it turned out, it was not until much later, when Joe Crosson was assigned to search, that things began to happen, mainly due to his emotional commitment.

By mid-November concern for Eielson and Borland had intensified. Gleason, as radio operator on the *SS Nanuk*, copied the daily press reports from the large coastal radio stations at San Francisco and San Diego. These showed that the disappearance of the well-known Eielson was now a nationwide concern.

The first real news came on November 18 when two Chukchi men from a settlement on Eielson's route arrived at the *SS Nanuk*. Gleason gleaned and reported the following information:

> On the 9th, the day Eielson took off from Teller, Natives had gathered at one of their houses sixty miles from us. They saw Eielson come over just as it was getting dark; visibility was poor. Eielson had circled the house twice but did not land. A Russian trapper, fifty miles from North Cape, heard the plane go over him but he could not see it.

These men also reported the visibility down their way had been good for the past few days. This led those on the *SS Nanuk* to suspect that Eielson and Borland were in trouble. This, in turn, led them to hope that it might be something minor such as too much snow for wheels, poor field, or even a damaged landing gear. Still, anxiety was growing. Naturally, the press releases received on the *SS Nanuk*'s radio, showing the nation's concern, added to the feelings of those marooned on the vessel. Olaf Swenson, the trader on the *SS Nanuk*, sent out two dog teams to search the area where Eielson's plane had been seen and heard but by the end of November they had not yet returned.

Also by November 18, just two days before the sun would disappear below the horizon and not return again until January 16, Alaskan Airways manager for the Interior, Charles Thompson, laid out a plan to get men and planes to Teller for an organized search. The two-week deadline had not yet arrived but his knowledge of Dorbandt's failed attempts to cross the Bering Strait probably moved him to start

Dog team at the Nanuk. *(Crosson Collection/Courtesy R.W. Stevens)*

early. Thompson's plan to get even a single plane as far as Teller was thwarted by a combination of weather and damaged planes.

This changed when Joe Crosson took off from Fairbanks on November 29 in an open-cockpit Waco 10, NC 780E. On his way to Teller, he landed at Ruby, where he caught up with Ed Young flying a New Standard and Harvey Barnhill in a Zenith 6. The two pilots, also on their way to search headquarters at Teller, were holding for weather. In an attempt to reach Nome, and having to return because of weather, Young damaged the New Standard's landing gear. Crosson, arriving at Ruby, surveyed the situation, dispatched Barnhill in the damaged New Standard back to Fairbanks, instructed Young to fly the Zenith to fulfill other Alaskan Airways obligations, then took off for Nome. Arriving there with a heavy load of mail, he unloaded it and quickly took off for Teller. He arrived there the same day, November 29, after having flown a total of five hours and thirty-five minutes. No small feat considering that the sun had hardly risen above the horizon before dropping back down again.

Crosson's actions since he left Fairbanks on November 29 were those of a man determined to find his close friend, Ben Eielson. The next morning, after long hours in the air the previous day, Crosson took off in his open-cockpit Waco with Dorbandt following in the heavier, enclosed Stinson. Their goal? to cross the difficult Bering Strait. Never mind that the *SS Nanuk* was reporting 35 degrees below zero, 40 mph winds and no visibility. He was determined to cross the greatest hurdle, the Bering Straits, then fly a short distance up the

Siberian coast to Cape Serdte-Janeb. This is where Eielson and Dorbandt had landed on their way out with the first load. With his determination to find Eielson, with plenty of gas back at Teller, and with a belief that weather isn't always as reported, he took off "to have a look." This time the weather was bad and drove them back to Teller. Crosson, with Dorbandt, tried again on December 3 and again were driven back. On the third attempt, December 6, the two planes, overloaded with extra gas for the return trip, hit just the wrong spots of rough ice and suffered gear damage on takeoff—Crosson's Waco just slightly and was immediately ready for another try. Dorbandt's, however, was damaged to where it had to be flown to Nome, and then on to Fairbanks, for repair.

Dorbandt's previous failures to reach the *SS Nanuk* and the greater damage to his plane might suggest lesser piloting skills or, perhaps, an unconscious avoidance of another crossing to the Siberian coast. A simpler explanation points to the heavier load the larger plane was required to carry.

The damaged aircrafts led Crosson to an immediate decision. Weather was beyond human control; the surface of the runway was not. With the help of locals, he found a nearby sheltered spot where the wind had not formed snow mounds on the ice.

Cape Prince of Wales. *(Frank Dorbandt Photo/Courtesy R.W. Stevens)*

During the next few days Dorbandt flew his Stinson to Nome, Crosson worked on the new ice runway while also keeping a weather vigil, and Thompson struggled to organize a solid search.

At that particular moment, on December 8, the Aviation Corporation in the East purchased three Fairchild 71 cargo aircraft to be sent to Alaska. These monoplanes had enclosed cabins, powerful 425 hp Pratt and Whitney Wasp engines, 800-mile range, 100 mph airspeed, equipped with extra-wide skis and were crewed by pilots and mechanics experienced in winter operations; all this indicated the Aviation Corporation executive's intent to provide the best that money could buy in the search for their Alaska manager and his mechanic. At this same time the Russian government was providing two Junkers F-13 monoplanes and crew to aid in the search. And it was on Monday, December 9, that Alaskan Airways dispatched two more planes to join the search. Ed Young, flying an enclosed Stinson Standard, NC 877 was sent and under his supervision, the unlicensed, inexperienced young pilot Harold Gillam was flying an open-cockpit Stearman, NC 5415.

At this point the resources within the aviation community as distant as the East coast of the United States and Canada as well as Moscow in the Soviet Union were mobilized to search for "two of their own." No one knew then that back on November 9, at 3:30 P.M. the Hamilton aircraft, with its pilot and mechanic, had smashed into a hidden hillside of the Siberian coast, killing its occupants instantly. Neither did anyone know that following the crash, strong winds had quickly covered the bodies hurled into the snow. Then the plane itself was covered except for a single wingtip pointing awkwardly toward the sky.

Had all this been known, then what? Left with the certainty that there were no survivors, there would have been no hope. And hope was the driving force behind all the effort. The bodies would eventually have been found and, with dignity, laid to rest in that same plot of ground. No difference in the final results. However, without that lingering hope there would have been no intense struggle, the struggle that in the minds of the men involved might have made the difference between life and death. Without hope there would have been no example of human courage and human effort against impossible odds, the likes of which have seldom been seen before or since. And among the men so engaged, the two who clearly demonstrated such courage and tenacity were Joe Crosson and Harold Gillam.

Chapter 12
THE SEARCH
What is man that thou art mindful of him?
(The Bible, Psalm 8)

On December 9th, 1929 Gillam was on his way to Teller as part of the Eielson-Borland search. Yet as recently as November 22 he had announced his plan to launch an air service in the Copper River region and that he would move to that area in December to begin actual service. On December 2, after having installed a new Warner-Scarab, 110 hp air-cooled engine in his Swallow biplane, he

Gillam and his Stearman; an inexperienced pilot faces the elements. (courtesy T.M. Spencer)

flight-tested it with the intention of flying it in his new venture. On December 7, just two days before leaving for Teller, the Aviation News section of the *News Miner* reported Gillam making a freight flight to Fort Yukon on the Yukon River. The article also mentioned his appointment as agent for Swallow airplanes for all of Alaska, stating he had already sold a Swallow trainer to fellow Fairbanks pilots Percy Hubbard and Art Hines. Certainly all these activities suggest an intention other than what he finally ended up doing on December 9.

What changed his mind? Obviously the answer relates to the decision of Alaskan Airways, both locally and within the parent company, to initiate a full-scale search. This decision strongly suggested Eielson and Borland were in serious trouble. True, because safe landing sites near settlements existed but these had no radio by which such safe landings could be reported, Eielson had directed that no organized search be initiated until two weeks had passed. Also, it was known that the plane carried full survival gear in case of a landing not near any Chukchi settlement. Extra gasoline carried on these trips could be used in the plane's firepot s for emergency heating.

Thompson, the Fairbanks manager, had attempted positioning planes for a possible search, even though the circumstances made it possible for most people to take a wait-and-see attitude. Meanwhile, stateside newspapers were carrying reports of the missing Eielson who was known to be an important figure in the aviation world.

It was during this period that Gillam continued with his plans for an air service. Obviously, the happenings immediately before December 9 brought an abrupt change in attitude, especially in the local aviation community. This changed attitude no longer allowed a guarded hope that Eielson's and Borland's lives were not in danger.

Hubbard and Hines with Swallow purchased from Gillam, they installed 225 hp Wright Whirlwind engine. (Courtesy R.W. Stevens)

Now the flying community which undoubtedly included Gillam, finally felt a terrible anxiety. However, Gillam never surrendered hope as long as even a remote chance for life existed. It was this hope, reinforced by the additional bond of friendship, that gave both Gillam and Crosson their intense dedication toward finding the missing airmen. Their faint but powerful hope simply rejected any thought that the airmen might not be holed up somewhere, alive.

How did Gillam react to this sudden change within the flying community? We know that on December 9 he was off to Teller under the watchful eye of an experienced pilot. How did this happen? How could the management of Alaskan Airways with its financial obligation to its stockholders authorize a young, unlicensed pilot with little or no experience in either cross country or weather flying, to take one of their planes on a search mission? A search mission to be carried out under the worst possible arctic flying conditions?

Jean Potter, based on her interviews of those involved in the search, reported that even young Harold Gillam, who had previously made only one cross country flight, was present. "Give me a ship, give me

113

a ship," he begged Alaskan Airways officials in Fairbanks. "I want to look for Ben."

His emotional commitment to the task that lay ahead certainly made a favorable impression. Yet, those officials had more on which to base their judgment. Gillam had worked for the company for over a year as a mechanic. This, along with his progress toward a flying license, which involved pilots who flew for the company, formed a solid basis for a positive judgment. Finally, Joe Crosson, who had frequent and personal knowledge of Gillam's attitude and skills relating to flying, also had something to say. His view would have been particularly valued since he was already acting informally as chief pilot for the search at the time he left for Teller on November 29.

Gillam's flight to Teller went well. After landing at Nulato for an overnight stay, the planes went on with a stop at Nome and then to Teller. Flying as a team with Ed Young, an experienced pilot, gave Gillam badly needed cross country and weather experience.

Although planes and pilots were in place at Teller by December 11, the first concentrated effort to cross the Bering Strait was not made till December 18. Also on that date, the Aviation Corporation in the East appointed Alfred Lomen, a well-known Nome business man, to replace Frank Dorbandt as overall search director. In turn, Lomen immediately appointed Crosson official chief pilot for the operation. A plan was then devised to use the two open-cockpit planes for the actual searching. These were faster and used less fuel. Important, since fuel was in short supply at the *SS Nanuk*. The heavier, enclosed planes would be used to freight gas to the *SS Nanuk* and to Cape Serdtse-Kamen on the Siberian side. On their return flights they would be freighting out furs.

Weather was a factor in delaying any attempt to cross the Strait. Time, however, was also needed to get Dorbandt's damaged Stinson to Nome and bring up its replacement from Anchorage.

Finally, with everything in place on December 18, four planes took off toward the Bering Strait. The two lighter, open-cockpit ones-a Waco and a Stearman-were flown by Crosson and Gillam. The two heavier, enclosed planes-a Stinson Detroiter and a New Standard-were flown by Ed Young and Harvey Barnhill. None of the planes made it across, due to severe snowstorms over the Strait. It is interesting to note that the two less experienced pilots returned first. These were Gillam, with little total experience, and Barnhill, a recent hire with little Alaska experience. The fact that they returned together indicated Gillam was still under the direction of another pilot. His assignment to a pilot with less Alaska experience was undoubtedly deliberate, the assumption being that Barnhill would be less apt to challenge severe weather and thus would keep himself and Gillam out of harm's way. This then, allowed the two experienced Alaska pilots to make a deeper penetration into severe weather. And that is the way it turned out. Except that Crosson came in last, and alone, having spent two hours in the air.

That evening Crosson, as chief pilot, evidently did some thinking. It must have been apparent that trying to hold together a formation of four planes in obscured visibility was unrealistic, especially when the formation included slower and faster planes. So the next morning the two faster planes, which used less gas, were sent out. And who would the pilots be? It was an easy matter for Crosson to assign himself to the Waco, but what about the Stearman? Assigning it to Ed Young, with his considerable Alaska experience, would have made sense. But he didn't. He chose Gillam. Why? There were practical considerations. Barnhill had decided to ride out with Matt Nieminen who was making shuttles between Teller and Nome, hauling gas to Teller for the search and handling regular freight and passenger traffic. From Nome, Barnhill would take off for the lower-forty eight. At that particular moment, only one pilot was left to make hauls to the SS Nanuk in one of the larger, slower planes. This job was important. Right then fish for the sled dogs, used in a limited way on a ground search, was in short supply; as was gas for the planes to be based at the SS Nanuk for the main search. Although important, this flying did not directly affect the finding of the missing airmen. Probably the most important factor in choosing Gillam was his emotional commitment. This commitment happened to parallel Crosson's own. Also, both men apparently felt their faint hope for the missing airmen was not totally unrealistic. This would not be the first time that men had been rescued after all but a few had given up hope.

So the next morning at 10:00 a.m., December 19, the Waco and the Stearman lifted off the ice with heavy loads of extra gas and emergency gear. On March 13, 1930, shortly after the search ended, Gillam was asked to dictate to a public stenographer the details of the actual search in which he was personally involved, and he was involved in almost all of it. This is the only piece of Gillam's writing, except for a letter to his father, that has ever been found. It contains a full report on this successful flight and the weather encountered.

Almost in its entirety, the report deals with facts. Yet his words, although not intended to, create in the reader's mind images that speak of skill, courage, and a total determination to "get through." Today this might be criticized as "get-home-itis". Back then, Gillam and other pilots reached out to their limits in order to give air transportation a reasonable degree of reliability. However, this was not done recklessly. They did not throw away their lives or disregard safety. These pilots used every flight, whether in good visibility or "not so good," to acquire competence. In the words of Don Gentile, World War II fighter-pilot ace, "Confidence comes from competence which, in turn, stems from diligent practice." In those early bush pilots, it was diligent practice that led to their competence. This, in turn, gave them the confidence to press on into marginal weather and thereby add to the airplane's reliability. The almost total lack of weather-related flight fatalities until well into the 1930s, speaks clearly to those early Alaska pilots' concern for safety.

Reading Gillam's account of this particular flight as described below, one cannot help but wonder how he could have achieved Gentile's confidence and competence without the necessary thoughtful practice.

December 19,1929. Joe Crosson flying a Whirlwind-powered Waco and myself a Stearman, left Teller at 10:00 a.m. Each plane carried sleeping bags, Primus stoves, and enough rations to subsist on for thirty days. Besides this, we had thirteen 5-gallon cans of gasoline each.

Crossing Bering Strait-most difficult part of the route; open leads frequently resulted in fog. (Frank Dorbandt photo, Mary Burrows Collection/Courtesy R.W. Stevens)

At this time our flying light was limited to four hours on clear days and much less on cloudy days, so we set our destination for that day's flight, the village at which Ben had stopped on his first trip from Cape North. We were anxious to get in contact with anyone speaking English so that we might interest them in the search. We started to climb immediately after taking off and had reached 6,000 feet when we started across the Bering Strait. We could see the Islands plainly, also the tops of mountains in Siberia. Our flying time from Teller to the Diomedes was just one hour—we were making excellent time. From the Diomedes on we ran into a haze which we could see through by looking straight down but we could see nothing looking ahead. The visibility changed depending on the nature of the floor. Over water, which showed black, everything was fine, while over the white ice, we could see nothing. We came down to within 200 feet of the ice opposite Whalen. From Whalen to Cape Serdze, precipitous bluffs formed the shoreline and, as they showed black, served as a real good mark to fly by. At Serdze, the fog opened up a little and we climbed up on top. We stayed on top for 45 minutes before finding a hole large enough to go through. We had seen nothing of the beach for 45 minutes and did not know what our ceiling would be, but fortunately, we went through over an open lead, the water giving us a chance to judge our distance accurately. Flying now at 100 feet, we started looking for a place to land. The villages along here are only about ten miles apart. The Chukchi houses showing dark gave us a chance to check our altitude. We were flying close together and were out of sight of each other most of the time. It was getting thicker with the fading of daylight so we landed at Pelikii without locating our objective.

Joe and I congratulated each other several times that night on getting through and both vowed we would wait for better weather.

December 21, the next day, as we had crossed the International Date Line.

On this morning our thermometers registered thirty-six below zero with about a twenty-mile North wind blowing. We prepared to leave while still dark. By ten a.m. it was light enough to take off and we left. Visibility was slightly better than on the preceding day and a streak of light in the east made us believe it would improve as the day became older.

We climbed to 2,000 feet and started across Koluchin Bay. That slender streak of light was all we had to fly by and we had to get about 2,500 feet to clear the hills on the west side of Kolchin Bay. After crossing the bay, the hills under us would be visible for a few seconds at a time and the light in the east was gradually fading. After a few minutes at 2,500 feet, we swung north, trying to locate shoreline so we could get down out of that fog. It was while flying north that I missed Joe. He was slightly higher and a little behind me. I turned south and caught a glimpse of him—he seemed to be going down. I returned to the place where I thought he had gone through but could not see down so I decided I would look for a better place before going down as I knew we were still over hills. I flew around in circles until I finally sighted a frozen stream directly under me—so down I went. No sign of Joe but, believing he would proceed on to North Cape, I climbed back out of this valley and headed north. I believed it impossible to return the way we had come. In about ten minutes I sighted an open lead and knew I was away from the hills so went down to within two hundred feet of the ice. I was between VanKarem and Onman. These two capes are about twenty miles apart and between the two is a smooth stretch of ice running along the shore. I flew to VanKarem, then returned to Onman thinking Joe might have flown out to shore-line and landed. Not seeing him, I turned around and proceeded to Cape North arriving at 1:45 p.m.

Joe had not gone down as I thought and, seeing me turn, thought I was following him so it was some time before he realized I was not. He then turned around and began searching for me but after we had lost sight of each other for so long a time and both turning, it was impossible to find each other. Joe finally returned to Pelikii, the village we had stopped at the night before, and came on to North Cape the next day.

Though attention is not drawn to it, this report indicates that Gillam did receive his "baptism of fire," that is, he received the necessary experience that gives a basic competence which then leads to confidence. There is evidence that from then on he committed himself to increasing his confidence.

To obtain a more immediate and emotional sense of what happened that morning of December 19, contrast Gillam's factual account with Jack Warren's (Teller roadhouse operator) and Joe Crosson's view as given to Jean Potter in an interview some ten years later. She wrote,

On this stormy morning of December 19 Crosson and Gillam loaded a Stearman and a Waco with extra gas and provisions to last several weeks. "This time we'll make it through," Gillam confidently declared. The others looked on morosely. "No one in his right mind," says Jack Warren, "would have started out to Siberia in that weather." Since the pilots had no radio contact, Gillam was to follow his more experienced partner, and would land wherever Joe did. Heavily bundled, they climbed into their open cockpits, waved goodbye, and flew into the gloom.

We made it that time," Crosson told me. "We managed to sneak across the Strait." Heavy fog boiled up from the broken ice. Winds funneling through the international channel "seemed to blow in twenty-three directions at once." He and Gillam flew low, fighting for control. Visibility was almost zero but they managed, by following the black streaks of open leads, to continue their course. They proceeded in this near-blind fashion for two hours, till they sighted a snow-covered bluff, Siberia. The fog was thinner here, but darkness was nearly upon them. They followed the winding, white, treeless banks in search of a place to land. After some time, Crosson sighted a village in the dusk and brought his Waco safely down upon the ice before it. Gillam landed in his ski tracks close behind.

How did Gillam come to survive that first, all-out battle with the demon weather without the gradual introduction most early bush pilots went through? One can get an idea of the answer by comparing Gillam's experience with Don Gentile's first flight into combat against skilled, confident German pilots. Ira Wolfert in his *One Man-Air Force*, Don Gentile's biography, explained how this "budding ace" stayed alive during his first combat flight, a flight through which many inexperienced pilots did not survive. Gentile explained he was fortunate to be under a flight leader who literally "took him under his wing."

> I was flying # 2 to Colby King. "Just stay with me," King said, "until you get confidence. If you keep on my wing I'll take care of you." Gentile did, and each time out he gained experience. Then, one day his flight leader was shot down and Gentile found himself alone, except for a German fighter on his tail. Certain death lay seconds away. Gentile, knowing the structural strength of his P-47 and his own steady nerves, rolled over and dove straight for the ground. As the G's increased and it seemed certain the plane would disintegrate, Gentile held on and the German broke away. With his life saved by his own action, he felt confidence growing inside him.

In Gillam's case, the example of air combat seems not to apply. Yet Gillam did have a flight leader, Joe Crosson, to help him through his first encounter with extreme weather. Gillam also lost his wing man at a crucial moment and found himself alone. Certainly, right then, he needed all his limited strength and his fearlessness, as reported by his friend Cecil Higgins, to get himself safely to the *SS Nanuk*. His report also shows that, while struggling to find his way out of a difficult situation, he never lost concern for his wing man.

Don Gentile also mentioned the confidence he gained upon discovering his exceptional eyesight. He states,

> And I had found out another thing about myself to give me confidence—the quality of my eyes. On that day over Dieppe I found out just how useful it was to have better vision—that half-second or one-second advantage it gives you over the enemy in picking the black speck of him out of a scud in the sky…it is the difference, other things being equal, between killing and being killed.

Chuck Yeager, well-known test pilot, made the same explanation for his own apparently uncanny abilities as a fighter pilot. He stated, "It's in the eyes" (Mark Twombly, October 1992, AOPA Pilot). James Doolittle was another exceptional pilot who acknowledged his exceptional eyesight. Len Morgan, World War II and commercial airline pilot, in the September 1996 issue of *Flying*, concurs with this statement, "The successful pilot must have a quick eye and steady nerves." The circumstances and the outcome of Gillam's December 19, 1929 flight to Siberia indicates that he possessed these traits very early in his flying career.

This first Siberian flight also may have begun Gillam's status as a legend. The *News Miner* for December 21, 1929 carried an extra bold and large headline which read: Gillam At Cape North.

On that same day the Aviation News section carried the following:

Praise for Harold Gillam was expressed on all sides yesterday afternoon when word of his arrival at the fur ship was received here. The youngest pilot in the fleet searching for Eielson and the least experienced, Gillam completed a flight which is acknowledged to be just about as difficult as could be attempted.

This article does no more than give well-deserved praise. It is a statement of admiration honestly felt by the people back then. Yet, over time, distortions crept in. For example, established journalist JoAnne Wold in her article published by the *Alaska Journal* in 1956 stated,

Crosson touched down at North Cape twenty-four hours later, and he was less than enthusiastic about Gillam's successful, if not foolhardy flight. He was worried about his young charge.

Use of the word "foolhardy" encourages the reader to believe that Crosson may have been "less than enthusiastic" because he may have felt Gillam's actions stemmed from a desire to gain recognition. In Gillam's report, he showed a concern for his friend Crosson while at the same time striving to bring himself safely out of a dangerous situation.

There is no better witness to Crosson's true feelings on finding Gillam safe at the *SS Nanuk* than Bob Gleason, who was present when both Gillam and Crosson landed. In an interview at his retirement home in Maryland, he was asked about Crosson's reaction on seeing Gillam alive at the *SS Nanuk*. He responded with, "very happy when he landed at the ship and found Gillam there; no anger, no rivalry, just caring." This was also the view held in his book published back in 1977.

So how do distortions, large or small, arise? Certainly it was not the writer JoAnne Wold's doing. She merely reported on the emotions and recollections of people she talked to. It seems to have something to do with unusual people who do unusual things and are remembered. As time passes, these people become more unusual than is justified. That may well be how legends come into being. Unfortunately, this tendency can produce legends which lack authenticity. The purpose in this biography is an attempt to separate the basic truths, which may well involve heroic actions, from that which may have been distorted by the passage of time and by vivid imaginations. Other examples of possible distortions of Gillam's behavior will be considered later.

Gillam's report on that first flight to the *SS Nanuk* shows that he tends to stay with the facts. It is Gleason who gives a feeling for the emotions of those stranded and waiting for some word. Gleason was one of those stranded and his account of the progress of the search which follows derives authenticity from his gracious sharing.

Radio contact with Teller gave people on the *SS Nanuk* immediate news of efforts to reach them. The three Fairchilds with their arctic-experienced crew had arrived at Seattle, had been placed on board a Coast Guard cutter, and were being rushed to Seward, where a waiting train would move them to Fairbanks. There they would be assembled, and complete their passage to the *SS Nanuk* by air.

Of even greater interest to those on the *SS Nanuk* was news that on December 18 (19 in Siberia), with fair weather at both ends, four planes had taken off from Teller. Hopes were high, but then faded as singly and in pairs they returned.

The following morning hopes arose once again as word came that Crosson and Gillam had taken off at 9:30 a.m. These hopes grew as darkness slowly settled in and the planes had not returned to Teller. They must therefore have made it across the Strait. Finally, darkness made further flight impossible. Still, the marooned hopefuls kept the oil in their barrel-markers burning. As the markers darkened, hope for arrival shifted to the next day. The flyers had not returned to Teller so they made it across to Siberia but had to land. They would make it in this coming day.

That next day's first light came at 10:00 a.m. and brought with it overcast skies but fair visibility. Again they took up their vigil. The hours dragged by. Then, at 1:45 p.m., just as darkness was near, we heard a plane's engine and saw the little biplane approaching in the dusk. There was only one.

The pilot landed nicely and pulled up to the *SS Nanuk* and said he was Harold Gillam.

Gillam explained what had happened. He also stated again and again that he was sure the veteran pilot, Crosson, was okay and would arrive soon. He did. The next morning, while Gillam readied for his first search, Crosson landed next to the Stearman.

After the happy reunion reported by Gleason, Crosson was taken to the *SS Nanuk* to rest. Gillam, with the fur buyer Olaf Swenson as observer, took off to the southeast where the Eskimos had reported smoke. It turned out to be a reindeer camp.

That evening Gillam and Crosson shared the details of their crossing.

Gillam arrives at SS Nanuk Dec. 21ˢᵗ 1929- Crosson arrived the next day. (Bob Gleason Photo/ Courtesy R.W. Stevens)

The next morning they were ready to continue the search. The people on the *SS Nanuk* were still marooned but now there was a different feeling in the air.

Because of weather and lack of sunlight, the pilots were only able to make two flights before Christmas. This did not mean they relaxed while on the ground. Gleason, in his interview, referred to the high state of frustration felt by both Gillam and Crosson. This frustration obviously stemmed partly from inability to be up in the air, searching. Yet part of it may have resulted from an unacknowledged feeling of futility.

Nature was perhaps kind by providing a fierce storm over Christmas. No hope of a letup led to a partial relaxing as the pilots took time to celebrate. The special day was briefly noted by Gleason's comments:

> Christmas brought a severe storm, and we spent it together. Bill Bissner, who had become chief cook after Crichton's departure, fixed us a big reindeer roast and fruit compote. Marion's (the fur trader's teenage daughter) presence cheered us all, and everybody liked our new companions, Crosson and Gillam.

By December 30 the severe storm had worn itself down enough to where visibility would allow a search. Both pilots prepared for take-off by applying the open flame of a firepot (plumber's furnace) against the cold metal of the engines. Normally the heated engine started, the throttle was advanced to get the oil circulating, then takeoff followed. Crosson and Gillam had already discovered that with the extreme cold, resulting from absence of the sun to warm the earth, the engines would keep running only at full throttle. This led to the unsafe practice of starting the engine, immediately advancing to full throttle, and quickly taking off. That was the procedure the two pilots had to resort to the morning of December 30. Crosson, with Olaf Swenson as his observer, got off without incident. The engine on Gillam's Stearman, however, balked briefly after starting but he was able to bring up the rpm's and took off. Just after lift-off the engine quit and Gillam had to set the plane down, straight ahead, on rough ice. Both landing gear struts were broken, and damage was done to the left lower wing and the cabene supports.

"He was chagrined,' was Gleason's summary of Gillam's reaction to the crash. Put in more down-to-earth language, he was probably just plain mad at himself. He was also a person who didn't waste time "cursing the darkness." Instead he set out to light a fire. This translated into his surveying the damage in detail, and walking three miles across the ice to the

Gillam's Stearman engine quits on takeoff; plane slightly damaged. (Bob Gleason Photo/ Courtesy R.W. Stevens)

Stavropol, a Russian steamship also frozen in for the long winter. Knowing there was a machine shop on board, he asked the ship's captain for help. By the time Crosson returned from his search, Gillam had inventoried the tools needed to remove the broken parts, which ones they had at the *SS Nanuk*, and which needed to be obtained from the Stavropol. Both Crosson and his sister, Marvel, had been putting together airplanes from spare parts in their parents' backyard all through their growing-up years. As a result, Crosson developed practical engineering knowledge. His more specialized background was combined with Gillam's practical knowledge. This combined expertise became even more effective through their joint emotional motivation. Their strong motivation also led them to eagerly seek Russian help. The Russians immediately committed themselves to do this. As a result, within twenty days, the Stearman was back in the air.

Those twenty days were busy ones. Crosson, once sound contact was developed with the Russians, spent those days keeping his Waco at the ready should weather and visibility permit a search. He was able to search only twice during that time but was determined to have the plane ready just in case. He also kept the Fairbanks office informed, giving and receiving information on the search and considering future plans.

Gillam's expertise as an aircraft mechanic was vital since the Russians, though fully willing to help, were seamen. So it was that every waking hour found Gillam walking across the ice to the Stavropol, working and directing the men, and in general making sure no time was lost getting his plane back in the air.

Russian seaman aboard steamer Stavropol give important aid to get Gillam's Stearman back in the air. (Crosson Collection/Courtesy R.W. Stevens)

This twenty-day effort was also but one example of the Russians' full cooperation and concern, which went on despite the lack of diplomatic recognition between the two countries. The human concern that overcame official barriers was suggested in the following comment by Gleason: "Gillam's plane was ready on the 20th, and we watched anxiously as he took off on his test flight. The repairs held."

Meanwhile, what happened to the three Fairchild 71s shipped by Coast Guard cutter and rail to Fairbanks? The Coast Guard had moved the planes rapidly, leaving Seattle on December 21 and arriving at Seward on the 25. A waiting train loaded the planes and traveled nonstop to Fairbanks, arriving there on the 26. There, the assembly was somewhat delayed because one of Alaskan Airways' hangars had burned to the ground on December 22. This left only one

Burning of the Bennett-Rodebaugh hangar delays assembly of new search planes. (Crosson Collection/Courtesy R.W. Stevens)

hangar in which to assemble the planes. Originally, the Fairchilds were chosen because of their folding wings, which allowed them to be moved by surface transportation without major disassembly. These folding wings proved their worth not only during the transportation phase but again in Fairbanks where less time was needed in the only hangar available to get each plane readied for flight.

Two of the Fairchilds were ready for takeoff to Teller on January 2, 1930. There was no hurry getting the third one assembled since it was only a backup and mainly to be used to get Alaskan Airways' other flying commitments back on schedule. As it turned out, however, this plane was needed immediately as a backup.

On the morning of January 2 both planes stood ready; heavily loaded with extra gasoline, emergency equipment, and so forth. Pat Reid lifted his Fairchild into the air first and circled while waiting for Gifford Swartman to take off. In the following few minutes tragedy struck. Swartman, although experienced in arctic flying, evidently felt rushed. He hurried his heavily loaded

Fairchild 71, on the way to join the search crashed on the takeoff at Weeks Field on January 2nd, 1930. (Jessie Rust Photo/ Courtesy R.W. Stevens)

Fairchild into the air before getting engine temperature high enough to produce full power. It left the ground but was unable to climb. Instead of forcing the nose up and into a stall, he simply let the plane sink back to earth. The damage was substantial but neither pilot nor mechanic were hurt.

The third plane was now quickly assembled and readied. Matt Nieminen was the Canadian pilot assigned to it. At the last minute, anticipating the need for an expert welder as well as necessary equipment needed to repair Gillam Stearman, Hutch Hutchinson was sent along.

On January 4, both Fairchilds were on their way to Teller. Good weather and a tailwind took them almost to Nome before a snowstorm blocked their

Fairchild repairs completed at forced-landing site. (T. M. "Pat" Reid Photo/Courtesy R.W. Stevens)

way. Nieminen turned back and landed at Nulato. Reid kept going and was reported missing. Weather prevented an aerial search and it was not until January 11th that a dog team located the plane on a creek bed. Reid had landed the plane safely with no injuries. However, one wing tip was severely damaged when it hit the creek bank.

With skilled repairmen on board, they used their ingenuity and available materials, including gas boxes, tree branches, and so forth to repair the wing. The repairs were completed by the time the dog team found them. Reid took off from the less than desirable spot and ferried the plane to Unalakeet, then on to Nome.

Lomen brought in all available planes and pilots from the area to Nome. The purpose was a meeting on how to allocate resources between the search and the more general flying obligations of Alaskan Airways. The only ones not present were Crosson and Gillam.

At the meeting Young and Reid, with the Fairchilds, were assigned to freighting gas and supplies from Teller to the *SS Nanuk*, then bringing back furs. After the damaged Fairchild received additional repairs at Nome, the two planes and their crews arrived at Teller on January 21. On hearing that Gillam already had his Stearman repaired, Hutch and his welding equipment were shipped back to Fairbanks.

Landing of Russian Junkers at the SS Nanuk show strength of that aircraft. (Bob Gleason Collection/Icebound in the Siberian Arctic)

Due to weather delays the two Fairchilds did not arrive at the *SS Nanuk* with badly needed gas until January 28 (*SS Nanuk* time). As it turned out, two Junkers F-13 monoplanes arrived there the following day. Back in November, the government in Moscow had promised these planes to be part of the search. Delay of their arrival involved several factors, weather, of course, being one. A more important reason was the Soviets' policy requiring any decision, even relatively minor ones, to be approved in Moscow.

Gleason's firsthand account of the Russian pilots' emphasis on high-speed approaches and landing is most interesting.

> One plane came in downwind at the southwest end of the bay. He landed about halfway from the shore and headed toward the stern of the *SS Nanuk* on heavily drifted, hard-packed snow. The first hundred feet were fairly smooth, but then the plane began to hit the bumps, still going fast because the pilot had landed tail up. The plane bounced time and again ten and fifteen feet in the air, clanking like a steam engine. It hit an especially big bump and the right landing gear strut broke. The plane came down on its right wing and stopped.
>
> The second plane made an equally spectacular landing, stopping

just before a sand spit, but without damage. To show that the German-made Junkers were more sturdily built than Gillam's Stearman or the Fairchilds, the second plane carried a spare shock absorber strut. This replaced the broken one. Since there was no damage to the ski or wing of the first plane, it was quickly made flyable—no twenty days of strain and struggle.

Now to fill in with what happened at the *SS Nanuk* between January 20, when Gillam-test flew his Stearman, and the arrival of the Fairchilds and Junkers on the 28 and 29. The sun was again making an appearance but only briefly. Snow and wind kept both planes on the ground from the 21 to the 25. On January 26 Crosson and Gillam continued their search. The following was taken from Gillam's official report:

> January 26, 1930. We left Cape North. This was the first flying day and the visibility was excellent. Joe was flying about six miles inshore and I about two. After one hour, I saw Joe start down in a spiral. Flying over, I found that Joe had recognized the left wing of the Hamilton and was looking for a place to land. We landed about 500 yards from the wreck.
>
> After one look at the tangled remains of the Hamilton, any hope we had entertained regarding the fate of Pilots Ben and Earl was replaced by the feeling that at least they had met their end instantly.
>
> We dug around the cabin of the plane for an hour and, failing to locate any trace of them, took off for Cape North to enlist the aid of Captain Weeding and Mr. Swenson in organizing a working party to uncover the remains.

These were the bare details. And again, Gleason added a touch of feeling.

> Marion called, "Here comes a plane."
>
> We thought they had struck fog down the coast and had been turned back. Marion ran and I skied over to the plane as Joe landed and taxied to the ship.
>
> He said, "The search is over, we found the plane."
>
> It took a minute to sink in. Joe pointed to the forward cockpit,

to a piece of corrugated aluminum. It was part of the wrecked Hamilton…Harold landed a few minutes later and we all went to the after cabin for a conference. The pilots were looking pretty peaked; a glass of vodka braced them up a bit. Then we got the story.

Especially noteworthy in Gillam's report is his statement that it was

At last the crash site located.
(Crosson Collection/Courtesy R.W. Stevens)

Crosson who spotted the wreck. Yet in some articles appearing later, credit was given to Gillam. For example, Ted Spencer's article in the January 1995 issue of *Senior Voice* stated, "Gillam sighted the missing Hamilton on January 27, 1930." So again over the years, distortion which favors the subject's achievement, has crept in. Is it possible that such exaggerations in themselves point to persons who have achieved legendary status?

One final reference to Gillam's formal report. On page 2 he made the following admission: "but I will say that we never would have seen the Hamilton without the aid of the sun." It is highly doubtful that he would have entertained such a thought during the heat of the search.

There is irony in the fact that the sun's appearance, the promise of better weather, along with the appearance of the Fairchilds and the

A shelter from the savage winds. (George King Collection/Courtesy R.W. Stevens)

Junkers all came together just when the search ended.

There was, however, much work left to be done. Gas needed to be flown in to replace that which the Russians had loaned; the furs still needed to be flown to market; and most important, the bodies needed to be found and flown out to their final resting place. It was the last-mentioned responsibility that proved the most difficult.

During the first days after the plane was discovered, Crosson and Gillam took a few workers with shovels out to the wreck site, assuming the task would be quickly finished. This proved not to be so. It was not until three weeks later that the last body (Eielson's) was recovered.

During that time, Russians from the Stavropol were brought to the wreck site by dog teams and by planes. Also, the Russian pilot, Mavriki Slepnyov and his mechanic, Fabio Fahrig, landed their Junkers F-13 at the site and built a snow block igloo under one wing. This proved to be a much-needed shelter for the workers during their long stay.

The men spent most of their time chopping through wind-packed snow, not knowing exactly where the bodies might be lying. Also, the men endured days of idleness, waiting out the demons wind and weather. Then, after each storm, new drifts had to be dealt with.

During those weeks Gillam had the routine duty of flying daily, if the weather permitted, from the *SS Nanuk* to the wreck site, some 90 miles to the southeast. This was directly on the course that Eielson had plotted before his first flight. Since there was no radio contact between the site and the *SS Nanuk*, it was Gillam's responsibility to report progress at the site and to bring needed items to the workers.

The search for bodies. Nature resists giving up its secrets. (Crosson Collection/ Courtesy R.W. Stevens)

Shortage of gas was always a problem until the last plane left on May 10, 1930. Gillam's plane was used because it consumed less fuel but even then, he skipped days to conserve it.

Just before the three weeks ended and the work was completed, another misfortune occurred. Reid, in the second Fairchild, misinterpreted a visual signal and attempted a landing at the site. His Fairchild still lay at the site with a collapsed landing gear; waiting for Hutch Hutchinson to return with his welding torch to set things right.

It was Slepnyov and his Junkers that flew the bodies from the wreck site to the *SS Nanuk*. There they were placed in the only building on North Cape. Here the Russian doctor from the Stavropol straightened the limbs, laid the bodies in a natural reclining position, then allowed them to freeze again.

It was at this point that the formal ceremony of transfer began. It is difficult to visualize these formal activities being carried out in this barren and isolated spot. Yet dignity was preserved and respect shown by all present—Russians, Canadians, and Americans. Russian and American flags were displayed at the cabin and a watch made up of one Russian and one American was stationed there. An American flag on the *SS Nanuk* was flown at half-mast. As Bob Stevens stated,

February 26, 1930. The bodies of Eielson and Borland, their faces exposed, lie on Chukchi sleds covered with American flags sewn by Siberian women from red and blue muslin and white canvas. The two sleds were drawn between two loosely formed lines composed of Americans and Canadians on one side and Russians and Natives on the other during the transfer ceremony.

After the ceremony the bodies were placed in Ed Young's Fairchild, the windows covered and all was ready for the flight out. The Russian and American governments gave permission for Slepnyov's Junkers to be a part of the funeral flight, as a token of respect from the Russians. Gillam's Stearman, with Pat Reid as passenger, was really part of the funeral flight. However, his plane left early because

Gillam had to take on gas from Reid's Fairchild, still stranded at the wreck site. They made a second landing for gas at East Cape where Reid had cached additional fuel. They arrived at Teller that same day, February 25 (Nome time).

Crosson left his Waco at the *SS Nanuk*, not having enough fuel to fly it out. He flew out in the funeral plane.

The transfer of bodies. In this wild setting; a formal gesture. (Donald E. Young Photo/Courtesy R.W. Stevens)

The flight itself was delayed at the *SS Nanuk* due to weather. While waiting for it to arrive at Teller Gillam flew Reid to Nome on March 3, where plans were made to salvage the Fairchild. On his return to Teller, Gillam brought in Lomen, who wanted to be there to meet the funeral flight. It was expected that same day. After the funeral flight made it in, it was delayed at Teller for a few days, again because of weather.

On March 5, Gillam was the first plane off from Teller, carrying Lomen back to Nome. The other two planes were delayed another day for weather. Taking off the following day, they scheduled a stop at Nome for a ceremony planned by the people there. Hard-packed snow ridges discouraged a landing and the flight continued to Ruby. Gillam, who had landed at Nome the previous day, took off that morning and arrived at Ruby ahead of the others.

All planes overnighted there because of weather ahead but took off and arrived in Fairbanks the next day. With Gillam now accompanying the other planes, the funeral plane and its two escorts circled over the town in formation before landing. A large crowd waited in silence while the Fairchild taxied into the hangar.

Here the bodies paused in their homeward journey to allow the people of Fairbanks to pay homage to their fallen flyers.

Gillam, who had left Fairbanks in the Stearman as an inexperienced pilot, now returned in that same plane as someone who had been tested and found worthy, especially in the ability that bush pilots valued greatly—flying weather. To some degree he possessed the confidence to challenge weather, combined with a wisdom to determine when to proceed and when to change course 180 degrees. If "change course" was to be the decision, then competence to do so entered in. Finally, if "proceed" was to be the decision, then he possess the flexibility of an open mind. Underlying all of these was *confidence*—a confidence and steady nerves that would allow sound decisions to be made and executed.

Landing at Weeks Field; the air journey ends. (Eleanor Stoy Reed photo/Courtesy R.W. Stevens)

Later, legend has it that Gillam flew through all types of weather. Not so. Here, at the beginning of his flying career, he had learned to "turn back." For example, in his formal written report, he stated, "February 25, 1930. I started (*SS Nanuk* to Teller) but poor visibility forced me to return."

As he accumulated hours and polished his skills, there were still occasions when he held, or returned, because of weather. Any honest legend regarding his weather flying should read, "He did turn back because of weather, when necessary. However, he seldom found it necessary. This was even true on his last flight.

Finally it should be noted that the Eielson-Borland search gave Gillam his first practice in flying weather. In turn this practice gave him both competence and confidence and was carried out

Gillam's Stearman at Weeks. (Crosson Collection/Courtesy R.W. Stevens)

without endangering the lives of others, at least not the lives of trusting, paying passengers.

Gleason, in the final pages of his book, paid personal homage to the individuals with whom he had close association during the Eielson-Borland search. He stated,

131

From almost every standpoint the voyage had been a disaster. Less than half the furs had been taken out; two lives had been lost; one airplane had been destroyed and three other airplanes damaged. Despite all this, I felt as though I had participated in an unselfish, heroic adventure. The dedication, perseverance, and tenacity of the crew, pilots, and mechanics, and the ability of men without adequate equipment and facilities to cope with cold, wind, darkness, and adversity, made this a tremendous experience, which I did not —and never will—forget.

Gillam's faithful Stearman as enshrined at Alaska Aviation Heritage Museum Anchorage Alaska. (Author Photo)

Chapter 13
MOUNTAINS, GLACIERS AND WEATHER

People seemed…Rather wholly resigned to take
life as it came; until such time as the weather cleared.
(Emil Goulet, "Rugged Years on the Alaska Frontier")

It was on Saturday, March 8, 1930 that Gillam and the funeral planes landed at Fairbanks' Weeks Field. Just ten days later, on Monday March 18, he would lift his own plane, *The Arctic Prospector*, off the same airfield and begin his delayed venture in the Copper River region. Those ten days would be busy and also emotion-laden. The focus would be on final tributes to the two airmen, now departed. Final rites were

Mt. Blackburn-a challenge for Gillam Airways. *(UAF Archives)*

held on Wednesday, March 12, at the Moose Hall Auditorium. Here Gillam served as pall bearer for Eielson's casket, along with fellow aviators Crosson, Young, Slepnyev, Nieminen, and Reid. On the evening of that same day, the air crews involved in the search were invited to the Alaska College to address the students. The *News Miner* reported, "Pilots Joe Crosson and Harold Gillam were present but were not called on to speak by their own request."

Search aviators receive a welcome. *(Crosson Collection/Courtesy R.W. Stevens)*

A guard of honor stood watch throughout that night. The next morning, Thursday, March 13, the *News Miner* reported the departure of the bodies,

Air Comrades in Four Planes Dip Over Funeral Train as a Last

Respect. As the train, a double-header, steamed out of the station, four planes of the Alaskan Airways with pilots Crosson, Gillam, Young and Nieminen at the sticks, dipped and zoomed and led an air path down the valley. The large crowd that had gathered early on the station platform quietly dispersed.

Now Gillam faced a difficult decision—when to leave. Getting ready wasn't a problem. Like any bachelor of that day, he had few personal

Russian airmen, Slepnyov and Fahrig, bid farewell. (Crosson Collection/Courtesy R.W. Stevens)

belongings. Those, along with tools and extra gas, could easily fit into the front cockpit. Ideas and dreams of what to do next had been carefully considered, sorted, and were waiting—ready for recall when needed. Holding him back were the seemingly never-ending days during which the people of Fairbanks were determined to express their gratitude to the Russian flight commander, Mavriki Slepnyov, and his mechanic, Fabio Fahrig. These two, through their total moral and physical support during the recovery of the bodies, had formed a close bond with the American airmen, especially Crosson and Gillam, with whom they'd had the closest contact. Gillam, of course, joined in the social activities. However, when the farewell dinner was delayed until April 9, Gillam's impatience won out and he made a painful decision. He would leave on March 18, three weeks before the final farewell of his Russian comrades.

A message, waiting for him on his return to Fairbanks, figured importantly in his decision. It stated simply, "Your crated airplane was off-loaded at Valdez the last week of February." This factory-new Swallow, with its 225 hp Wright Whirlwind air-cooled engine had been ordered before he made the sudden decision to join the search. The waiting plane weighed heavily on his mind as he said his good-byes.

He did not find out till later about the honor bestowed on him at the farewell dinner. The front page of the *News Miner* for April 10 reported it as follows:

> One of the bright spots of the evening was the presentation to three Alaska aviators, Joe Crosson, Ed Young, and Harold Gillam of a medal, one that had been given to Commander Slepnyov by his government as its does to all its airmen who have made flights aggregating 100,000 kilometers without accident, either to flier or machine. The medal was mounted on a silver plaque for the presentation to the group. At the top of the plaque were inscribed the names of Crosson, Young, and Gillam and beneath, the words, "To brothers and friends, from Slepnyov."

The people of Fairbanks also gave recognition to Gillam for his outstanding contribution during the search. Membership in Pioneers of Alaska was restricted to those who had helped shape the Territory of Alaska by living there for at least thirty years. Young Gillam could obviously not qualify. The members, however, felt strongly that he should be recognized as one of them. Therefore, on February 20, 1930, even before he returned from the search, they took the rare step of granting him honorary membership. And so, to this day the name, Harold Gillam, Senior # 1525, is listed under the special category of honorary member on the permanent roll of Pioneers of Alaska, Igloo # 4.

Recognition of a more personal nature came also to Gillam. Following the search, Ben Eielson's father visited Earl Borland's parents in Seattle. While there, he made it a point to visit Gillam's mother. His purpose was to express gratitude for her son's courage and tenacity while attempting to find the missing plane.

Also of a personal nature, and stemming from a close association during the search, was the special recognition to Crosson's and Gillam's efforts by Olaf Swenson, owner of the *SS Nanuk*. The *News Miner* carried this statement,

> Mr. Swenson praised especially pilots Joe Crosson and Harold Gillam, who flew from Teller to Cape North in the shortest days of the year and carried on the search by themselves for a long time under the most trying conditions. Over an extended period, even when the weather was at its best, they had only about four hours of semi-daylight to fly in.

These recognitions were well deserved. Still, one cannot help but wonder if Gillam did not obtain even greater satisfaction from his successful flying through weather. Any satisfaction he may have felt did not lead to overconfidence, however. This was evidenced by the weather decision he made during that first flight from Fairbanks to Valdez on the morning of March 18. This flight would be over unfamiliar terrain, unfamiliar at least from the air. Also, there would be no Joe Crosson up ahead to make decisions. Gillam and A.A. Bennett had flown as far as Copper Center the previous October on their way to Chisana to pick up an injured miner. From Copper Center they turned east toward McCarthy. Gillam's course lay straight ahead to the south, over unfamiliar terrain and into a snowstorm.

Anxious to assemble his new Swallow, he tried making it through Thompson Pass which lay between him and Valdez. However, not knowing the terrain that lay beneath him, and faced with obscured visibility, he turned back. Coming back into the clear, he followed the Lower Tonsina River till he got to the roadhouse. It was open, so he landed thinking to wait out the weather.

Weather bad? Gillam gets through by steamship which brings him to the Valdez dock. (Valdez Museum)

The roadhouse had a radio connection with Chitina and Gillam soon found out the weather was expected to be around awhile. He didn't waste time waiting for it to improve. The roadhouse owner gave information Gillam needed. The weekly train heading south to Cordova would get into Chitina that same evening. The train would connect with the *SS Yukon* on its way to Valdez. It could get him there by evening of the next day. Getting to Chitina was the only thing left to think about. He could fly there but didn't know anybody to leave the plane with. Once he got the new Swallow flying, he wouldn't need the old *Arctic Prospector* for a while. The matter was settled when the roadhouse owner agreed to let him tie the plane down next to the building and leave it there as long as he wanted to. He also dug up a dog team to get Gillam into Chitina in time to catch the train.

With everything settled, Gillam relaxed and got into Valdez the next evening as planned. Knowing his time and date of arrival, the people of Valdez held a reception and dance in his honor that same evening. This gave him an opportunity to share with them his experiences in Siberia while at the same time telling of his plans for the first air service in the Copper River region.

Gillam's new Swallow makes an impression. (Clifton Library Photo/Courtesy R.W. Stevens)

Owen Meals, the local Ford dealer, who was also agent for the Eagle Rock Aircraft Company, had already cleared his garage. There, early the next morning, he and Gillam started assembling the Swallow. By April 1, 1930 the plane stood ready, flight tests completed, and citizens gathered round the plane for publicity shots. Shortly thereafter, Gillam was climbing to 10,000 feet before heading toward Chitina, McCarthy and his first contract.

Gillam's first contract was to move men and materials to a remote mining site. This was consistent with his long-range goals. From its beginning, Gillam Airways' purpose was to provide Alaskans with transportation where it didn't exist or where it was inadequate, and to provide this transportation with safety and reliability. For this reason he did not locate his air service in Fairbanks. Not only were air services provided there but they were, to a degree, competitive. This implied there were more than enough planes and services. Instead, Gillam chose the Copper River region, which had no air services and had a definite need for them. The reasons why this need had not been met before Gillam's arrival were extremely mountainous terrain and severe weather conditions.

On the other hand, Interior Alaska was sheltered from the severe coastal weather patterns by two parallel, east-west mountain ranges— the Alaska and Brooks Ranges. Also, because of its relatively flat surfaces, the Interior provided an extensive network of navigable rivers. These rivers allowed large boats to meet transportation needs in the summer. In winter, the ice on these same rivers provided trails which dog teams used to meet transportation needs. This explains why almost all outlying villages of the Interior are found on the banks of these navigable rivers.

In the Copper River region extremely mountainous terrain led to less navigable rivers which, in turn, led to less population in the outlying areas. Even in the outlying villages that did exist, high costs limited communication, travel, and movement of goods. It becomes obvious why air transportation was needed to open the Copper River region to trade, communication, and to allow exploitation of its mineral resources.

To accomplish the above, however, would not be easy. The same barriers to land and water travel were, to some degree, also barriers to air travel. This may well explain why the airplane was slow in making its appearance. Weather, an area in which Gillam was to demonstrate exceptional competence, presented a special barrier to air transportation, especially when combined with mountainous terrain. Gillam must have been aware of these challenges but this did not deter him.

Gillam's first contract provided an immediate challenge to his resolve. For example, the cargo to be moved had to be flown off, and then landed on non-airport strips. Also, the flights had to be made either over or around the Wrangell Mountains, a range that contained peaks reaching heights from 12,000 to 16,000 feet. Going over this formidable range also meant being isolated from any human habitation between takeoff and landing. When loaded with passengers or freight, Gillam tended to follow the advice of old timer, Noel Wien, "Whenever possible, fly near a trail and know which direction leads to people; just in case you have an unexpected landing." Returning with an empty plane he favored a quick climb to altitude and back across the mountains. Here, the stout 225 hp Wright Whirlwind engine in the new Swallow gave the extra power needed.

Having completed his first contract, Gillam took steps to introduce commercial aviation to Cordova. On April 17, 1930 he made a quick trip on the Northwestern and Copper River Railroad to that city and addressed the city fathers. He stressed the need for an adequate airport in order that his company might better serve residents of the Copper River region. Referring to his two Swallows, he emphasized further a need for action by stating, "I plan to enlarge this fleet as soon as conditions justify aggressive expansion." *The Cordova Times* supported Gillam's efforts by giving his visit a headline reading, "Gillam Urges Construction of Landing Field in Cordova."

Unfortunately, this promotional effort bore little fruit. Gillam had recommended developing the ballpark site, which would be close to the town. Although the Territorial Legislature would pay 80 per cent of the cost, developing the townsite would cost more and would not

Called the "Million Dollar Bridge" it really cost more. Only the Kennecott Copper Co. could afford such an investment and did so because of the return on that investment. (UAF Archives)

meet the preferred length set forth by the U.S. Department of Commerce. After further deliberations, the site at Lake Eyak (17 miles out of town, on the railroad) was decided on. On June 13, a committee,

By taking the train Gillam demonstrated the need for an airport at Cordova. (UAF Archives)

including the Territorial highway engineer, visited the Lake Eyak site and found it eroded and unusable. Gillam's visit did achieve immediate temporary improvements and he was able to land on the strip on June 24 to pick up cable. From there he flew it far to the north, across

139

the lofty Wrangell Mountain Range and landed at the Nabesna mine, where the cable was urgently needed.

Although water takeoffs and landings were made on Lake Eyak in summer and-ski equipped planes used its ice for those purposes in winter, the actual strip was seldom used, except by Gillam, who used it only when necessary. Even the inaugural flight of Gillam's new

Miners need Gillam Airway. *(Harold Starkel Photo)*

Zenith in June 1931, when he hosted the Chamber of Commerce members on a trip to Fairbanks, had to take off and land on the inadequate strip. Not until mid-1934, when the Alaska Road Commission completed a new airport (also on Lake Eyak) and Cap Lathrop underwrote the building of a large hangar, did competing air services focus on Cordova as a base for flights to Anchorage, the Interior, and on to Nome.

April also saw Gillam making flights out of McCarthy to an unimproved landing site in the nearby Bremner Mining District. The purpose? To move prospectors and their gear to a spot that might just turn out to be an elusive bonanza.

The month of May brought many "bread and butter" flights, some involving administering the law, like bringing in law officers, witnesses, and indicted persons (possibly some on the same plane) for a trial in Valdez. The town was referred to as the "court city" because it was the headquarters of the Third Judicial District of the Territory.

Other flights had no visible purpose. For example, because Gillam had been surprised suddenly by a deep love of flying, it was not

Gillam and his Swallow using the mud flats to take Valdez residents for their first airplane ride. *(Clifton Library Photo)*

surprising that he would take every opportunity to bring others into this happy state. Thus finding himself in Valdez on a sabbath day, specifically May 11, 1930, he proceeded to spend that afternoon taking local citizens aloft. On every flight the front cockpit was filled to capacity, two passengers—some anxious, some not. On the final flight, which landed at 4:35 p.m., one of the passengers, a Miss Anna May Dolan, was on her second venture into the air that afternoon. Robert Stevens, a pilot himself, recorded the following feelings of a person present that day, "In fine weather, with the sound of the motor reverberating among the shining peaks, the flights were a joy to all, both on the ground and in the air."

Gillam, being at that time the only active commercial pilot in the Copper River region, was kept busy. One particular flight at the end of May showed his support for the mining prospector whose hopes and dreams regularly outran his abilities to finance them. Also, this flight demonstrated Gillam's willingness to take chances on off-airport landing s. The bare facts pertaining to this flight were given by Stevens who stated,

> Harold Gillam took Mrs. Martin Harrais from McCarthy to the head of the Chitina River on Monday, May 26, 1930, landing on a gravel bar which turned out to be pretty rough. The woman's husband, who was doing patent work on a group of mining claims in that section left at the same time as his wife, going overland, but did not arrive until days later. After landing, the pilot spent some time clearing rocks and driftwood from the bar to make a better landing spot.

The following is a view of the same event as experienced by Mrs. Harrais, who recorded it in her diary,

> I'll admit feeling apprehensive, wondering how we were going to land, and that feeling deepened as we circled the field several times. I held my breath. Being all ready for a bump, I was agreeably surprised at the smoothness of the landing, thanks to Harold Gillam's skill as an aviator. I asked whether it was a successful landing. He replied that any landing you can walk away from is a successful landing, but that he wouldn't land on the field again until the Territory did some more work on it.

The next major event during Gillam's first month in business involved a trip to Fairbanks to take the airmen's examination being administered by Wylie R. Wright, the U.S. Department of Commerce inspector. He passed the examination and received his air transport pilot license.

Gillam left Fairbanks to be present at a meeting of the Valdez City Council on June 2. The meeting dealt with improving the airfield, extending the runway, and building a small hangar. Gillam agreed to build a machine shop adjoining the hangar. Ultimately, he saw Gillam Airways being headquartered at either Cordova or Valdez but he had as yet not made his choice.

At this time A.A. Bennett, former joint owner of the air service bought by Alaskan Airways, and Gillam had been thinking about joint ownership of

141

an air service for the Copper River region. This idea was finally dropped by mutual agreement. Such an arrangement would have been fraught with problems since they were both committed to "being their own boss."

As to the immediate headquartering of Gillam Airways, the tentative plan was to choose Chitina because it was a railroad stop and division headquarters for the Alaska Road Commission. However, since it had no airport, flight operations were limited to use of the winter ice on Town Lake and, in summer, chance landings and takeoffs from a Copper River gravel bar near town. McCarthy, with an airport, was also thought to be a suitable base for the planes. Yet McCarthy had a short runway and

Gillam Airways used a flat piece of ground to establish its head-quarters at Copper Center. *(Clifton Library photo/Courtesy R.W. Stevens)*

high nearby mountains, which led Gillam to settle on Copper Center as his base. It was no farther from Chitina than McCarthy but was surrounded by relatively flat land. It also had a long, flat former hay field next to the roadhouse that made an ideal runway. Another advantage was its location at the intersection of the Valdez Trail (soon to be named the Richardson Highway) and the trail from Chitina. Also, plans to purchase an amphibian for water landings at Chitina and Cordova would still allow it to land at Copper Center for servicing. With location of the base finalized, Gillam made immediate plans to build a hangar.

All this thought and activity did not prevent him from returning to Fairbanks on June 7 to help celebrate the marriage of fellow pilot

Elliot's Chariot. (Crosson Collection/Courtesy R.W. Stevens)

Grant Elliot and Miss Barbara Nud, who had just arrived from the States. Gillam had gained the reputation of being a serious person. He was, most of the time. Still, he was willing to relax and even engage in frivolity, especially if initiated by fellow pilots. The accompanying photo showing his participation in a trial run of "Elliot's Chariot" is evidence of this less-known aspect of Gillam's personality. He was also a member of the "Airport Gang." All members who were in town attending the wedding used the occasion to hold a reunion and pose for a picture.

July 4th was a flying day for the president and chief pilot of Gillam Airways. At the end of that day he brought two passengers from

Gillam at home among fellow airmen. (Crosson Collection/Courtesy R.W. Stevens)

Copper Center to McCarthy. While there, he added to the festivities that evening by taking sightseers over the spectacular Kennicott Glacier and the more familiar (from the ground) Kennecott mines.

To show that Gillam's successful efforts in bringing air transportation to the Copper River region had not gone unnoticed, the editorial in the September 23, 1930 issue of the *Cordova Times* paid special tribute to him. It stated,

> …the success of Gillam Airways should prove inspiring to all Cordovans and all Copper River valley residents. There still are untried enterprises of commerce in this undeveloped region which will bring success and prosperity to those who dare to leave the beaten trails…

The above editorial was written during the Great Depression of the 1930s. That depression was worsened because there were no jobs. And there were no jobs because those who had money were afraid to put it into projects that would create jobs. They were afraid of losing their money so they simply sat on it.

The editor singled out Gillam because he had the courage to put money, his own at first, into a project that gave people something they needed: transportation. At the same time his project, in a small way, put people back to work. Then what happened? People wanted more transportation than Gillam could supply so he had to buy more planes and hire pilots. This got the Territorial government to build small airfields where they were needed and supplied part of the money to larger towns so they could build larger airports with hangars and needed services. Now other people, with money, began using it to organize air services both large and small until there were enough to meet all needs. At that point Gillam slowly and quietly withdrew and moved Gillam Airways to another area, where the need was greater. By its very nature, such an area involved the challenge of pioneer work, which suited Gillam's basic temperament.

During that beginning year, he found September in the Copper River region to be a time of last-minute work before closing up for the winter. This was especially true of mining and the Alaska Road Commission. Gillam Airways was there to take care of these last-minute emergencies. Yet it was also able to meet the need of big-game hunters. This need also arose just before winter set in. Getting hunters and their guides out to isolated areas was of special interest to Gillam and he performed well in doing it. The September 29 issue of the *Cordova Times* reported,

> White River hunt perfect says Eckart (of the Sun Oil Company). Flown in by Gillam Airways, Ekart was enthusiastic about the area for its big game trophies and because flying there saved a week of travel time.

Gillam's picking up passengers from steamships stopping at Cordova, then flying them to Fairbanks, would be repeated often in future years. The trip on October 17, 1930, however, had a special significance for all concerned. As the *Times* put it,

> Joe Crosson and bride fly to Fairbanks with Gillam. The flight from Cordova to Fairbanks was an unexpected ending to their tour and was planned by Pilot Gillam, who flew over from Valdez yesterday to meet them here.

A four-hour flight instead of three additional days of travel by boat and train was indeed a pleasant surprise for the two weary travelers anxious to move into their first home. Gillam added to the event by arranging a relaxing overnight stay at Ma Barnes' Roadhouse at Copper Center, then landing them at Weeks Field at noon the next day.

Having established a thriving air service in a few months, Gillam flew to Valdez on November 6, 1930, secured his Swallow, and boarded the steamship Alameda. His purpose? Travel to the lower-forty eight to obtain another plane, an amphibian, and a pilot. A second pilot was urgently needed. The lack of one resulted in his second Swallow, the *Arctic Prospector*, seeing little service that first summer. Gillam had changed it from skis to wheels on April 24, when it was still at the Lower Tonsina Roadhouse. The snows had melted by the beginning of June when he flew it up to the Copper Center airport. There, except for a few flights, it languished at its tie-down.

An expression of friendship; Gillam flies Crosson and his bride, Lillian to their new home. (Crosson Collection/ Courtesy R.W. Stevens)

Search for an amphibian took Gillam to the East Coast. Previous correspondence with the Sikorsky Aviation Corporation in Bridgeport, Connecticut impressed him sufficiently to travel cross-country to inspect and fly their Model S-39. This firsthand experience heightened his interest. This heightened interest was somehow distorted and caused the *Cordova Times* to report that Gillam had purchased the plane. Actually,

Now able to also land on downtown Chitna's town lake in summer. (Adena Knutson Photo)

after leaving the Sikorsky plant he traveled to San Diego, still the West Coast aviation hub, where he was given a first-hand experience with the Ireland Neptune. This is the amphibian he finally bought.

Approximately 100 miles north of San Diego, at Midway City, California Gillam contacted the Zenith Aircraft Corporation. There he purchased a Zenith Z-6, perfect for his needs. It had an enclosed cabin for six passengers and a 220 hp Wright Whirlwind air-cooled engine. Unfortunately, the idea of allowing the pilot to fly without the wind in his face dies hard. So in the Zenith back in 1931 the pilot still sat, all alone, above his passengers and in an open cockpit.

Gillam's long trip to the East Coast was not totally without reward. While there, he visited the postal authorities in Washington, D.C. There he made a plea for applying the newly adopted Star mail routes in the Territory of Alaska. This method of mail delivery allowed postmasters in specific areas to choose the most efficient method of mail delivery without having to obtain approval from the more remote higher authority. In Alaska, with so few roads and almost total isolation during the winter months, the airplane would obviously be the most efficient, but only if it would prove reliable. Reliability happened also to be Gillam's concern.

He had two reasons for stressing reliability on his mail routes. First, any indication that airplanes could not reliably deliver the mails would raise doubts in the selecting postmaster's mind as to their efficiency. Gillam's second reason for stressing reliability was personal. He felt a responsibility to those relying on him to deliver the mail. His sense of responsibility reached out especially to those living in the outlying areas, whether it be miners or ordinary people living in villages.

Incidentally, without any awareness on his part, his exceptional reliability in delivering the mails contributed immensely to his legend as a weather pilot.

Finally, before leaving Seattle on the SS *Northwestern*, Gillam and Carl Whitham—owner of the Nabesna Mine—made a similar pitch to the postal authorities in that city which considered itself "the gateway to Alaska." There can be little doubt that these efforts regarding the mails brought positive results to those living in Alaska's outlying areas.

Thus, by early January 1931, Gillam had finalized orders for two planes; the five-place Ireland Amphibian to be delivered in April and the six-place Zenith to arrive in June. Also important, he brought with him a young pilot, Adolph Dieterle.

Good news also awaited his return. The post office had awarded Gillam Airways a mail contract for Interior Alaska. This included mail and the right to carry passengers from Cordova to Chitina, to McCarthy, to Kennicott and return to Cordova, service to begin February 28, 1931.

Gillam also spent time in January amending the formal structure of the company by authorizing issuance of stock and to sell a maximum of 100,000 shares at a value of $1.00 per share. The purchase of shares by those within the Copper River region who directly, or indirectly, had an interest in Gillam Airways' services would be the first evidence of community support. The *Times,* therefore, made every effort to publicize the stock sale.

Because he was president and manager of the company, it probably crossed Gillam's mind that selling stock meant he would no longer be completely his own boss. There would now be stockholders who, quite naturally, might want to know what he was doing with their money. Yet, at this point, good will led to trust in his leadership. After all, he had spent his own money to get the air service started and there was perhaps no one who questioned the need for it.

Still, Gillam undoubtedly sensed an obligation to the people who supported his goals and dreams by investing money in Gillam Air-

Gillam and his Swallow are first to land on the Town Lake in downtown Chitna. *(Adena Knutson Photo)*

ways stock. For this reason he took every opportunity to attend functions where he could explain his future plans and allow questions.

That was probably on his mind on January 17, 1931 when he landed his Swallow on Town Lake 's ice in the heart of downtown Chitina. This was the first time that even he had landed there. Since the town had no airport Gillam, in summer, landed on nearby gravel bars on the Copper River. Now, in winter, he made do by landing on a lake that needed more length and that was often frequented by winds which made landings hazardous (in fact, it was on this lake some five years later that Gillam's faithful Zenith would meet its tragic end).

He probably gave little thought to such things on that day in January when he landed and attended the luncheon at the Commercial Hotel. He talked about his plans to make the airplane safe, reliable, and useful to the people of Chitina. Certainly he touched on the need for an airport.

Superintendent Shepherd, head of the Alaska Road Commission's district office, attended the luncheon and heard. For the record, Chitina did not receive its airport until 1937, through no fault of the superintendent, who saw the need for an air service and would be a stock-holder in Gillam Airways. The problem lay with a number of well-meaning and prominent people who simply believed that communities that were served by a railroad had little need to invest in air services. Such thinking may well explain why Cordova made such slow progress in developing an adequate airport.

However, for the most part, people saw need for the airplane. So in 1931 it was Gillam's task not so much to justify air transportation but to justify how it could best serve the people. Thus Gillam talked, explained, and answered questions. More than that though, it was through his actions that he sold people on the idea of buying stock shares in his company.

Those first months of 1931 saw Gillam Airways doing much of what it had been doing during the previous year. The focus continued to be service to the mines and now, mail delivery. Having obtained a second pilot meant that both Swallows would be flying. As it turned out, both would be needed.

Because Gillam was intent on establishing reliability on his mail delivery, he looked on the weekly mail flights out of Cordova as his major responsibility. Since Adolph Dieterle had 800 hours of flight time in the populated area of the western United States, Gillam was mainly concerned with building the new pilot's Alaska experience. To this end, Dieterle was assigned the Swallow with its lesser horse power (the Warner-Scarab 110 hp) and would take on the more local flights out of Copper Center, where work had started on a hangar.

As it turned out, prospects for gold in the Bremner Mining District had recently improved and requests would soon be coming in to drop off individual miners and their gear within that district. The district lay not far south of McCarthy, which had an airport. However, the particular areas of interest had no airstrip of any kind.

Gillam had successfully dropped off prospectors and their gear the previous summer but such ventures were always hazardous. The pilot must use judgment as in how close he can bring the prospector to his desired area. Sound judgment can come only with experience.

Fortunately, prospectors did not go out in midwinter and Gillam spent some time during that winter with Dieterle in the front cockpit. The terrain appeared different when snow covered the ground but making low approaches in likely areas gave some sense of what it was like to make off-airport landing s. The rest would be up to Dieterle. Gillam reminded him to study the general area of the Bremner Mining District as he went back and forth on regular flights; this was part of his homework.

Gillam's own flights to mines focused on Nabesna, where preliminary prospecting had been done by Carl Whitham. Heavy equipment had been brought in during the winter and the mine had begun operation on a limited scale. Supplies and passengers for the mine were sent from Cordova to McCarthy on the railroad. There Gillam loaded them in his 225 hp Swallow and flew them around or over the mountains of the Wrangell Range. In winter, when the daylight hours were few, it wasn't unusual to fly direct. This involved passing by Mt. Blackburn, which reached up to 16,390 feet, then dropping down to cross over Nabesna Glacier before landing at the mine. Obviously, the Swallow needed that more powerful engine to make it across.

While making trips over the Wrangell Range to Nabesna, Gillam also made exploratory flights farther north toward the Canadian boundary to the Forty-mile country. This included Jack Wade Creek and Chicken (originally the latter location was to have been called "Ptarmigan," now the official State bird, but no one was certain of the spelling so it became known simply as "Chicken").

By April 1, Gillam had obtained a contract to deliver mail twice monthly to these mining communities. There was now an obvious need for the two additional larger planes. This was even more apparent when the day for the first mail delivery (February 28, 1931) arrived. It was to begin and end at Cordova, The stops included Copper Center, Chitina, McCarthy, and Kennicott. On that same day, six passengers from Chitina and McCarthy decided to book passage to Cordova. Using both Swallows and assigning Dieterle an additional flight, along with the blessings of good weather, resulted in the mail obligations being carried out on schedule.

Dieterle was kept busy on his local flights and was at the same time growing in his knowledge of Alaska flying. Meanwhile, Gillam had undoubtedly recognized his innate qualities of superior eyesight and unusual awareness of geographical location in situations where visual clues were almost totally lacking. There is evidence that he also deliberately set out to sharpen these innate qualities through practice. Oscar Winchell, who worked for Gillam at Copper Center (1931-32), commented to Jean Potter on these innate qualities and Gillam's deliberate practice of them. In her *The Flying North*, she wrote,

> For some reason," says Winchell, "Harold seemed to like to fly in the dark. He woulda got killed but I think he had abnormally sharp eyes. I always grabbed a flashlight to walk from a field to the roadhouse but Gillam would never bother. He'd step along on a pitch-black night, sure footed as a wild animal.

Then Winchell went on to tell Potter about Gillam's ability to sense physical location.

149

"Once," Winchell says, "he and Gillam were circling at 16,000 feet above a sea of clouds. Mountains were hidden below. There was only fifteen minutes gas left in the tank. He was sittin' there, lookin' around, found a few breaks in the fog but none big enough—there wasn't a worry on his face. Finally he pulled back the throttle and took her down. We could see a little, then she was too thick, we was blind awhile again, right in the mountains—then we broke out in the clear, just over the field...."

Gillam, like all bush pilots of that time, took advantage of every flight, to learn what would make him better able to fly when darkness or weather obscured normal visibility. Mercy flights, where he came to the aid of those needing medical attention, were particularly helpful in giving him firsthand experience. Flying a medical emergency assumes a life-or-death situation which justifies risk taking beyond the ordinary.

Such was the case on March 17, 1931 when the *Times* reported that Gillam made an emergency flight rushing a Mrs. Gerald Clark—with her husband sharing the front cockpit of the Swallow giving whatever comfort and assistance possible—from the Kennecott hospital to Cordova. Here the *SS Yukon* delayed its departure for two hours waiting to take the stricken woman on board.

Shortly thereafter, different circumstances but also involving a life-or-death situation, involved Gillam's concern and special skills. Fred Moller, a relatively inexperienced pilot, planned a flight from Fairbanks to Nabesna on March 9. When he failed to arrive, an extensive search was initiated over his intended route. On March 25, 1931 Gillam, flying in the area and keeping a sharp eye on things below, found the wrecked plane on the Chisana rather than the Nabesna River. Apart from being marooned so many days, the two occupants were in good condition and the event had a desired ending.

Because Gillam was at first the only available pilot in the area, one might assume he was called on often in emergencies. This did not happen immediately simply because residents of the area did not realize such help was available. Even when word of mouth passed on Gillam's willingness and ability to respond, the result was not a great increase in emergency calls. Instead, this knowledge resulted in a sense of security which slowly enveloped those living in the outlying areas. The strong sense of self-reliance remained, but added to it was the quiet confidence that outside help was waiting.

Of the anxiously awaited planes, the Ireland amphibian arrived first, in mid-April. It was accompanied by A.J. Valley, an experienced seaplane pilot hired by Gillam when he bought the Ireland in San Diego. The plane was unloaded on the dock at Cordova and assembly began immediately under Valley's supervision. On April 15,1931 after testing, Valley took the Ireland on its first commercial flight, carrying four passengers to nearby Katella. The plane was to be available for coastal charters and, of course, for flights to and from Chitina during the summer since it had no airport. Town Lake, located in the heart of Chitina, would serve as a convenient base of operations. Valley would be the pilot in charge but this did not keep Gillam from flying the Ireland to gain seaplane experience and to visit locations not otherwise available to him.

Valley's specific knowledge of seaplane flying combined with Gillam's high motivation and quick grasp of piloting led to a rapid and smooth transition to flying the Ireland. In spite of his involvement in this new learning, along with regular flights in the Swallow, Gillam still found opportunities to publicize the Ireland's versatility. One of these was publicized in the following June 8 front-page article in the *Cordova Times*,

> Plane Beats Boat By Four Days On Trip. Gillam returned to Cordova yesterday evening after making the first airplane landing at Yakataga. Gillam made the flight in one hour and forty minutes and arrived there a few minutes after a boat which had left Cordova four days previously. The flight was made possible without difficulty through the amphibian equipment. Gillam said he took off from Lake Eyak (at Cordova) in his boat and landed on wheels on the beach at Yakataga, the heavy surf making it dangerous to attempt a water landing.
>
> Gillam left Cordova late last night for Copper Center to make a flight into the Nabesna country. He will then fly to Valdez to accept delivery on the 6-place Zenith cabin plane.

While Gillam was making this special trip, misfortune finally came upon Adolph Dieterle. He had been carrying out the usual Gillam Airways flying assignments, dealing successfully with both weather and unfamiliar terrain. All the while he paid particular attention to the Bremner Mining District, looking for possible temporary landing sites. Thus, when approached by Bill Berry, a prospector, to land him close to a particular spot, Dieterle took him there to look things over. Not far from the chosen area they located what appeared to be a level spot covered with green vegetation. On it Dieterle proceeded to land. It was a mistake. The green, inviting vegetation turned out to be a boggy surface which was both rough and soggy. The plane nosed over but not before damaging one landing gear slightly, and the propeller, of course.

After looking the area over carefully and locating a safer landing site, Dieterle walked out. Back at McCarthy he got Bud Seltenreich's older brother, Ted, to help him. Gillam had taught Ted to fly and the brothers then bought a Swallow aircraft. Ted loaded Dieterle and materials needed to straighten the prop and repair the landing gear,

then flew out to the wounded plane. With Dieterle's careful directions in his mind, Ted landed safely and they eventually got both planes back to Mc-Carthy.

Meanwhile, Bill Berry proceeded with his prospecting. Nudged into action by this

Gillam gave the Saltenrich brothers their start in aviation. *(Bud Saltenrich photo)*

mishap to the Gillam Airways operation, and knowing the mining operations in the Bremner Mining District were growing steadily, the Alaska Road Commission finally began working on a small airstrip to serve the area, and had it completed by October 24, 1931.

While all this was happening to Dieterle, Gillam made it back from Nabesna to Valdez in time to help his old-time pilot friend, Owen Meals, move the crated Zenith from the dock to the garage where it would be assembled. Meals was a qualified mechanic and would do the assembly and testing while Gillam continued with his flying.

A week or so earlier, two women on their way to work in the canneries at Dillingham, had gotten off the ship at Cordova with the idea of chartering Gillam to take them on from there. He agreed to do so as soon as the Ireland amphibian and Valley had caught up with their charters. Gillam wanted to be back from this trip by the time the Zenith was ready. Meals estimated it would be flying by June 22. So, giving himself a day or so for possible delays, he took off with his two passengers for Dillingham. As it turned out, he needed the extra day because weather held him up at Seldovia. The *Cordova Times* for June 20 carried a front-page article, "Gillam Safe at Dillingham; Was Delayed by Bad Weather." This brought some wag to remark, "When Gillam doesn't make it through bad weather, it's front page news."

This delay was yet another example of Gillam's careful approach to weather flying. He apparently used his innate qualities—keen eyesight and geographical orientation—but also did not hesitate to use the bush pilot's time-honored practice of using greater caution when flying over unfamiliar terrain in obscured visibility.

In any case, using caution and delaying flight due to weather did not keep him from arriving on schedule to pick up his Zenith. On Monday night, June 22, he checked out in the plane at Valdez and then, during the long daylight hours of summer, flew to Cordova. There he picked up priority items for the Nabesna Mine and made the long, high flight to that destination.

Arrival of the Zenith created excitement, especially among the city fathers—specifically members of the Chamber of Commerce. These influential individuals were genuinely involved in promoting the economic growth of the town. Concern for its growth was especially important when one remembers that the early 1930s found the United States as a whole in a deep depression. Perhaps lives of Alaskans were not as profoundly influenced because, for many, "food for their table" came directly from the land. Yet many people in the Cordova area depended on employment for their livelihood. Naturally, the city fathers felt an obligation to promote employment through economic growth. To them, the success of Gillam Airways suggested a way to promote such growth. Gillam undoubtedly agreed, since their goal coincided with his goal of providing safe and reliable transportation where it was most needed. Still, conflict between Gillam and the city fathers was a possibility.

Gillam's new Zenith; passenger comfort finally arrives. (Courtesy T.M. Spencer)

Gillam may well have contributed to this possible conflict. To promote the new aircraft and its future service to the region, he announced, when the crated Zenith arrived at Valdez on June 11, an inaugural flight which he would sponsor.

The flight would carry five Chamber of Commerce members to Fairbanks and return as part of an official visit to the Chamber there. This trip would parallel a scheduled air route that some Chamber members hoped Gillam would establish as the next step in his planning. Such a route would obviously shorten the travel time between Seattle and Fairbanks as well as to the rest of the Interior, including Nome on the Bering Sea. Without making any reference to it, they hoped this route would also effectively cut much of the surface traffic now moving through Seward and Anchorage. In turn, this would make Cordova, rather than Anchorage, the transportation hub for the Interior. This possibility was not lost on Chamber members in either town.

And where did Gillam stand in the matter? The inaugural flight would not take place until June 28, some three weeks after it was announced. This provided considerable time to talk about it and its implications for the future direction of air transportation in the Copper River region and, specifically, the role Gillam Airways would play in this future development. As early as June the *Times* spoke of the arrival of Gillam's Zenith and that it would start operations from Cordova to Chitina and then on to Fairbanks, and that this service would begin about the middle of June. The same article openly pointed out that this service would reduce travel time from Seattle to Fairbanks by two and one half days.

Gillam sells Cordova-Fairbanks business men on commercial air travel. *(Courtesy Fairbanks Pioneer Air Museum)*

It is not known whether Gillam agreed with the content of that news item but it is apparent that he was caught up in the excitement of the inaugural flight. He was at that time invited to become a member of the Chamber. All this was heady stuff and may have, at least for a moment, taken his mind off his long-range goals. Did Gillam actually ponder basic questions such as, Is reduction of travel time from Fairbanks and the Interior to Seattle more important than the needs of the mines in the Copper River region for emergency parts and supplies, or the needs of outlying areas for mail and for fresh produce?

Perhaps Gillam did not have time to ponder such questions between June 22, when he began flying the Zenith, and June 28 when the inaugural flight began. Another factor that Gillam probably didn't have time to consider was any subtle pressure he may have felt to agree with the Chamber, of which he was now a member. This pressure may have stemmed from an obligation he may have felt toward those people who had shown their confidence in him by buying stock to support his venture, or from the goodwill extended by the *Cordova Times* in promoting the stock sale and in general giving generous space to publicize Gillam Airway services. Whether such pressures were felt by Gillam will never be known but their possible existence cannot be discounted.

In any case, the trip was a complete success. The weather cooperated during the entire three days. The scenery from the plane's windows was magnificent. They saw the Wrangell mountain range with

Fortunately, weather did not interfere with a beautiful view of the mountains of the Wrangell Range. (Courtesy Valdez Museum)

individual peaks reaching up to heights of over 16,000 feet; then there was Mt. Wrangell, still an active volcano in 1931; all this stood out in the clear sunshine of those long summer days.

The party left Cordova on a Monday morning at the reasonable hour of 9:00 a.m.. The flight each way was only slightly over four hours but Gillam arrange a stop at Copper Center to relax and enjoy a leisurely lunch at Ma Barnes' Roadhouse. They arrived over Fairbanks in early afternoon. A full day of meetings followed in which cooperation between the two towns was discussed and surely direct transportation between them came up.

During that brief Fairbanks visit, an episode took place not involving business but showing Gillam's sense of humor which some would deny he possessed. This is the report given by the *Cordova Times*:

> Pilot Harold Gillam of the Gillam Airways recently flew the members of the Cordova Chamber of Commerce to Fairbanks. It so happened that he arrived the same day that Wiley Post and Harold Gatty

155

were closing the circle of their round-the-world flight, and it was a gala day in Fairbanks. Shortly after the arrival of Post and Gatty at the Nordale Hotel, a lady entered and, walking up to Gillam who was standing in the hotel lobby, said: "Are you the flyer?" Naturally thinking of his flight from Cordova, Gillam nodded assent, at which the kindhearted old lady threw here arms around his neck and with a hug and a kiss said: "My, but you are a brave boy to attempt that long flight around the world. I sure am proud of you."

The genial aviator's attempt at explanations was not a success. The enthusiastic lady gave him a final hug and smilingly departed, after which Gillam decided that Harold Gatty should be paged.

On Wednesday the delegation returned, with beautiful weather allowing them again to enjoy the scenery. Again they had a rest stop for lunch at the Copper Center Roadhouse. And they were still able to land at the Cordova airport on Lake Eyak by mid-afternoon. From there, the five passengers and their pilot traveled those last seventeen miles on a railroad speeder, an automobile of sorts which rode the tracks. A change of transportation that truly brought them all "back to earth."

On the days following, the *Times'* pages were filled with the delights and importance of the trip and with praises for Gillam, who made the event possible. Also, some of the statements suggested the trip had proven the feasibility of a direct air link connecting the steamship traveler with Fairbanks and other parts of the Interior.

We will never know what went through Gillam's mind as he was singled out for all this attention and praise, knowing that some of the Cordova businessmen who were bestowing this attention were also hoping he would put his new Zenith to work making scheduled Flights between Cordova and Fairbanks.

We don't know what he thought but we do know what he did. We know that he immediately put the plane to use serving the mines and hauling the mail to outlying areas. Up to this point mail contracts dealt with deliveries during the winter months when the Northwestern and Copper River Railroad was closed down. Now, however, Gillam was contracted to carry mail to mines across the mountains, to the Nabesna Mine and then farther north to the Forty-mile country. And now he would be delivering mail during the summer months also.

Gillam continued to serve the Copper River region's mines and outlying areas, and his efforts led other pilots to begin serving this region also. And throughout all this, Gillam continued to grow in competence as a pilot—especially in weather flying. In this way what appears to be a legend continued to build.

156

Chapter 14
MEETING CHALLENGES
Go confidently in the direction of your dreams. (Anonymous)

As the second half of the year 1931 moved on, the physical base of Gillam Airways was firmly established at Copper Center. From there the planes flew in and out; there a hangar stood waiting for them. And in that hangar the mechanic, Earl Wood, worked to keep those planes flying. Also, Gillam was headquartered at Copper Center. Yet an important part of that air service lay many miles away at the seaport town of Cordova. There the weekly mail flights began and ended; there Cordova businessmen bought Gillam Airways stock; and there the *Cordova Times* publicized Gillam Airways' service to the town and to the entire Copper River region.

Zenith; Gillam's work horse. (Courtesy T.M. Spencer)

To keep close contact between the two locations, Gillam provided radio communication between Copper Center and Cordova and later to Chitina, an important village in need of air transportation.

Everything worked smoothly until, not long after the successful inaugural flight of the Zenith to Fairbanks, an unforeseen event sent a tremor through Gillam's organization. The Anchorage paper reported it on the evening of July 8, 1931. The Ireland Neptune, after a flight from Valdez and Seward, flipped over during a landing at Anchorage's Merrill Field. Pilot A.J. Valley had first landed on the water at Anchorage's

Lake Spenard. Next, with mechanic Jack Moton as passenger, he took off and extended the wheels for a landing at nearby Merrill Field. The wheels lowered but the left one did not lock properly. On touching down, that wheel gave way and the plane flipped on its back. Neither pilot nor mechanic were hurt, although the mechanic, because he had not fastened his seatbelt, was bruised a bit from being tumbled about. The Ireland received minor damage, mainly on its left wing tip. Perhaps because of the awkward position in which it came to rest, the plane appeared to have suffered considerable damage.

Overturned Neptune; don't blame this one on Gillam. *(S. Mills/Courtesy Sourdough Sky)*

Gillam, who happened to be in Anchorage, came and saw the plane still on its back. This prompted him to say, "Looks like a good time to clean the bottom." Gillam had a tendency to introduce humor into otherwise serious situations to ease tension. This seems to have been a trademark of his personality. The humor, however, almost always came at his own expense.

This dramatic setback did not deter Gillam or his organization. The injured Ireland was disassembled, put on a small ocean-going tug and hauled to Valdez. There mechanic Earl Wood and newly hired Oscar Winchell loaded it on a truck and hauled it over the Richardson Highway to Copper Center. By the beginning of August, Wood and Winchell had the Ireland hangared and both worked full-time to get it back in the air. By the beginning of September it was ready. At this point Gillam owned three planes, all of them airworthy. The smallest was the open-cockpit Swallow with the large 225 hp engine. The older *Arctic Prospector* had been sold to Reuben James who worked at the Kennecott Mine. James had arranged a lease-back so Gillam could use it, if needed. The two larger planes were the six-place Zenith and the newly repaired five-place Ireland amphibian.

A quick resurrection. (*UAF Archives*)

The Zenith, being the best performer in terms of speed, takeoff, and load-carrying capacity, was flown by Gillam most of the time. This changed in mid-September, about when the Ireland was again airworthy.

Gillam had been busy flying gold ore concentrate from the Nabesna Mine to Copper Center. From there it was taken by road to Chitina, then by railroad to Cordova where it was put on a steamship and taken to a refinery in the Seattle area. On one of these flights from the mine, Gillam came in after dark and crashed when the heavily loaded plane ran out of runway. As Oscar Winchell, who was there, described it in his biography,

> It was dark by the time they walked out of the hangar. Gillam buzzed the field, then approached for a landing as if there were miles of runway, and then CRUNCH !!! over the end he went with the Zenith.

These few words strongly suggest an overconfident, if not reckless, pilot. These words may well have laid the groundwork for the view that Gillam was a reckless pilot. Jean Potter, in her book *The Flying*

Recent photo showing what remains of Gillam's Copper Center hangar. (**Author photo**)

North, after interviewing people some twelve years after the crash, made this report:

> One night people at Copper (Center) heard the roar of Gillam's engine and looked out their cabin windows. His Swallow (Zenith), its navigation lights flashing against the bluffs, was circling to land. Men hurried down the trail to mark off the field with lanterns. But Gillam did not wait for their aid. His ship, heavily loaded with ore concentrates, descended and crashed. It rolled violently over a bank and a large stump broke through the windshield, missing him by inches.

The people interviewed seemed to communicate, as did Winchell, a feeling that Gillam, as a pilot, acted hastily and showed lack of judgment.

On the other hand, Harold Starkey, who worked at the Nabesna

Nabesna mine will play an important role in Gillam's flying, while in the Copper River region. (Harold Starkey photo)

Mine during the time Gillam flew there a lot, was interviewed recently. He gave a different view of what caused the crash. First he pointed out, as did Winchell, that Gillam flew often at night. Starkey went on to say that in winter, with few hours of daylight, he landed regularly on a small lake next to the mine. He did this more as he got to know the layout of its location. The crew working there firmly believed that since he flew out of Copper Center regularly and made night landings there from time to time, Gillam should have made a normal landing. They felt he didn't because some well-intentioned person, trying to point out the field, directed the beam of a high-powered flashlight at the plane as it made its final approach. For a moment, this may have disoriented Gillam and caused the crash.

This explanation has credibility since there is no record of Gillam making an intentional landing resulting in a crash. This includes a precautionary landing he made at night in the arctic, which happened in unfamiliar terrain.

What really happened will never be known because Gillam simply never laid blame on others for what happened to him while flying.

Gillam's response after the crash, as reported by Jean Potter, gives an insight into the tenacious nature of this man; not unlike his response after the Danforth crash.

> He unbuckled his seat belt, climbed out and dourly surveyed the wreck…"I'll be damned," he said, "If I think there's any money in this business." Yet, the next day he began figuring what parts could be salvaged to rebuild the plane.

As it turned out, the damage was not as severe as it first appeared. Wood and Winchell began recovering the wings immediately and had the Zenith rebuilt by mid-November. While the Zenith was being worked on, Gillam took over the Ireland since it was a better load carrier than the Swallow. It also had an enclosed cabin.

Then, on November 17, 1931, Gillam Airways suffered another setback. On that day, Gillam took off in the Ireland from Valdez airport for Cordova. A short distance from Lake Eyak Airport the engine quit. Gillam was able to make a forced landing without injury to passengers and without putting the aircraft over on its back.

The *Cordova Times* reported the forced landing of the Ireland on its front page. However, in doing so it was able to put the episode in a positive light—both praising Gillam's skill as a pilot and the safety of air travel even when the unexpected happens. The *Times* reported,

> Pilot Gillam has crackup near railway. Makes perfect landing when motor stalls: passengers hardly felt the jolt.

> Water vapor in the gas line which froze, stopping the engine, resulting in Gillam making a forced landing at mile six or seven. No injuries but considerable damage to the Ireland amphibian. The safety of air transportation was well illustrated when Pilot Gillam, with a dead engine, picked out a suitable spot to land, without injury to his passengers—or himself. Landed in brush, tore off lower wing. Ship will be towed to hangar at Lake Eyak for repairs.

Certainly Gillam Airways and air transportation in general were happy to receive a word of support at that time.

Now Gillam Airways was down to one plane. There had also been a change in the pilot roster. Adolph Dieterle had left; probably soon after his unfortunate encounter with off-airport landings. Oscar Winchell replaced him. He was hired in August, 1931, to be both mechanic and pilot, whichever was needed at any given time. Winchell had considerable hours as pilot but none involved Alaska flying. A.J. Valley, also without Alaska flying experience, had been hired mainly for his seaplane background. He was kept busy until that unfortunate event at Merrill Field. The Ireland was not available for him to fly after that, either because it was being repaired or, when it was airworthy once more, because Gillam commandeered it during the time the Zenith was being repaired. Apparently due to these circumstances, Valley dropped out and flew for Star Air Service in Anchorage. This left Gillam and Winchell as qualified pilots. With only the Swallow airworthy, Gillam took it to begin his winter mail contract. So the unhappy Winchell was left, yearning to fly, but doing what he had been doing since he arrived—repairing airplanes.

Winchell finally did make one flight of an emergency nature from Copper Center to Valdez and back. This happened when Gillam began flying the newly repaired Zenith and found its engine needed an urgent overhaul. He did make it into Valdez. There, with passengers and mail needing to be moved and feeling the Zenith engine no longer trustworthy, he called Winchell. The instructions were for him to fly the Swallow down to Valdez, switch airplanes and fly the empty Zenith back to Copper Center. The following dialogue, taken from Winchell's biography, expresses both Winchell's frustration and Gillam's impatience,

> There (at Valdez) Oscar found Harold Gillam sitting comfortably at the potbellied stove warming himself. He was ready to leave for Copper Center as soon as he saw Oscar.
>
> "Don't go tonight," Oscar pleaded, "we've got to take time out and discuss the Zenith. What are you going to do with it?"
>
> "I'm not going to fly it; it can't take it anymore."
>
> "Earl says that we could take the engine off the amphibian you left at Cordova."
>
> "Fine, fine," answered Gillam. "But why can't I have the Swallow?"
>
> "It's got a cracked induction chamber and must be changed. You'd never make it."
>
> "Okay…okay, we'll change it in the morning and then I can get going. And then you can get that other engine off that amphibian and get it to Copper Center," Gillam said.
>
> "Oh, brother, errand boy again," Oscar thought as he bid his boss good night.

After a quick change of parts, Harold Gillam took off and Oscar was left with the crippled Zenith. He waited for clear weather before returning to Copper Center.

Winchell did get the Zenith with its tired engine back to Copper Center without too much delay. Meanwhile Wood cannibalized the engine out of the Ireland, got it to Copper Center and installed it in the Zenith. While all this was going on Gillam flew the Swallow with its open-cockpit and smaller load-carrying capacity. These flights were both longer and uncom-

Winchell finally flying. *(Courtesy Mills and Phillips; Sourdough Sky: Superior Publishing Co.)*

fortable. Both passengers and Gillam were happy to have the big plane back on line.

No sooner was the Zenith ready when it was called on to make a "mercy flight." Old-timer John McCrary, the storekeeper at Copper Center, who had never been sick as long as anybody could remember, started staying in bed for part of the day. He still insisted there was nothing wrong. One day when he closed the store around noon, somebody contacted Gillam when he got back from a flight.

The townspeople loaded McCrary into the Zenith and Gillam took off for the Kennicott hospital, some 125 miles to the east. It was almost the shortest day of the year, and visibility was poor due to blowing snow, which made it anything but an easy trip. Landing at the McCarthy airfield (5 miles from the hospital) after dark was probably the hardest part. It was known to be short and there was only one way in. However, to Gillam a life was at stake and he had plenty of practice flying at night and in poor visibility. The doctor had been notified and operated immediately. He found a perforated ulcer. McCrary had been losing blood for a number of days and the doctor didn't give him much of a chance to live. The news got to the son, Nels McCrary, who was fire chief at Cordova. Nels asked Gillam to pick him up. He also told him the ice on Lake Eyak was thick enough to land there. Knowing that visibility was still not the best and that the sick man was now in the hospital, Gillam held off for a few hours so he would be flying toward daylight (as Cecil Higgins, Gillam's buddy, said, "He doesn't take unnecessary chances"). Gillam landed the ski-equipped Zenith on the lake before noon, loaded the son and took off. Even so, darkness had fallen when he landed at McCarthy. By the time Nels McCrary got to the hospital his dad was already sitting up, ready for Gillam to take him home. As the people in Copper Center said, "That Honest John is a tough old bird."

Gillam had saved a life and probably only he could have flown those trips safely. It is interesting to note that, although the facts in this event show it to be a dramatic one that points to Gillam's skill and courage, the people involved seemed to feel a need to add details that make Gillam's efforts even more dramatic. Jean Potter's account of the mercy flight in *The Flying North* again quoted the people involved who were interviewed some twelve years later.

> Gillam loaded the groaning man into his plane, took off at dusk and flew 125 miles through driving snow to Kennicott. The doctor there said the patient might not last the night. Gillam left Kennicott after midnight and flew another 200 miles to fetch McCrary's son from Cordova.
>
> As the plane came down on the lake at Cordova one wheel broke through the ice and it sagged over. A spar of the lower wing was cracked. It took three hours to pull the ship out and drag it to shore. Meanwhile a telephone report came from Kennicott; McCrary was sinking fast.
>
> A worried group watched as Gillam poured gas into the tanks.
>
> "You taking off, Harold," asked one, "with that busted spar?"
>
> "Ice is awful thin," said another.
>
> "Oh, that's okay," Gillam told them as he screwed on the gas cap. "I think it'll be all right."
>
> He motioned his passenger in, took off on the rubbery ice, and returned to Kennicott.

It is apparent that Potter wrote in a journalistic style to enhance reader interest. However, as a correspondent for Time-Life Publications back then, she had an obligation to not embellish the facts. It is reported that she firmly upheld that obligation. Therefore, it was the participants who embellished. Why? Since twelve years had passed, they may have remembered it the way they told it. There is also the possibility of "legend building" at work. Legends are developed around exceptional people accomplishing exceptional tasks, and around such a person facts tend to be embellished. In the McCrary incident the people may also have felt a thankfulness that Gillam had saved the life of someone they held in affection. Or they may simply have stood in awe of his skill and courage as an aviator and this may have affected their memory. It would seem legend, although based on fact, holds an element of mystery also.

The year 1932 opened with Gillam using the Zenith to carry out the usual weekly mail flights.

Passengers were also carried on these mail flights. This particular year many travelers needed flights that did not fit the weekly mail schedule. Since Gillam Airways was still the only company serving the Copper River region, these needs had to be met. To meet them, Winchell was assigned the Swallow to take care of special flights as they arose. Winchell was of course delighted with an arrangement that put him back into flying.

Earl Wood. In Gillam's view a good mechanic makes a pilot look good. *(Clifton Library photo/ Courtesy R.W. Stevens)*

Except for major work on the Ireland, Earl Wood could use the hangar to do routine maintenance. The plan for the Ireland was to have it brought from Cordova to Chitina by railroad when it began operations in early spring. Then, with the wings off, it would be transported by truck to the hangar at Copper Center for repair. As it turned out, when it arrived in Chitina and Wood went there to give it

165

a closer inspection, he found that repair of the bulkhead would require special equipment. The plane, with the wings removed, was stored at Chitina and was never flown again.

One of Gillam's February 1932 flights showed how he went out of his way to interest kids in flying. It turned out young Carl Carlson wanted to fly from his home in Chitina to McCarthy, which was close by. Gillam didn't have any passengers to drop off or pick up at Chitina on the return trip so he told young Carlson he could fly with him from Chitina to Cordova and then from Cordova to McCarthy and all he would pay for was the short, 65 mile trip from Chitina to McCarthy. Most adults might not think that kids would be thrilled by such an offer. Not so, The following is part of an article published in the school paper, *The Chitina Weekly Herald:*

> Little Carl Carlson lately had a fine chance that any boy or girl in Chitina would give their pair of false teeth to have gotten…So friend Carlson got a free ride of 262 miles to Cordova and return. "Why can't we all be like that bird?" It was in the Zenith six-passenger plane.

It was also in February that Winchell had his first bad experience with Alaska winter flying. On February 21, while flying Swallow 430N with mail and one passenger from Cordova to Chitina, he tangled with a snowstorm while following the railroad. As the visibility got worse, he turned back. That didn't help matters and he landed straight ahead in the deep snow. There were no injuries and the plane suffered only a bent prop. The passenger, having more knowledge of the area than Winchell, determined they were about three miles from the track-walker cabin at Mile 101. Using the one pair of snowshoes, they finally made it to the cabin. There they called Chitina and reported what had happened. Meanwhile the track-walker made them comfortable for the night.

Returning to the plane in the morning, they found the wind had blown it part way over and now both the propeller and the skis were damaged. While these were being repaired, the wind managed to blow the plane all the way over, this time damaging a wing. Using a Ford Snowbird (a Model T Ford modified to use tracks instead of wheels), they got the Swallow into the hangar at Copper Center. There Wood and Winchell had it repaired by the end of March.

Shortly after that, Winchell went to work at McGee Airways in Anchorage, as pilot.

Soon after Winchell left, Gillam hired M.D. Kirkpatrick, who was also both pilot and mechanic. Gillam first got to know Kirkpatrick when he was superintendent at the Swallow Aircraft Company at the same time Gillam became the company's agent for Alaska. Kirkpatrick moved with his wife to Copper Center. There, with the milder weather of summer approaching, Gillam took time to check Kirkpatrick out in the Zenith. This gave him a good start in his Alaska flying. With the winter mail contract finished, Gillam and Kirkpatrick worked together in the Zenith and Swallow to get men and supplies to the mines.

It was during one of those early spring days that Gillam left his regular flying to make another mercy flight. The following headline and article from the *Cordova Times* may seem overly dramatic to today's reader. Nevertheless, back then, a pilot's and his plane's ability to save a life was indeed dramatic. The headline and article read,

> Gillam Airways Wins Race With Death: Patient Saved. Airplane transportation again played a leading role in possibly saving a human life yesterday when president Harold Gillam of the Gillam Airways flew to Chitina with Doctor Shore of the Cordova General Hospital, and returned later in the evening with Amos Fluery "Frenchy" who was suffering from acute appendicitis...Fluery was operated on at the hospital this morning and late this afternoon his condition was reported as satisfactory, it being believed that he now is entirely out of danger.

At the end of May 1932 Gillam bought a Keystone Leoning amphibian from Alaskan Airways. Immediately after that purchase he made a quick trip to the lower forty-eight in his Leoning. He left with a passenger, John Rosswog, a merchant of Cordova, on June 10 and returned on June 24. Some may have wondered why he left, even for a quick trip, with the mines opening up and with a definite need for his newly acquired amphibian. We will never know, since Gillam wasn't much at giving reasons for what he did. Since he had a tendency to become familiar with any plane he bought by "trying it out" on an extended trip, this may have been a factor. He was also interested in pioneering a route between Alaska and Seattle. A route which provided fuel and airstrips that would allow smaller planes to be flown up rather than being disassembled, shipped on a slow steamship, and then reassembled.

Probably his main reason for making the trip was to find a load-carrying plane as backup for the Zenith. At that time Varney Airlines, headquartered in Portland, Oregon, was surplusing its 525 hp Stearman Mail Winds and replacing them with newer twin-engine passenger-carrying types. The Stearman would serve Gillam's load-carrying needs and, being surplused, would be less expensive than buying a new Zenith. In addition, since this plane previously owned by an airline, it would have instruments for blind flying installed. Alaska planes were still not equipped with these. Gillam saw modern instrumentation as an important step toward safe and reliable air transportation. He would, of course, not make a heavy investment without a firsthand knowledge of the plane's performance. Perhaps he might even get a chance to fly one. Then there was also the matter of talking to the people involved as to availability, cost, and so forth.

He must have made such explorations during his quick visit, because within six months he was able to make another trip, this time to pick up a Stearman from the Varney people. He was fortunate to have made arrangements in advance because another emergency arose which again took the Zenith out of service.

Whatever Gillam's reasons for the trip in the Leoning, he was not delayed by weather. His time in the air was shortened because, flying an amphibian, he was able to use the coastal route via Juneau, Ketchikan, and Prince Rupert (in Canada). Taking the coastal route did not prevent him from gathering firsthand knowledge of the Interior route via Prince George, Hazelton, Telegraph Creek, Skagway, and then on to Cordova. It was this land route that he used in bringing up the Stearman in November. It was also the route he used later in bringing up his other planes, none of which were amphibians.

After returning to Cordova with John Rosswog, he checked Kirkpatrick out in the Leoning, then went back to routine flying.

The 4th of July celebration is an important one for Alaskans. It was the only one during the short busy summer when all work stops. Work did not stop on the 4th of July, 1932 for Gillam. He spent it putting on his own airshow and giving rides afterward.

During that summer and into fall, Gillam and Kirkpatrick cooperated in routine flights which included the twice-monthly mail trips to the forty-mile country. Those flights were thought to be anything but routine by those served by Gillam Airways. A particular one Gillam made in late July was described by Goulet in his book *Rugged Years on the Alaska Frontier*. Goulet was at that time, like other miners, searching for the strike that would make him rich. He not only communicated how important Gillam's trips were to the miners but also pointed out the hazards involved for pilot and plane, especially for the plane.

> Before the storms increased in intensity, Bob and I made a Pilgrimage to Slate Creek to stock up on supplies. Gillam, an aviator based at Copper Center, had flown to Slate Creek that day with a load of fresh eggs and vegetables. In landing on the river flat he broke the carriage and wrecked a wing. The closest telephone was 40 miles away, at Paxson. The Slate Creek mine owner loaned Gillam a horse

to get him to Paxson, but he had to go with him to get the horse back, since they would need it to get back out in the fall. I imagine the young pilot thought horseback travel over those flats and through the brush pretty slow compared with his own method. The point, however, to this story is that Bob and I had fresh vegetables and eggs for the first time since the previous fall, almost a year before.

The damage was not as great as it appeared to Goulet. Before leaving, though, Gillam did clear a space of loose rock to assure a safe landing for the Zenith when it returned with him, Kirkpatrick, and materials needed to make temporary repairs. Surely, appreciation for what Gillam had done to improve the morale of the mine workers was part of the reason the mine owner willingly gave a day of his precious time to help Gillam.

After the Swallow was flown back to the Copper Center hangar to get further attention, Gillam and Kirkpatrick kept the Zenith and Stearman flying. Again things went well, until a cold morning in early November. The usual procedure on cold mornings was to heat the engine with the open flame of a plumber's firepot placed under a cowling cover which kept the heat in. This was being done to the Zenith that morning as it sat in the hangar. The young man designated to keep constant watch for any stray flame trying to reach out toward the fabric, failed to watch carefully. In spite of the cold, a flame did flick out and ignited a spot on the highly inflammable fabric and spread quickly.

Fortunately, the alarm was given, the firepot turned off, and waiting empty burlap sacks soaking in buckets of water served as fire extinguishers. Cool heads put out the fire immediately, but not before it charred much of the fabric on the wings and on parts of the fuselage.

Chapter 15
CHANGES; IMMEDIATE AND ON THE HORIZON

Man can learn nothing except by
going from the know to the unknown.
(Claude Bernard)

The year 1933 saw air transportation both grow and change in the Copper River region. However, a disruptive change within the Gillam

Cordova. Gillam gradually moved his headquarters here. (R.W. Stevens photo)

The 225 hp Swallow could handle the short, rough McCarthy airstrip. (M.J. Kirckhoff photos)

organization required his full attention and caused him to ignore the broader changes going on around him, changes that would have serious implications for his future operations. This immediate, disruptive change involved neither planes nor pilots.

In early spring 1933, Earl Wood, who had been mechanic for Gillam from the beginning, moved to McGee Airways in Anchorage. This was a blow for Gillam, since he believed that the success of any air service depended to a great extent on its mechanic.

The blow was softened somewhat by Bud Seltenreich. Gillam had first known him as the eleven-year-old boy with questions. This encounter took place at the Anderson garage in McCarthy during the winter of 1923-24. Gillam was then still working for the Alaska Road Commission as a crawling tractor operator.

As it turned out, when

Gillam returned as president and chief pilot of Gillam Airways he made many stops at McCarthy, since it had the only airport and overnight accommodations in the area. Bud was now a young man of seventeen with a natural mechanical ability that had been sharpened by a natural interest in mechanical things. Bud and his two older brothers, Ted and Fred, had bought a Swallow airplane and later Gillam taught the oldest, Ted, to fly. Bud was now old enough to hold regular jobs but managed to find time to hang around the airport when Gillam showed up. In summer he'd help with things like fueling and checking oil. In winter there were extra things to do, such as handling wing covers and fireproofing.

Bud started young and in his lifetime did much for Alaska aviation. (Wings over Alaska/Alaska Aviation Heritage Museum)

In this way, Gillam got to know him better, his abilities and his intense interest in airplanes. It was natural then that Gillam would hire him as mechanic when Earl left. Bud, interviewed when he was eighty-five and still sound in mind and body, talked about his experiences working as Gillam's mechanic. He said, among other things,

"We were both mechanics at heart. He was older and knew more. I learned a lot, especially when we worked together. That was past the time when pilots took a mechanic along to fix things in case of a forced landing. Of course Gillam was a trained mechanic but he wanted me along when he took those big planes like the Stearman and the Pilgrim onto river bars and little strips. Then he needed help to turn them around. I'd hook a rope around the tail wheel and pull like the devil to bring it around while he opened to full throttle and worked the rudder, and brakes, if it was summer."

During that session he paused for a moment, then added, "I never felt safer in the air then with Gillam. He was the best." After another pause and with a twinkle in his eye he went on, "You might say he was even a better pilot than me."

Another change came shortly after Earl Wood's leaving. Kirkpatrick left to fly on his own and not long after, became involved in organizing the Cordova Air Service. His leaving related directly to the Copper River region's need for more air transportation. This need stemmed mainly from the growth in mining. Nabesna Mine was now in full production. The Romer Brothers in the Bremner Mining District near

Cordova were moving toward full production. Also, Eastern capital had bought out the small mines on Dan and Chitutu Creeks near McCarthy. These holdings were then consolidated and formed the Pardner Mining Company.

This greater activity in mining finally moved the Territorial legislature to appropriate money for a new airport at Cordova. The Alaska Road Commission then moved men and equipment to the old airport site and began construction in 1933. Summer 1934 was to be the completion date..

With a new airport at Cordova in sight and Cap Lathrop (a financier located in Fairbanks) supporting a large, modern maintenance hangar there, a number of air services planned to move into the Copper River region. One of these was the new Cordova Air Service with Kirkpatrick now as its head.

Surprisingly, Kirkpatrick's leaving Gillam Airways to head up Cordova Air Service involved no animosity. Merle Smith, who later flew

Gillam's Zenith moves up the ramp into Cordova's new maintenance hangar. *(Bud Seltenreich photo)*

for Cordova Air Service, states in his biography, *Mudhole Smith, Alaska Flier,* that a number of Cordova businessmen with a financial interest in the Romer Brothers mine wanted an air service that gave priority to that mine's needs. Gillam was unable to meet the growing needs of the entire Copper River region. In addition, his priority was on providing mail deliveries.

Gillam seemed to have no problem with competing air services moving into the new Cordova airport. His decision was to remain in the Copper River region and provide reliable mail service through Cordova, especially to the outlying areas. Since Cordova would be the central distribution point for the region's mail, it explains why he gradually moved his headquarters from Copper Center to that seaport town.

There may also have been in Gillam's mind a desire to follow through on his dream of providing scheduled passenger service between Cordova and Fairbanks.

Kirkpatrick's leaving Gillam Airways during the summer of 1933 posed an immediate and practical problem. Kirkpatrick had adjusted quickly to the special requirements of Alaska flying and proved himself a valuable asset to Gillam Airways. Now Gillam was faced with the situation of having four airworthy planes but only himself as pilot. To resolve the problem he hired Johnny Moore, again a pilot with a good number of hours but no Alaska experience.

Gillam stayed particularly busy that summer and fall of 1933. Besides his regular flying and working with Bud when there was more maintenance than usual, he gave extra attention to training Johnny, especially in the Stearman.

Although busy, Gillam found time to handle emergencies when they arose. In mid-September, 1933 Reuben James, who worked for Kennecott and bought Gillam's old *Arctic Prospector,* was flying it to bring an injured miner to the Cordova hospital. Weather caused him to crash in Thompson Pass. Neither he nor his passenger suffered injuries from the crash, but the plane was destroyed. A motorist brought the stranded pilot and injured miner to Valdez, where Gillam appeared and flew them to Cordova. In this instance, the miner died at the hospital but Gillam had done all he could.

Gillam was still providing reliable mail service with his faithful Stearman. *(UAF Archives)*

Between mail flights, Gillam taught Johnny Moore special techniques for getting the Stearman in and out of short mining strips. Instruction was brief and to the point. Don't carry more gas than you safely need. Assume you'll have a heavy load coming in for a landing. Aim for the first few feet of the strip. Carry power and hold the edge of a stall. When safely on, chop the throttle, stall the plane, and get on the brakes. Takeoffs are fairly easy. Come out empty if at all possible. Wide open throttle, stand on the brakes, let go, steer it and let the 525 hp engine lift you off.

Johnny learned all this well. It was weather that got him into trouble. In the middle of January 1934 Gillam made his first of two monthly flights to the forty-mile country and had just started his weekly flights to nearby towns on the railroad. Then it happened. Johnny, flying the Stearman to Cordova, made a precautionary landing on a slough because of weather. Pilot skill brought the plane in without harm to pilot or plane. Moore struggled with high winds for over an hour before getting the plane secured. Then, while walking to a cabin for help, the heavy Stearman broke through the ice, which severely damaged it. For the moment it could not be salvaged or repaired.

Loss of the Stearman may well have been a factor in Moore's decision, at this time, to leave Gillam Airways and fly for McGee Airways in Anchorage. Not to be overlooked is the possibility that Moore, as well as other pilots who left Gillam Airways to fly out of Anchorage, saw it as a less hazardous location in which to do their flying.

Now he was the only pilot. Hardly three months later, another blow fell. Gillam, flying the Zenith with the last mail for the winter contract, landed at Copper Center to refuel and work with Bud to fine-tune the Leoning amphibian. He fell off the wing and ended up with a sprained wrist and bruised leg. Wanting to finish the final mail flight, he took off for Valdez. In Thompson Pass, only 30 miles from his destination, the engine lost oil pressure. Hoping to save the en-

Flying in the Copper River region takes experience. (Harold Starkel photo)

gine, he landed on a makeshift strip next to the Richardson Highway (the old Fairbanks Trail). After deciding the engine would need to be worked on before he moved the plane, he tied it down in a sheltered spot and caught a ride into Valdez.

What had happened? The young man servicing the Zenith had left the oil cap off. Bud insisted Gillam did not overlook preflights. That he could tell at a glance if anything was out of place. However, this time, probably because of distractions, his system failed, and it was a costly failure.

In Gillam's defense we can refer to Charles Lindbergh who had a similar experience. Here also, distraction led to a poor preflight, followed by drastic consequences.

After his solo flight across the Atlantic, Lindbergh made a goodwill tour to Mexico. While there he met Anne Morrow, his future wife, the U.S. ambassador to Mexico's youngest daughter. To have a quiet moment away from reporters, Lindbergh borrowed a plane and they flew out to a secluded spot for a picnic. Before taking off for his return trip one would assume, knowing his careful nature, that he did a careful preflight. He didn't. After the plane lifted into the air, Lindbergh saw the right wheel still rolling along on the ground.

His immediate concern was justified. Regardless of skill, the plane would certainly flip over on landing and this trusting young woman might well be injured. He knew the injury could be serious because many enclosed planes of that period had no seatbelts. His borrowed plane was one of these. Knowing this, he directed his young charge to gather all loose cushions, arrange them behind his seat and place herself among them. Having made these preparations, she would then hang onto the back of his seat during the landing.

As expected, the crowd and reporters awaited their return and the plane did flip over. However, young Anne escaped unscathed; but the stalwart young pilot did not. Wanting to keep his body and seat in place, in order to provide additional protection for Miss Morrow, he braced himself

(United Press Int'l photo. Courtesy Harcourt, Brace, Janovich)

with his free arm. In doing so he dislocated his shoulder and had to carry his arm in a sling for a time.

The moral of the above example? Even the most level-headed pilot can become distracted in a preflight and the consequences for such a lapse can be serious. As someone once said, "Aviation is not inherently dangerous, but like the sea, is terribly unforgiving."

With both of his load-carrying planes now out of service, Gillam made a quick decision to go outside, purchase another Stearman from Varney, and fly it back. His decision to fly the Leoning out, sell his Swallow before leaving, and to be gone an entire month seems a bit strange.

It had been rumored that Gillam was suffering financially, not only because of plane losses, but also due to loss of previous investors. Many of these were now supporting another air service, one, that would give priority to their mining interests. Possibly lack of money would account for his selling the Swallow to J.D. Finley, who planned to use it to mine out of Valdez.

On the surface, flying the Leoning out and remaining in the Seattle area for a full month are more difficult to explain. True, Gillam had made arrangements for the mail contract to be flown by Lyle and Dorrance Air Service, now located at Copper Center. Also, Gillam knew the air transportation needs of the region would be met by Cordova Air Service and others. He was, in a sense, putting Gillam Airways on hold during the month of his absence.

What did Gillam intend to accomplish besides buy a Stearman and fly it back? A small part of that month would be needed to fly out and then back to Cordova. Flying the Leoning out would be faster than going by ship but would necessitate leaving the Leoning in the Seattle area. Or he may have had in mind selling it to finance the purchase of the Stearman. In any case, he didn't sell it.

Flying out and back from Cordova and buying the Stearman would take up only part of the month allotted for the total trip. What else was planned? Looking back over what was actually done during that month makes it appear as though it was part business and part personal. First there were two passengers aboard on the way out. Gillam's close friend, Tom Donohoe, a Cordova lawyer who was also a prominent community leader and strong financial supporter of Gillam Airways. The other passenger was Donohoe's sister-in-law who would be returning to her Grass Valley home in northern California.

Leoning; Gillam's ability to fly weather proves capability of small airplanes for long distance and business travel. (courtesy T.M. Spencer)

Once in the Seattle area, the first stop was to pick up Gillam's mother and take her on her first airplane ride to visit a sister at Corvallis, Oregon, not far from Portland. At Portland, the Stearman purchase with Varney was finalized. From there it seemed a natural progression to fly south to Grass Valley, California to drop off Donohoe's sister-in-law, then to proceed north to pick up and return Gillam's mother to her home in Seattle. At that point they would have completed all their business and personal obligations and could have prepared for their flight back to Cordova. Had they done this, the total trip would have been shortened by almost two weeks. It wasn't. They returned to Cordova on June 5, 1934, exactly one month after their departure.

The fact that Tom Donohoe accompanied Gillam on this trip suggests that it had another important purpose. It so happened that during the summer in which Gillam made the trip to pick up his second Stearman, American Airlines was in the midst of surplusing their ten-place Pilgrims. These were being replaced with the modern twin-engine airliners being manufactured by Boeing and Douglas. American was flying these surplused Pilgrims to their maintenance headquarters at Tulsa, Oklahoma, to be displayed and sold at that location. This was an important event in the aviation world and Gillam, who made it a point to keep abreast of aviation news, would have known these details.

The Pilgrim would have been the perfect plane for scheduled passenger service in Alaska. However, Gillam was not, at that time, ready to venture into such an enterprise. He still had the obligation to the mail service. Also, getting the planes would involve planning and, most important, financing. On the other hand, this ideal plane was being surplused and available for a reasonable price, now.

There is little question that he discussed all this with his close friend and supporter. This led Donohoe to accompany Gillam so they could explore the Pilgrim together and first-hand assess its suitability, its cost, and the matter of financing. Obviously, if Donohoe had a firsthand knowledge of all this, and was satisfied with the business possibilities, he would be in a good position to promote the idea among his business associates in Cordova.

So it would have been a natural thing for them to head east in the Leoning, after drop-ping off the sister-in-law in Grass valley, and do their exploring at the American Airlines maintenance headquarters in Tulsa. After that,

Gillam and Dono-hoe; future plans. (Alice Harris photo/Courtesy Sourdough Sky)

they would have returned Gillam's mother from Portland to her home in Seattle and then proceeded north in the Stearman along the Interior route to Cordova.

That they did indeed do the exploring and did promote the idea in Cordova is evidenced by the fact that just one year later Gillam picked up his first Pilgrim at Tulsa and flew it to Alaska.

Purchasing that first Pilgrim in the summer of 1935 did not mean Gillam was ready to plunge into his dream. However, he did continue to hold firmly to his long-range goal of providing reliable and safe air transportation. He knew that providing a safe and reliable scheduled passenger service would be quite a different matter when compared with the usual Alaska bush pilot operation. Bush pilots provided a specific flight, on request, and when reasonable weather conditions prevailed.

Gillam's knowledge of worldwide aviation events also forcibly reminded him of the hardships involved in establishing scheduled passenger service. In America it was achieved under Lindbergh's direction of Transcontinental Air Transportation (TAT) in 1928-29. Even with his name, careful preparation, and substantial financial support, the struggle was long and hard before it became successful and finally merged into Transcontinental and Western Air.

TAT's beginning was plagued with loss of life and aircraft. Many lives were lost in a single crash because airliners were being built to carry more passengers. The crashes, for the most part, stemmed from encounters with weather, simply because maneuvering larger aircraft in reduced visibility was difficult.

Anne Morrow Lindbergh, in her book *Hours of Gold, Hours of Lead*, describes poignantly the tragedy of TAT's first two crashes. She also described in detail the money, time, and effort the company management spent to overcome the public's innate fear of flying. This included such things as color and decor of the plane's interior, dress and demeanor of the flight crew, as well as brochures laying out the route being flown over, and a variety of other activities to occupy the mind. On the ground the traveler was met with every luxury conceivable—courteous personal attention, attractive and comfortable waiting rooms, good food and so forth. And all this to overcome a basic fear, encapsulated in the trite expression, "If God had meant humans to fly he would have given them wings." Yet in Gillam's later attempts to inaugurate schedule flights, following the example of the earlier airlines by appearing before his prospective passengers in immaculate dress, some suggested he was making himself attractive to the ladies.

This fear persisted with the passing of years. It was fed by the very real persistence of airline crashes. For example, the May 25, 1935 issue of the *Cordova Times* carried this item: "Royal Dutch Airline (later, KLM) crash kills 13. Third such crash within six months. Fog a factor." It was no wonder then that Gillam postponed his dream until he had modern planes equipped with the most recent navigational devices. He also delayed until he was totally familiar with the terrain to be flown over and had integrated the newest navigational technology into his own weather-flying experience.

On Gillam and Donohoe's northward journey, the newly purchased Stearman touched down on June 5, 1934 on the nearly completed new Cordova airport. Although Cordova Air Service was in full operation, Gillam had plenty of flying waiting for him, and not just the mail contracts. Preferring to fly with Gillam did not just apply to miners who could only get to where they were going by flying. It included such people as the Cordova merchant Rosswog, Gillam's friend Tom Donohoe, and Donohoe's sister-in-law who could have traveled by steamship. They flew with Gillam over a pioneering route because they had trust in his flying skill, especially in weather. Perhaps even more important, they trusted his judgment to fly only when it was safe for him to do so. As Bud Seltenreich said, "I never felt safer in the air than with Gillam. He was the best."

On June 22,1934 the new Cordova airport, still on Lake Eyak, opened officially. The weather on that day gave Gillam an opportunity to demonstrate his ability to arrive on schedule. The following statement on the front page of the *Cordova Times* spoke directly to Gillam's prowess as a pilot, and as a pilot who was able to fly weather.

Gillam uses his newly acquired Stearman to demonstrate his prowess as a weather pilot. *(Courtesy T.M. Spencer)*

Cordova Airport officially opened…Ceremonies last evening dedicated new airport; Entire town attends function…It had been the hope of the committee in charge of ceremonies to have several planes here from neighboring towns but adverse weather did not permit their arrival. However, Pilot Harold Gillam who had been in Chisana (on the other side of the Wrangell-St Elias Range) arrived in McCarthy late last evening and hurried to Cordova, thus establishing the record of being the first pilot to land on the new airfield.

He experienced no difficulty in bringing his large Stearman plane onto the field. Striking it about 200 feet from the end, he rolled another 150 feet and came to a stop, using barely one fifth of the extensive field.

Some might cite Gillam's actions as grandstanding. Not true. It was a personal gesture of joy, rarely exhibited except when mysteriously triggered from within. In this case it probably stemmed from a wish come true for himself and for all people living in Cordova and in the entire Copper River region.

A flurry of air activity followed the formal opening of the airport. One of these was the arrival of a special Pan American flight on September 10. It brought a group of postal authorities who were surveying for possible Star mail routes in Alaska. Harold Gillam was one of the delegates organized to meet the postal officials. As a Star Route mail pilot, he was recognized as one who helped establish reliability in delivering mail by air.

Also in September 1934, Gillam's friend Joe Crosson brought the renowned round-the-world flyer, Wiley Post, to Cordova as a jumping-off point for a brown bear hunt. Arrangements had been made for Gillam to land them on the beach at Yakataga. He found pleasure in flying hunters into remote spots accessible only by air. This flight was made especially memorable when he returned some two weeks later to that same beach for the pickup, and found the hunt had been successful.

In November of that year, Goulet in his book *Rugged Years on the Alaska Frontier*, gave a particularly graphic and personal view of how important Gillam's flying was for the Alaska Road Commission and how a first-time air passenger felt back then as he observed a pilot at work.

November found us through with our season's work. Winter closed in, the last train left for the coast, the crew was laid off, and the camp closed down. Mr. Cameron...and I were too late to get to Chitina by train, since we had to see everything in order for winter at the camp before we left. So Gillam, a Cordova flier, was sent in to get us. The ceiling was practically nil, but it seemed Gillam could fly in almost any subarctic weather condition and reach his destination.

Along with two miners, who were stewed to the gills, Gillam picked up Cameron and me. He locked the two drunks in the freight compartment behind us, and took off about 2:00 p.m. on November 20. He followed the river flat until he could gain altitude. Then climb as fast as the old crate would climb. Completely surrounding us were mountains. Cameron and I sat on pins and needles, expecting any minute to smack into the side of one in the fog, while the two inebriated soldiers of fortune in the rear yelled, sang, and celebrated, neither knowing or caring that we were flying blind. Thirty minutes of climbing put the fog beneath us. At that altitude all we could see was the top of Mt. Wrangell, the highest peak of the Wrangell Mountain Range. While it was a relief to us to be able to see, it was no solution to the problem of landing on the Copper River airfield, our destination, and no larger than a city block. Poker-faced Gillam calmly held his course. We both watched him apprehensively, for we didn't see how he could get that crate down through the fog and land himself and his passengers alive. Soon he saw an opening in the clouds, which looked to us to be about ten feet square. As he dove like a hawk after a chicken, we thought he had lost control of the plane. It seemed to me we would surely hit the ground at any moment, yet it seemed an eternity going through the opaque nothingness about us. When we did see ground, the pleasantest sight of a lifetime met our eyes: the Copper Center Airfield and just below us. Gillam circled twice and glided for his landing.

Copper Center Airfield as it looks today. The exact spot where Gillam glided to a landing is still there. *(Courtesy T.M. Spencer)*

Goulet's description was indeed dramatic and personal but also gave the impression that Gillam's ability to fly through weather involved an element of mystery. Bud Seltenreich, who flew with Gillam often in adverse weather, explained away much of the mystery. Yes, Gillam did have a keen sense of geographic location and never seemed to stop studying the terrain of the Copper River region. Bud also pointed out that Gillam installed the latest "blind-flying" instruments in his planes. So, taking off in severely impaired visibility and climbing above the overcast was not a problem.

Getting back down through an overcast was much more difficult. As Bud explained after his own lifetime of flying, Gillam had worked out a scientific approach to that problem. When above an overcast, he always had a general idea of the terrain's layout below. It was then a matter of following the contours of a mountain or hilltop that projected above the overcast; looking for slight breaks in that overcast where it lay against the terrain. This indicated a river, stream or moving water of some sort running into a valley; that is, flowing into lower terrain. Flying over it, he would probe to determine if it provided sufficient visibility to move under the overcast. It took a skilled pilot, one completely oriented to the terrain, to apply this method. Gillam became skilled by practicing the method under ideal conditions where he knew exactly what lay beneath the overcast; as in the case of the Copper Center airfield. During this same, recent interview, Bud admitted he'd felt no uneasiness flying with Gillam when he probed weather conditions in this way.

It was during one of the numerous talks with Bud in his retirement home in Anchorage, Alaska that he told of a medical emergency in which he accompanied Gillam. It was during the first days of December 1934. They had finished a long day of flying. It was dark when they secured the Zenith on Town Lake in Chitina and walked to the Commercial Hotel. There they were told that the respected black woman, owner of the local restaurant, had a heart condition needing immediate treatment, which was available only in Fairbanks. Gillam did not hesitate, sending Bud out to get the still-warm plane ready while he and the townspeople prepared a makeshift stretcher and loaded the patient. Except for the 40- below temperature, weather was not a problem. In fact it was a clear, moonlit night.

While climbing to get through Isabel Pass before dropping down into the Tanana Flats, the engine slowly started losing power. Gillam, seeing Paxson Lake clearly outlined in the moonlight, decided to land and trace the trouble. The two discovered the engine was running cold and used the firepot to throw heat directly under the cowling. They then quickly took off. Now, being through the pass, they dropped to a lower altitude and warmer air on the Tanana Flats. This brought them safely to Fairbanks. Bud did admit to anxious moments until Weeks Field came into sight.

Word had gotten to Fairbanks, where a hospital vehicle and nurse whisked the patient away. While walking to the hotel, Bud remembered Gillam saying, "We need to be up early and get out of town in case somebody decides to attach the plane." This was a sure indication that the rumors of Gillam's financial problems were true. It is safe to assume that most of those concerned about their investment in Gillam Airway lived in Cordova. Yet it is interesting to note that Gillam's fears of having his plane attached did not focus on the good citizens of that town.

On December 6, shortly after the medical emergency to Fairbanks, Gillam responded to another call for help. This time it involved his old friend Carl Whitham, owner of the Nabesna Mine. He had fallen down a shaft, suffering a number of broken bones and possible internal injuries. This incident, like others before and after, contributed to the Gillam legend. In this incident, however, the drama and Gillam's courage in responding to it, were in no way exaggerated. During a recent interview, Harold Starkel, who worked at the mine during that time, gave his account of what happened. It corresponds with the accounts given in the *Cordova Times* of that time. In addition, his account brings back to life those moments at the mine as the bookkeeper's message reached out from the Nabesna Mine to the faraway places of Anchorage and Fairbanks; and as his request for help was turned down. No pilot and plane could make it through the wind and snow roaring through the whole Copper River region. And in a few hours, darkness would add to the danger.

Aerial view of Chitina (during daylight) flying north toward the Nabesna Mine. (Adena Knutson Collection)

Gillam happened to come into the train station at Cordova when the same request for help came through. The wind off the water was particularly fierce and rattled the windows in the warm station as Gillam listened. Then he said simply, "If nobody else will, I'll go."

Volunteers went with him on the railroad speeder out to the airport. He needed them to help move the Zenith into the wind for takeoff. With the plane lined up on the runway and the throttle wide open, the men let go. In seconds it lifted off the ground and climbed into the gathering dusk. Later, the people at Chitina heard the plane pass over, but blowing snow and darkening skies hid it from view.

The mine heard from Chitina and got ready. The wind on their side of the Wrangell Range had died down and cold weather had settled in. Lights from the mine on the hillside were turned on just to help Gillam get his bearings for a landing on the nearby lake. No lanterns on the lake itself; they knew how Gillam wanted it.

Minutes after landing, the plane was fueled, Whitham loaded and Gillam lifted the Zenith into the air again, heading north to Fairbanks. Waiting for him there would be people from the hospital. In addition, there would be a surprise meeting for Gillam and two of his comrades from the Eielson-Borland search. Joe Crosson and Bob Gleason happened to be testing a rotating beacon on top of a station wagon to determine how effective it would be in guiding airplanes to the airfield. After the Zenith landed, and with Whitham in the hands of the hospital staff, the three men held a reunion of sorts. During their visit, Gillam told them how he was able to see the flashing beacon a considerable way off. That he was then able to home in on it rather than follow the bends and curves of the Tanana River.

Witham lay in the enclosed cabin of the Zenith; Gillam, as pilot, sat in the open cockpit. (UAFA Archives)

Whitham recovered fully, but it was months before he returned to the mine. Gillam was able to do his friend yet another favor. The shaft of the mine's main diesel engine broke a day after Whitham was injured. A quick call to Cordova and then a radio message to the lower forty-eight brought a new shaft by steamship on December 22. Gillam then flew it directly from Cordova to the mine. The shaft weighed 2,250 pounds and was too long to be carried inside the Stearman freighter. So Gillam rigged a sling and hung it outside the fuselage (between the landing gear) and flew it in. Had it not been flown in, the mine operation would have been closed down for months.

The year 1935 began with Gillam still the only pilot flying for Gillam Airways. He usually flew the Zenith on mail flights and the Stearman for hauling freight to the mines. The Leoning was still in the Seattle area. It was not heard from again until the fall of 1941 when his log showed local flights out of Fairbanks. Also, Gillam's second son, Donald, remembers back to age six when his dad took him along when he flew out to rivers and lakes and landed on them.

And why didn't Gillam hire another pilot? It may have had something to do with his inability to train non-Alaska pilots to fly his planes without damaging them. Certainly the Copper River region was a rugged land, not suited for flight training. In any case, on April 6, 1935 his beloved Zenith was totally destroyed in a freak wind on Town Lake. This ended for the moment

Stearman with replacement shaft hung below the fuselage; keeping the Nabesna in operation. (Bud Seltenreich photo)

any need for another pilot. Supposedly, this happened while Gillam was landing it. As the *Cordova Times* described it, a wind from the rear upended the plane and tossed it into the on-shore brush. The facts so far cannot be disputed. There is some question, though, as to whether Gillam was actually flying the plane when it entered the throes of the freak wind, or whether it was securely tied down when the wind did its damage. Certainly such a wind could well have torn the plane from its tiedown. The view that Gillam was flying the plane when the wind destroyed it is somewhat discredited by the accompanying photo. It shows the Zenith on its back in the brush. So far, the photo could be used to support either view, but it also shows the cowling cover clinging to the nose of the plane. The plane would never be covering the engine during flight, and there would have

been no reason for putting it there once the plane had been destroyed and lying on its back in the brush. It would be more logical to assume that the plane had been secured after the day's flight and the cowling cover put in place in readiness for fireproofing the next morning. It was prob-

The only thing salvaged was the engine. (Harold Starkel photo)

ably after this was done that the freak wind came through.

As usual, it was not Gillam's way to correct someone else's explanation regarding his flying and especially not if the explanation questioned, even indirectly, his skill as a pilot. As with his crash of the Zenith in the night landing at Copper Center, he would never defend his flying ability by blaming others. Even if the blame lay, as in this case, with a freakish wind.

No matter how the cherished Zenith met its end, the fact that it lay beyond repair, except for the engine, was yet another event that brought Gillam one step closer to activating his dream.

Gillam Airways was now down to one pilot and one plane. Its single plane, combined with Gillam as pilot, was an ideal pair to provide reliable mail service and to provide other air transportation as the need arose.

Since air transportation needs were now being met by other carriers such as Cordova Air Service, it meant Gillam would no longer feel an obligation to buy additional planes and hire additional pilots to meet such needs. He was now free to fly the Stearman with its advanced instrumentation, and practice integration of his practical skill in weather flying with the modern instruments as found in the Stearman. At the same time, this practice would result in even greater reliability on his mail flights. In turn, this emphasis on greater reliability in flying the mail route would naturally lead to greater reliability on any future scheduled passenger service. Thus, keeping Gillam Airways a one-pilot and one-plane operation while planning ahead for a change in direction probably made sense to Gillam.

Meanwhile, the possibility of obtaining American Airlines' surplused Pilgrims at a reasonable price would fulfill an important requirement for a scheduled passenger service. The plane had been built specifically to American Airlines' specifications. This included adequate number of seats, comfort, range, and modern instrumentation. To obtain this plane and a backup, though, would require time for negotiations and financing. As was mentioned earlier, Gillam and his close friend and financial advisor, Tom Donohoe, were already working on this and would soon succeed.

Over the years, Gillam Airways had gradually changed its headquarters from Copper Center to Cordova. This was a natural occurrence as more emphasis was placed on mail deliveries where the flights started and ended there. Now, with the intention of changing to passenger service out of Cordova, the change of headquarters was completed. To that end Gillam established an office in the Donohoe Building in downtown Cordova.

Gillam kept flying the Stearman continuously, building time and experience using the newest navigation instruments found in it. These included the turn and bank, Sperry's artificial horizon, the Kollsman precision altimeter, and the Sperry directional gyro. The radio navigation devices were not available in Alaska until immediately before World War II. Meanwhile, Tom Donohoe continued work on the financing and purchase of the first Pilgrim. In midsummer the purchase was finalized, Gillam made arrangements for the mail deliveries during his absence, and then left for Tulsa. By coincidence, Gillam's logs beginning with his June 16, 1935 entry until his final flight in January, 1943, were made available to the author through Ted Spencer, former head of the Alaska Aviation Heritage Museum and the University of Alaska Fairbanks Archives. The June 16, 1935 log entry, the date Gillam began his flight from Tulsa to Cordova, indicated the tremendous range of the Pilgrim. It recorded a nonstop flight of 1,000 miles between Amarillo, Texas and Los Angeles. The log also showed two passengers on board for the trip to Cordova. One more boarded in Seattle. There is some question whether the third was a paying passenger. The Seattle paper gave the following interesting, and somewhat humorous, account surrounding that passenger.

> Girl, 19, Flies as 'Stowaway'.... When Harold Gillam, Cordova airplane pilot, took off from Seattle the other day with two passengers for Alaska, Miss Geraldine O'Neil was given permission to accompany the party as far as Vancouver, B.C., "just for the ride." But Miss O'Neil, without telling anyone, had made up her mind that she was going to visit her former home at McCarthy, Alaska.

> So as soon as they left Seattle she began entreating Gillam to take her all the way. He was adamant at first, but finally said he would consent if she telephoned her father.

> At Vancouver she skipped off to a telephone booth and returned a few minutes later announcing it was "all set."
> So on to Alaska she went—and it wasn't until her arrival at Cordova that Gillam learned she had been unable to reach her father, as he was out of town that day. But she hadn't prevaricated—she really was "all set."

Arrival of Gillam and his Pilgrim at Cordova was given front page coverage in the *Cordova Times* for July 5, 1935. It stated:

> Gillam Brings Large Plane to Cordova. Ten place Pilgrim to be used in coast interior service. Arrived here last night from Seattle via the Interior aviation route. Brought in three passengers; purchased in Tulsa, flew it to Los Angeles then Seattle...Hazelton, Prince George and Juneau. Pilgrim is a comfortable passenger plane

with large seats and plenty of cabin room. It is complete with bathroom and shortwave radio, Pratt and Whitney engine.

The article mentioned the Pilgrim was to be used in coast-interior service. This did not happen immediately. Gillam was still getting ready. His log showed a number of trips between Cordova, Seward, and Anchorage, almost all with a full load of passengers. This suggests he made steamship connections. His log also showed the Pilgrim's prowess as a load carrier. It recorded a load of six passengers and 1,800 pounds of mail on a flight out of Cordova.

In August 1935, not long after his return with the first Pilgrim, he went out to pick up a second one. This could suggest more

"getting ready" for scheduled flight but it also may have indicated a complete commitment to the Pilgrim as best suited for his Alaska flying. The fact that almost all of his flying from then on was in Pilgrims strongly indicates a prefer-

Gillam's first Pilgrim; one step closer to his goal of safe reliable commercial air transportation.
(Bud Seltenreich Photo)

ence for this type aircraft. The following article in the *Cordova Times* suggests that Gillam was still promoting flying, and his new Pilgrim, among the citizens of Cordova:

> A pleasure flight over the city was made last Saturday afternoon in the Gillam Airways Pilgrim by H.W. McDermott, Mr. and Mrs. T. Donohoe, Miss Lucille Wolfe, A.J. Dimond, and Thomas Nestor. They reported that Cordova and environs were a beautiful sight with its sparkling mantle of snow.

The article did not include a human-interest element that shows Gillam's human side. Tim Eakstrom, a high school sophomore, spent a great deal of time out at the Cordova airport, helping out or just hanging around. On that day, Gillam found room in the Pilgrim and put Tim on board for his first airplane ride. Interviewed recently in his retirement, Eakstrom said, "I'll never forget that day and that ride." After a pause, he added, "He was thoughtful toward me. Gillam is okay in my book and you can quote me on that."

On November 22, 1935 the *Cordova Times* announced that Gillam Airways had been awarded the Cordova-Copper River mail contract for the fourth year in succession. It would start on December 1 and end on March 31 of the year following. This indicates that Gillam planned to continue hauling the mail, a weekly trip in the Copper River Valley, as he proceeded with his plans for a scheduled passenger service. The year 1935 ended on a slightly jarring note. With Gillam at the controls, the ski-equipped Pilgrim 733N did not quite gain lift-off speed before reaching the rough ice on Lake Eyak. One wing tip was slightly damaged but the plane was back flying within two days.

The year 1936 was a hectic one for Gillam but began by his mixing goodwill and business. It involved the Tibbs family living in Cordova except for a son in McGrath. The plan was for the son to fly in from McGrath for a Christmas gathering. Bad weather intervened and he got only as far as Anchorage. In order not to abort the reunion altogether, Gillam loaded the Pilgrim with nine family members and flew them to Anchorage on January 2. After a belated gathering, he brought the plane load back to Cordova on January 4. The new year got off to a good start.

Chapter 16
HOME AND FAMILY

For this is the journey men make: to find themselves. If they fail in this, it doesn't matter what else they find. Money, position, fame, many loves, revenge are of little consequence...
But if a man happens to find himself - if he knows what he can be depended on to do, the limits of his courage, the positions from which he will no longer retreat, the degree to which he can surrender his inner life to some woman...then he has found a mansion which he can inhabit with dignity all the days of his life.
(James Michner, "The Fires of Spring")

Little or nothing has been said about Gillam's personal life, about those waking hours when he was not flying or getting ready to fly. Was flying the total focus of his life? Certainly most of his spare moments were taken up with reading and study pertaining to advances in aviation; especially those relating to instruments that would

Gillam, Nell and children.
(Gillam Collection)

permit flight without visual references outside the plane. His was not just a study of theory. His energies also took in installation and experimentation with these instruments.

Yet he did find time to socialize. In the beginning such socializing involved mainly talk, and listening, in the company of fellow pilots. In a sense, this was just an extension of learning his craft. He had no interest in "killing time" with small talk. This led people to classify him as cold and aloof. He was anything but that. He took an interest in introducing young people into the world of flight.

And this interest was not limited to the young. Frank Barr, who was quoted in connection with participation in "hangar flying" sessions, said, "Harold would sit slightly in the background, grin at some of the more humorous remarks, and once in a while interject one of his own..." Gillam was at his best, though, in showing his outgoing nature when in a position to encourage an inexperienced young pilot who needed help. This was Mudhole Smith's situation when he came to Alaska and started flying out of Cordova for Kirkpatrick (Gillam's competitor). In his biography, *Mudhole Smith,* he talked about running into weather on his first Alaska flight:

> As Smitty piled up experience flying the Copper River over the next few months, he found that the lingering sense of self-doubt he had felt that first day stayed with him...he never seemed able to shake that lingering doubt until, later that year, he had a long talk with Harold Gillam.

> The point of no return was what Smitty had passed that day on the Copper River when he couldn't get back to McCarthy.

> Gillam swore, "That goddam point of no return has killed more pilots than anything I know. I just forget it. If you get beyond the point of no return, you have to try harder, and usually you make it to where you're going."

Smitty followed that advice and not only did he make it through, but found he was more relaxed when he forgot about the point of no return. Also, his confidence began to build again.

Some five years later, in 1942, while flying the mail on the Kuskokwim River for Gillam, he still remembered that advice. In the same biography he explained,

> Smitty had plenty of chance to reflect on Gillam's advice about ignoring the point of no return. He landed at Minchumina, the last stop on his way home, and took off on a compass course for Nenana. He was in the air about five minutes when it began snowing. He'd turned on the landing lights, and all he could see was thick whirling white flakes...

> "No ice," he thought, but the wings were thick with snow. "Maybe I'd better go back and land at Minchumina."

> He made a 180-degree turn, plotted a reciprocal course on his compass and headed toward the place he had just left.

> He could see nothing at all and began to worry. "What if I miss Minchumina? There are no lights there, and I don't know the country very well."

So he changed his mind, turned around once more and headed for Fairbanks again....

Time stretched on and on and where was Nenana?

Then he saw a little flicker of light. He burst into a clear spot and below him were the lights of Nenana. Ahead of him from Nenana to Fairbanks stretched the broad "highway" of the Tanana River, a frozen white trail, easy to follow.

Smitty wondered what might have become of him if he had persisted in trying to find Minchumina in the dark and the snow. He decided there was such a thing as playing it too safe.

This example involving Mudhole Smith makes it clear that Gillam was quite willing to share his valuable experience with others and ready to give aid when needed. But this is still about Gillam's life as a flyer. Wasn't there any outreach toward others unrelated to aviation?

The answer can be simply stated. For a considerable period of his adult life Gillam's world was pretty much restricted to the people he came in contact with during his working hours.

As an adult, he always became intensely interested in whatever work he chose. Deep sea diving had been no exception. He probably volunteered because it presented a challenge and an opportunity to learn. In this case, staying alive gave him an additional motivation.

Then came his work with the Alaska Road Commission just when it

was changing over from horsepower to power delivered by engines. This allowed him to develop his natural aptitude for operating and maintaining mechanically powered machinery. It also satisfied his natural curiosity to learn how they functioned. This explains why he became involved in studying the operation and functioning of the "crawling tractor" while

Road machinery, its operation and maintenance becomes the focus of Gillam's life. (*Alaska Road Commission/courtesy Fairbanks Pioneer Museum*)

it was still in the hold of the steamship which was carrying both him and the tractor to Cordova.

Thus began a three-year period of learning to operate and maintain every type of powered machine in the Alaska Road Commission inventory. The crawling tractor, being the most difficult to operate and understand, became his favorite. Here again, intense involvement in learning led him naturally to limit his human interactions to those working on the road crew. This included Cecil Higgins, his lifelong friend.

Next came flying. It was especially suited to giving free rein to his natural aptitude and interest in the operation and maintenance of machines. In addition, flying made him aware of his untapped gifts— keen eyesight, exceptional coordination and balance, along with an uncanny sense of geographic orientation. Perhaps most important, flying gave him an immediate feeling that total mastery would never be achieved. Working toward mastery would be a lifelong affair.

Flying brought one more significant change into Gillam's life. Like any boy growing into manhood, he had an awareness of the opposite sex and its attractiveness to men. Up to this point, however, his natural attraction to women was held at bay by an equally natural tendency to learn about the wondrous world of work.

Back then, more than now, it was expected that men would make overtures to begin a relationship and women would have their own subtle way of responding, perhaps even encouraging. How different this must have been for Gillam, who had always engaged most of his intelligence, his will and, yes, even his emotions toward the examination, study and operation of mechanical things. Of course, he spent time interacting with men as they worked and talked. But that was different. You didn't have to think about what to say to men who, like his friend, Cecil Higgins, were taken for granted.

As it turned out, flying, in which he immediately became totally involved and which required all his time, talent, and energies, would also be the vehicle responsible for introducing him fully into the mysterious world of women.

This is how it happened. The pilots who met on Sunday afternoons at Joe Crosson's cabin had as their purpose, to talk about flying. Of course, Gillam joined them. Then, in a natural chain of events, Joe's sister, Marvel, came to visit. She also happened to be a pilot with an avid interest in flying and in building airplanes. Back then relationships between young men and women developed at a slower pace. Yes, there was a shortage of women, which one could assume would stimulate competition among the men and speed up the process. This didn't happen. It seems that in a gathering of men where there was a feminine presence, everyone benefitted.

Our informant with regard to what happened in these mixed gatherings was the young college student, Lillian Osborne, later to become Mrs. Joe Crosson. She pointed out that these mixed gatherings did not involve men bringing dates. Instead, since young people had to provide their own entertainment, word would get out about an informal party at a certain date, time, and place. Someone volunteered to make minimum arrangements. Since there always was a shortage of girls, men always asked women to bring along any girls they knew. Social events not being too plentiful in that pioneer community, young women gladly accepted these invitations. After such informal efforts, a lively party followed. Usually the activities involved dancing, games, and just informal mixing. These provided entertainment while giving members of both sexes an opportunity to become comfortable in each other's company. All this was preliminary to dating and possibly, after much passage of time, a formal commitment to marriage. Lillian Osborne was an example of this slow process in such matters. Joe Crosson first caught her eye and interest when the steamship he was on stopped at Cordova in August 1927. They were married in August 1930.

Social events for young people included roller skating and masquerade parties.
(Bunnell Collection/courtesy UAF)

And how did Gillam fit into this picture of young men and women socializing at these informal gatherings? His involvement began somewhat late, at age 24. His initiation into the process came with the Sunday afternoon gatherings, after Joe's sister, Marvel, arrived on the scene. She made it a painless process by having a common interest with the men. This allowed the unmarried men, including Gillam, to enjoy a feminine presence without awkwardness.

There can be little doubt that Gillam appreciated the advice and help Marvel provided in shaping his first steps into flying, especially her establishing a base for him in San Diego at Joe and her parents' house. This, however, did not justify a movie script on the Internet which dealt with Marvel's being a pilot in the first women's transcontinental air race and in which her engagement to Gillam was stated. An attempt was made to locate the author of the script for an explanation of this supposed romantic involvement. When the effort failed, Lillian Crosson, now a feisty 91, was contacted for verification of the relationship. She quickly set the record straight. No, they were not engaged nor was there any kind of romantic involvement. She went on to say that, in her opinion, Gillam was somewhat shy around women. Yes, he did attend party functions, mainly because the men were mostly pilots or at least interested in flying. Eventually he took it upon himself to enliven these gatherings by acting out skits, and so forth. Lillian felt justified in responding to the questions since Gillam was a close friend of her husband, so she knew him over an extended period of time.

The attribute of shyness seemed to enter in when people were asked to comment on Gillam's attitude toward women. Another of Gillam's attitudes toward women might be termed, "chivalrous." The dictionary defines it as considerate, generous, or courteous, especially toward women.

Such an attitude was evident toward his mother while he was in the midst of danger and uncertainties during the Eielson-Borland search. Knowing she would be concerned for his safety, he reassured her through brief radiotelegrams. The first, dated December 17, 1929, sent from Teller, Alaska, read, *"Am with Eielson relief expedition…expect to leave for Siberia tomorrow. Do not worry if you don't hear from me for a month. May be impossible to communicate. Love, Harold."* This was followed by a message dated December 21st, sent from the stranded *SS Nanuk*. It read simply, *"Arrived North Cape okay, Don't worry, Love, Harold."* Then on Christmas Eve, 1929, he remembered her with a wire reading, *"Merry Christmas"*.

Another action in connection with the Eielson-Borland search also shows his consideration. A young woman from Seattle had recently visited Fairbanks. While there, she had met various pilots, some of whom became involved in the search. On being interviewed by the Seattle paper, she commented that Mr. Gillam had taken time to inform her on the activities of the pilots she had come to know while in Fairbanks.

Not only do these actions suggest a considerate attitude toward women, but they were also not attempts to draw attention to himself. In the case of the radio messages, the communication became known to the public only through an examination of Robert Gleason's radio log on the *SS Nanuk*. The communication with the young woman became public only after she made it known through the interview.

Because of his tendency toward privacy in his personal life, it is not surprising that Gillam was able to begin a more intimate, but secretive, association with a Catherine Jacobs. This association eventually led to marriage. Yet it did not, at that time, become known to the community. Only now, in a recent interview with Vernice Reid, the then-nine-year old daughter of Catherine Jacobs, were the beginnings of the association made known. As it turned out, aviation was the setting for the beginning romance. Vernice told how she and her mother came to

Fairbanks from Cordova, and became connected with the aviation community through her mother's friendship with Earl Borland's wife. Borland was then an aircraft mechanic. Vernice and her girlfriend used to hang around Weeks Field after school to watch the planes. She remembered Cecil Higgins, who evidently got Gillam to take them for an airplane ride. To get permissions and that sort of thing, it followed naturally that her mother, Catherine, and Gillam met.

All this happened shortly before the Eielson-Borland search. During that time, Gillam had also made plans for his air service in the Copper River region. His plans to begin this air service were postponed when he volunteered to search for his friend, Ben Eielson. Evidently there was another postponement—his marriage to Vernice's mother.

It appears that Gillam demonstrated an unusually impetuous nature when it came to courting a woman toward whom he felt strong emotions. He simply did not conform to the usual slow development of a relationship between a man and a woman, which would then end in marriage.

Chitna's Town Lake an important part of Gillam's aviation career.
(Adena Knutson photo)

As it turned out, the search lasted longer than expected. This search, itself, placed a strain on all involved but was felt more deeply by Gillam because of his private concern, to marry Catherine as soon as possible, a concern unknown to others except for Catherine. It is easy to imagine the frustration he felt on being delayed even longer in Fairbanks when the people there held a number of events to honor the Russian airmen as well as the American pilots such as Crosson and Gillam. And so now we know there were two reasons why Gillam strained to get to Valdez—waiting there for him was not just his new Swallow but also his bride-to-be.

The delay in the marriage from December until March was caused by Gillam himself when he volunteered for the search. So when he finally did arrive in Valdez, he probably would have preferred to get married the very next day. However, even a simple civil ceremony required paperwork and the need to obtain the services of a judge, in this instance, Judge Reed. All this delayed the marriage until March 22, 1930. Meanwhile, before the marriage and after, Owen Meal and Gillam worked on assembling the Swallow. This made possible an April 8 departure for his first airfreighting venture.

Gillam's preoccupation with assembling the Swallow and early departure on his first commercial flight made good business sense and demonstrated once again his total dedication to flying. From a marital standpoint, however, it demonstrated a total failure to understand a woman's point of view, especially that of a newly married woman. From the beginning, the marriage faced another impediment, one that helps explain why it did not last long. Copper Center was chosen as the headquarters for Gillam Airways, and

Ma Barnes' Roadhouse; after a modern face lift. (Author's photo)

Gillam assumed that this tiny rural village would be an adequate first home for him and his wife. Again, his focus was on his new flying venture and he failed to take into consideration how Catherine, who was accustomed to living in larger communities, would react to living in a cabin without modern conveniences. Such as electricity, running water, indoor flush toilets and finally, the convenience of not having to rely on heating and cooking on a wood-burning stove. It was to Gillam's credit, considering his limited contact with women, that he immediately saw the impossibility of such a situation. So he moved himself and Catherine into Ma Barnes' comfortable roadhouse. Here there would also be social contacts—important when Gillam was away on flights.

The situation left much to be desired. Fortunately, most of Gillam's flights did not involve long distances, which allowed him to be home most evenings. In summer, though, long hours of daylight kept him in the air many more hours. On the other hand, building a hangar that first summer encouraged him to reduce his flying somewhat. In addition, there were flights into Fairbanks, which did not involve flying passengers or hauling freight, for example, Gillam's flight to Fairbanks at the end of May to take his airman's examination. Then, on June 7, 1930, the flight in to celebrate the marriage of fellow pilot Grant Elliot. Here Catherine was able to accompany her husband and spend a few days in Fairbanks with friends.

For his fellow airmen Gillam shed his shyness. (Crosson Collection/ Courtesy R.W. Stevens)

As spring turned to summer and summer moved toward fall, Catherine's pregnancy became more obvious. The decision was made that she travel to Seattle to have the baby. There she would be with family and have the best medical care. Harold Jr. was born on August 16. After the baby's arrival, Catherine returned to Alaska but not to Copper Center. She stayed in Valdez. This decision could have been prompted by a concern for the baby. Living at the roadhouse would now not be an option, nor would living in an isolated cabin without conveniences.

Then strangely, on November 1 1930, a few month after her arrival in Valdez, Catherine Gillam filed for divorce. It was not contested and the final decree was issued on November 10. Gillam agreed to child support and provided $25.00 monthly until his death, even after Catherine remarried. Gillam's concern for his son was also demonstrated when his mechanic and best friend, Tom Appleton, as administrator of the estate, provided for Harold Jr.'s college education.

Obviously, the early breakup of the marriage came mainly as a result of circumstances which both husband and wife failed to anticipate and were unable to cope with. Unlike in so may cases of divorce, there appeared in this instance little or no animosity. A year later, during the winter of 1931-1932, Oscar Winchell, then employed by Gillam and working at Copper Center, reported the following in his biography: " Oscar was too busy to wonder who visited the undaunted pilot, although it was a known fact that Gillam had an ex-wife and a small son who visited him frequently during the winter."

It is interesting to note that nine days after the final divorce decree was issued, Gillam flew to Valdez on November 19, tied down his Swallow, and left for the lower forty-eight. Outwardly he was intent on expanding Gillam Airways. One can not help wondering, though, how he felt about losing his newly founded family.

The five years that followed found Gillam focused entirely on flying. This didn't mean he did not interact with others. He did. However, it was almost always related to his world of work—aviation. Young Bud Seltenreich was not the only one who held the view that Gillam was a good listener and that he looked for opportunities to reach out to others. Another example was the young high school student Tim Eckstrom. In this instance Gillam worked things out so that, on a routine sightseeing flight paid for by a prominent Cordova resident, the boy got his first airplane ride, free. With fellow pilots, he shared willingly advice and support. Mudhole Smith admitted freely how Gillam had offered understanding and advice on a serious problem. Other examples have been given to support his openness to others as it pertained to flying. Probably Gillam's most important "reaching out" were his many mercy flights.

Yet in those years from 1930 to 1936 his personal life did not, to any great extent, include the world of women, except for his immediate family, basically his mother and sister. Ma Barnes, owner of the Copper Center Roadhouse, interacted with him daily somewhat in the role of a surrogate mother. She may have been right in describing him as being a bit on the shy side around women.

Considering Gillam's possible shyness in the presence of women, it seems strange that a rumor to the contrary persisted. This rumor, voiced mainly among men, claimed that he was a "skirt chaser." Such rumors are hard to track down because there is usually no specific evidence. Skirt chasing, by its very nature, suggests a man who gives time, attention, and energy looking for opportunities, and possible opportunities, to satisfy his lechery.

This would seem to eliminate Gillam since there are few men who would deny that his focus was on flying. He was always looking for new techniques and equipment. Whereas the skirt chaser is intent on searching out possible conquests. Gillam's spare moments were focused elsewhere.

Additional evidence against the rumor comes from women, intended victims of a sexual predator. There was Lillian Crosson. Some might say her view is not valid because Gillam was a close friend of her husband. However, there were other females, also young and attractive back then, who in recent interviews rejected the rumor.

Alaska Linck is one of those. She remembered back to the high school dances when popular Ben Eielson attended these. She remembered how enamored the girls were with this handsome pilot. And here it should be mentioned that Ben Eielson was not a skirt chaser. He also was too busy with his love of flying. Alaska Linck didn't remember Gillam ever attending these dances. She did remember him well as a pilot who tried to win away potential passengers from Pan American flights (previously Pacific Alaska Airways) to the coast. As a loyal young employee of Pan American, she felt it her responsibility to not let this happen. To avoid this she would, before each coastal flight, visit various business establishments in Fairbanks to encourage flying with Pan American. She admitted to bravely entering cigar stores for that purpose. Cigar stores were considered off limits to women. Naturally, she made her visits brief and businesslike. In any case, she recalls Gillam made no effort to introduce a personal element into their interactions.

Kay Kennedy, a journalist who died a few years ago, rejected the rumor. Her exact words on this subject come to us from the past. To begin with, Kay Kennedy was an exceptionally beautiful young woman, as attested to by Helen Van Campen, who spoke of this beauty in the November 1, 1936 issue of the *Fairbanks News Miner*. She states,

> Men have been the bright figures in Alaska history. Now the women merit a spot beneath the north land's glorious sun, and its searching rays shine upon young Kay Kennedy, feature writer for syndicates and outside publications....

> Kay, with sweetly serious grey-green eyes and abundant dark, wavy hair, slender and lovely, is a heartbreaker along the trails. She doesn't try to do it, but she can't dodge, and casualties are heavy as they pile up in her wake...She has boldly pushed into gold strikes and oil camps, asking no odds...

Evaluating Gillam, as a pilot and, most important, as a man, Kay reported on her first encounter with him in the following article for the *Anchorage Times* aviation issue:

> In those days (1936-1937) the Anchorage Grill was a 24-hour-a-day—open cafe where most people frequented. One day I popped in there for coffee and onto a counter stool beside a good-looking young man with dark, direct eyes under shaggy eyebrows.
>
> I chatted freely and he gave with a few comments. "Oh, you must be Harold Gillam." He acknowledged that he was. We chatted a bit and I began to realize that he was his own man—not cocky, but sure of himself in such a quiet way.
>
> He paid for his meal—and my coffee—(notice here his chivalrous attitude) and went on his way.
>
> Some two years later Gillam had a charter to Aklavik to bring out a load of white fox skins and looked for me all over Fairbanks to take me along for the ride (notice how he did a similar thing for the young high school student in Cordova) but I was out at Livengood. My loss. He wouldn't have talked. He just was himself, quiet and complete.

Kay Kennedy, not as young as in 1936, but still beautiful. (UAF Archives)

> There were men who learned to fly and men who flew with a few hints and directions. Gillam must have been one of the latter.
>
> Gillam was a lone eagle. He flew with supreme confidence in himself or whatever he believed in, right to the last. He seemed to be one with the storm and the weather.

Kay Kennedy's words should forever put an end to that unjustified rumor regarding Gillam as a skirt chaser. Her words should also put to rest the suggestion that Gillam strove for excellence in all he did because of an inferiority complex, especially regarding his height. Pat Wachel in the June 1966 issue of *Alaskan Northern Lights,* although speaking positively of Gillam as an aviator, did suggest feelings of inferiority as the basis of his achievements. "Charles Harold

Gillam, a man of small stature, challenged life as though he were invincible…His flights were a desperate effort to prove he was just a little bit better than other pilots of his time."

Kay Kennedy, who lived back then and wrote based on personal knowledge, speaks of Gillam's unusual inner confidence that simply does not fit any psychological theory.

Some who still persisted in this negative rumor, spoke of Gillam's immaculate dress when meeting ships at the Cordova docks, looking for passengers. This was true, but so did Noel Wien when he was bent on the same mission. The motive for this fancy dress-up was simply to overcome fear of flying. Inducing passengers to give up the safety of travel by ship and train for the reward of reaching their destination a day or two sooner was no easy task. These pioneer Alaska pilots were trying to instill confidence in air travel in much the same way that Charles Lindbergh did when he began transcontinental air travel in 1928-1929. And it was for much the same reason that today's airlines have their air crews dressed in immaculate uniforms.

Careful dress to help passengers overcome fear of flying. (Crosson Collection/ Courtesy R.W. Stevens)

A final statement to discredit the rumor of Gillam's inordinate sexual interest in women comes from a man. Bud Seltenreich, Gillam's mechanic who flew with him often and observed firsthand his activities on overnight trips, was asked, "What about Gillam and women?"

He answered, "Women liked him. But they liked all pilots. There was something romantic about what they did to earn a living." Enough said.

It was not until 1935, five years after Gillam's divorce, that he again became involved with a woman. And again, it appears to have been a sudden courtship culminating in marriage. He met Nell McGee sometime in 1935 in Anchorage. At that time she was working as a waitress to support herself after a 1934 divorce from Linous (Mac) McGee (owner of McGee Airways). After a brief courtship Gillam and Nell were married in Palmer, Alaska on February 5, 1936.

Gillam's entry into this relationship with Nell McGee led to another rumor. This a more serious one—that he had entered into a sexual relationship with a married woman. And in the case of Nell McGee, that he was a home wrecker. Again there were no specifics. An example showing that the rumor existed is found in an otherwise innocent statement in the first chapter of Beth Day's biography of Bob Reeve, *Glacier Pilot*.

> Frugal of speech, withdrawn, but warm to his friends, swarthy, gypsy-eyed Harold was a favorite of children, air-crazy boys, and especially women. "Everybody loved Harold" explained one old-timer, then added sagely, "except maybe a few husbands!"

The "old-timer" remains anonymous and the rumor is strengthened. The fact that Gillam took up with Nell when her name was still McGee gave credibility to this rumor. Back then, women did not retain their former married name and certainly not while engaging in serious contact with other men. This rumor arose from an honest misunderstanding involving names. Nell's maiden name was McGee and she married Linous (Mac) McGee. When they divorced sometime in 1934 she took back her maiden name which happened also to be McGee. Some honestly believed that Gillam had entered into an adulterous affair with Linous McGee's wife. Others, having accepted the rumor of Gillam as a skirt chaser, found it easy to accept the report as but an extension of his sexual escapades. It is a fact that Linous McGee had remarried before the first of January 1935. This is verified in the January 3, 1935 issue of the *Cordova Times*. It stated, "Linous McGee and Mrs. McGee, the daughter of Mr. and Mrs. Custer Seaberg, were on their way outside on a six-month combined business and pleasure trip." The wife in this article is referred to, rightly, as Mrs. McGee. It is obviously not Nell. Her maiden name was McGee, not Seaberg. Thus Linous McGee had already remarried before Gillam took up with his former wife, Nell.

The Gillam marriage took place about the time he transferred his flight base to Fairbanks. There followed five years of married bliss. Gillam built a home in Fairbanks and he and Nell began raising a family which grew to three children, not including his first son, Harold Jr. This son lived with his mother. The second family included one son and two daughters.

Articles on Gillam made favorable comments on his new role as husband and father. Jo Anne Wold, in her 1986 *Alaska Journal* article stated,

> Mature, business-minded Gillam emerged in Fairbanks. His youthful daring was tempered by a more stable, determined approach. He was in his mid-thirties, married, and the father of a young son-also named Harold-who later became mayor of Fairbanks.

Pat Wachel, in her June 1966 *Alaska Northern Lights* article on Gillam, stated,

> Although he was gone from his family a great deal, Florence Winchell, wife of his former employee and friend, recalled that Harold made a conscientious father as the number of his second family grew. There were three children by 1942.

That he had matured in his personal life during the five years since his first marriage is evidenced mainly by the way he deliberately made time to share with his children and especially in how he worked out ways to give his wife "breathers" from her constant care of the children. For example, he took up photography as a hobby, including setting up his down darkroom in their house. In working with his hobby, he automatically involved himself with the children. In this regard, the oldest daughter, Maurine, in a recent interview, remarked, "He was always around taking pictures of us. Then he would develop them and give us a chance to see ourselves."

Gillam isn't in the picture. He's the photographer. *(Gillam Family photo)*

Another example of Gillam working out ways to be involved with his family was most unusual. This happened when Don, the first child in his second family was still a baby. In this case he not only gave Nell a breather but also introduced the boy to the world of flying. It happened on one of the commercial midnight-sun flights he had inaugurated. Helen Van Campen was among the passengers on the June 21, 1939 flight and gave a feel for the wonders of what happened and how "Baby Gillam" participated. In her *News Miner* article, she stated,

> Nine could go, not counting a very little boy to chink with. He nipped inside Harold Gillam's ship, rapidly decided whose lap to invade, and rapidly changed to another. Nobody minded, except to resent the next one getting Baby Gillam, who briefly said, "sun!"

> His pilot father came aboard, forward and took the controls. Baby

Gillam chuckled at some private joke of his own, left the lap of a person who had tickled him, and bright-eyes enjoyed the ride along the field....We were high over clouds now...A violent red eye looked from the tops of candy clouds, and the light flared and flamed until there was only blinding brilliance.

"Sun!" said Baby Gillam, waking from a quick snooze on the warm chest of a pleased man...

This was certainly an interesting example of how Gillam was able to be a pilot-in-command and a father at the same time. It also points to the mother, or perhaps both father and mother taking time to stimulate a two year-old to focus on words, such as *sun,* in connection with this experience.

He also took time, as the boy grew older, to introduce him to his father's work on the ground, in the Gillam hangar. Don, now recently retired from his own career as a helicopter pilot, recalled being around the hangar. He especially remembered the spanking that came after he got too close to the caged polar bears (more on these bears in a later chapter). Don felt sure it was Tom Appleton who gave the spanking and seemed to recall that he got more than one.

Nell, trying to control dog team, not too successfully. *(Gillam Family photo)*

These experiences indicate that Nell and Harold Gillam worked together to create a harmonious home life. Although Don was the oldest, he readily admitted that Maurine was the one in the family with an exceptional memory. Even at age four, she remembered moments of affection between her mother and father. She also remembered a short-lived argument with her mother who had bought Maurine a new-styled dress that buttoned up the back (no zippers back then). Maurine, being fiercely independent, insisted she could button her own dress. When her efforts ended in failure, she preserved her dignity by instructing her mother she was not to buy Maurine any dress that buttoned up the back.

And so the five years passed with the family growing in size and harmony. This harmony was expressed in the feelings of Nell in a letter written to her mother. This letter, although written on March 18, 1941, was not made available to the Gillam family until August 1997. It was not until then that Winona, the youngest in Gillam's second family, was finally successful in making contact with her mother's people, the McGees. It was then, at a family reunion, that Winona received two letters. The March 1941 letter, quoted below in its entirety (except for the last two paragraphs, which mention people outside the family), shows Nell's family interactions and her emotional response to her in-laws.

Fairbanks, Alaska
March 18, 1941
Dearest Mom,
I don't know who wrote the last letter but what's the difference. I owe you a lot of them.

Harold's mother is still here. I guess she is staying until after Harold's sister, Elsie, is married, which is April 8. I sure wish it was April 8 today and his mother was ready to go outside again. I am getting sick of her; she is one of the kind that likes to cause trouble but I know she isn't going to be here much longer so I am keeping still, After all, she is old and Harold and I are happy so I shouldn't be writing about it ever but sometimes it just gets under my skin. Well, so much for that.

Donald is learning to ice-skate, he's so darn cute about it. The very first time on them he stood up like he had been on them all his life. Maurine is a little young yet for skates but by next fall she can have some too. Winona is growing like a weed. She is getting so cute, but dear, can the three of them ever keep us busy. Well, it's almost time to cook again. Seems like that is all I ever do anymore is cook and wash dishes. I still have Mrs. Swanson who comes in three days a week and does my washing and ironing and the cleaning. I don't think I could get along without her now.

I am having a garden this summer; some of my plants I want to start in the house pretty soon now. Flowers grow so darn pretty up here. Our season is terribly short up here but they sure grow while it lasts. The weather has been just grand. The snow has started melting. Will I ever be glad when I no longer have to put so many clothes on the youngsters when they go out to play. Skookie (dog) stays out and plays just fine—but Maurine is coming in every few minutes and wants her things off. Then she sees Skookie doing something and she has to go out again. Wish you could see my family. I think they're pretty swell but I don't want any more.

We have sent East or to Ridgefield Conn for a Saint Bernard pup for the kids. I just mailed the letter about a week ago but Donald is expecting his dog to come every day, but I know they are going to be plenty thrilled when it does come. Will I have fun now, three kids and a big dog.

The kids are asleep now so I guess I can go mail my letter. Write soon. With all my love,
Nell

Her words certainly spoke for Nell's feelings about her family. She and Harold are happy. Then the every day happenings of the kids, as only a contented mother could tell them. Followed by the significant comment, "Can the three of them ever keep us busy." Obviously, she and Harold were working together. Then the typical complaint about housework followed by her inclusion that Harold thoughtfully provided her some relief. Her reference to the coming of spring and her plans

This is the only known photo of the Gillam children taken by a professional photographer. (Gillam Family photo)

for a garden suggested she had made a complete adjustment to living in the north country. News of the St. Bernard tells something about the relationship between the parent's and their children.

The family's summer plans changed unexpectedly when Gillam decided to go out to Houston, Texas to get his instrument rating. His decision to take the whole family with him was surely met with enthusiasm by all. To give his wife a two-month vacation away from Alaska and normal family routine must have been a major consideration in Gillam's decision. Dropping off the baby, Winona, at Grandmother Gillam's was also obviously part of that major consideration.

Don, the oldest and then almost five, remembered little except that

"Uncle Willie," with whom the family stayed, had a Stagger-wing Beech, in which he flew them out to a fancy fishing camp. Maurine, a year and a half younger than Don but with a much better memory, remembered important things, like staying in a fancy home with servants. Both of them remembered that their mother was there with them but Winona was not.

The family left Fairbanks in early May and spent a leisurely month traveling and visiting. Then Gillam spent June obtaining his instrument rating while the family vacationed with Uncle Willie and his family. The month of July found the Gillams traveling northward. Again at a leisurely pace with a probable visit to Nell's people in Oregon. They arrived back in Fairbanks in early August.

After a few business-pleasure flights in the Leoning amphibian (Don remembered being taken along and landing on lakes and rivers), Gillam entered into a relentless flying schedule. His hours doubled those flown in previous years. It should be remembered that the attack on Pearl Harbor was only months away and that the United States had, to a great extent, neglected preparing for the military defense of Alaska.

In Gillam's personal life it meant being away from home more than before. And when he did come home, there was only time to get ready for the next flight. It was in the midst of this hectic time of military preparedness and Gillam's participation in it, that Nell wrote a second letter, this one to her sister, Clara. Postmarked November 6, 1941, it was brief and contained the tragic news of the collapse of Nell's close-knit family. Given here is the entire content of this one-page letter,

Dear Lara,

Things are a mess; Harold is mean as hell but I stopped in Anchorage and saw a lawyer. He told me to come home and to just sit tight.

Harold won't get my coat out and won't give me any money. I will have to borrow some so I can pay you back. I thought sure I could send it now but can't. I have a job in Anchorage. If things don't work out will take the kids and go back there. Will write and let you know how things are going. I really don't know yet what will happen but I do know I am not giving the kids up. Will write again in a few days.
Lovingly, Nell

Note that in this short, one-page letter, she stated twice her determination not to give up the children. Unfortunately, she gave no reason for the sudden collapse of the marriage. And so after the passage of sixty years and after much research the cause of this catastrophic event remains a mystery. Circumstances were uncovered that suggested a cause but none established a credible one. Still, these circumstances may well be worth examining, if for no other reason than to demonstrate how deeply caring individuals, individuals with the best of intentions, can destroy what they love most.

Might Gillam have played a role in precipitating this tragedy? As has been shown, flying to him was what he loved to do most. Yet, unbelievably long hours of flying combined with the responsibility he felt for his role in preparing the nation for war, along with an awareness of neglecting his family—could all these factors have led to an unreasonable attitude toward his wife? Especially if that attitude involved the children, to whom he was particularly attached and who were now almost totally the responsibility of his wife?

And Nell, how might she have been part of the cause? Beginning comments in the letter to her mother dated March 18, 1941 gave a hint. In it she referred to her mother-in-law as "one of those kind that like to cause trouble." Then she apologized (to her mother) for harboring such thoughts. Yet she found it difficult to keep her feelings under control as she went on, "She isn't going to be here long so I am keeping still, after all she is old..." The question is, Could she keep to her good intentions and not unload the suppressed feeling on her already overburdened husband?

The matter was further complicated by Gillam's sister, Elsie. She had just married and had moved into a house directly across the narrow Chena River. Here she had a close view of the Gillam home. It is a known fact that both Gillam's mother and his sister held narrow and rigid views on serious matters of right and wrong. An example of the mother's rigidity was her total rejection of alcohol, even an occasional social drink. Therefore her husband, although a conscientious family provider, was not allowed to have one drop of alcohol, even beer, in their home. She held to this view both before and after the period of legal prohibition. As a consequence, after providing his wife with a comfortable home and monies for daily living, he found reasons to travel in search of work. One example of this was when he joined with his son and Cecil Higgins to work in Alaska. Traveling to find work was also an excuse to avoid his wife's tyranny when at home. That his life was made unpleasant by his wife's rigid and narrow views is suggested in a letter Gillam wrote to his dad in 1929, soon after the father's divorce and remarriage. In it, Gillam stated, "Well, I was surprised to hear of your marriage. Please let me congratulate you. I thought it would take a shotgun to get you again..."

Gillam, in spite of his traditional respect for his mother, felt free to suggest that she had indeed made life anything but pleasant for his father.

Gillam's sister, Elsie, held the same rigid views. This was evidenced by strict rejection of alcohol in her home during an eleven-year marriage. Her husband complied with this restriction until his wife's death. Thereafter, the Gillam kids, now older, noticed the appearance of beer in the refrigerator.

Elsie's rigid and narrow views also related to child-rearing. Some of this came out much later when she obtained official custody of the children (this will be explained in the final chapter).

Winona, now an adult, volunteered that her Aunt Elsie seemed to possess a "mean streak." Don, who did the most to defend his aunt's behavior, stated she always provided for the kids' physical needs but was totally incapable of demonstrating love toward them. Don's remarks established clearly that Elsie was not an evil person, but was simply a person who would not allow her beliefs to be tempered by compassion. As a result, she was capable of sacrificing a human life or a family's happiness if those should stand in the way of her beliefs.

These factors, which might have contributed to the sudden tragedy in the Gillam family do not reveal what particular event set things in motion. Nor does it fathom the agony it brought to the two individuals who had the most to lose, Harold Gillam and his wife, Nell. The spark that set things off, whatever it was, released a deep anger in Gillam. This is evidenced by Nell's own words as given in her November letter. However, such intense anger is difficult to understand when one considers the warm, loving relationship that had existed between them during the five years of their marriage. In any case, Nell's response to this unreasonable anger was, in turn, a powerfully emotional one. This emotion was dominated by anger and fear that, in her husband's anger, he might attempt to take their children from her.

Fortunately, it did not come to that. Gillam must have had second thoughts, possibly thoughts on what would be best for the children. Nell, on her part, took the lawyer's advice and went back to Fairbanks.

Gillam, meanwhile, was in the process of being hired by Morrison-Knudsen Company, which was mainly responsible for military airfield construction in Alaska. He was hired as executive pilot to be in charge of all the company's air operations in the Territory and would be flying out of Anchorage, M-K's headquarters.

Since Gillam had to be based in Anchorage, there must have been an agreement between him and Nell that she would remain in Fairbanks with the children. This gave them the security of living in a home in which they had been born and raised, at the same time allowing powerful emotions to subside.

Although Gillam was flying more hours than ever, he was still able to schedule himself for overnight stops at Fairbanks to see his family. Even after war was declared on December 7, 1941, Gillam found time and ways to keep contact with his children.

Both Don and Maurine remembered an unusual example of this in their adult years. Probably somewhere in March 1942 he took the two of them in the newly acquired twin Lockheed 10 on a quick trip to Dutch Harbor. Again, although younger than Don but with an exceptional memory, Maurine recalled details of that trip.

She remembered Don sitting up front in the cockpit next to his dad, while she was strapped into one of the passenger seats. As she remembered it, wanting to find out what was going on up front, she finally wiggled out from under her safety harness and made her way forward. While she was hanging onto her Dad's seat, he finally turned his head and saw her. She remembered clearly his firm scolding but she also remembered his firm arm around her holding her close while he did the scolding. After they landed, their dad picked them both up and carried them down the steps to the ground. Both of them remembered they were never afraid when flying with their dad.

A dramatic change for the children occurred in 1942. According to a statement made by Grandmother Gillam before she died, the three children were sent to her in Seattle in September of that year. The two older children remembered going there but did not, of course, remember the date. This sending the children away from their mother in Fairbanks to their grandmother in Seattle may be seen by some as an indication of a widening rift between Gillam and his wife. This does not make sense, however, in view of Nell's determination (remember her letter dated Nov. 8th, 1941) to not be separated from her children. She would not have allowed her children to leave her home in Fairbanks without some legal document which would have required her to do so, and there was none.

What might have moved Nell to send her children away? Probably their physical safety. The time was perilous and the place dangerous. Dutch Harbor had been bombed on June 3 and 4, 1942. Four days later the Japanese invaded Alaska. They captured the island of Kiska on June 7, followed by the capture of Attu on June 8. During that same summer the Federal Government began evacuating the Aleuts from their homes in the Aleutian Islands.

The fear of a Japanese takeover of Alaska was heightened by the continuing success of the Japanese in their war effort. The attack on Pearl Harbor, and the naval engagements immediately after, gave them supremacy in the South Pacific. Their ground forces, aided by their navy, allowed them to capture the Philippines, British Malaysia, and the

Dutch East Indies in a matter of months. By July 1942 they had gained a foothold on Guadalcanal in preparation for invading Australia.

American military setbacks since Pearl Harbor, the Japanese victories, and adding to this, the unpreparedness of military forces in Alaska, all created among Alaskans an emotional state bordering on panic. Many families with children struggled to get the children stateside and the Federal Government supported their efforts.

Under these circumstances there can be little doubt that Gillam and his wife had a genuine concern for the safety of their children. This would have led Nell to agree that the children should be moved to where they would be safe from any wartime action, even if it meant sending them to Grandmother Gillam, with whom she had deep differences.

Thus both Gillam and Nell undoubtedly saw this move as a temporary one. When the war ended, attempts at reuniting the family could be given full attention. That the move was considered a temporary one is supported by the fact that there was no divorce or any type of legal separation. If there had been, there would also have been a custody contest and the courts would have rendered a written legal decision as to who would have custody of the children.

Unforeseen events later changed this intent of a temporary move.

Chapter 17
NEW PLACE, NEW START

*Courage is not the absence
of fear, but the conquest of it.*
(Anonymous)

This chapter returns once again to the details of Gillam's life as a
pilot and its challenges. On January 4, 1936 Gillam, after providing
the Tibbs family with a belated Christmas reunion in Anchorage,
landed his Pilgrim # 733 at the Cordova airport and delivered the
family to their homes and their everyday living. Gillam Airways' in-

*Various stories of how "sinking" Pilgrim came to the attention of those
on shore. Some accounts are wilder than others but in all accounts a
boat was used and the men saved.* (Stephen Mills, Arctic War Birds, p136)

ventory of planes at that time included one Pilgrim, one 525 hp Cy-
clone-powered Stearman Mail Wind and a 4-place Keystone Leoning
amphibian. Gillam was the only available pilot. The flights during
that first month of 1936 were routine—flying mail, freight, and passengers within the Copper River region, perhaps a few longer flights
to Anchorage and Fairbanks. An entry in Gillam's log for January 5 is
of particular interest. It read simply, (returned—snow). Never before
had such a note appeared. This involved a proposed one-hour flight
between Valdez and Chitina over terrain well known to the pilot. Yet,
forty-five minutes into the flight and some fifteen minutes short of his
destination he "returned because of snow." Gillam was known to
have said more than once, "Weather is often not as bad as is reported. So he made a practice of taking off and finding out. This two-

word notation in his log shows that, if conditions warranted, he would turn back.

Sunday, February 2, 1936 was anything but an ordinary day for Gillam. What happened that day came to be known as the "Inlet incident" and added considerably to the growing Gillam legend.

Bud Seltenreich, Gillam's mechanic, who has given many reports of his boss' activities, gave a firsthand account of what happened that Sunday. His own words in the FAA publication, *Trapline,* told the story as no one else could,

> One time about February 1936 I came to Anchorage with Gillam and one passenger. I was a mechanic for Gillam Airlines in those days. We had a load of mail and cargo to take up to the Interior on the regular mail route contract. It had rained a week or so in Cordova and all the snow was off, so we had to put wheels on the airplane. We couldn't land in the Interior with wheels; so we came over here (Anchorage) with the idea of landing, putting the skis on and completing our trip up to the Interior...

> It was a Sunday when we left Cordova. The bulk station was closed so we couldn't get any gas without going to a lot of trouble getting someone out to open the station. Deciding we had enough gas anyway, we headed out to Anchorage.

> It was good, clear weather all the way until we got over the mountains, coming in from Seward. This whole valley was fogged in. We looked around trying to find Merrill Field. Couldn't find a place to get down and couldn't find the airport. It was just a blanket, pretty solid down there. It wasn't so thick, maybe a thousand, fifteen hundred feet. We were desperate because we didn't have enough gas to go back.

> We came down through the fog and broke out underneath all right, about where Elmendorf is now. There were farms over there. He spotted this field and about the time he got the wheels on pretty good he saw a big ditch about eight feet deep, up front coming across the fields. He gave it the power and pulled up again. Of course that put us back in the fog. He kept pulling up and made a right hand turn. About the time we got our turn completed the engine quit. We were out of fuel and over the Inlet.

> The Inlet was solid with ice. Not solid ice. It was icebergs all pushed together. We came down and broke out of the fog over the Inlet

and landed on the ice. It was nothing but icebergs. As soon as we touched down they spread out and the airplane went down underneath. The airplane was full of air, and it just popped right back up again. We jumped out and got on top of the wing. The airplane was kind of nose down, sinking very rapidly. Water was coming up on the wings. The tide was going out quickly, we could see the shore but not the town. Seeing railroad cars, I said, "Hey, there's a train going by over there." Well, the train wasn't going by, it was parked box cars, and we were going lickety-split with the tide.

As the airplane sank further and further we decided that wasn't going to work. We got some seat cushions, figured we could use them for flotation. There was a pretty good size iceberg close by. I said to Harold, "I'm going to jump on that iceberg. It looks better than the airplane." He said, "Not a bad idea." So we all three jumped. That worked fine. In fact our only worry was that it was going out to sea. We figured if it got out there far enough the iceberg would melt.

The happy ending came when men on shore saw the plane land, broke into a cannery to get a boat and pushed through the loose ice to rescue them. When talking to Bud he said, "We thought a lot about having to drop into that ice-cold water but they got us out and we didn't even get wet."

The crowd on shore did more to help. They loaded empty fifty-gallon barrels onto boats, tied them under the wings to keep the plane afloat, then tied a long rope to the tail to keep the whole thing from going out with the tide. At low tide a taxicab pulled the plane to shore. The next day Bud moved it to a hangar and by late summer he had it ready to fly again.

During the interview Bud also mentioned that he knew if anybody could get them out of that pickle, it would be Gillam. He also remembered sitting there watching Gillam do just the right things at just the right time. Then, thinking back, he added, "I guess we should have bothered somebody on that Sunday morning to open up the bulk station."

While Bud went to work on the plane, Gillam made plans to pick up another Pilgrim through a broker in Texas who still had surplus ones for sale. But before he left, there were things to be done. He flew the Stearman on the mail route for a few days until the Lyle and Dorrance Air Service in Copper Center could take over.

Then, during this hectic time, he still fulfilled a commitment made before the Inlet incident. He married Nell McGee at Palmer, Alaska on February 5. He then flew her to McCarthy and got her comfortably settled in this tiny, out-of-the way community. There they spent a short honeymoon before making his quick trip to Texas. His failed first marriage and the six years since that failure seemed to have somewhat increased his awareness of what a husband should contribute to a marriage—in addition to being a good provider.

Gillam and his bride escaped the "airport gang" by honeymooning in secluded McCarthy. *(M.J. Kirckhoff, "Historic McCarthy")*

Gillam's subtle sense of humor was demonstrated again in the Inlet incident. Here, when Seltenreich, in a particularly life-threatening situation, said, "I'm going to jump on that iceberg, it looks better than the airplane," Gillam replied, "Not a bad idea." His humor is conveyed in his particular choice of words and their delivery. Bud felt they tended to reduce the tension building up in what was obviously a dangerous situation.

In connection with marriage, it seems out of character for Gillam to have shown a lack of humor in responding to what his friends thought of as a joke. They, in humor, sent him a lengthy telegram of congratulation and sent it collect. For some reason it upset Gillam and when approached by the *Cordova Times* reporter, he virtually denied the event took place with this statement,

> Friends in Anchorage thought it would be a swell idea to start the story and when I was in Chitina they sent me a long telegram of congratulations. The worst part was that it was collect and since I was expecting a wire, I paid for it.

Not only was the statement so out of character for him, his denial was contradicted when, after three weeks, he returned with Pilgrim # 739 from Texas. At that time the March 14 issue of the *Times* reported, "Gillam arrived here in his own plane late yesterday afternoon from McCarthy. He was accompanied by Mrs. Gillam."

Gillam's log book showed a slightly less hectic flying schedule after his return from Texas. This might be interpreted as a further awareness of his responsibilities as a newly married man. He could have hardly overlooked his new wife's desire to establish a home. Soon after their marriage, when interviewed by the *Times* staff, Mrs. Gillam confided that they planned making a home in Cordova soon.

On the other hand, gaps in Gillam's flying as shown in his log between May 16 and June 3 1936 may well have been connected with another important step in his flying career. On March 23 the *Cordova Times* reported the Federal Communications Commission had notified Alaska's Territorial representative, Anthony Dimond, that Harold Gillam had been granted temporary authority for installation and operation of radio stations at Cordova, Chitina, and Kennicott and also for one aircraft unit, or station. This is another indication of Gillam's efforts to make air transportation safer and more reliable. Pacific Alaska Airways (a division of Pan American) had already intro-duced air-to-ground com-munication by Morse Code. This required a radio opera-

From the beginning it was clear to Gillam that radio communication would make commercial air transportation safer and more reliable. (Fairbanks Pioneer Air Museum)

tor on board their flights. Gillam was the first to install and make practical use of air-to-ground voice communication. He used it exten-sively in his Weather Bureau contract flights.

At this point, mid-May 1936, Gillam decided to put into operation scheduled, safe, reliable air transportation between Cordova and Interior Alaska, specifically Fairbanks. The schedule involved meeting the steamships as they docked at Cordova on their way to and from Seward, Alaska. Gillam's Pilgrims would be available to fly Fairbanks-bound passengers directly to their destination. Or Fairbanks passengers bound for Seattle could fly the Pilgrims from Fairbanks directly to Cordova and there board steamships heading for that city. The task of providing reliable air service connecting with the steamship schedules would not be an easy one, considering that weather conditions might interfere at any time.

Keeping the schedule for Cordova-Fairbanks passengers would be the easiest. Since he was based at Cordova, it would simply be a matter of having plane and pilot available when the Seward-bound steamship docked. Should weather interfere, the Fairbanks-bound pilot and plane could go part way and complete the flight in stages.

The passengers arrival in Fairbanks by air would still be sooner than if they'd continued travel on the steamship to Seward, enduring the inconvenience of changing from ship to train, and then completing the two-day trip by train.

Completing the air schedule from Fairbanks to Cordova to connect with a Seattle -bound steamship would be more difficult. Once the Fairbanks-Seattle passenger made a commitment to travel by air, the train connecting with a steamship at Seward would have already left Fairbanks. If weather kept Gillam's Pilgrim from reaching Cordova in time, the traveler would in a true sense "miss the boat." If this happened often enough, not only would Gillam's goal of reliability be shattered, but prudent travelers would soon return to the slower, more reliable surface transportation.

Gillam studied these problems and took precautions. He now owned two Pilgrims, which gave him a backup. Both planes had been spe-

The Pilgrim would be the "backbone" of Gillam varied future flying.
(Fairbanks Pioneer Air Museum)

cifically built for American Airlines to serve as state-of-the-art airliners. To assure safety, both planes had been factory-equipped with the latest instrumentation. With regard to pilots, it was perhaps fortunate that Gillam Airways at that time had but one, Gillam. This reduced overhead expense, true. More important, the owner-pilot was particularly qualified to provide reliability and safety. He had also prepared himself specifically for this task. By now, his ability to fly weather had become legendary. He had also flown in this area for at least five years and knew it well. Finally, he possessed an almost mystical sense of direction and geographical location (Mudhole Smith once said of Gillam, "He must have a compass built into his head").

It may seem strange, but it is possible that Gillam wanted this pioneering effort to be a one-man operation. He probably felt a need to personally work out any problems that might arise. Given his motivation and his preparation, he undoubtedly felt that he was the most qualified to protect the lives of his passengers. Providing reliability would, in turn, bring success to this experimental effort.

Also a factor in support of a one-pilot operation was Gillam's inability to hire pilots competent to fly in the Copper River region with its lack of landing sites and its extreme weather. This was true even when adhering to a schedule was not a factor.

Except for M.D. Kirkpatrick, his hired pilots had made more than their share of mistakes, as had Gillam. The hired pilots had then chosen to relocate to areas where flying requirements were not as demanding. Gillam, on the other hand, stayed, gained experience, and learned from his mistakes. Probably the most important factor favoring a successful outcome for this new venture was the season of the year. The long daylight hours of summer would be a welcome help in maintaining a set schedule.

Gillam's mail contracts had been completed by March of 1936, except for a short trip out of Cordova to Katella and Yakataga. This freed him to give full attention to his proposed scheduled coastal service. However, since he was still based at Cordova, he would continue making flights to Valdez, Copper Center, Chitina, and McCarthy when his scheduled Flights permitted.

This flat ground used by Gillam as his landing field was used earlier to harvest hay which was then stored in these barns. They also housed horses that traveled the Richardson Trail. (Author photo)

Gillam soon introduced a unique addition to his newly scheduled Flights. During June 1936, when these flights began, his log showed simply "Cordova-Fairbanks" and "Fairbanks-Cordova" with no intermediate stops. Beginning July 2, 1936 the log showed intermediate stops, usually at Copper Center.

These stops served an important purpose. Since the flights took a full four hours in the air, Gillam left Fairbanks a day before the steamship left Cordova for Seattle. This resulted in free hours and Gillam used them effectively. If weather should prove a problem, though it seldom did, he could use them to assure timely arrival. If arrival time was not a problem, the extra hours would be used to provide passenger comfort. Gillam knew most travelers saw the hours in the air as an ordeal. An ordeal to be endured in exchange for time saved. For those passengers apprehensive about flying the ordeal obviously worsened. Since Gillam's log showed none of the stops involved overnighting, and since the Pilgrim required no refueling, it is apparent that motive for the stop was to make the trip a more relaxing experience.

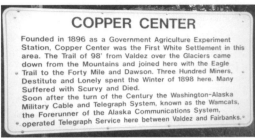

COPPER CENTER

Founded in 1896 as a Government Agriculture Experiment Station, Copper Center was the First White Settlement in this area. The Trail of 98' from Valdez over the Glaciers came down from the Mountains and joined here with the Eagle Trail to the Forty Mile and Dawson. Three Hundred Miners, Destitute and Lonely spent the Winter of 1898 here. Many Suffered with Scurvy and Died.
Soon after the turn of the Century the Washington-Alaska Military Cable and Telegraph System, known as the Wamcats, the Forerunner of the Alaska Communications System, operated Telegraph Service here between Valdez and Fairbanks.

Copper Center figured importantly in the U. S. efforts to provide a totally American route to the gold fields. (Author photo)

Copper Center was chosen as the stopover for good reason. It lay directly on the flight course. More important, during the years it served as Gillam's base of operations a friendship had developed between him and Ma Barnes, the roadhouse owner. She now found special ways to make the travelers welcome. Copper Center had an interesting history and Ma Barnes gladly shared her knowledge. It was the first settlement for those wishing to reach the goldfields over American soil. The first trail from Valdez to Fairbanks, now called the Richardson Highway, passed through the village. Surrounding it lay flat, fertile land. Here hay was harvested to feed the horses that provided year-round transportation. The barns that sheltered the horses and stored the hay are still standing today but in a derelict condition. Some travelers enjoyed relaxing in the rustic setting, others enjoyed a short walk to view the scenic Wrangell mountains. If there was time, Gillam provided ground transportation for a more extended tour. Tourists especially enjoyed this addition to their travel plans.

There were already signs of competition for the steamship trade and one might attribute Gillam's concern for passenger comfort as his desire to best the competition. But did real competition exist? There is evidence suggesting the answer is, yes, although not at first. In early 1930 Gillam organized Gillam Airways to serve the Copper River region, which included Cordova. Prior to that time, no one had thought about encouraging passengers traveling by steamship between Seattle and Fairbanks to fly part of the way. The reason? Planes had not developed sufficiently for such travel and as a result, passengers were reluctant to fly unless absolutely necessary. Along with this, terrain and general weather conditions discouraged such flying activities.

The following article in the March 13, 1928 issue of the *Fairbanks News Miner* gives dramatic evidence of the total lack of air travel between Fairbanks and the two coastal towns of Cordova and Valdez,

> Another page would have been written in Alaska's aerial history today had not a blinding snowstorm prevented crossing of the Alaska Range and completion of a flight from Fairbanks to Cordova, a hop never before attempted. The vice president of the F.E. Company was trying to catch the *SS Yukon* at Cordova. A.A. Bennett (one of the top early pilots) used all his weather skills but couldn't make it. The *SS Yukon* was holding for the vice president's arrival but to no avail.

This situation gradually changed as suitable planes became available. Change was also helped along by Gillam's determination to provide air transportation where there was none and where such transportation was needed. While serving the Copper River region he also began flights that connected the coastal towns of Cordova and Valdez with Fairbanks. As noted earlier, his first such effort involved flying Cordova Chamber of Commerce members to Fairbanks on June 28, 1931 to meet with members there, then flying them back. Gillam, even back then, showed concern for passenger comfort by landing the delegation at Copper Center for lunch and a leisurely break. He did so both going and coming.

The Chamber trip plus other flights between Cordova, Valdez, and Fairbanks led naturally to other pilots doing the same. However, a full blown interest in such flights between the coastal towns and the Interior, especially Fairbanks and Nome, came slowly. An editorial in the April 28, 1936 issue of the *Cordova Times* indicated that such a full-blown interest had arrived. It referred to a Northern Air Transport trimotor flying in from the Interior twice in the previous three weeks and Pacific Alaska Airways flying in with its twin-engine Lockheed just the previous week. The editorial went on,

> Looks very much like the beginning of a new phase of Cordova aviation history. It looks as though Cordova is becoming the relay point between coastal steamers and interior aviation...These big planes carry people to Nome for something around one hundred dollars.

So by spring and summer 1936 various air services were competing for passengers willing to leave the steamship at Cordova and fly to the

Interior. At this point, however, Gillam was the only one who set up a regular schedule based on the coastal steamships docking at Cordova.

Gillam was obviously skilled in the use of salesmanship. (Fairbanks Daily News Miner 6-29-36)

The following ad appearing in the June 29, 1936 issue of the *Fairbanks News Miner* indicates the regularity of his schedule, as well as his courage in stating the Pilgrim would definitely leave on a certain date and that it would connect with the steamship. Finally, besides listing the fare, he made a "tongue in cheek" statement comparing the advantages of flying over driving the Richardson Highway from Fairbanks to Valdez.

That Gillam was successful in acquiring passengers is indicated by the following item in the *Fairbanks News Miner's* "Airport News" section for June, 1936:

> With nine passengers, Pilot Harold Gillam of the Gillam Airways flew from Fairbanks Saturday morning to Cordova. All of the passengers boarded the *SS Aleutian,* southbound for Seattle.

The same issue of the "Airport News" carried the report of a Gillam competitor. "Seven passengers left Fairbanks early yesterday for Juneau on the Lockheed Electra of Pacific Alaska Airways." PAA was a Gillam competitor in this instance because passengers taking that regularly scheduled flight to Juneau could board a Seattle -bound steamship there. This would cut out traveling across the rough, open waters of the Gulf of Alaska by steamship and shorten the total travel time to Seattle. Another advantage: the flight would be made in a modern, fast twin-engine plane.

The main disadvantage to the Juneau flight was uncertainty of arrival. PAA, as a subsidiary of Pan American, had strict rules regarding weather flying. Juneau added to the problem, being surrounded by coastal mountains that rose steeply out of the water. This was in addition to the fog and low ceilings often encountered there. As a result, PAA frequently failed to keep its schedule. The frustration relating to getting in and out of Juneau was expressed by Jack Jefford in his biography *Winging It*. He states,

> But I couldn't get out of Juneau as easily as I'd planned. Bad weather prevented the arrival of the Lockheed Electra that flew

the Juneau-Fairbanks run with an intermediate stop at Whitehorse, in Canada, Yukon Territory.

After three days of baggage drill—packing my bags, checking out of the hotel, and going to the airport to find that the flight had turned back to Whitehorse—I began to wonder if I were ever going to get out of Juneau.

Gillam, on the other hand, not only maintained scheduled flight as did PAA, but he had an unfailing record of getting passengers connected with steamship departures. This not only built further confidence in him, it also demonstrated to the pilot and business communities that scheduled Flights between the coastal towns of Cordova, Valdez, and the Interior were possible. This is not to say that Gillam's fellow pilots were as successful as he. Michael Kennedy stated in *Transportation in Alaska* (p.211) "Gillam's unique methods of conquering the elements were not answers that any man could use."

Gillam did more than just fly the Pilgrim. *(Pat Franklin Photo/ Courtesy Dirk Tondoff)*

One can, however, say that Gillam provided a goal and his fellow pilots, in time, also achieved that goal. And, surprisingly, with little loss of human lives.

Chapter 18
A SPECIAL CHALLENGE
I see the stars, I hear the rolling thunder...
Stuart K. Hine

All went well with Gillam's one-man scheduled air operation until July 9, 1936. On that date the Federal Government publicized a unique bid for an airplane to make a series of pioneering experimental high-

Gillam house built 1937- a home for members of the Gillam family to the present. (Author's photo)

altitude flights for the United States Weather Bureau. These flights were to determine the condition of arctic air masses. In turn, the data gathered would be used to more accurately forecast weather in the United States as a whole. The flying was to be done between September 15, 1936 and March 15, 1937. This would be during the coldest, darkest time of the year when the general weather conditions would be at their worst.

Gillam's interest in the project, besides the money involved, stemmed from the rigorous requirements to which both plane and pilot would be subjected. Besides the requirement stated above, the flights were to be made twice daily in the darkness before dawn and after dusk, regardless of weather conditions. Each flight would attain an altitude of 16,500 feet. Both climb and descent rates would be exactly 300 feet per minute. Instruments attached to the aircraft would record not only the weather data but also the plane's track through the air. Noncompliance would result in penalties based on a percentage of payment for that flight. Gillam, during his two-year participation in the program, missed only one flight and was late in complying only twice.

This type of flight had been attempted before but in a less rigorous manner. Frank Pollack had made similar flights but only a total of five during a month. Also the compliance requirements were less rigid. The flights under these more exacting conditions would be challenging but Gillam was determined. So it was that even before August 22, when Gillam was awarded the contract, he was ready. His two Pilgrims were equipped with the latest instrumentation—directional gyro, sensitive altimeter, artificial horizon and, most recently, air-to-ground voice radio. He had also practiced blind flying under an improvised hood, whenever he was flying empty. Probably Gillam's most important decision was to use the heavy Pilgrims. Frank Pollack had used lighter aircraft and the general opinion favored their use because they were less expensive to operate and maintain. On the other hand, Gillam felt the greater cost of using heavier planes would be offset by reduction in performance penalties. The Pilgrims would be more stable in turbulence and prove more manageable while flying in instrument conditions. He was proven right by his high completion rate.

Obtaining a second pilot proved to be his most important and most difficult task. He was committed to keeping his scheduled coastal flights. By obtaining a third Pilgrim he now had a plane for each assignment plus a backup. By inquiring about previous weather flights he was able to hire Bert Lein, who had flown such observations in North Dakota. Though he stayed only one year, he proved to be an exceptional pilot in both the weather observations and in maintaining the coastal schedule.

To complete the needed crew for both assignments Gillam hired Tom Appleton as mechanic. Appleton was one of the best and stayed on to become what might be considered a general manager. He was credited by Gillam as well as others for Gillam Airways' accident-free record. During all the years of the Fairbanks operation, not one engine failure occurred to any of the Airway's planes. Gillam expressed his appreciation of Appleton by confiding to a friend,

"I'm paying him four hundred a month (a large amount at that time) and I'd pay him twice that much if I could afford it." In time he became Gillam's trusted friend and, on Gillam's death, was appointed executor of the estate.

Gillam flew the initial weather flights and during one of these a problem arose. After completing the morning takeoff, climb, and descent, a strong wind and dense overcast prevented him from locating the field. In case this happened, Appleton was to monitor the plane-to-ground radio and, by listening for the sound of the engine, would give Gillam an approximation of his location. Using this information, Gillam would work his way to the field. In this instance Appleton could not make radio contact. The October 20, 1936 *Cordova Times* reported the incident as follows:

Pilgrim returning from one of its harrowing weather flights. *(UAF Archives)*

Five gallons of gas...remained in the tanks of Harold Gillam's big Pilgrim plane when he landed at the Fairbanks Airport this morning after nearly three hours of flying. Unable to locate his position in the dense clouds and fearing to come down to look at the ground because of the low ceiling, Pilot Gillam flew blind trying to establish communication with his radio station at the airport.

Signal Corp radiotelephone finally reached him...Pilot Gillam says he saw both Cleary Summit and Dunbar but could not get under the clouds to reach Fairbanks. Signal Corp directed him to Hard-ing Lake where the clouds were scattered and he came in following the highway.

After that episode, Gillam devised his own ADF (automatic direction finder) by hooking up a battery charger in front of a radio transmitter located at Weeks Field. This transmitted a signal that Gillam could home in on. Appleton reported it knocked out any radio in the area and upset the Signal Corp people.

After the weather flights were well established, Bert Lein took over and Gillam gave attention to his coastal flights. This coincided with the midwinter months with their limited daylight and stormy weather with which Gillam was more comfortable. During that time he managed to do some charter work out of McCarthy and Skagway into Canada, especially Whitehorse and the Kluane Lake area. Apparently this involved getting hunters into prime game areas.

Fairbanks 1930s, the Gillam family home 1936-1942. (Candy Waugaman Collection)

Soon after the weather flights began, Gillam had moved his wife to Fairbanks, where they rented a place next to Weeks Field. This was to be temporary, for Gillam planned to establish a permanent home by building a house that following summer, which he did.

Fairbanks, the town Gillam brought his new wife to in 1936 as winter approached, was a small town. By the last census its population stood around 2.000, but growing steadily. Gold-mining revival using large dredges, along with airplanes making the town a transportation hub, accounted for this growth. Rapid growth led to modern conveniences such as telephone, electricity, a radio station, a hospital, churches, clubs, and so forth. What a difference between Fairbanks and Copper Center as a home for a newlywed woman. Yet Nell Gillam was introduced to a winter which she had never before experienced, a winter as described by Merle Colby in his *Guide to Alaska, Last American Frontier*. His description gives the reader a feel for a Fairbanks winter as Nell must have experienced it. Colby stated,

As winter comes on and nights grow longer, the air becomes breathlessly still and the thermometer drops to the bottom of the tube. The light snow remains poised on telephone lines and bare branches of trees in motionless bands inches high, unshaken by a breath of wind. Deep tracks are worn to woodpiles outside the door, the stove glows red in the early afternoon twilight, and under the lamp grown men pour over treatises on mining and agriculture to make a passing mark in their courses at the University of Alaska. Fifty-inch logs crackle in the fireplace in the lobby of the Nordale Hotel and the North Pole Bakery freezes thousands of loaves of bread that six weeks later in remote outlying camps, after thawing in the oven, will be as fresh as when baked. Kerosene freezes thick and white, and dogs learn to turn aside when petted to avoid the tingle of a spark of static electricity jumping from the human hand to their noses.

Beginning of a new family. *(Fairbanks Daily News Miner, Dec 3rd, 1936)*

And it was during this winter of 1936, specifically December 3, that Nell Gillam gave birth to a son, Donald. The first child in Gillam's new family.

Perhaps his accepting the weather observation contract and moving his wife to Fairbanks were indications to the Cordova community that, even though he would continue flights between their town and Fairbanks, he would no longer belong to them. There seemed to be a feeling among the people of Cordova that some tribute needed to be paid to this man who was beloved by everybody in the Copper River region. The tribute came naturally on a stormy Tuesday morning, November 24, 1936. Gillam came to Cordova that day doing what he had been doing well for some years, bringing safe and reliable air transportation to the people of the Copper River region. The *Cordova Times* for that day reported on Gillam's arrival in a poetic, dramatic, and almost reverential tone. It began with this bold print,

> Gillam Here From the Interior With Pilgrim (then went on) surprises residents when he appears out of mist; making a dramatic appearance in a howling wind shortly before noon today. The large Pilgrim of the Gillam Airways gave Cordova residents a breathtaking thrill when it suddenly loomed up only a few hundred feet above the town.

> It had been announced over the railway telephone line that Pilot Gillam had passed over Mile 89, and considerable anxiety was felt, as the visibility here was practically zero and with the strong wind blowing, there was a possibility of the ship being damaged on the field, should it be able to get through this far.

> The plane flew so low that it could be seen bobbing around in the strong currents, and one observer on the ground said that when it swung around into the wind to make a landing it practically stopped and appeared to be suspended in midair, "fluttering like a great wild bird" to use Miss Irene Cooley's expression.

The landing was made successfully, however, and Gillam stated that he would leave again with passengers for Skagway via McCarthy as soon as flying conditions improved.

This lengthy, emotional response is indeed a tribute.

In 1930, when Gillam returned from the Eielson-Borland search, the people of Fairbanks had also reached out to him with their hearts. Six years later, when he returned, he was still looked on with love and respect by Fairbanksans. The previous quote from Jo Anne Wold, in *No Kill'em Gillam*, deserves repeating here because it expresses so well this feeling about him. She stated,

> A mature business-minded Gillam emerged in Fairbanks. His youthful daring was tempered by a more stable, determined approach. He was in his mid-thirties, married, and the father of a young son...

What Wold wrote was true. Yet this did not keep him from building on the legend that began when he left Fairbanks for the Eielson-Borland search. His accepting the challenge of the weather flights did just that. As noted earlier, newspapers reported almost daily on the problems Gillam faced as he carried out the rigid schedule of flights into the darkness of winter, where weather reduced visibility even more and required him to rely on instruments alone to keep the plane from spinning into the ground.

The dog Gillam is holding tells something about the man. (*Fairbanks Pioneer Air Museum*)

Ordinary citizens of Fairbanks were aware of what Gillam was accomplishing. Alaska Linck was mentioned earlier with regard to protecting her employer, Pan American, from Gillam's usurping that company's passengers. In a recent interview she recalled as a young woman walking to work in the cold winter darkness and hearing Gillam's Pilgrim taking off into the dense ice fog.

Also in a recent interview, Richard Wien, the son of Noel Wien who was one of the first bush pilots in Alaska aviation, remembered that his father marveled at Gillam's ability to keep the twice-daily schedule—which often required going up through the overcast and ice fog—and to get back down again. This awe came from a pilot who was at that time pitting his own skill and courage against the elements.

Gillam's fearless nature has been mentioned by his lifelong friend, Cecil Higgins, as well as by others. This has led some to conclude that his nerves of steel resulted in a human being without compassion. Alaska Linck spoke of his compassion. She was at Weeks Field when a Pan American flight, carrying passengers enroute to connect with a Seattle -bound steamship, nosed over in the deep snow. Gillam was there and loaded these passengers into his Pilgrim so they wouldn't miss their connection. As it turned out, they ran into heavy turbulence and the plane returned. Alaska Linck was there when the plane landed. As a young woman, she was impressed as she listened to the passengers tell what happened. It seemed that, as the turbulence grew more violent, Gillam gave full attention to flying the plane.

Yet he still found time, in a calm voice, to reassure the passengers. He kept repeating, "We'll make it through okay." In spite of his calming voice, two of the passengers panicked and began screaming. At that point Gillam, still in a calm voice but loud enough to be heard said, "Okay folks, we'll have to turn back."

In the waiting room, those who panicked were still upset but the other passengers spoke in praise of Gillam's ability as a pilot in this difficult situation and for his compassion toward those passengers who had lost control of their emotions. So many years later, this elderly lady spoke in praise of the man who, as a pilot, had been a competitor of her employer. This episode had become part of a legend and can be heard in different versions. However, Alaska Linck was in that waiting room, heard the correct version, and from it gained respect for Harold Gillam.

By the end of January, 1937 Gillam had taken over almost all of the weather flights. Bert Lein then moved over into flying the coastal schedule. This made sense, since increased hours of daylight and the accompanying improved weather made it easier for a pilot with less Alaska experience to keep to the schedule. This change could also have been prompted by Gillam's desire to be at home every night and thus play a more important role in his new son's life.

When March 15, 1937 and the end of the weather contract arrived, Bert Lein returned to the lower forty-eight and E.E. (Elbert) Parmenter signed on with Gillam Airways. Like Lein, this was another fortunate choice. From the beginning he handled the coastal flights well. Like Lein, he stayed only a little over a year. Both were also exceptional in flying weather. The fact

E.E. Parmenter, a competent pilot at a critical time. (UAF Archives)

that neither were involved in any incidents or crashes can be attributed not only to their piloting skills but also to Tom Appleton 's competence as a mechanic.

Also, neither pilot was called on for landings at marginal sites. Gillam took these simply because of his years of experience. He still engaged in flights to off-airport locations as shown by his round trips to Coal Creek— this was the site of a new gold dredge operation near Fairbanks.

At the end of the weather contract, both Gillam and Parmenter kept busy with the coastal schedule. Gillam also became involved in special assignments. In one of these, during April 1937, Republic Pictures hired him to fly its camera crew while they shot air scenes for one of the studio's movies. After removing the Pilgrim's door, Gillam had the exacting task of moving the plane into positions which allowed the camera crew to get exactly the right shots.

Jensen To Build Gillam's Hangar

Joe M. Jensen, Fairbanks contractor, is to build a hangar for Gillam Airways on the south side of Weeks field, according to Harold Gillam.

Work on the hangar is to start soon, Mr. Gillam said. The building will be 50 by 64 feet, large enough to house a Pilgrim plane for servicing.

Gillam Airways operates three Pilgrims.

Gillam obviously made a total commitment to meeting the terms of this mail contract. (Fairbanks Daily News Miner, September 25th, 1938)

On June 21, 1937, the longest day of the year, along with the days immediately before and after, Gillam developed another use for his plane, one he repeated in years to come. He personally took passengers on a local flight to high altitudes where they could see the sun moving along the edge of the horizon, but not quite dipping below it. This new enterprise, referred to as "midnight sun flights", was successful. A total of 18 passengers made the first night's trips.

The summer of 1937 was an exceptionally busy one, involving more than just flying. As soon as the snow melted, the Gillams planned and contracted for a house to be built. That house still stands next to the Chena River at 104 Second Avenue, only one block from the well-kept cemetery where Gillam's grave can be found among those of other early Alaskans. The house, during most of its existence, was lived in by Gillam's oldest son, Harold Gillam Jr. and his wife Janet.

The improved Valdez airfield in Gillam's time. (Valdez Museum)

The hangar was also built that summer but not finished until October. It was built on what is now Gillam Way.

The hangar was an impressive sight, big enough to hold two Pilgrims, with a rounded roof giving it a modern appearance. Sturdy weatherproof construction combined with a furnace inside made it comfortable on the coldest winter days. A small apartment provided a place for either pilot or mechanic to get a few hours' rest before starting another long day.

A strike on the Copper River and Northwest Railroad in the summer of 1937 left food and other supplies for mines and backcountry settlements stranded on the steamship docks. Gillam and Parmenter set up a base at Valdez for well over a month to meet an emergency need for air transportation. Gillam showed a concern for his wife and young son by bringing them down with him for a brief vacation.

During the first part of August, Gillam, Parmenter, and Appleton lengthened their already long working days to overhaul the engines on all three Gillam Airways Pilgrims. Special attention was also given to the all-important air-to-ground radios. These had become an important company trademark. This attention to the well-being of the Pilgrims proved to be an important step in the immediate future.

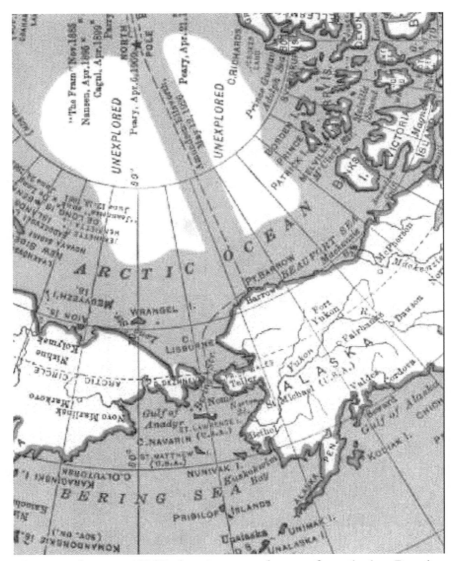

Circumpolar map 1947 showing search area for missing Russian plane. *http://www.explorenorth.com/library/maps/n-polarmap1947.htm. The map was scanned from Collier's World Atlas and Gazetteer (New York: P. F. Collier and Son, 1947).*

Chapter 19
FLIGHT INTO THE ARCTIC NIGHT
There's only one way to fail, and that's to quit.
(Anonymous)

The world's attention was drawn to the arctic north on August 14, 1937 when Sigismund Levanevsky (the Soviet Union's "Lindbergh of

Russia") and his five crew members were reported missing on a polar flight from Moscow to San Francisco with an intended stop at Fairbanks. Final radio contact was made after the plane crossed over the Pole and approached Alaska. A search was begun which in-volved a number of nations. Gillam's life was immediately af-

Levanevsky had flown from Russia to United States more than once but never over the North Pole. (Courtesy of Evelyn Boker)

fected when the Russians contacted Alaska's Territorial delegate to Congress, Anthony Dimond, for a recommendation of the most qualified pilot to haul radio equipment and other vital supplies from Fairbanks to Barrow. Dimond recommended Harold Gillam.

The Russians were setting up a base at Barrow, on the southern shore of the Beaufort Sea. They would use aircraft for a physical search and set up a radio station with specialized equipment to pick up possible signals from the downed aircraft. The Russian icebreaker *Krassin* moved toward Barrow with many barrels of gasoline to service the planes. It would also become headquarters for the search.

During the early years of flight few pilots had flown in the arctic region surrounding Barrow. To mention a few, there was the ill-fated

Wien expedition in May 1928. The Lindberghs' exploratory flight for Pan American during the summer of 1931 landed at Barrow before proceeding on to the Orient. Then there was the Wiley Post-Will Rogers flight in August 1935.

All of these had taken place during the summer months with their long hours of daylight and relatively mild weather. Gillam would be

The Lindbergh's wisely chose summer for their polar penetrating flight. (Wide World photo/Courtesy Anne Morrow Lindbergh "Hour of Gold-Hour of Lead)

making his flights as winter approached and, as it turned out, through the dead of winter, when total darkness covered the cold, wind-swept, and snow-covered land.

Now he had to deal with another matter: how to carry out the Barrow flights, accomplish the weather observations, and fly the coastal passenger schedule. Fortunately, Parmenter had already proven himself competent in flying Alaska weather on the coastal passenger schedule.

With regard to being able to fulfill all three flying obligations, it was probably to Gillam's advantage that competition had been steadily growing on the coastal flights. No longer were these passengers dependent on Gillam's schedule. Interestingly though, with increased competition came an increase in demand. It seemed as though, as more air transportation became available, more and more adventurous souls overcame their fear of flying and opted to travel by air.

All this did not mean Gillam's scheduled service faltered. As it turned out, his reputation prevailed and his Pilgrims carried a fair share of the passengers. Also, to keep travelers posted, Gillam placed ads in the *News Miner* stating when his planes would be leaving. As much as possible he kept Parmenter at Cordova, where he would be in a position to fly northbound passengers to Fairbanks or Anchorage.

The weather observation flights were less of a burden in the winter of 1937-38. The contract called for only one flight every third day. Balloon observations were used in between. This lighter schedule allowed Gillam to be available for the Barrow flights, which involved only two days for each trip, that is, unless complications arose. This did happen.

The first Barrow trip, flown between August 27 and September 1, 1937, went well. With adequate daylight and the weather co-operating, he flew directly to Barrow without refueling at Alatna. Although the weather held for the return trip, Gillam showed farsightedness by overnighting at Alatna. It gave him a chance to gain firsthand knowledge of the roadhouse facilities, adequacy of the fuel supply, and communicate to the roadhouse owner his intention of using Alatna as an intermediate stop in future

The Arctic takes its toll even during summer flights. (Charles Bower "Fifty Years Below Zero p298)

flights—should darkness and weather require fuel and a possible overnight stop. It probably occurred to Gillam that such a stop would not only add safety to the flight but also make it relaxing and more comfortable for any passengers he might be carrying. This would not be too much different from his arranging to have Copper Center serve as an intermediate stop on the coastal flights.

Shortly after the Barrow trip, on September 3, Gillam flew to Aklavik at the mouth of the McKenzie River in Canada as part of his contract with the Russians. The explorer, Hubert Wilkins, had established a base there and was using a long-range Consolidated PBY amphibian (capable of staying in the air twenty-four hours without refueling) to search out over the Arctic Ocean near the Pole. This flight to Aklavik was also uneventful due to adequate daylight and good weather. On returning to Fairbanks on September 7, Gillam was moved to make the following positive statement which appeared in the September 10 issue of the *News Miner,*

> During my stay at Aklavik I was provided quarters by the Mounted Police and must say their hospitality was unlimited and I could not have been treated better. The boys are a splendid lot of fellows, living up to all the traditions of the famous force.

Gillam's second trip to Barrow, September 18 to 20, was again routine. There were fewer daylight hours but weather was especially docile and no stop was made at Alatna either going or returning. Only one newsworthy event occurred. Charlie Brower, an ex-whaler who had established a trading post at Barrow some fifty years previously, decided with his daughter, Sadie Brower, to board Gillam's Pilgrim for Fairbanks. From there they would go on by plane and boat to Seattle. This was a rare event because Brower seldom traveled outside Alaska, since six months were required for a round-trip by boat.

On Gillam's return from that second Barrow trip he made another of his rare public announcements, which was carried by the *News Miner.*

> "I believe the members of the Levanevsky party, or some of them at least, are still alive," declared Pilot Harold Gillam, who returned to Fairbanks from Point Barrow. "Even if they had been forced down in water. The polar flyers probably have climbed onto the ice, and if they had supplies, they would be safe."

The flyers had been unreported for over a month but Gillam's statement reflected his deeply held conviction, evidenced during his involvement in the Eielson-Borland search, that searches for lost airplanes in remote areas should not be abandoned prematurely. The Russians who expended time and effort in pursuing the search, reflected this same attitude. Gillam possibly remembered the Russians' sending planes and pilots to help in the Eielson search. This may have moved him to make his views public.

The third flight to Barrow, from November 18 to 20, went well, although the hours of daylight were reduced considerably. Since Gillam had over the years deliberately flown at night, for him darkness alone presented no problem. However, darkness mixed with bad weather and its further limits to visibility would be quite a different matter. On this trip Gillam was bringing in sophisticated radio equipment used to pick up very faint signals which had been especially requested by

Hubert Wilkins. On the return trip he brought back an unusual cargo—three polar bear cubs.

Cargo on the fourth trip (December 10 to 17) was mainly mail and goods pertaining to Christmas. This led to Gillam's being referred to as an "aerial Santa Claus." Unfortunately, bad weather did mix with an almost total lack of official daylight and led to harrowing moments for plane, pilot, and mechanic. Under these circumstances the lack of visibility led even Gillam to land at Alatna, refuel, and stay overnight.

The next morning, Gillam and his mechanic, Eddie Wissler, prepared their Pilgrim and stood ready to take off in order to utilize the little daylight available. Stormy weather lay across their path of flight but they took off, planning to fly around it. This proved more difficult than anticipated.

They ran out of daylight just as they were entering the bad weather with its additional limitation on visibility. Gillam flew on, not being able to see the ground, and relied entirely on his instruments to keep the plane flying level. It was then that his keen sense of geographical awareness suggested he had wandered out over the treacherous Arctic Ocean ice pack. There was no hope of making a safe landing. He immediately turned back to shore, giv-

Charlie Brower, known as king of the arctic. *(Associated Press photo/Courtesy "Fifty Years Below Zero" P299)*

ing up all hope of finding Barrow. Flying east, he came out of the weather and found himself along the coast at Cape Halkett, some 90 miles east of Barrow.

He had no intention of flying back into the storm and darkness in an attempt to find Barrow. Instead, using reflection off the snow, he made a safe landing. However, the ice was rough and when the plane came to a stop, an inspection showed minor damage to a wing tip. He had a piece of canvas and dope to repair the fabric tear and an abandon ship's hulk could supply a metal rod to finish temporary repairs.

The plane's powerful radio now reached out to Barrow, where Stanley Morgan (radio operator) received the good news of the safe landing. Gillam gave his position and asked for a dozen hacksaw blades needed to repair the wing tip. He also asked dog teams to come out and haul back the Christmas mail. This would lighten the damaged plane for the takeoff.

Morgan got the Presbyterian minister, Klerekoper, to recruit Eskimos and their dog teams, then took off in his fast sno-go

with the requested hacksaw and blades, additional gas, plus other items that would be both helpful and appreciated by the stranded airmen. Morgan made the trip in thirteen hours and the three men set to work immediately making repairs. Gillam, while

Eskimo dwelling built to conserve heat during the long, cold winters. (Crosson collection/ Courtesy R.W. Stevens)

waiting, had explored the beached hulk and found a metal rod that would serve for the temporary repairs. All was ready for the hacksaw and blades.

When the temporary repairs were completed, the dog teams arrived. The plane's cargo was loaded onto the sleds and the teams headed back to Barrow. So with a blessing of reasonable weather but little daylight, Gillam brought the empty Pilgrim to Barrow on December 16. Landing there in the dark became complicated when the temporary lights failed. The Eskimos formed a dark line with their bodies. This contrasted with the moonlight reflecting off the snow. Gillam then brought the powerful Pilgrim in for a gentle touchdown.

Additional work was done on the wing tip with a welding torch to strengthen it for the flight back to Fairbanks. The next day, December 17 at 11:00 a.m., as all the Eskimo men and their dog teams stood lined up in silent tribute, Gillam and his mechanic took off in the empty Pilgrim into total darkness, except for a full moon reflecting off the snow. With the radio reporting good weather at both ends, the flight would have been direct except for frost on the wings, which Gillam reported by radio to his home base. The frost did not allow the Pilgrim to reach the needed altitude so he chose the pass through the Endicott Mountains, landed at Alatna, then proceeded to Fairbanks.

The *Fairbanks News Miner* carried the front page story: "Gillam

Makes Historic Moonlight Hop," and went on "He was the first air-man to soar through the arctic night."

Gillam was able to postpone the next Barrow flight until the end of January, 1938. He used this darkest time of year to help Parmenter with the weather and coastal flights. When the call came for additional radio equipment and supplies, the daylight hours at the Fairbanks latitude had increased significantly. However, when Gillam took off on January 31, the sun was still not rising above the horizon at Bar-

Trading Post at Barrow. (Arnold Liebes/ Courtesy of Brower)

row. On the other hand, his radio was not reporting any storm activity at his destination. He also knew that, above the arctic circle, the moon does not drop below the horizon during the months of December, January, and February. Having this information, Gillam decided to fly direct to Barrow.

Problems arose, though, when he passed over peaks of the Brooks Range, then dropped down toward the Coast. Here he encountered reduced visibility due to a fog-like condition. True, he had already mastered flying by instruments. Yet it must have crossed his mind what happened during his last encounter with instrument flight on his way to Barrow. Also, this time he had not refueled at Alatna. In any case, he found the first likely spot and landed, this time without damage to the Pilgrim.

Again, his reliable radio came into play. Gillam reported himself and his mechanic, George Saunders, in good condition and no damage to the Pilgrim. He also reported that he could not proceed to Barrow after the weather cleared without getting gas. In giving directions for the dog teams he thought his position to be some 60 miles south of Barrow and on the Meade River. He also added, "not entirely certain of my location." This is as close as Gillam came to admitting he was lost. It turned out, the position he reported was fairly accurate.

He then came up with a creative idea to help locate the plane. He would light a smudge fire at noon every day and set off flares exactly at midnight. Although severe storms prevented the dog teams from leaving Barrow immediately, they did find the downed Pilgrim on the night of February 4, 1938. Fueling up the next morning, and with good weather helping things along, the delayed flight arrived in Barrow on February 5.

At this time a party of Eskimo seal hunters were stranded on a drifting ice floe. Gillam stayed an extra day at Barrow in case his plane could help in effecting a rescue. That same afternoon, the ice floe, with the men on it, drifted closer to shore and a rescue party took them off in a skin boat. Gillam left the following day.

The *News Miner*, reporting on Gillam's and Saunders' circumstances while awaiting rescue stated, "The flyers suffered no privations. They had plenty of food and warm clothing."

Gillam and Saunders saw things a bit differently. Their views were expressed in a February 8 article after arriving in Fairbanks. After the cold days and nights on the tundra, Gillam decided in favor of more fur apparel than he usually carried and he returned with new mittens and a parka made at Barrow. The pilot and mechanic had only one sleeping bag and the weather was twenty below or colder and windy. Saunders' memories of the trip are of cold nights on the bleak, flat tundra, beans cooked in a 5-gallon can over a gasoline firepot, and more beans.

When the Eskimo mushers arrived at the plane with a reindeer mulligan, bread and butter (sent by Mrs. Stanley Morgan) and the drivers heated the mulligan then made a big pot of coffee—that was about "the furtherest north" in Saunder's estimation.

Although the Russians closed off their search out of Barrow and moved it to Siberia, Gillam still made charter flights there. The approaching summer with its milder weather and long hours of daylight made these trips routine. The one made on April 9,1938 to take Charlie Brower and his daughter back home from their trip "outside" provides an opportunity to contrast a newspaper report of an event and what actually happen according to the people involved. The April 9 news account read,

> "Flyer Forced Down On Way to Barrow": bad weather today forced Pilot Harold Gillam to set his airplane down at Alatna while on a flight from Fairbanks to Point Barrow with Charles D. Brower and his daughter, Sadie Brower.

The following explanation for the stopover at Alatna is given in Brower's own words as put down in his book, *Fifty Years Below Zero,*

> Then, on Saturday, a flight over the mountains with my pilot friend, Harold Gillam, who had worn this air route smooth while flying for the Russians the year before. Dusk was falling when Alatna hove in sight ahead of us and far below.

> "We can spend the night here or go on," said Harold, "How about it Charlie?"

> Up to that moment you couldn't have got me to Barrow too soon.

Suddenly a queer notion struck me.

"Let's stay over," I said.

"Plenty of gas," he reminded me.

"I don't know, but -"

Why try to explain that a sentimental old idiot, homeward bound, wanted to prolong the thrill by making an extra night of it.

Gillam's performance during his winter Barrow flights added significantly to his growing legend. Even his failure to arrive on two of

Gillam takes friend Charlie Brower home to Barrow. *(Photo courtesy Hana Kangas)*

those flights added their share by demonstrating his ability to get down without harm to man or machine. Then, once down, his skill and tenacity resulted in completing the missions. This legend-building process must also take into account the statements of witnesses who actually flew with him when he demonstrated his exceptional weather-flying skills. An example is the view expressed by Dan Cathcart, former United Airlines pilot, who was later hired by Gillam. His view was reported by Rudy Billberg in his, *In the Shadow of Eagles.* Billberg's account read,

Gillam made regular supply flights to Barrow in a way that other pilots could hardly credit. Dan Cathcart, a United Airlines pilot, rode with Gillam on one of these flights. Cathcart said that Gillam left Fairbanks and climbed his Pilgrim high and flew above unbroken clouds for six hours with no view of the ground. At the end of six hours, Gillam pointed the big potbellied Pilgrim down through the clouds and landed on the lagoon at Barrow. Cathcart had seen nothing to indicate where they were, no land, nothing. He was incredulous when the buildings of Barrow appeared nearby in the fog as Gillam landed. There had been no radio contact between the Pilgrim and Barrow.

How can Cathcart's account be justified when contrasted with the struggles Gillam engaged in during two of those Barrow flights just mentioned? Cathcart did make that flight with Gillam and he was amazed. The flight with Cathcart on board, of course, was made toward the end of March, 1938 when daylight had replaced darkness and there was no indication of a storm. He didn't use his radio? He didn't need to. He obviously would have had a long talk with Stanley Morgan at Barrow, using the radio in Gillam's hangar. The weather information obtained must have satisfied him that the overcast mentioned by Cathcart was something he could handle. And what if he couldn't? If he had to go elsewhere? By the time of this trip he undoubtedly had in place the reserve tank that Maury Smith of the *Fairbanks News Miner* described in his flight to Barrow with Gillam. The 50-gallon, removable tank that Smith described was installed in the forward part of the cabin along with a hand pump. If extra gas was needed, the hand pump would transfer it to the wing tank. This innovation probably resulted from his running low on gas during one of those flights into weather.

It seems reasonable to say that, before Cathcart flew to Barrow, Gillam had already learned much from first hand experience flying to that village under the worst wintertime conditions. Do these explanations detract from Gillam's exceptional skill in flying weather? Is there not an element of mystery that cannot be explained away?

Tom Appleton, who knew Gillam well, had his own view which he expressed to Jean Potter in 1944 and which she reported in *The Flying North*.

"Gillam," Alaskans like to say, "was part bird." Even Tom Applegate, Gillam's ruddy-cheeked, matter-of-fact mechanic, was baffled by his navigation in stormy weather. "The mysterious part," Applegate declared, "was that when he said he was going somewhere he nearly always did. And he nearly always got home the same way. I'd get a telegram saying he'd be in. The fog would be on the ground and every other ship on the field would be sitting by its hangar. By golly, just at that time he'd wired I'd hear a roar and that old gray ghost would come whistling in.

Going back to Gillam bringing the polar bear cubs from Barrow to Fairbanks, why did he do it? Eskimo hunters at Barrow had shot the mother, then brought her cubs into town. There they got into trouble. Charlie Brower, the trader, told Gillam that if somebody didn't fly them out of the village they would have to be shot. Gillam, having a kind streak in him, brought them to Fairbanks.

When they first got there, people used to ask, "What are you going to do with them?" Gillam, with his subtle sense of humor, answered, "Thought I'd enter them in the Fairbanks Dog Derby next spring." Then, with a twinkle in his eyes, he added, "The female is real gentle. Might keep her as a pet. My wife always wanted a polar bear in the house."

So how did the bears take to their new home? After a big pen was built for them outside the hangar, they felt right at home in the cold and the snow. But not all the humans took kindly to the bears. Tom Appleton probably suffered most with the appearance of the "bear family." Although his title was "chief mechanic," he was also good-natured, friendly, and competent. Gillam, on the other hand, was totally involved in the actual flying part of Gillam Airways. That combination made Gillam Airways effective and naturally resulted in Appleton's handling almost anything that came up—including polar

Polar bear feeding time-more work for Tom Appleton (Pat Franklin/ Courtesy Dirk Tordoff)

bears. He soon got used to scrounging stale bread from the bakery and leftovers from the restaurants. Then came summer, warm days arrived and the snow melted. The bears didn't know what to make of this. They stopped frisking about and acted like they were homesick. Somebody thought of a way to cheer them up. This prompted an article in the *News Miner*. It read,

> To keep the Gillam Airways trio of young polar bears happy, Norman Cameron, radio operator, and D.V. Cathcart, pilot, have installed an oversized tub in the cages at the company hangar on the south side of the Fairbanks Airport.

The sheet iron tank, a 10-by-10-foot rectangle, is three feet deep. Cameron and Cathcart sank a well to supply water for the tank, and the bears are just like that advertised animal, the contented cow. Playful beasts, they had a lot of fun spluttering around in the water.

The contentment didn't last too long. Before fall, they started exploring and found the ground wasn't frozen any more. This led to more exploring and mischief. One evening they dug a hole under one side of the cage big enough to crawl through. The next day the *News Miner* told what happened. Bob Reeve, who had moved with his family to Fairbanks, gave the facts as presented in the newpaper but made them more interesting with his talent for storytelling. The following is his account as told in Beth Day's *Glacier Pilot*,

One summer morning a carload of police roared up to Tom's cabin at the edge of Fairbanks. "Bears are loose!" Tom got a rifle and a car and drove into town.

Since it was summer, the citizens of Fairbanks had their doors open, and the cubs were busily running up and down the narrow alleys, emptying garbage pails, then sticking their huge, sharp-nosed, curious faces into the open doors of houses. Tom started chasing them, trying to herd them out of town. But the bears were having much too exciting a time, poking around, making people scream. Tom gave up chasing them, got a whole fish, cut it up, bought Nembutal tablets from the druggist, laced each piece of fish with the drug, then scattered the pieces of fish to the outskirts of town...the biggest one collapsed, asleep, before he made it to the cage. Tom had to get a cat tractor and haul him in.

Tom Appleton must have been pleased when a front page-article in the December 7,1938 issue of the *News Miner* told of Gillam's interest in getting the bears to a zoo, that they were now about 200 pounds and were eating him out of house and home. He was offering the bears to any reliable person or institution willing to pay for crating and shipping them.

Actually, the editor was pleased with the presence of the bears and in the editorial for that same day pointed out that the bears, and Gillam's desire to get rid of them, were creating much publicity for the city. The editor even authorized the following positive reference to the bears to be printed in the regular news section of the paper:

The dinky locomotive at the Alaska Railroad Station formerly was the most photographed subject in Fairbanks, but the polar bears are getting far ahead of the old engine in popularity.

In spite of what Gillam said, he didn't seem in a hurry to see them go. Then, on January 18, 1939 all that changed. The *News Miner's* front page for that day brought the tragic news to the community of Fairbanks. It read,

> "Polar Bear Hanged As She Plays In Den": Kate Snow White, a 300-pound polar bear acquired by Pilot Harold Gillam during an arctic flight to search for the lost Russian transpolar flyers, died by accidental hanging in her den yesterday.

> Kate was frolicking with two other polar bears, Gillam reported, when she caught her head between two bars at the top of the den. Her struggles broke her neck and she died instantly.

Immediately afterward, the two remaining bears were shipped off to a zoo. Knowing Gillam, one wants to believe that he didn't wait for any monies to be forthcoming before sending the bears to a better home.

In the spring of 1938. With the Levanevsky search closed down at Barrow, Gillam once again gave full attention to his scheduled coastal flights. Demand tended to increase with increased passenger confidence in air travel. This kept both Gillam Airways and its competition busy.

After Kate's death the bears were staked outside. (Pat Franklin /Courtesy Dirk Tordoff)

It was while making one of these coastal flights, on March 21,1938, that an incident occurred in which the passengers involved gave Gillam special praise for his piloting skills. On that Saturday, a steamship had docked at Valdez. Jack Jeffords, flying a fast Lockheed Vega on skis, was loaded with passengers for Nome, his home base. In his biography, *Winging It,* he explained his problem. The snow was wet and sticky, which would make takeoff with a full load questionable on this marginal-length runway. The problem was complicated by a sloping runway with the wind favoring an uphill takeoff. Jeffords asked Bob Reeve's advice, which was an into-the wind uphill take off. Jeffords did so, but used all the runway and when he finally lifted off, his wheels brushed against the low brush at the end.

Jeffords circled and watched as Gillam with a full load of nine passengers taxied out and made a downslope, tailwind departure. Jeffords saw him get off successfully but the plane seemed to hesitate as it passed over a power line, then climbed normally again. At this point Jeffords noticed that the front restraining cord on one ski had broken and that ski pointed downward. Gillam circled, then turned northward toward Fairbanks.

In addition to this eyewitness account of the takeoff, a statement by the passengers in the Pilgrim, made after their landing, was reported in the *News Miner*. The passengers were in agreement as to what happened. None mentioned contact with the power line simply because those on board were not aware that it had happened. Once the offending ski was brought to the passengers' attention, they were unanimous in praising Gillam's dealing with what could have been a dangerous situation. Below is the event as described by the passengers and as published in the *News Miner*,

> "Passengers Loud In Praise of Pilot Gillam's Skill": great piece of flying skill was performed Saturday by Pilot Harold Gillam of Gillam Airways according to passengers arriving here from Valdez, when he set his plane down at Rapids, not withstanding a dangling ski.
>
> It appears, judging from recounts, that in taking off from Valdez Saturday with nine passengers, Gillam was forced to run the entire length of the field and in taking off a shock cord attached to the toe of one ski broke, leaving the ski dangling.
>
> While there was no particular danger involved, passengers were loud in their praising Gillam's landing on the ice at Rapids. The tail was put down first, then slowly he settled the ship on the skis, favoring the one which, while hanging, was in the right position for a natural landing.
>
> The group remained at Rapids overnight, repaired the ski in the morning, and flew to Fairbanks Sunday.

This story was embellished with the passage of time and added to Gillam's legendary status (Gillam, ever attentive to passenger comfort, provided a relaxed evening at the roadhouse before flying on to Fairbanks).

Soon after that, starting on April 19, Gillam was confronted with a need to repay kindness to the Presbyterian minister, Pastor Klerekoper, at Barrow. It was he who recruited Eskimo men and their dog teams to make the rescue searches when Gillam was forced down. Now word had come over the radio that Klerekoper, who had been having problems with his appendix, might be in need of an emergency flight to Fairbanks for surgery. Gillam, although his competent pilot, Parmenter, was away temporarily, was determined to make this emergency flight if the doctor at Barrow asked for it. Fortunately for all concerned, the crisis passed during a week or so and Gillam was notified of this on the very day, April 25,

Gillam remembers Pastor Kelerekoper's favor. (Charle Bower, 50 Years Below Zero p230)

1938, that his first daughter, Maurine, was born.

It so happened that also on that day Gillam made a coastal flight to Cordova and returned the following day. His log showed many such flights during that period because of Parmenter's absence. Nevertheless, it suggested a real conflict between his flying and his family obligations.

Fortunately, this situation improved somewhat on April 30 when Cathcart, the United Airline pilot who had flown with Gillam to Barrow, was hired. His hire proved only a temporary reprieve from Gillam's over commitment. Parmenter, after returning from a trip to the lower forty-eight, married a Valdez school teacher on May 27, 1938, then resigned and began flying for Wien Alaska Airways. To show there were no hard feelings, Gillam flew the newly married couple from Valdez to Fairbanks.

In spite of his pilot hire problem, Gillam was able to continue his Midnight Sun flights. These began on June 19. Not long after their completion, on June 29, Cathcart quit.

Stork Calls At Gillam's

That fabled bird the stork called in Fairbanks early this morning, leaving a nestling in the Gillam aerie.

Pilot and Mrs. Harold Gillam are the parents, and the infant is to be called "Maurine Carol," a beautiful sister to handsome little Donald Gillam.

Maurine Carol weighed 8 pounds and 1 ounce at birth. She arrived at 12:25 a. m. today in St. Joseph's hospital. Mother and daughter are getting along very well.

Mr. Gillam is the owner-operator of Gillam Airways.

First daughter in the Gillam family. (Fairbanks Daily News Miner, April 25th, 1938)

From that date until he hired R. Clemons as pilot, Gillam seemed to be content to keep up the scheduled coastal flights and take on a few special charters. One of these charters ran from August 12 to 20 and involved short trips between Cordova and nearby Strawberry Point. Since this took him away from Fairbanks and put him in Cordova, he brought his wife and children down with him—another indication of concern for his family.

A special charter, involving only one day with five hours of continuous flight, showed people and organizations relying more and more on Gillam to carry out special and difficult assignments.

On this day Gillam was to fly a group of scientists, including Bradford Washburn and G. Dallas Hanna, on a visual and photographic observation of the St. Elias mountain range. The flight was sponsored by the National Geographic Society. A report of the flight was written up in the *Journal On Nature of Man-Pacific Discoveries*. The following excerpt gives G. Dallas Hanna's reaction to the flight and also indicates Gillam's ability to make such flights safely,

Flying straight down the coast we gradually gained altitude until 15,000 feet was reached when we were directly in front of the stupendous mountain itself. At times it seemed that we could almost reach out

and touch the jagged rock walls, so windswept not even snow would adhere to them...while we were up there we thought we might as well go on around Mt. Logan and see what was on the Yukon side. There we cruised alongside a great cliff, so nearly vertical, snow will not

A distant view of the awesome mountain.
(Author photo)

cling to it, dropping 10,000 feet from the top of the mountain down-down-down into the depths of a great canyon so far below us we could not estimate the distances.

It was probably engine performance on flights like these that prompted Gillam to pay Tom Appleton $400 a month.

In one of Gillam's last special charters in September he flew to Aklavik to pick up six passengers, brought them to Fairbanks and then flew them to connect with a steamship docking at Cordova. The fact that it was a five hour trip each way, and that radio contact was maintained with Gillam's hangar during the entire trip made it worthy of *New Miner* coverage on its departure September 9, 1938 and on its return September 12.

It is interesting to note that just one month before the Kuskokwim mail contract was to begin, it appears Gillam did not intend to drop the coastal flights while fulfilling it. This intent was indicated by the following ad appearing in the September 30 issue of the *News Miner.* It read,

> Gillam Airlines will start regular passenger service to Valdez and Cordova. The big 9-passenger, radio-equipped Pilgrim service will leave Fairbanks to make connections with both north-and-south-bound boats. For reservations call Gillam hangar or Pioneer Hotel.

Clemons, the new pilot, had served as pilot and mechanic for Cordova Air Service and was familiar with weather and terrain in this area. Perhaps his special qualifications moved Gillam to believe he could carry out both his mail schedule and the scheduled coastal service. Integrating the two would prove a formidable challenge. A challenge that led Gillam to reconsider.

Chapter 20

THE NEXT STEP

*Somewhere out there the mailplanes were struggling. Their night
flights dragged on — like an illness needing to be watched over.*
(Antoine de Saint-Exupery, "Vol de Nuit" Night Flight)

Eight years had passed since Gillam chose Copper Center as headquarters for his newly created Gillam Airways. His basic goal then
was to provide air transportation to an area that had none, the Copper River region. During those eight years he had achieved his goal.
Evidence of this was highly visible. Cordova Air Service had been
established to provide additional services to the mines. With the passage of time, more than enough air transportation had become available in the Copper River region and Gillam turned to more challenging and pioneering flying projects.

The first of these projects was Gillam's dream of reliable scheduled Flights between Cordova and Fairbanks connecting with the
steamship arrivals and departures. This project began in earnest
June 1936. To do this, he moved his base to Cordova and Lyle and
Dorrance Air Service established itself at Copper Center. Gillam had
informally been grooming this company to carry out the mail and
passenger flights to the outlying areas and, most important, to do
so with a dedication to reliability. At first Lyle and Dorrance was
called on infrequently. However, the company was called on more
often as Gillam engaged in special projects or was reduced to a
one-pilot operation.

Gillam committed himself to another special project almost before
he was able to get the scheduled Flights running smoothly. In August
of 1936 he signed a contract to carry out the highly structured flights
for the National Weather Service. Now he was required to move his
operations to Fairbanks. This fit in with his long-range plans. From
the domestic view, his wife wanted to put down roots and build a
house. Gillam agreed, but did not want Gillam Airways to be located
permanently in Cordova simply because its services were no longer
needed in the Copper River region. True, Fairbanks also had adequate air transportation. Here, however, he could continue his reli-

able scheduled air transportation as he was doing out of Cordova and at the same time meet the challenges of demanding National Weather Service flights that few, if any Fairbanks air services would be qualified to carry out. Being a one-pilot operation; keeping up his scheduled Flights, moving to Fairbanks, and preparing for the weather flights wasn't easy. Yet, by September 15 when the weather contract began, he was ready. Bert Lein, with actual experience in making the weather flights, was hired. Most important, Tom Appleton became Gillam's chief mechanic. Gillam Airways now had three Pilgrims, which over the years, Appleton kept in perfect mechanical condition. Also, he took over the day-to-day administrative detail which Gillam simply wasn't interested in. His only desire was to obtain flying contracts and to improve his competence in successfully completing them. In any case, on March 15, 1937, with the weather contract completed, Bert Lein returned to the lower forty-eight and Gillam hired E.E. Parmenter, an experience pilot who was able to carry out the scheduled Flights while Gillam gave attention to building a house and a large modern hangar. Parmenter's Alaska flying experience became particularly valuable when Gillam

Gillam's concern for reliable mail delivery resulted in his getting this mail and passenger route for life. (Courtesy Dermot Cole, "Frank Barr: Bush Pilot)

began another project when the Russian government asked him to make winter supply flights to Barrow in support of efforts to find a downed Russian plane and its crew. The special weather flights for that winter were drastically reduced and eased the flying burden so that all contract obligations were successfully completed by spring 1938. At that point only the scheduled Fairbanks-Cordova flights needed to be flown. This was fortunate because Parmenter left and Gillam Airways was once again a one-pilot operation.

All this changed when on April 28, 1938 the *Fairbanks Daily News Miner* announced that the United States Postal Service had awarded Gillam Airways a contract for the Kuskokwim winter mail route. This contract involved 26 weekly round trips between Fairbanks and Bethel with 11 intermediate stops in each direction. Each round-trip required 1,080 miles of travel, which totaled 28,000 for each contract period. This would be the most challenging contract that Gillam Airways had ever entered into.

It should come as no surprise that Gillam was awarded this important contract. He began carrying the mails as early as 1931. It was the beginning of the Star routes in Alaska where postmasters at the local level could make decisions as to the most efficient way of delivering the mails. During the winters in Alaska there were only two choices— by dog team or by air. Back then, when airplanes were so undependable due to weather, the postmasters found no difficulties opting for dog teams. Gillam changed all this. He soon proved to the postmasters and to the people in the outlying areas that he could deliver the mail regularly, faster, and more often than any form of surface transportation. Gillam's record of reliability discouraged other pilots from bidding on contracts as did an unclear grasp of what bid would assure a profit. There was also the need to assure the postmaster that the pilot had adequate equipment and the needed skills.

Gillam also made it a point, when he needed the services of a subcontractor to help out, to choose one who possessed the competence and the dedication needed to not disappoint those who were dependent on the mail service. This led him to choose Lyle and Dorrance Air Service as a subcontractor. When over a period of time its personnel clearly demonstrated a high level of competence and dedication, and Gillam moved his operation to Fairbanks, he recommended that this air service be granted the new contract. Gillam's competence and conscientious attitude in fulfilling his obligation to the United States Postal Service resulted in a solid reputation. A reputation that stood him in good stead as he became involved in obtaining the important Kuskokwim mail contract. His commitment was a heartfelt one stemming from a determined, lifetime goal of providing air transportation where it was most needed. People in the outlying areas deeply appreciated this commitment to them and their needs.

Gillam's conscientious attitude led him to prepare carefully to assure contract compliance in his new venture. His base of operation would be the Gillam hangar on Weeks Field. This hangar could house two of the three Pilgrims the organization now owned. In addition to the three Pilgrims, three additional 575 hp Pratt and Whitney Hornet engines were available as spares. Besides the regular mechanic, Tom Appleton, an additional one was employed to accompany the mail plane. A repair shop connected with the hangar was fully equipped with all facilities needed to repair engines and aircraft. The main structure also included a small apartment for anyone working long hours on some emergency project. A furnace provided heat throughout the hangar for comfortable winter operations.

A 100-watt aeronautical radio station (KAZA) operated out of that same hangar. It included a homing device for radio navigation, voice ground-to-air radio communication, and a full-time operator/technician in charge. This radio section provided both routine and emergency communication. This was not just for the mail flights but also for any other planes having the voice-radio capability. In this regard, Jeff Jeffords mentioned in his biography, *Winging It,* the aid provided by Gillam's radio station on a night flight with a sick person on board. After explaining his predicament of bad weather and being low on fuel, he stated,

> I worked the CW set and was able to establish communication with Gillam Airlines in Fairbanks. I radioed our predicament to Tom Appleton. He sweated it out with us as we tried to find our way into town.
>
> Appleton rounded up as many people as he could find and had them park their cars along the perimeter of the strip. The headlamps, along with a bunch of flares carefully placed by Clyde Armistead of Alaska Airmotive illuminated the unlighted field. Tom also stationed some friends around the city at various listening posts— hoping to hear our engine and direct us to town.
>
> After what seemed like hours, Appleton radioed that they'd heard us; we were in radio range of Fairbanks. We were lucky and discovered Chena Slough, following it right through town. About three-quarters of a mile out, I saw the glow of the flares and headlights from the cars at Weeks Field. In moments we were on the ground.
>
> Kalland and I climbed down and helped load Frank Alba into the ambulance Appleton had called.

With all these facilities and personnel, it appeared Gillam was ready for the mail flights. The operation did have one weakness, though. It had only one pilot—Harold Gillam, Senior. He lost Parmenter, who stayed slightly over a year, and then Cathcart, who stayed only a few months. It is to Gillam's credit that in this instance his commitment was total. He personally flew each of those weekly flights with their 11 intermediate stops for three years. And according to the postal service's official report had, during those three years, a 100 per cent completion record.

Always, in his special projects of the past, he tended to lapse over into a new one before the current one had been completed. This couldn't help but weaken final results.

In this instance there was no wavering, though opportunities presented themselves. For example, the threat of World War II loomed on the horizon. Along with this came warnings from leaders at the Territorial level such as Anthony Dimond, Alaska's delegate to Congress, and from national military figures such as Billy Mitchell. All stressed

Alaska's strategic importance in the event of an invasion of the United States. They also pointed to the total lack of Alaska's military preparedness in case of such an event. As war possibilities came closer, Congress finally did act. Monies were appropriated and the world-renowned, American construction company Morrison-Knutsen was singled out to build military air bases throughout Alaska. This work was to be done on an emergency basis. Since there were hardly any roads in the Territory over which to move men and materials, M-K pleaded for pilots to become part of this war preparedness effort. Gillam's legendary skills as a pilot who could fly weather were well known. Yet Gillam held out until he was able to find a replacement for the Kuskokwim mail delivery; a replacement he could trust to

Anthony Dimond, Territorial delegate to Washington advocated preparation for war. (Stephen Mills, Sourdough Sky, p107)

carry out the schedule and who would be committed to staying with the job for the foreseeable future.

At the end of three years Gillam found that pilot, a man who had the commitment and the skill. This man, though, did not necessarily agree with Gillam as to how the job must be done. It

Hap Arnold, commander of bomber flight to Alaska advocated military preparedness in Alaska. (Stephen Mills "Sourdough Sky" p120)

was a credit to both that, given their differences in temperament and outlook, they were able to compromise; and the basic conditions of the mail contract would be complied with. This man was Frank Barr, the pilot who eventually became Gillam's replacement.

All this careful and thorough preparation aimed at conscientiously carrying out the conditions of the Kuskokwim mail contract seems to be at odds with the previously mentioned September 30, 1938 ad in the *Fairbanks News Miner*—just one month before the first mail flight was to begin. It stated clearly the intent to continue the scheduled Fairbanks-to-Cordova flights. Gillam's resolve in this direction was weakened by an important event which occurred in August 1938, an event which would have a dramatic influence on Gillam Airways' future. On August 22 the federal government created the Civil Aeronautics Authority (CAA). It, in turn, created a Civil Aeronautics Board (CAB) which immediately held hearings on the matter of regulating commercial air transportation throughout the nation, including Alaska. These regulations would establish scheduled Flights, designate and assign routes, and propose subsidies to be paid to assure schedules were kept and strict safety standards maintained. Mail contracts were to be a part of this package.

The proposed regulations were to bring order out of the chaos that then existed in Alaska's commercial aviation. For example, certain outlying areas had no scheduled passenger, freight, and mail service while others, such as Fairbanks and Anchorage, had a surplus of such services. This resulted in unfair competition in which neither the air services nor passengers benefitted.

Gillam's attempt to set up his scheduled coastal flights fell victim to just such competition. First he established a need for the coastal flights. Then, even if Gillam Airways had provided additional planes and pilots as demand increased, other air services would have moved in and provided an oversupply of planes and pilots. As it turned out, such incidents did happen and the ensuing competition resulted in price cutting and "deal making" in which the air services lost money and the passengers were not able to determine what price to pay.

Gillam and fellow-pilot, Reeve, imbibing "branch water" in a bar. (*Courtesy T.M. Spencer*)

Although the pilots would have been happy to see such competition removed, they were an independent lot who were especially opposed to the federal government telling them what they could or could not do.

Unfortunately, although Congress approved setting up the CAA (Civil Aeronautics Act) on August 2, 1938, and the CAB immediately began writing regulations and laying out routes, actual CAB hearings explaining their content to the pilot community did not come to Alaska until August 1939 when the first one was held in Anchorage. Given the distrust of federal regulation, many of the pilots and air services did little until the Anchorage hearing was announced. At that time the pilots did come together to determine what they should do. By this time, though, little could be done.

Gillam, on the other hand, did not waste time opposing what would soon be the law of the land. Actually he favored the regulations because they supported his own goal of providing air transportation in Alaska where it was most needed. Whether government direction would be successful was a debatable issue as it still is today. In any case, back then and for Alaska, Gillam wanted to give government regulation a chance.

To support a theory is one thing but Gillam was also a practical man. He wanted to know the immediate effect these regulations would have on his business. Here he was fortunate in having his longtime friend and lawyer, Tom Donohoe, willing to give legal advice. A crucial part of the new regulations was a "grandfather clause." It stated simply that any pilot or air service that provided regular flights over a given area between May 14 and August 22, 1938, would retain exclusive rights to serve that area from that time on. The only stipulation was that they apply for that right within 120 days after August 22, 1938 and that, when issued a certificate for a route, the provider was obligated to maintain adequate flights and would charge a reasonable price. Government subsidies would be granted where providing adequate air transportation to an area did not provide an adequate financial return.

At this point Gillam was given a bit of good news. His constant attempts to provide air transportation where it was sorely needed was to be rewarded. For some seven years he had been bidding on mail contracts to outlying area and had followed through with wholehearted efforts to fulfill those contracts. His reputation with the postal service had led to his being granted the current Kuskokwim River mail contract, which was signed in July 1938. It must have come as a complete surprise when he was told that his signing this latest mail contract gave him exclusive rights to the route as outlined—Fairbanks to Bethel, including all 11 intermediate stops. And this route, which had had no regular service previously, would be his by law as long as he did what he had been doing since his first mail contract—conscientiously providing mail, passenger, and freight services to these outlying areas and its inhabitants.

So how did the August 1938 Civil Aeronautics Board's decision to regulate air transportation in Alaska help Gillam decide against continuing his scheduled Fairbanks-Cordova flights? There may have been a doubt in Gillam's mind. The CAB had promised the Kuskokwim mail and passenger route to him from that time forward, if he provided reliable service. Yet he did not have a formal certificate of authorization. Possibly he might loose this important right through some technicality. In fact this did happen. The Anchorage postmaster did award the 1941-1942 mail and passenger contract to Star Airlines of Anchorage. This was done on the technicality that the temporary certificate had not yet been issued (the certificate was issued in October 1942 and the proper rights were restored to Gillam Airways). On the other hand, under the new federal regulations Gillam had a right to apply for a permanent certificate for the scheduled Fairbanks-Cordova route which he had initiated and maintained for a number of years. Certainly his lawyer-friend, Tom Donohoe, would have noted that such a certificate might not be issued to Gillam because there were a number of competitors who had also flown that route during the prescribed period and would also be applying. Probably what moved Gillam most toward dropping the idea of applying for the Fairbanks-Cordova route was this: if an application for the route were approved he would then be faced with the unenviable task of providing adequate (safe and reliable) air transportation over two routes. This meant increasing the size of Gillam Airways—especially it's pilot population. It might even require him to become basically an administrator with limited opportunities to fly. Fortunately, good sense prevailed and he chose the mail route. Here, for the next three winters and one summer he would hone his weather-flying skills and practice his flying depending on instruments alone. And always anticipating the day when navigational devices on the ground would unite with those modern instruments already in his plane and allow true instrument flight—from takeoff to landing.

The first mail delivery on the route left Fairbanks on Wednesday, November 2, 1938 at 11:00 a.m. The pilot, Gillam, sat perched above the engine while Walley Burnette, the mechanic, found a spot among the bags of parcel post and freight. The plane was to have returned on Friday but did not make it till 5:00 p.m. Saturday. The next trip would not leave till the following Thursday in order to take along any first-class airmail arriving via PAA from Seattle and Juneau.

The overall plan to make the round-trip in two days, with one overnight, frequently extended to a third day. This happened often when short daylight joined up with heavy snowstorms or other bad weather. The flights were routine for Gillam, although the terrain was not completely familiar to him during his first few round-trips.

The first unusual happening came on the morning of January 25, 1939. While he was firepotting the engine before taking off from McGrath, the open flame spread and burned the ignition wiring. The plane was now disabled and a lengthy delay seemed likely. Gillam immediately made use of his radio to contact Tom Appleton at the hangar in Fairbanks. After explaining what happened, he instructed Tom to contact Frank Barr, who would fly Appleton with needed tools and materials to McGrath in the standby Pilgrim. Gillam would then take it to continue on the mail route. Barr, after temporary repairs were made, would fly Appleton back to Fairbanks.

Firepotting is a hazardous but necessary procedure during winter flying in Alaska's bush. *(Courtesy Dermot Cole,* "*Frank Barr: Bush Pilot)*

That Frank Barr was available to help Gillam in the emergency was the result of an emergency of his own. Barr had ten years experience flying in the north country—including Southeastern Alaska and the Yukon Territory in Canada. Soon after buying a surplus Pilgrim in Texas (from the same source that sold Gillam his), he moved with his wife to Fairbanks. There he got a contract flying barrels of diesel fuel from Big Delta, near Fairbanks, to a mine on Jack Wade Creek. On August 4, 1938 an engine failure caused a forced landing in a remote area. The landing did considerable damage to the plane's tail assembly. Barr's plan was to rebuild the plane's tail in Fairbanks during the winter. Then, the following spring, he would return the rebuilt part to the crash site and weld it onto the plane. After that, the Pilgrim could be flown back to Fairbanks for additional repairs. Meanwhile, Barr was without a plane needed to pay his bills. Gillam knew of his situation and hired him to fly for Gillam Airways as jobs came up. This happened quite often after the November 1938 mail contract began and Gillam had no second pilot. Barr was not only experienced in flying a Pilgrim, he had also done much flying to Alaska mines and other off-airport locations. Circumstances seemed to have worked things out well for both Barr and Gillam.

Although the two had little in common with regard to outlook and temperament, they did share a love of flying and especially love of flying the Pilgrim. Certainly in their early contacts, Gillam had no thought of hiring Barr to do mail flights. Nor did Barr show interest in that direction. His goal was simply to work on getting his own Pilgrim back in the air. Then he could take on flying assignments that would be a more reliable source of income.

Things changed, though, as Gillam had a chance to observe first-hand Barr's flying skills and his ability to handle problem situations in the air. On this particular assignment of bringing the crippled Pilgrim back to Fairbanks, a problem did arise. Appleton was not able to repair the fuel gauge or the airspeed indicator. To make matters more difficult, a strong head-wind put them in the air longer than expected. With the fuel gauge not working there was no way of determining how much more fuel they had left. In this situation Appleton began fidgeting but Barr just sat there flying the plane—much as Gillam would have done. He finally set it down at Weeks Field with two gallons remaining in the reserve tank.

On the surface, Barr was more relaxed, but both he and Gillam had a confident coolness in emergency situations. It was this confident coolness, in turn, that instilled confidence in their passengers.

Frank Barr, at this point still flying his own Pilgrim.
(Courtesy Dermot Cole, "Frank Barr: Bush Pilot)

They both also had an underlying concern for people. Barr's relaxed manner made it easier for him to communicate this. But Gillam's caring surfaced often. About this time, another event illustrates this caring. Bob Hansen now lives in Anchorage, retired after working 47 years in Reeve Aleutian Airways' maintenance section. As Bob likes to tell it, when he retired in 1995 he was the only non-family member to become a Reeve stockholder. In a recent interview he told about starting to work for Gillam the day before Pearl Harbor. He was a green kid who had never worked anywhere but in the family mine at Manley Hot Springs. He remembered well an incident that told him how human Gillam really was. It was a cold morning and Bob had worked in the hangar only a few days. He rolled a drum of fuel oil inside to refill the holding tank on the furnace. The oil was cold and didn't flow well. The drum lay on its side on a platform where the oil would run into the holding tank. Instead of standing around waiting for the oil to warm up and flow more freely, he got busy with something else. Sometime later, Gillam came in and saw the holding tank overflowing. About the same time Bob looked over and saw the mess on the floor. Right away he thought, "It's my first job and I'm going to get fired for sure."

Instead, Gillam didn't even chew him out. He just smiled and said, "I'm sure glad they don't make those oil drums any bigger." He was still smiling when he turned away and went about his own business. So many year later Bob remembered the incident and said, "He must have known how I felt."

Gillam also showed consideration of others during that first mail contract. The Winter Ice Carnival came at the end of March and he rearranged the mail schedule a little so people could fly in for the celebration. This he was able to do without messing up his 100 per cent completion record.

Bob started as a mechanic with Gillam way back when, but still remembers "that act of kindness."
(Marguerite Keiss, "Miners at War, Bob Hanson", The Alaskan Miner February 19, 1996)

As he and Barr worked together, understanding seemed to grow and when the time arrived for Barr to take over, both pilots were ready to let it happen.

In his biography by Dermot Cole, this is how Barr saw it,

> The two men never became close friends but they got along well most of the time.
>
> He never told me how to fly or when to fly or anything else. I just flew the mail back and forth. I didn't know I had a boss, even. I never tried to fly like anybody else did. I knew what I could do and I knew my plane's limitations.

As for that first year's contract, the last flight ended on April 14, 1939. In the April 18 issue of the *News Miner*, the residents along the Kuskokwim mail route expressed their feelings toward Harold Gillam and his mail deliveries. The article stated,

> People along Harold Gillam's Kuskokwim mail run have been well

satisfied with the service given them. Word reaching Fairbanks through Kuskokwim residents is to the effect that winter nights were made a lot brighter by the mail that they received at regular intervals.

No wonder the Kuskokwim people appreciated Gillam's delivery. Before, PAA would fly the mail from Fairbanks to Bethel. From there it was delivered by dog team to the villages along the Kuskokwim. Only first-class letters were delivered; packages were kept by the Seattle post office until spring, when the rivers were open to boat traffic. Gillam's mail delivery was weekly and included parcels as well. He was required to take only one thousand pounds of mail out of Fairbanks each week but was able to keep the Fairbanks post office free of parcels. Can you imagine the emotions an entire family felt on receiving a Sears mail order package during the winter when they usually had to wait till early summer to receive it?

Gillam was free of mail contract obligations during the summer of 1939. Strangely, though, he did not seem to make many coastal flights. Apparently other carriers were providing sufficient flights and did not need him to provide additional competition. Instead he arrange more distant flights, including Barrow and Aklavik. These charters probably provided a challenge even during the long daylight hours of summer. He did find time, though, to carry out his Midnight Sun flights.

The first flight on his second mail contract (November 1939-April 1940) struggled out of Fairbanks on November 1. On that day the News Miner reported all aviation in the Interior stalled by snowstorms. The November 1 issue stated,

> Aviation Halted By Snowstorm. Aviation in Alaska was at a standstill today as snowstorms swept the Interior. In Fairbanks airlines cancelled out flights scheduled for the day, and awaited clearing skies. Airmail between Fairbanks and Juneau was held over, keeping planes aground in both cities.

Four planes were reported idling at McGrath until more favorable conditions permitted their taking off for their respective bases. These were ships of the lines of Jack Peck, Ray Petersen, PAA and Star Airlines.

Gillam was not listed because he arrived at McGrath during the storm, although he did decide to overnight there rather than fly through heavy snow in the dark. He did take off the next morning and continued on his route.

The News Miner carried a short note on Friday the third, stating, "Harold Gillam was reported on the homeward trip from his first winter mail flight to Bethel and waypoints and there was a possibility he would arrive in Fairbanks late today."

Actually he landed at Fairbanks the next day. Gillam flying through

Notice Gillam does not mix darkness and snowstorms. *(Courtesy Fairbanks Pioneer Air Museum)*

a snowstorm to complete his route might be the one Ray Petersen referred to in a recent interview. He mentioned miners trying to get out to Anchorage and then on to Seattle after the mining season closed. Early November (the time of the storm) would be about the right date.

Later flights on the mail run became routine, although the *News Miner* did mention Gillam flying in perishables to the bush villages for Thanksgiving. This again suggested that Gillam continued to find ways to personalize his flights to the Kuskokwim villages.

Frank Barr was now being mentioned in the *News Miner* as flying to outlying areas in his own Pilgrim. It appears that Barr was no longer dependent on Gillam Airways for special jobs. In fact, it appears that, over time, Gillam Airways became dependent on Barr for help in carrying out flights not related to the mail route.

An experimental mail contract was put out for bid involving weekly flights between either Anchorage or Fairbanks to Bethel with intermediate stops. This was for the summer of 1940. Gillam was awarded the contract, which kept him busy. He did find time, though, to again carry out his Midnight Sun flights.

The Leoning amphibian which Gillam flew out to Seattle in the summer of 1934, and left there, seems to have appeared once again in Alaska as part of the Gillam Airways fleet during the summer of 1940. It was flown back by pilot Vernon Bookwalter. He did not, however, become one of Gillam's pilots. This meant he was still relying on Barr and his Pilgrim to handle extra jobs while Gillam kept busy with his mail contracts.

During that busy summer of 1940, specifically on July 12, Gillam's second daughter, Winona, was born at St Joseph's hospital.

Mrs. Gillam Is Mother Of Daughter

-Harold Gillam, well-known aviator, is "up in the air" today he is so happy over the birth of a daughter to Mrs. Gillam at 7:45 o'clock Thursday evening in St. Joseph's hospital.

The infant weighs 7 pounds and 8 ounces.

Mother and child are doing well.

The News Miner *forgot to include the young daughter's name: it is* **Winona.** *(Fairbanks Daily News Miner)*

On November 6 Gillam began his first trip on the November 1940-April 1941 mail contract; with him was a new flight mechanic, Austin Joy. The flights continued without incident until March 11, 1941. On that date the *News Miner* reported that a snowstorm over the Interior brought air traffic to a halt. Gillam, however, continued to fly and made the round-trip in three days.

It was during March 1941, near the end of his mail contract that Gillam gave the first indication that he would tie in with Morrison-Knutsen. He made plans to take the summer off and travel to Houston, Texas with his family and get his instrument rating. And what would happen to his Kuskokwim mail contract? After putting in three years of his flying life to make it a success, he certainly had no plans to abandon it, especially since his certification for the mail route and its intermediate stop was approved by the CAB on December 19, 1940. This meant he was entitled to that route, exclusively and from that time on, unless he failed to provide the service.

Obviously, Gillam expected to receive the mail contract for both the summer of 1941 and for the year November 1941-April 1942. However, since he would not be continuing as pilot for the route, Frank Barr would probably do the flying. A statement in Barr's biography supports this assumption. It read, "Barr made a few more flights for Gillam before he put him on the payroll full-time in 1941."

It was apparent then that Gillam planned to have Frank Barr take over mail flight responsibilities for Gillam Airways. There had been enough interaction between the two that Gillam accepted Barr for the job.

There may have been some uneasiness on Gillam's part over the fact that Barr had applied for a route certificate in the Delta, Forty-mile country. Since he had not flown his plane over the route during the magical dates of May 14-August 22, 1938, (his plane was disabled during that time due to a forced landing) he was not eligible under the "grandfather rights" clause. This would have automatically certified his application. His being certified for that route under normal procedures was highly unlikely. This proved to be the case when the CAB denied his application on August 22, 1942.

Then came what must have been a surprise for both Gillam and Barr. The March 15, 1941 issue of the *News Miner* stated: "Star Airline given the Kuskokwim mail contract." It seems the authority to choose the best bid had been transferred from the Fairbanks postmaster to the one in Anchorage. The postmaster there had decided to make Star Airline of Anchorage the chosen contractor. It was to have both the summer of 1941 and the November 1941-April 1942 contracts.

How could this be? Gillam's application for a certificate to fly the Kuskokwim mail and its intermediate stops had been approved by CAB on December 17, 1940. On the other hand, Beth Day, in her Reeve biography noted that "it was not until October 1942 that temporary certificates were actually issued to Alaska carriers." Of course public reaction in Fairbanks, saw it as "politics." Anchorage had the largest population and with it went the political clout. Obviously, though, there was a technical point involved. When, exactly did Gillam's certificate became valid?

Fortunately, Gillam chose not to question the technical point. Gillam Airways' newly hired pilot, Frank Barr and his Pilgrim, would have enough flying to do. Indications of war were becoming ever more evident. Congress was finally appropriating monies for the Territory's defense. More immediate, M-K was charged with airport construction throughout Alaska and was hard strapped for both pilots and planes.

Gillam, although not a public person, was a patriotic one. Here was a new challenge and helping to meet it would determine the fate of his nation. He was indeed ready to more directly aid the war effort with his special flying skills.

What about the Kuskokwim mail contract? Would dog team delivery once again become its fate? No, the route in the year ahead would be served by an air carrier; it just wouldn't be Gillam Airways. The following year, though, it would be Gillam's again and he had already carefully chosen the pilot who would do the flying. Then the Kuskokwim mail route would be in good hands.

Meanwhile, Barr and his Pilgrim were kept busy moving men and materials needed to build an airport at Boundary—later called Northway. The following year the mail contract did go back to Gillam and stayed. It was still there when Gillam Airlines became part of Northern Consolidated Airlines and was still active when Northern Consolidated became part of Wien Consolidated Airlines.

Frank Barr and his Pilgrim were the last to finish the Northway Airport Project. Mudhole Smith, who also flew for M-K and Gillam at Northway, finished early and Gillam asked him to get the Kuskokwim mail contract for November 1942-April 1943 started on time. In the first part of January 1943, Gillam moved Smith to an M-K project at Nome and Barr took over the mail route and stayed. His last flight on the route was on September 16, 1945. He may not have achieved a 100% completion record but he kept delivering the mail regularly and satisfied the residents who depended on him.

Gillam did get his instrument rating at Houston during that summer of 1941. By taking his family with him and spending three months away from home, he probably intended this to be a sort of vacation for all and especially for his wife, Nell. As noted earlier, a definite rift had developed between him and Nell between March and November of 1941. No one knows exactly when it happened or what caused it. Quite likely part of the cause stemmed from his inability to give enough time to his family. If that was indeed part of the cause, the three months' vacation of sorts may have been Gillam's attempt to remedy matters. They returned to Fairbanks in August and for a few days he made local flights in the Leoning amphibian, during which he took his youngest son, Don, with him. Then he plunged back into his flying with an intensity deepened by thoughts of war which came on December of that year. The rift between him and Nell remained unresolved as his flying life became ever more hectic.

Information about the Kuskokwim mail flights was abundant. What about the emotions—the pilots' as well as that of the passengers? Here we could hardly turn to Gillam. For as Barr said of him, "He would never offer anything about his own experiences." To some extent this was also true of Barr. However, a passenger, Henretta McKaughan, a newspaper reporter whom Barr invited to accompany him on one of his weekly flights, gave the emotional reactions she experienced while flying the route.

With three small kittens in a ventilated box and mechanic Bob Vanderpool as fellow passengers, Mckaughan squeezes in with a mountain of cargo on her late-winter flight. Lake Minchumina was the first stop...Vanderpool unloaded the mail and exchanged greet-ings with those who met the plane...The first major stop was McGrath.... They went to the McGrath roadhouse... while planes taxied about, the travelers had a cup of coffee...Before leaving McGrath the mail sacks were readjusted to make room for mechanic Vanderpool's wife and niece...they were going home to Crooked Creek. The mail sacks for Stony River and Sleetmute were placed on top

The Kuskokwim River ice makes a convenient landing site-during the cold winter months. (Dermot Cole, "Frank Barr"/courtesy Fairbanks Pioneer Air Museum)

of the pile for an air drop. Barr didn't plan stopping at those two villages until the return trip. So Vanderpool would just kick out the sacks as they flew over. Barr changed his plans, however, when he learned by radio that there was a sick child at Sleetmute...Passengers who climbed into the Pilgrim for the return trip included a woman just out of the hospital, bound for Sleetmute, and the child who had had the bean removed from his ear, and his teacher...As was often the case, the flight was a rough one. It was so windy that Barr de-cided it was unsafe to land at Kalskag. He landed on a slough outside the village, knowing that the villagers would have heard and seen the plane and would send dog teams out to get the passengers and mail...

This partial recording of the first day's events as taken from Dermot Cole's biography of Frank Barr suggests the experiences were anything but ordinary. One can imagine what it would have been like for the passenger, had the flight encountered a severe snowstorm.

Chapter 21
FINAL FLIGHT

The urge always to seek and to know is strong within us and
is part of the challenge and the inspiration that keeps us flying.
(Sir Gordon Taylor, "The Sky Beyond")

As this biography and Gillam's life draw to a close, there seems an urgent need to, in some preliminary fashion, bring together his personal life and his life as an aviator.

The March 18, 1941 letter written by Nell Gillam to her mother in Oregon suggested harmony in the Gillam household. That same year marked Gillam's decision to get his instrument rating in Houston, Texas that summer. Although getting the rating took only a bit over two weeks, he took the family with him and made an extended va-

Anchorage: future headquarters Morrison-Knutson Construction, Gillam's employer.
(U. S. Air Force/Courtesy Mills, "Sourdough Sky")

cation of it, especially for his wife, Nell. The family returned to Fairbanks in early August, 1941. His log shows him making local flights in the Leoning amphibian. It had finally been flown back to Alaska from Seattle by a friend. These flights in the Leoning seemed to serve no urgent purpose. This was supported by the then-young son, Donald. He remembered flying with his dad and landing on various lakes and rivers.

After that, Gillam's log from September 6 through October 16 showed no flight activity. This period probably involved preliminary contact with Morrison-Knutsen. Such contact undoubtedly dealt not just with flying but also with leasing his Pilgrims to M-K. This seems like a valid conclusion since he and his Pilgrims, first NC 711Y then NC 733N, flew continuously from that time on until year's end; and especially since his destinations varied and strongly suggested preparations for war.

A few of these destinations were his usual ones—Fairbanks to Cordova and return. Most, though, suggested a new direction. For example, entries from November 23 through December 2, 1941,

 show a series of flights from Fairbanks to Nome via Galena and a return also via Galena. December 7 (Pearl Harbor) found him flying from Fairbanks to Barrow via Bettles with the same stopovers on his return. Then from December 11 through December 17, a series of flights from Fairbanks to

Shows clear view of second runway. *(Crosson Collection/Courtesy Mills, Sourdough Sky WeeksField))*

Nabesna and return to bring in materials for construction of a newly authorized radio range. To finish off the year, Gillam made another trip from Fairbanks to Barrow via Bettles with the same intermediate stop on his return. Then on the very last days of the year he flew to McGrath and back.

Meanwhile during that time while Gillam was flying continuously, Nell had mailed her second letter on November 6, this one to her sister with the news of her close-knit family falling apart. Was there a connection between this apparent crisis in Gillam's personal life and his deepening concern to help his country prepare for war? The cause for the crisis is not completely explained. Fortunately, it is not necessary to know the details of the cause in order to consider its effect on Gillam's life as a pilot. It would be easy to make a psychological interpretation. The disruption within his all-important family probably had an immediate effect. It may have distracted him from his flying tasks which he had always given himself to totally. This distraction then may have led to the tragedy of his final flight, which was about to unfold.

However, Gillam and his wife were both trying to agree on compromises regarding the family crisis as it unfolded within the broader crisis of the nation at war. Their compromises dealt mainly with their children, and would have held out hope for the future. This hope, in turn, would have given Gillam comfort as he plunged into an effort to serve his country.

What was Gillam's situation when the year 1942 began? War with Japan had been formally declared. The Territory of Alaska, although unprepared, was readying itself for a possible invasion. In early January 1942, M-K had hired Gillam for a special role. The company's obligation was to construct airfields throughout the Territory in the shortest possible time. Gillam's role, although not completely finalized, would require his flying out of headquarters in Anchorage. This meant he

Nell and the children would remain in the family home while Gillam was at M-K headquarters in Anchorage. (Authors photo)

would have to locate there. As was noted before, Gillam and his wife, Nell, had agreed that she would stay in Fairbanks so the children would not be uprooted from the place where they had been born and which had always been their home. Also a consideration, flying to all parts of the Territory would result in his spending little time at headquarters in Anchorage.

On January 13, 1942 Gillam arrived at Cheyenne, Wyoming to inspect a Lockheed Electra for possible purchase. He inspected, purchased, and was checked out in it by January 15. He then flew it to St. Paul, Minnesota where the engines and the plane itself would be given a complete overhaul, with particular attention to the instruments needed for all-weather flying. At the outbreak of World War II commercial aircraft were in great demand and this was particularly true of the Lockheed Electra with its modern design, which combined speed with load-carrying capacity.

Gillam recognized the rundown condition of the aircraft but knew M-K would authorize getting the engines and airframe in perfect condition. He knew all this but it undoubtedly involved more time than he expected. After 17 days in the shop he took the plane up but was not satisfied. After 20 more days in the shop he again flew it and found performance according to his expectations.

The model he purchased had two weaknesses that could not be corrected. It was powered with 400 hp Curtis Wright engines. The manufacturer later replaced these with 450 hp Pratt and Whitneys.

Also, its props were constant speed but not full-feathering. This meant the props would windmill with an engine out and produce additional drag. This was also corrected in later models. Obviously both these weaknesses would reduce single-engine performance.

After final checkout of the plane, Gillam spent four days and eight hours in the air getting personally familiar with its specific flight characteristics and performance.

On March 5 he took off from St. Paul and arrived in Anchorage on March 7. He made a short detour to Fairbanks. Although it was a brief stop, it indicated his family had not been forgotten.

By the end of 1942 he had logged approximately 700 hours in the Electra.

Log entry shows fast trip St. Paul, Minnesota—Anchorage via stop at Fairbanks; flying Lockeed Electra. *(Gillam's log/ Courtesy T.M. Spencer)*

Although the plane was considered part of M-K's executive fleet, Gillam was the only one checked out in it. At first he flew it mostly to haul equipment and supplies where they were urgently needed. It was fast, could haul a good load and, with Gillam at the controls, it was able to get in and out of rough and marginal fields.

When Gillam first returned with the Electra, a strange arrangement existed with regard to his role at M-K. In August 1941 Leon (Slim) DeLong, the general manager of M-K in Alaska, hired Herman Lerdahl to be his executive pilot. As Lerdahl admitted in his biogra-

Electra at work moving men and materials for the Northway Airport project. *(Courtesy T.M. Spencer)*

phy *Sky Struck*, DeLong was not happy with his executive pilot's willingness to fly weather. Things finally came to a head and Lerdahl was sent, at company expense, to get an instrument rating. He left on January 20, 1942 and received his rating on March 22. This was approximately when Gillam, who had obtained an instrument rating on his own in June 1941, returned to Anchorage with the Electra.

As it stood, Lerdahl, with his instrument rating, would fly DeLong and other supervisory staff to and from the various airport construction projects throughout the Territory in all types of weather. A new, sleek single-engine ten-place Vultee was obtained for Lerdahl to fly. Thus Lerdahl was the executive pilot and Gillam with his Electra was available wherever and whenever needed.

As time passed, and without any special effort, Gillam proved himself an exceptional and versatile pilot. Since he was constantly visible to the company's top brass, they could not help but be impressed with his ability to use the sleek, fast Electra to move materials quickly and, most important, in any kind of weather. By summer, he was made chief pilot for the Nabesna-Northway airport construction project. He hired pilots to fly heavy loads from Nabesna, at the end of a makeshift road, to Boundary or Northway, where the airport was being built. Flying such loads off and onto im-provised strips re-

Pilots who flew the Nabesna-Northway run for Morrison Knudson Construction during summer of 1942: From left; Merle (Mudhole) Smith, Rudy Billberg, John Waltka, Frank Barr, Don Emmons, Jack Scavenius, Frank Krammer, and Herman Lerdahl (Lerdahl was also executive pilot). (Johanna Walatka Bouker photo/Courtesy of Rudy Billberg, In The Shadow of Eagles p 101)

quired pilots with "bush" skills and Gillam knew where to find them. Two of them had flown for him before, Mudhole Smith and Frank Barr.

During the Northway Project Lerdahl's position gradually changed. Part of his time was spent hauling heavy loads in the Pilgrim. Gillam had leased his Pilgrims to M-K but had kept one to fly the Kuskokwim mail contract, which would be returned to him for the November 1942-April 1943 year. By the end of 1942 things had worked themselves out. DeLong had ac-

Gillam, as chief pilot, was heavily involved in building the Northway airport in the summer of 1942. (Rudy Billberg, In The Shadow of Eagles)

cepted a commission and moved into the Army. Robert Gebo moved up as general manager of M-K in Alaska. Lerdahl accepted a job as pilot with Northwest Airlines. Gillam then took over officially as chief pilot for M-K.

There was unanimous agreement among the top staff of M-K regarding Gillam. All had had a chance to fly with him in all sorts of situations, especially those involving difficult weather. William Loftholm, who

Spartan Executive, purchased to replace fast 10 passenger Vultee. (Spartan School of Aeronautics photo/Courtesy Bilsteins "Flight in America" p 114)

273

took over as superintendent when Gebo retired and is now also retired, consented to an interview. He gave a firsthand endorsement of Gillam's ability as a pilot. Loftholm felt his most outstanding quality was an ability to instill confidence in any tense situation. Quiet confidence in himself seemed to transfer to others.

To illustrate this point, Loftholm told of Gillam's gathering staff from various outlying areas with the company's Grumman Goose. He was to assemble them at Bethel, then bring them to Anchorage for sort of a celebration of the 1942 Christmas season. As would be expected, in mid-December with the shortest day of the year close at hand, darkness and snowstorms prevailed. Gillam managed to get them all to Bethel. There blowing snow and limited visibility made things grim. Loftholm, along with the rest, felt a bit anxious. All were eager to arrive in Anchorage. But for those like Loftholm, planning to fly with Gillam to Seattle and from there get home for Christmas, the tension was considerable. Gillam walked into the room and said quietly, "The weather here is bad but everything's okay. We'll take off on instruments. We're equipped to do that. The weather at McGrath and Anchorage is clear so we don't have to worry about ice. We'll make it okay." It wasn't just his words that dispelled the tension. It was more than that. They trusted him.

On their arrival at Anchorage, everybody enjoyed the get-together. Since Gebo had arranged for the Electra to leave right after the party, Gillam left to make sure everything was ready for the flight.

Merrill Field; still an active airport in spite of being completely surrounded by buildings of the downtown area. (*U. S. Air Force photo/ Mills, "Sourdough Sky" p117*)

Later that same evening the Electra, with Loftholm on it, took off for Seattle. Gillam's log shows a stop at both Juneau and Annette— in Juneau probably to pick up more staff who wanted to be with family for Christmas; and in Annette most likely to make certain there would be enough fuel, regardless of winds aloft.

The plane arrived in Seattle at 2:40 the next afternoon. From there, happy passengers left for home. Gillam, whose kids were now living with their grandmother in the Seattle area, went there for Christmas. It would obviously be a lonely holiday season for Nell.

On Tuesday, January 5 at about noon, people started coming together near the Pan American hangar on Boeing Field. A young ap-

Boeing Field dedication 1930, not too different in appearance from when Gillam landed his Electra there in December 1942. *(E. Miller photo/King County Int'l Airport Boeing Field)*

prentice mechanic for that airline, George Clayton, helped open the doors of the hangar where the M-K Electra was parked. He then took in the scene; not for any particular reason other than that he was already hooked on becoming a pilot. When interviewed recently, as a retired airline pilot with 24,600 hours in his log books, he remembered well that day back in January 1943. He remembered a station wagon pulling into the hangar next to the Electra. People and packages flowed out of the station wagon and into the plane. George recognized Gillam as the pilot by the way he checked the plane over, then got in last and latched the door. A tug pulled the Electra out of the hangar with Gillam now in the cockpit. George followed the plane out and kept watching. No one told him to get back to work so he watched while Gillam taxied out to the other end of the runway. Pretty soon he heard the whine of

A rare sight, Gillam in business suit, relaxing at M-K headquarters in Anchorage. *(M-K photo/ Em Kayan, March 1943 Issue)*

those twin engines racing toward him. During the interview, George added, "There just isn't a prettier sound than a twin coming at you with the throttles wide open and the props set for high rpm."

Visibility was pretty good as the Electra lifted off and climbed up over the downtown Seattle office buildings. George was probably the only one who kept watching as the plane disappeared to the northwest. He then hurried back to work.

What happened on board the M-K Electra that day has been told mainly from the viewpoint of Robert Gebo, who was not only on board but was given the privilege of serving as copilot. His interest in flying got him into the copilot's seat and from there he got a clear picture of what happened during the flight. The information came mainly from Gebo's answers to questions asked by Ethel Dassow, which were then published in an article entitled "The Gillam Plane Was Missing". This came out in the July 1943 issue of *The Alaskan Sportsman*. A small part of the information not reported in the article was given by Gebo directly to the CAB investigators (an official copy of the CAB report is attached to the end of this chapter).

Gebo's opening statement set the stage and provided basic information about the flight and its passengers. He stated,

> We had no sense of impending doom as we boarded the plane for a flight from Seattle to Anchorage. It was mere routine for me. I had flown the same route many times before; and, despite the disastrous interruption of that ill-fated journey, I shall probably fly it again...

At this point things were normal and Gebo continued with an introduction of those on board as he temporarily assumed the role of a modern-day flight attendant by handing out lunches. He went on,

> Harold Gillam, our pilot was a veteran of the Alaska airways...I'd been in Anchorage as construction engineer with the Morrison-Knudsen Company, and was returning there from spending the Christmas holidays with my wife and small son.

> After about a half-hour I went back into the cabin and distributed a lunch to the other passengers. The three husky men were no novices to the air. Percy Cutting of Hayward, California, was returning from a vacation at home. Joseph Tibbits, a CAA mechanical maintenance man at Anchorage, had been to Ogden, Utah, to visit his sick mother. Dewey Metzdorf, resident of Anchorage, had been Outside on a business trip.

> Miss Susan Batzar, a young stenographer from Idaho Falls, had joined the CAA only recently and was on her way to work in the Anchorage office. Whether she had flown before, I don't know.

276

One passenger, William Loftholm, who was mentioned earlier in this chapter, missed the flight by three hours. The person driving him in to Seattle had miscalculated the wartime gas rationing coupons needed and was delayed getting additional ones.

Gebo continues his relaxed narration of the flight.

We passed over Alert Bay at about 10,000 feet. The weather was clear and the flight uneventful…Gillam went on instruments about four hours out of Seattle. In about fifteen minutes we picked up the Annette Range on our radio and followed the A side of the beam. About forty-five minutes later, after computing time and average speed, I advised Gillam that we were thirty or forty miles from Annette Island where we expected to land.

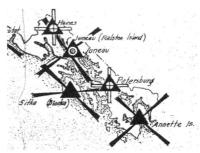

Low frequency radio ranges were new to Alaska in 1941. (Civil Aeronautics Authority- Airway Engineering Division)

Referring now to the CAB report, Ketchikan Radio noted that Gillam was making proper turns for an instrument landing but the compass headings to be followed were incorrect. This caused Ketchikan Radio to comment, "Gillam and Gebo were at least temporarily lost."

The incorrect compass headings stemmed from the Coast Guard's making various heading changes for the Annette Island Radio Range. These changes were duly noted on a revised chart which was then published and made available to pilots. Gillam had not obtained the most recent chart showing the changes, nor had he noted them on the chart he usually made notes on, the one he always carried with him in the cockpit.

The CAB report continued, "According to Gebo both were confused by the radio range signals they were receiving and Gillam was preparing to use his radio direction finder equipment at the time the left engine stopped."

In other words, as soon as Gillam was unsure of the radio range's reliability for the instrument landing he immediately made the decision to switch to his ADF. He was obviously prevented from doing so by the left engine's failure. The CAB report, therefore, cited the engine failure as the primary cause of the accident. It of course, also cites Gillam's failure to have current charts in the cockpit as a strong contributing factor. How strong a factor it turned out to be is discussed in Chapter 23.

The reactions of one passenger, Percy Cutting, right before the crash appeared in *Alaska Life* and is given below,

> The pilot was preparing for an emergency landing. We all knew we were going to crash, but there was no sign of hysteria. Everyone was cool and calm. The pilot leveled off to about 70 miles an hour. I said to myself, "This is the end," and I braced myself for the end like you brace yourself in a dentist's chair to have your tooth pulled. The side of the mountain seemed to meet us and we crashed.

The CAB report gave the following accurate and detailed account of Gillam's actions in this emergency situation,

> ....at an altitude of 7,000 feet the left engine stopped. Pilot Gillam called Ketchikan radio and advised them that their left engine had failed and he thought they were in trouble. About this time a violent downdraft caught the aircraft and the pilot became so busy in an attempt to recover normal flight attitude that further effort to communicate with Ketchikan by radio were abandoned. The plane broke out of a ragged overcast at an elevation of 2,500 feet, headed in a northerly direction and parallel to a ridge of mountains. There were other mountains ahead. Gillam turned off the right engine, headed toward a clearing on the side of the mountain, and pulled the plane up into a stalled attitude for a crash landing. The right wing contacted and sheared two tall trees at mid-height and the plane swerved to the right about 90 degrees, struck the ground on the stub of the broken right wing and bottom of the fuselage, and stopped in an upright position.

All lives aboard the Lockheed Electra were saved by Harold Gillam's last acts as a pilot during the forced landing in the rugged mountains of Southeastern Alaska. The following chapter will deal with the unbelievable heroism of those survivors. The survivors include one young woman whose life Gillam could not save. The CAB report told it well when it stated, "The accident resulted in critical injuries to Miss Susan Winch Batzer which proved fatal about 48 hours later for lack of medical attention." She died of blood loss from a severed artery in her hand which was trapped in the torn fuselage.

Considering Gillam's many years of safe flying with no loss of life, let's hope that it gave him comfort during those last few days of his own life to know that he had come so close.

Adopted: August 25, 1943

File No. 1299-43

REPOREPORT OF THE CIVIL AERONAUTICS BOARD
on the
Investigation of an Accident Involving Aircraft in a
Cross-Country Commercial Flight

An accident occurred on January 5, 1943, at approximately 6:30 p.m. on a heavily-timbered mountainside, about 30 miles east of Ketchikan, Alaska, at an elevation of approximately 2400 feet above sea level. The accident resulted in critical injuries to Miss Susan Winch Batzer which proved fatal about 48 hours later for lack of medical attention. Robert Gebo and Dewey Metzdorf were seriously injured, while Joseph H. Tippets and Percy Cutting received minor injuries. Pilot Harold Gillam was apparently uninjured in the accident but in an effort to summon aid to his injured passengers he perished by exposure and freezing. His remains were found on February 6, 1943, on the shores of the Boca de Quadra Inlet, approximately 7 miles from the scene of the accident. Gillam held a commercial pilot certificate with single and multi-engine 150-865 h.p., land, sea and instrument ratings, and had accumulated approximately 7412 hours of flying time, about 757 of which were in the type of aircraft involved. He was physically qualified, properly rated and certificated for the flight involved. Gebo, who was acting as copilot, was not certificated as an airman. The aircraft, a 10-passenger Lockheed Electra 10-B, NC 14915, powered by two 412 h.p. Wright engines and owned by the Morrison-Knudsen Company, a construction firm with a branch office at Anchorage, Alaska, was demolished.

Due to the unavailability of an Air Safety Investigator of the Civil Aeronautics Board in the Territory of Alaska, an investigation at the scene of the accident was conducted by E. S. Gull, a Senior Aeronautical Inspector of the Civil Aeronautics Administration, stationed at Anchorage. Accordingly, from the information furnished by the Civil Aeronautics Administration, which included statements of witnesses and survivors, the Board now makes its report as follows:

Pilot Gillam obtained clearance for a cross-country flight from Boeing Field, Seattle, Washington to Annette Island, Alaska, and after receiving weather data, took off at approximately 1:27 p.m. He plotted his course to follow the Victoria leg of the Seattle Range. According to Gebo, who occupied the copilot's seat and assisted with the navigation, and statements of two of the passengers, one a CAA inspector and the other an uncertificated aircraft and engine mechanic, the flight proceeded contact under broken clouds at an altitude of from 3000 to 3500 feet. After passing over Victoria, about 30 minutes after take-off, the pilot laid a course along the east side of Vancouver Island and climbed to an altitude of approximately 9000 feet and over the broken clouds. About 3 hours out of Seattle, over Alert Bay, the course was changed to 300° and the flight entered an overcast at about 5:10 p.m., then proceeded on instruments. At approximately 5:25 p.m. they picked up the Annette radio range and followed the "A" side of the southeast leg. At about 6:25 p.m. Copilot Gebo computed the speed and estimated their position to be 30 or 40 miles from Annette Island, their destination. According to Gebo, the course was then changed to the left to 245° compass heading and they proceeded until they crossed what they thought was the southeast leg but which was actually the east leg of the Ketchikan Range. A short time later they crossed what they thought was the cone of

279

silence and after flying on the same heading for 3 minutes, made a 180°
turn. It required 6 minutes to return to the same apparent position. The
then turned to a course of 11° and at an altitude of approximately 7000 fe
the left engine stopped. Pilot Gillam called Ketchikan radio and advised
them that their left engine had failed and he thought they were in trouble.
About this time a violent downdraft caught the aircraft and the pilot beca
so busy in an attempt to recover normal flight attitude that further effor
to communicate with Ketchikan by radio was abandoned. The plane broke out
of a ragged overcast at an elevation of 2500 feet, headed in a northerly
direction and parallel to a ridge of mountains. There were other mountain
ahead. Gillam turned off the right engine, headed toward a clearing on
the side of the mountain, and pulled the plane up into a stalled attitude
for a crash landing. The right wing contacted and sheared two tall trees
at mid-height, and the plane swerved to the right about 90°, struck the
ground on the stub of the broken right wing and bottom of the fuselage,
and stopped in an upright position.

The four survivors remained lost for a period of 29 days following the
accident, during which time an extensive air, land, and water search was
carried on over large areas east and south of Ketchikan and up into Britis
Columbia. After continuing the hazardous search during winter weather for
a period of approximately three weeks, the party was given up for lost and
the search was abandoned. On February 3, 1943, two of the survivors search
ing for aid came upon a United States Coast Guard patrol boat in Weasel
Cove on Boca de Quadra Inlet and the remaining two were rescued from their
camp on February 7, by civilian guides and Coast Guard personnel.

Investigation revealed that Gillam had consulted personnel of the
Weather Bureau at Boeing Field prior to his departure. He studied the
surface and winds aloft charts, the hourly reports and Pan American Airways
spot weather reports, and was advised that the overcast condition extended
over the coastal route with occasional breaks in the lower layers, occasio
al light rains and moderate icing and precipitation. After deciding to
take the coastal route, he was again cautioned about icing conditions to b
expected in clouds. He was informed that winds aloft would be around 270°,
with velocities of 30 to 40 m.p.h. above 6000 feet and reduced velocities
at lower levels. He was offered a copy of the United States and Alaska
codes for obtaining weather, which he declined, remarking that if he neede
further weather data he would declare an emergency and get the report in th
clear.

The Fraser River Aeronautical Chart being used by Pilot Gillam, and
which was recovered from the wreckage, was out of date and showed the
Annette Island Radio Range incorrectly. The southeast leg heading had bee
changed 5° from 117° to 122° magnetic, while the northeast leg heading had
been changed 39° from 27° to 66° magnetic, several months previously and
these new headings had been flight checked and were shown on the current
aeronautical charts. Evidently it was this change that confused the pilot,
although he had ample opportunity to acquaint himself with the current hea
ings. According to Gillam's chart, which had his proposed course outlined
in pencil, he had not made these corrections. He had also invited error
by labelling the bi-sectors, which he drew on the chart in true rather
than magnetic headings since the variation was 29° east. No attempt was
made en route to contact the ground stations by radio to verify the Annette
Island range headings or to report the progress of the flight. Radio

reception was good, according to Gebo, and their radio transmission was subsequently reported by the Army Control Tower at Annette Island as satisfactory. It is quite evident that Gillam and Gebo were at least temporarily lost. According to Gebo both were confused by the radio range signals they were receiving and Gillam was preparing to use his radio direction finder equipment at the time the left engine stopped. They had not used their direction finder equipment to establish their track or position at any time during the flight, nor had they reported their position since leaving Seattle, which made the unsuccessful search more difficult.

Just prior to their departure from Seattle, Gillam's attention was called to an oil leak on the discharge line from the vacuum pump vent to the top of the oil tank. As the line was one to handle overflow rather than a feed line the break was not considered serious. However, it was mended temporarily by the use of friction tape and shellac. According to the CAA inspector who examined the wreckage, this temporary mend had not parted and in no way could have contributed to the engine stoppage.

On account of the remoteness of the wilderness where the accident occurred the left engine was not returned to Ketchikan for examination to ascertain the cause of its failure, therefore, it was not determined whether the stoppage was due to lack of oil or fuel or to some mechanical failure.

While the stoppage of the left engine from an undetermined cause in extremely rough weather and over hazardous terrain undoubtedly was the primary cause of the accident, it is apparent that strong contributing factors were the pilot's failure (1) to equip himself with an up-to-date aeronautical chart and (2) to utilize the radio aids available to him to accurately establish the position of the flight while on instruments.

BY THE BOARD

/s/ Fred A. Toombs
Secretary

094

Chapter 22
THE RESCUE

We were human beings rather than impersonal objects of energy.
(*Sir Gordon Taylor The Sky Beyond*)

The details of what happened after the crash came directly from two sources. The first was Gebo, whose statements were published in the July 1943 issue of the *Alaskan Sportsman*. The other was Percy Cutting. His statements were made to Kathryn Eckroth and published in the August 1943 issue of *Alaska Life*.

What happened right after the crash was a bit chaotic. For a moment all were rendered unconscious from the impact. Cutting, though, seemed to recover more quickly and gave facts mixed with emotion. He stated,

> When I regained consciousness my legs were lodged in the seat in front of me. The only one I could see was Gillam, who was crawling out of the top of the ship...I finally extricated myself. Joe Tippets, Harold Gillam and I gathered around the plane—shaking each other, looking each other over frantically and asking wild questions like "Are you hurt?" "Sure you're all right?" "You're cut, Gillam." And "What's the matter with your leg, Percy?" We were in a dazed condition and seemed unable to believe we were still alive. (Even the reader must experience some sense of awe at the realization that all occupants of a fast twin engine aircraft crashing against a mountain side survived with but relatively minor injuries)
>
> Then we came to our senses and started looking for our companions. Bob Gebo was stuck in the copilot's seat and we pulled him out. We found Dewey Metzdorf among the baggage and rescued him. In order to get to Susan, we had to tear out all the seats....She was on the floor with her right arm sticking out through the side of the ship...Her wrist was broken and the bones were protruding. It was bleeding profusely.

At this point the men knew Susan's condition, although restricted to her right hand, was serious. Both Gebo's and Cutting's words communicated what those men, most of them also suffering injuries, did to save this young girl's life. And then, when they knew this was hopeless, what they did to make her next 48 hours as comfortable as if she were in a hospital bed. They did everything but give her the blood transfusions she so desperately needed.

Because Cutting seemed more emotionally moved by Susan's plight, what happened will be presented through his words,

> It took us two hours to free her and then we worked like madmen to stop the bleeding, but we all realized our measures were only temporary ones. We did everything possible to make her comfortable. She was put in one of the sleeping bags and all the available blankets were placed around her. It was impossible to move her, so we kept her in the plane.

> My injured leg was acting up so badly that I rolled up in a blanket near the pilot's cockpit.

Gebo, who had been up front in the cockpit with Gillam, suffered perhaps more than his share of injuries. Much later they discovered he had suffered a broken leg and broken arm. This condition led to less physical activity and naturally to frozen limbs. On the other hand, being physically incapacitated may have helped him recall and note with greater vividness the courage demonstrated by this small band of survivors struggling to keep each other alive.

To Cutting's narration of help and care given to Susan, Gebo added this detail,

> Tippets and Cutting had gone back with Gillam to free Susan…Tippets and Gillam spent all that first night working over Susan. They made her as comfortable as they could with seat cushions, and put a wing cover over the holes in the fuselage to keep the rain off her.

Cutting poignantly suggested additional ways the four men expressed their compassion for this girl in those hours before death overtook her. He stated,

> That night the rest of the party stood up all night under the other wing cover. The rain and sleet slashed down without a letup, making it miserable for them…I stayed inside the plane trying to help Susan. She was in constant pain, but I never in my life have seen

her equal. She was so brave that I had to brace myself to keep from breaking down in front of her...Susan was still conscious, so far. She had not been delirious. However, we could see that her strength was dwindling fast. She knew that she was dying, and I repeat that I had never seen her equal. She didn't utter a word of complaint. She had complete hold of herself until the last. At six that evening, she died quietly and courageously. We forgot thoughts of our own difficulties in tribute to this girl who met death so unflinchingly.

Of course life had to go on. Susan's body was moved gently to the tail of the plane and covered with her coat. There the body lay until, as Gebo so poetically expressed it,

Susan's body lay in the plane, beneath fall after fall of pure mountain snow. Early in March a Coast Guard party was able to reach the plane and bring her body down to Ketchikan, where it was taken to her hometown for burial.

On the day of Susan's death, Thursday, January 7, the second day after the crash, Gillam was already working on a comfortable shelter for the living. As Gebo described it,

On the third day Gillam made camp under the left wing. The wing was wedged up against the mountain, forming a shelter. He and Tippets scooped the snow out from under the wing, and left snow walls which made the shelter comparatively windproof. The space was four or five feet high, with room for four of us to lie down. With fir boughs and some seat cushions from the plane, we were more comfortable than we had been before....On Friday (January 8) we dug the shelter out a little more, Cutting was feeling better and able to get out of the ship. We had two sleeping bags and five blankets and all of us spread out on the snow floor of our shelter. It wasn't cold then. It rained all the time until Friday...

Friday, January 8 was the first clear day. It may have been Saturday, the ninth. Gebo's and Cutting's reports conflict on this point. Two search planes were sighted; one circled on a ridge some distance from them. Again there was a slight difference between Cutting's and Gebo's report on the survivors' reaction upon sighting the planes. Cutting reported magnesium flares were fired and the survivors were shouting. Gebo made no mention of this. Since Gillam was still at the camp on that date, it seems strange that he would not have set off magnesium flares. Perhaps not. These flares give off a white light which would have little chance of being seen in daylight against a background of white snow. He might well have cautioned against wasting this valuable signaling device.

In any case, were they disappointed at not being sighted? Yes. However, as Gebo stated,

> We felt sure they were looking for us, but we didn't feel badly disappointed that they didn't find us that time. After all, they were the first planes we'd seen, and we really felt encouraged. The attitude was still, "They will find us and we'll be okay."

Gillam apparently didn't agree with this optimistic view. Obviously he intended to take a more active part in their rescue. That next morning, Sunday, January 10 he left in search of help. Gebo gave the following account of his leaving,

> By Sunday the ground was frozen hard. Gillam and Cutting went up the ridge to see how the land lay…when they came back, Gillam gathered up a box of raisins, a can of sardines, a few bouillon cubes, matches, a parachute, and some magnesium flares from the plane. He said he would go back up the ridge and build a signal fire, as the weather was very clear. If he saw something favorable he would go on. He never came back, and no one ever saw him again.

Monday, the day after Gillam left, was still clear and a search plane came near. It was in the valley, though, and didn't see the survivors. Cutting kept a signal fire going all day. That Monday night it began raining again with some snow. This kept up till Thursday night. The men stayed in their shelter, talking and waiting. While talking, they must have discussed what favorable thing Gillam might have seen that moved him to leave camp. Cutting would have mentioned the water he and Gillam had seen from the ridge. The thoughts that developed during those days of waiting for the rain and snow to end were probably best contained in this statement by Gebo,

> This was Monday, the seventh day after our forced landing. We discussed the possibility of immediate rescue, and decided that the food might have to last us as long as two weeks. We put everything into one pile and each ate the same amount each meal.

Certainly survival was on Cutting's mind when, on the next clear day, he went back up to the ridge and saw the same patch of water he and Gillam had seen before. After coming back down, he made his report.

The next morning he took a sleeping bag, a little food, and the.22 rifle, then set off down toward the water. It took him the full day, Saturday, January 16, to arrive at what was later identified as Smeaton Bay. He set up a signal fire and stayed there Sunday and Monday. He returned Tuesday completely exhausted but with four spruce hens. Cutting felt his bad news—that he found no sign of life at the water—was offset by the four spruce hens. He was right. The lack of food was now becoming critical. Gebo stated,

> By this time we were feeling less optimistic about prospects of rescue. Two full weeks had past very slowly, just waiting in the snow. We talked the matter over and decided that our best hope lay in moving camp to the base of the mountain where our signal fires could be seen from planes flying low along the valley.

Gebo's statement indicated the survivors felt less hopeful about being found from the air. True, they mentioned that low-flying planes might be better able to see them. They were also discouraged by "just waiting in the snow." No planes had been heard or seen since the three appeared immediately after that first weekend. The hopes of the little band would have been severely shaken had they known why no additional planes were heard. There seemed to be an intuitive desire to move closer to the water, a feeling that water might bring about their rescue. In the end it did.

Meanwhile, the move down the mountain was put off until Cutting had regained his strength. He and Tippets were the ones who would mainly be depended on to do the job. The move took its toll as Gebo and Metzdorf, weakened by hunger and swollen feet, found it difficult to keep going. As Gebo said, "We were simply to weak to drag all our stuff any further. So we left about half of it along the way."

The ordeal of moving had almost been finished by Saturday afternoon, January 23. The urgent need for food, though, persisted. Again Cutting lifted the morale of all with his marksmanship. This time Cutting reported on the situation. He said,

> Around two in the afternoon of the next day, we arrived at the foot of the mountain. Our camp was established in an open area. I built a lean-to of the canvas from the plane while Joe continued to move bundles to the foot of the mountain. We just couldn't move all the stuff that night. Our spirits were bolstered again when I shot a squirrel. I boiled it and made soup. We all agreed it was "delicious."

Sunday was cold and snowy. Time was spent finishing the lean-to and moving the rest of the blankets. The rest of the day they spent around the fire, trying to stay warm. Their meal for that day was a bouillon cube and a small piece of chocolate each. The camp was now much closer to Smeaton Bay, but the food supply was down to almost nothing. On Monday, January 25, it was still cold and snowy and Cutting was weak from hunger, but went hunting. The events of that day brought a sudden change in Cutting's point of view about being rescued. He stated,

> I became more depressed when I didn't see any game. Right then and there I made up my mind that if we all stayed there waiting for help, we'd die of starvation. Someone had to go and find it, or we'd never be found on time.

> When I returned, I told Gebo and Metzdorf, "We can't last more than a few more days without food, so I'm going to try to get outside and locate help." Gebo then said, "If you most go, take Tippets with you. Two of you have a better chance of getting out alive."

This put Cutting in a bind. He explained it this way,

> I didn't go much for that idea. Neither of them could get around without crawling and I didn't like to leave them alone, but they insisted.

> So for the rest of the day Joe and I worked to get a supply of wood for them, to fill every container with water, and to put everything in reach of them.

> Before we left the next day (January 26), we gave them the remaining food. It consisted of a bouillon cube each and two tablespoons of tea. We each took a cup of hot water to warm us up.

> It was snowing hard when we set out. I was determined we would make saltwater that night or die in the attempt....All day long we hiked without a stop, for we felt that if we sat down for a rest we would never get up again. Just as we began to think that we could never make it, we saw the water ahead. Our hardships were forgotten temporarily as we ran toward the beach.

The joy they felt on reaching the bay may simply have stemmed from reaching their goal. Or it may have stemmed from a mysterious attraction this body of water held for them. No one can be certain. Cutting then explained what happened next,

We made our camp at this spot, which we found out later was Weasel Cove on Boca De Quadra Inlet. We had roasted squirrel for dinner, which was a tasty dish to say the least. It was an unforgettable night, so cold that we felt we would melt away like icicles if we ever warmed up.

The next morning, January 27, dawned with clear skies and the two men made plans to contact the outside world for help. Their first goal was to reach an unoccupied cabin on the opposite shore. It was only about 7 or 8 hundred feet across at this point.

Cutting and Tippets were relatively young men. Their exact ages are not known. It would seem reasonable, though, to assume that, given the dangers and hardships they endured during the nine-day period, from January 26 to February 4, they had to possess the stamina associated with youth. What else can be said about the basic nature of these two young men? Their courage and resolve were readily apparent from their actions. Perhaps not apparent was their subtle humor. It seemed to persist in the face of frustrating events. Quite possibly, it was humor that helped them persevere in the face of these seemingly hopeless situations. This humor was indeed subtle and showed only in carefully selected words—words that one would hardly expect to hear in the given situations. In addition, some of their attitudes and actions seemed to defy common sense. The term "reckless abandon" may well come to mind. Finally, through it all, their attitudes and actions conveyed, subconsciously for the most part, high ideals—loyalty, responsibility, and self-sacrifice among others, as they steadfastly pursued the goal of saving the lives of their helpless fellow-survivors as well as their own.

After some thought on how to reach the unoccupied cabin, they saw driftwood logs. This suggested a raft. By late afternoon the work was completed. They then set out toward the cabin. The raft, its logs bound together with strips cut from their highly prized blankets, refused to hold the intended shape needed for forward propulsion. At last, by leaving Tippets behind and by lying on his stomach and paddling with his hands, Cutting made it across.

What happened next was expressed in Cutting's words,

The cabin was abandoned…I found one can of cinnamon, one can of cayenne pepper and one cup of rice, with the weevils working on it. I was lucky to find a single-man dory, badly in need of repair, one pot of tar and some small boards.

With my booty loaded on my raft and the dory tied on, I began my trip back. In the middle of the stream, the tide and wind got hold of the raft. It took me downstream three miles. Poor Joe tried to follow me down the beach, but it was impossible because of the rocks, I finally made the beach...it was late at night and I was plenty tired. By poling and using the branches from the shore, I managed to get the raft within a mile of the camp...

At this point, Joe met me and I ambled along behind him to where our campfire was burning. It looked swell to us. We immediately cooked half of our weeviled rice and were so hungry we thought it tasted fine.

It was so cold that night that we spent most of the time jumping around to keep warm. Our blankets were down to two.

The next day, January 28, they ate the rest of their weeviled rice and started to patch up the dory with tar and pieces of their blankets. Their goal? Get over to the cabin. Cutting told what happened then.

About three o'clock, we finished repairing and began our voyage to the trapper's cabin. When we were 50 feet from the other side, one of the seams opened up and we started to sink. Out we went, swimming and pulling the boat in with us. Our rifle was wet and we were soaked to the skin.

In the trapper's cabin we made a stove out of an oil can. It was heaven to have a roof over our heads. We took off our clothes and wrung them out. Millionaires had nothing on us—we had a cabin, a stove, and three crows I had shot...

We never lost the urgent feeling, though, that the lives of the other two men depended on our getting help, so we were busy again the next day repairing our boat.

It was then that they sighted an old cannery about five miles down the inlet. They hurriedly finished the repairs and took off to explore. Nothing there, no food. Since they now had the cabin as a shelter, they thought of burning the cannery to get somebody's attention. Then they saw the sign, "Do not destroy" signed by the owner and figured some guy might be planning to make it his home. So they left and started back to their cabin. It took seven hours to make the round trip.

That same evening they noticed their inlet extended to the open sea. The next morning, January 30, they decided to try for the open

water. There they might get in touch with a passing boat. Again
Cutting described what happened.

> Bad weather was coming up, but we didn't have brains enough to
> stay put. After two hours' rowing, a sudden wind and ground swells
> swamped our dory. We lost our overcoats, cooking utensils, every-
> thing but the clothing we had on and our rifle. We swam ashore…As
> always in our worst predicament, it began to snow.

Their bodies seemed able to withstand the extremely cold water.
However, they wasted no time getting to shore and wringing out
their clothes. Then they started walking around the cove back to
their cabin. Before getting there, they heard a boat's motor and caught
sight of a Coast Guard patrol boat. It was on the inlet coming toward
them. But before they could get out and be seen, it turned away. It
was gone but they still had hope and built a fire in front of the cabin,
which they kept burning for three hours.
They went to bed without food that night, wondering what had happened to Gillam and thinking of the guys they left behind. Obviously
they were discouraged and Cutting made this clear.

> It was the 31st of January and we had been lost for almost a month.
> We were worn out and disillusioned. No more attempts to reach
> open water for us. We put a rag on a pole on the beach, prepared
> wood for future signal flares, arranged a continuous watch and sat
> down to wait for rescue. That day we saw the tail end of another
> boat going out of the inlet, too late to signal.

> We watched all day on the first of February for the sign of a boat.
> In the afternoon we were so weak from hunger we caught some
> mussels and prepared to die from poison if not from starvation.

> We ate about ten or twelve, questioning each other constantly about
> whether we felt any pains or signs of poisoning. It was funny that
> night. You know how a person's stomach rattles when it's empty.
> Ours did that all night, which seemed a sure sign to us that we
> were goners. It was quite a surprise to find we were still alive the
> next day. So we had some of the shellfish for breakfast.

The next day, February 2, they were up watching, listening, and
eating more mussels. Around five in the afternoon they heard a motor and ran to the beach, waved, and started fires. The boat kept right
on across the bay, up the inlet and out of sight. That setback was a

real blow. This time they had been ready and did everything right. They went back to the cabin not saying a word to each other. Cutting told what came next.

> Then we heard motors again. When we went to the door, we saw a boat coming out of the other inlet with lights. We immediately went out on the beach and prepared a big fire. The boat came north toward our camp, but it stopped about four or five miles away. We watched for three hours, keeping the fire burning with magnesium flares from the wreckage...The boat stayed there in a fixed position as though it were going to anchor there...

> Joe and I took turns watching that night. About six o'clock the next morning, it began to snow and fog came down over the inlet. We lighted another fire, feeling that if he had seen the previous one, he would know for sure there was someone in distress. As it grew lighter, I could no longer see the lights of the boat. In fact, I couldn't see the boat because of the background of mountains, timber, and rocks. We began to think he had started up in the storm and we hadn't heard him.

> Joe lay down heartsick and hungry...

> It came to me then that if I would only get a pan of mussels and roasted them, the boat would come for us and I wouldn't have to eat them. Our luck seemed to be like that. The harder we tried the more it seemed to buck our efforts. So I went ahead and put some on to roast. They were half done when I heard motors on the bay.

In order not to bolster any false hopes and disappointments, they kept telling each other that they didn't hear any boat motor sounds. Finally Cutting could hold out no longer. They both went outside and Cutting relates the happy ending,

> The boat kept coming closer and closer. We knew he had seen us. We dashed back to the cabin, picked up our belongings and were back on the shore in no time.

> It was a Coast Guard patrol boat and they were already launching a skiff. Our frayed nerves snapped. We acted like a couple of crazy loons, hugging one another, bawling and waving our rags frantically. It was the most wonderful sight in my life as the boys rowed the skiff to the rocks.

"Who're you?" they questioned us.

It seemed unbelievable that they wouldn't know who we were. "We're two of the survivors of the Morrison-Knudsen airplane crash almost a month ago" we managed to get out between sobs.

On board the *SS Tucson*, Captain A.W. Angellson thought we were a couple of trappers. We must have looked like a couple of filthy scarecrows to him. I had an old rag on my head for a hat and my clothes were so dirty that a self-respecting louse wouldn't have stayed on me. Joe was in the same condition. His feet were wrapped up in blankets, for he had no shoes. Our hands were blackened and badly cut up. Our whiskers were about an inch and a half long. Our eyes were haggard and we looked like a couple of bean poles.

From there the captain took over and the patrol boat was theirs. When they immediately told about the two helpless men waiting for help, he volunteered to lead his men to the survivors' camp and give them first aid. Both Cutting and Tippets insisted they needed to lead the rescue party to insure that the camp could be located as quickly as possible.

The Captain then ran the patrol boat full speed to the Ketchikan Coast Guard Base. Here medical staff would be standing by to prepare Cutting and Tippets for a morning departure as leaders of a rescue party.

The hospital staff met the patrol boat with waiting wheelchairs which the two men proudly refused. They walked themselves into the sick bay. The evening was completely taken up—first with medical attention, followed by what would make them feel more human: showers, shaves, haircuts, street clothes and so forth. Then came food, and finally, rest between fresh sheets.

Up to this point neither Tippets or Cutting knew for certain that Gebo and Metzdorf were still alive. In their hearts, though, they would believe nothing less.

And what was happening to the incapacitated survivors back at the camp while Tippets and Cutting were making their seemingly hopeless effort to locate and get help? Gebo could only give disconnected glimpses of what happened to him and Metzdorf during their nine-day ordeal of waiting. Gebo made these brief comments:

Meanwhile Metzdorf and I were just lying there in our lean-to. I had fallen and dislocated my wrist, and that, along with my swollen feet, left me nearly helpless. How the time passed I don't know.

Each minute seemed like an hour, and each hour seemed like a week. Once we made some tea, and another time we used the bouillon cubes. Once, too, which night I don't remember because they were all so much alike and it didn't seem to matter, we woke up to find three inches of water standing around us. It had turned warmer during the night, and the snow had started to melt. Everything was wet—our clothes, our blankets, and all.

We built a fire with the last of our wood, and dried out what clothing we could. We moved our bedding to the other side of the lean-to, putting canvas from the front of the lean-to underneath us, and our extra clothing on top of that. The wet blankets we spread over the lean-to door.

Meanwhile, it seems that an early attempt to reach the survivors by air, to assure them that help was on its way, failed. It happened this way. Captain Angellson had immediately notified the Coast Guard Base that he had two survivors on board but that two more were still at a camp in the valley not far from Weasel Cove and the Boca De Quada inlet. A young naval lieutenant, Gantry, took off in his float plane to see if he could locate the camp. He reported the weather was too thick and that he had to return without information. Actually, without seeing the camp, he had made his turn back to base near enough for Gebo to have heard the plane's engine as it turned back. Gebo stated the following:

On Wednesday neither of us even stirred from bed. At about dark on Wednesday a plane circled over the camp. We were helpless to do anything to attract attention, and we couldn't know then that Cutting and Tippets had been found, and that rescuers would soon be on their way. I can't describe the desolation we felt when the roar of that motor died in the distance. With that fading sound we composed our minds and prepared to die too.

Thus this humanitarian act, intended to assure the survivors that help was at hand, ended up having the opposite effect. The next morning, though, the good news arrived. Tippets had left in the patrol boat for Smeaton Bay while Cutting took off with Ray Renshaw of the Game Commission in his floatplane loaded with blankets and food. Once the fog lifted, Cutting immediately located the camp. He saw one man outside the shelter as Renshaw flew over and rocked the plane's wings. Cutting didn't recognize who it was but knew that if one were alive so was the other. As Cutting pushed the bundles out the plane's door, he was filled with a sense of completion. Now he knew that they knew. The waiting and the uncertainty were over.

Next, Renshaw landed by the patrol boat in Smeaton Bay and Cutting climbed aboard. After leaving the boat, the rescue party traveled overland for the remainder of that day and well into the night. As they came near the general location of the camp, darkness made movement difficult. This and the remote possibility they might miss the camp led the party to halt.

Courage of the group brought success. *(Coast Guard Reserve Party/Courtesy Alaska Sportsman July 1943)*

They fired shots to assure the survivors that their rescuers were near. Gebo described the meeting.

> That night we heard gunshots in the timber. Other human beings were within hearing. Oh, praise the Lord! Early Friday morning they came, twenty Coast Guardsmen under the leadership of Art Hook, Ed Higginbothem, and Fred Hill; and with them, in order to direct the party with the least possible delay, were Cutting and Tippets! Worn out as they were from their long ordeal, they still had managed to master enough strength to come back for our rescue.
>
> Metzdorf and I broke down and blubbered with reckless abandon. The others blubbered too. No one could feel ashamed of his emotions at such a time as that! The gratitude I felt toward those men is something I could never express.

Tippets and Cutting, with an escort, were sent back down and taken by boat to the hospital. The Coast Guardmen worked on a shelter for the survivors and themselves, while the base pharmacist concerned himself with medical matters. Another contingent of Coast Guardsmen arrived on Saturday, enough to carry the survivors out on makeshift sleds to a patrol boat. On Sunday morning, February 7, the survivors, bundled on sleds, were moved slowly down to Smeaton Bay, arriving there at 4:30 p.m. and arriving at the base hospital that same night.

So ended the saga. The Coast Guardsmen were rewarded by the emotional outburst toward them by the survivors. The survivors will be long remembered for their courage and loyalty to each other. There is, however, one person who, because she was a part of this saga but for a brief moment, would probably not be long remembered; but she should. Susan Winch Batzer has been cited earlier for her exceptional courage in facing her own death. But is it not possible that those who struggled with such courage and hope in

Competent hands, minds and hearts at work. (Coast Guard Reserve Party/Courtesy Alaska Sportsman July 1943)

situations that seemed so hopeless; might they not have been helped to do so by Susan's example? Is it possible that they made a subconscious connection between dying courageously and living courageously? Gebo said what many of the survivors felt in their hearts, *"My greatest regrets are for that prince of men, Harold Gillam, and for Susan Batzer, whose young life was so sadly interrupted."*

Gebo and the other crash survivors were influenced by Susan Batzer's courage as she faced death. However, as these men returned to their routine lives and after the Coast Guard brought Susan's body from the wreckage and it was sent to her home in Idaho for burial; after this chain of events one suspects she would be forgotten. Yet some 40 years later, in 1982, two men, Bucky Dawson and Gerry Bruder, visited the crash site.

Young guardsmen-something to ponder and remember. (Coast Guard Reserve Party/Courtesy Alaska Sportsman July 1943)

Dawson's vague reason was to perhaps salvage a piece of the plane to display at the Ketchikan Historical Aircraft Society Museum. He

came away with a fairly intact tail fin of the Electra. Bruder had no specific reason for visiting the site except, perhaps, to experience in some way the drama that had unfolded there so long ago. He was not disappointed. However, he was not prepared to experience the feminine presence of Susan Batzer. He had come with a knowledge of her courageous behavior but his closer association with her can be best explained through an excerpt from an article, "Crash Site Revisited" which he wrote for the Summer 1982 issue of the Alaska Journal. There he wrote:

A journey in time. (Gerry Bruder photo/Courtesy of The Alaska Journal, Summer, 1982)

> Back in the cabin area he (Dawson) found a white shoe, a glove, and some cosmetic jars-all apparently belonged to Batzer. I dug up several more cosmetic jars and a small perfume bottle among the soggy, crumbling remains of a leather suitcase that was partially buried next to the wing.

Bruder then made known his emotional response to Susan's femi-

nine presence with these words, "I wondered what Batzer had looked like, and what her dreams for the future had been."

Is it possible that these emotional responses to Susan through word of mouth and through the printed word being read now and, possibly in the future—that these might keep Susan Batzer and her courage from being forgotten?

A feminine presence recalls an event. (Gerry Burder photo/ Courtesy The Alaska Journal, summer 1982)

Gillam's body was found February 6, a day before all four of the survivors of his crashed plane arrived safely at the Coast Guard hospital. It was found one mile from Weasel Cove on the Boca De Quadra Inlet. This was not far from the spot where Tippets and Cutting camped that first night, and near where the Coast Guard patrol boat rescued them. It was as if, on that Sunday, January 10, he wanted to reach the spot where men in boats passed by; but didn't quite make it.

The attention of searchers traveling on the inlet, immediately after

Tippets and Cutting were rescued, was drawn to red underwear and boots hanging from a tree. When they got out to investigate, they found Gillam's body wrapped in a silk parachute. He must have been greatly in need of rest. Yet knowing his concern for the other survivors, and his purpose, which was to make contact with someone for help, he would not have lain down without first marking the spot in a way that would get a passer-by's attention.

What has been given thus far are facts, but his actual death is surrounded by mystery. Why did he stop at this particular spot, wrap himself in the parachute, apparently to rest? Some say it was pure exhaustion. However, with his intense obligation to find help, exhaustion alone would not have caused him to stop for rest. Why did he die apparently after he lay down to rest? Some would say that the head wound he received in the crash finally caught up with him. This seems an unlikely answer since he lived and actively participated in survival activities for five full days after the crash. Still, no autopsy was performed so the answer cannot be completely rejected. The best suggested answer would be a combination of exhaustion and hypothermia. Only such a lethal mixture could have lulled him into a sleep from which there was no awakening. Yet a definitive answer will remain unknown.

It seems not unreasonable that his body was sent to Fairbanks, where his aviation career had begun. There, last respects were paid at a funeral held on March 5, 1943 at the Elks Hall. The announcement in *Jessen's Weekly* stated there was a large attendance. The pallbearers were James Barrack, Clyde Smith, James Dodson, Noel Wien, Frank Barr, and Thomas Appleton. Most of these were his fellow pilots. His earthly remains were buried in the Clay Street Cemetery along with other pioneer Alaskans. This cemetery is located along the Chena River and but one block from the home he had built in 1937, Where he and his family spent five happy years of their lives. The epi-

A dignity deserved. (Authors photo)

taph on his headstone is brief and appropriate, GREATER LOVE HATH NO MAN.

Many tributes have been written to honor Harold Gillam Senior's memory. An especially heartfelt one was written by Bob Reeve, a fellow pilot, and a friend who often disagreed with Gillam. It was published in the May 1971 issue of *This Alaska*. It read as follows,

He rests in eternal sleep beneath a simple headstone in a Fairbanks cemetery. But this is not his only resting place, nor is the flyer's valhalla where he also lives, nor is his shrine in the Alaska Hall of Fame where he will live in perpetuity as one of Alaska's great. He will always live in the memories and admiration and esteem of Alaska's old-time flyers, as alive today as in the days he ruled Alaska's air in years gone by.

Chapter 23
LEGEND OR LUCKY?

Flying is some fundamental and satisfying
source of personal expression: acquiring a
sense of immortality, an ease of spirit, a confidence.
(Sir Gordon Taylor, The Sky Beyond)

Perhaps it seems trite to title this final chapter on Gillam's life as a pilot, "Legend or Lucky?" Perhaps not. In the very first chapter of this biography the question was raised whether Gillam's life as a pilot, especially his ability to fly weather, deserves legendary status. The chapters that followed narrated his significant flying achievements. It appeared Gillam did possess special aptitudes and applied these especially to achieve in his weather flying. Because of his exceptional success in this area, people talked about him. In the process, many may have exaggerated and thereby possibly given him an undeserved legendary status. Careful research tried to restrict this tendency to exaggerate. However, the author's own bias and the limited information available, made it highly unlikely that the effect of this tendency was eliminated completely.

The question arises, though—how might "luck" have influenced Gillam's exceptional achievements in flying weather? Up to this point "luck" has not been mentioned simply because no one had openly spoken of it as an explanation for Gillam's exceptional performance. It was not until after his final flight that such an explanation was brought forward. This suggests another question—Why did Gillam's final flight provoke individuals to openly challenge his right to legendary status as a weather pilot? Probably no clear answer will be found. However, a detailed examination of the views held by pilots who were Gillam's contemporaries might help us arrive at our own conclusions.

The first example involves Noel Wien, one of Alaska's renowned bush pilots. In a recent interview with his now grown son, Richard, he told how, as a boy, he remembered his dad marveling at how Gillam was able to fly in darkness up through overcast skies and then return to earth through that same weather and darkness. Since Gillam did it twice daily and for many months, regardless of weather, Noel felt chance or luck did not enter in. So he assumed Gillam possessed some unusual or mysterious aptitude combined with his skill. In a very real sense Noel Wien, without exaggerating, was contributing to the legend of Gillam as a weather pilot. Wien prob-

Wien's response to Gillam as a pilot. (Noel Wien photo/ Courtesy R.W. Stevens)

ably did not know that when Gillam had a serious problem getting back down, he devised a primitive radio homing device that helped position him and his plane over the field for future landing. Knowledge of this fact would probably have reduced somewhat the amount of mystery that Wien saw in Gillam's performance. Nevertheless, that the most respected bush pilot in Alaska believed that Gillam possessed, in some degree, a special geographic orientation which allowed him to land the clumsy Pilgrim under those conditions may have led others to reject luck as a factor in Gillam's performance.

Ray Petersen, fellow bush pilot. (Ray Petersen photo)

The second example giving a positive view of Gillam as weather pilot came from Ray Petersen who was a recognized bush pilot and later became president of Northern Consolidated Airways. In a recent interview he described a situation where he and other pilots were stranded by weather at Bethel, on the Kuskokwim River, where they were anxiously waiting to fly out a number of miners from the nearby mines. These men had finished their summer work and needed flights to Anchorage, where they could take the train to Seward, then a steamer on to Seattle where they would spend the winter with family. In the midst of the continuing storm, a plane was heard overhead. It was Gillam on his Fairbanks-Bethel mail route. As the incoming mail was exchanged for the outgoing, Petersen jokingly asked, "Well Harold, I suppose you plan to go back to Fairbanks?" Whereupon Gillam, in a serious tone replied, "No, just to McGrath."

Gillam's arrival and departure during the storm caused a number of the waiting pilots to try for Anchorage. No one made it. Some got partway, but most returned to Bethel. Then Petersen made an important statement. He said, "Most of us experienced pilots weren't embarrassed to admit that Gillam was just better at flying weather than we were." Here again, there was no mention of luck as a factor.

Certainly not all pilots agreed with Petersen's evaluation of Gillam's skills. Among some, a silent resentment may have set in. Such a resentment may have been partially justified. What was overlooked and made Gillam look better than the other pilots were the conditions that favored his success. Gillam had been flying his mail route weekly for a two-year period in good weather and bad. This is the kind of advantage that all bush pilots work toward. Many of the pilots in this example probably had not flown often in this area. Also, Gillam had the advantage of flying over relatively low ground in getting to his destination. The others faced a problem of crossing over the rugged Alaska Range through Rainy Pass. This made a big difference in the other pilots' weather decisions. Thus, a legend can be established not by exaggeration but by simply leaving out crucial data that allows someone like Gillam to fly where others must wait.

The third example is somewhat similar to the Bethel one except it took place at the McGrath Roadhouse. It also involved Gillam flying through on his mail route while the other pilots were holding because of weather. This episode was published in Jean Potter's *The Flying North*. She obtained her information from Dave Clough, the roadhouse owner. Potter, as a journalist, was able to introduce an emotional tone without distorting the facts. More details of Potter's account are included here to give the reader a feeling for the responses of the pilots who continued to "wait out the weather" while Gillam came and went.

Snowflakes whitened the windows of the roadhouse at McGrath. The panes rattled with the wind. The dim afternoon sun was turning to dusk. Besides the Yukon Stove a group of dispirited flyers settled down to another game of poker…They heard it faintly at first over the moan of the wind…No one wondered who the pilot was…the sound of the engine traveled back and forth, louder and louder…Finally the blurred shape of Gillam's Pilgrim appeared just over the runway and plowed to a stop in deep drifts. Gillam, bundled heavily in furs, climbed out and unloaded his sacks…"Where's the mail, Charlie?" he asked the gangly veteran mechanic. "Will you gas me up? I'm going on up to Fairbanks."

He asked for a cup of coffee and stood alone as he drank it, warming his back against the stove…He stood for a moment, hands in his pocket, watching the poker game. Then he walked out not saying a word…Gillam had turned on the landing lights for takeoff, a ring of brightness broke the stormy dusk. All eyes followed the Pilgrim as it came growling back in a trail of white. The plane slowed to a sputtering stop…Gillam tried again and failed. He walked back and asked Charlie to get a tractor. "Make a path just wide enough for the skis"…He sat alone in his ship as the chugging cat broke a runway. Then he gunned the engine and was gone…One of the pilots turned up the radio receiver as they went back to their game…When they woke the next day the snow was still flying, the wind still blowing…By afternoon the men began to worry…They sent a query to Fairbanks…Gillam had landed at his home base on schedule, as he always landed on schedule.

Potter set an emotional tone but allowed the reader to make his or her own judgements as to the waiting pilots' reactions to Gillam's decision to fly when they opted not to. What were the inner reactions of those pilots? Would their later outward expression support the Gillam weather-flying legend? Or would some harbor a silent resentment, having been made to feel lesser pilots than Gillam? The pilots who might have responded negatively, even though not expressing it, could endanger his legend. This seemed to happen in connection with Gillam's final flight.

This last dramatic portrayal of an episode involving Gillam's ability to fly weather also provides an opportunity to examine the whole matter of decision making in flying weather. Much is at stake each time a pilot makes a weather decision. In a very real sense, it can be a-life-or death matter. Wolfgang Langewiesche in his introduction to Robert Buck's *Weather Flying* (1988) gave an unusual slant to weather-flying decisions. After naming the many advantages involved in flying modern planes, Langewiesche pointed out that making weather decisions is still a serious problem, a problem that invites poor choices, especially for the private pilot. He stated,

But the weather is not often clearly impossible. When it is, we have no problem: back to the hotel. On the contrary (as Robert Buck points out) the weather is normally flyable. Again, no problem, or only easy ones. But every once in awhile, depending on season and part of the world, something is sitting out there that worries us. If you fly far enough in a straight line, you're likely to come against some problem weather that very day. How well we deal with those situations determine how well the airplane works.

Too bold, and we cause emergencies and accidents. Too timid, and we destroy utility of the airplane and let our skills as pilots atrophy. Then pretty soon we have to be more timid still.

These weather decisions can be painful to make because we really don't know how to go about making them. And we know we don't know! We make them often by a process which is a dumb confused struggle between "guts" and "judgement", ambition and fear. How it comes out depends on how we felt that day when we last had a good scare, whether the girlfriend is looking, or "the town is full, there is a convention on, you can't get a hotel room, let's go." Things like that tip the balance. And so we "drag the luggage back to town" often for no reasoned cause, or we "fling ourselves into the air" often with only a vague estimate of what's ahead.

Langewiesche pointed out not only that the pilot's weather decisions are important but also that many pilots do not know how to go about making them. Such a situation can lead to error, which in turn holds the potential for tragic results.

Applying Langewiesche's words to Gillam's situation at the McGrath roadhouse, it is obvious he had given thought to all relevant information and that the decision was made before he landed. He gave directions for refueling then relaxed with a cup of coffee while he waited. Obviously his decision did not partake of timidity. Was his decision too bold? Some would answer, yes. However, they are in no position to make that judgement. Only Gillam was entitled to that. Only he could assess the value of his thirteen-odd years of successfully flying weather and of having flown this mail route weekly for almost two years

Frank Barr, Pilgrim advocate; fellow bush pilot and employee of Gillam, makes a down-to-earth evaluation of Gillam as a pilot and as an employer. (Barr Family photo/ Courtesy Alaska Northwest Publishing)

through good weather and bad. Only he knew every flight characteristic of his beloved Pilgrim, its instruments, and their placement on the panel, along with his years of practice in their use.

Gillam's view on decision making in weather situations was not unlike that of Frank Barr, who stated in his biography, "I never tried to fly like anybody else did. I knew what I could do and I knew my plane's limitations." That Gillam recognized the need for his pilots to have the freedom to make their own weather decisions is clearly indicated in a previously quoted statement by Barr about his boss, Gillam. He said, "He never told me how to fly or when to fly or anything else...That's why I liked to work for him."

A pilot's weather decisions are terribly personal. No one but he can gather together the information needed to make such a decision. This is a case where it is easy to state the rule but difficult to practice it.

In the McGrath roadhouse episode being considered here, no one openly questioned Gillam's weather decision. Most did not because it would suggest they had a right to make someone else's weather decisions for him. And what of those who may have silently questioned Gillam's weather decision? These individuals convinced themselves they had a right to do so. Even more dangerous, though, they were subconsciously convincing themselves that they were as good weather pilots as Gillam. Such pilots would be better off remembering old-time bush pilot Ray Petersen's words, "Most of us experienced pilots weren't embarrassed to admit that Gillam was just better at flying weather than we were."

Does this mean that Gillam's weather decisions were not subject to error? Looking at his thirteen years of flying weather without a fatality might tempt one to give the wrong answer. Gillam was human and knew weather was an adversary that would not be soon overcome. However, he never did stop trying to overcome it. People who worked with him and knew him well—Tom Appleton, Cecil Higgins, even Bob Reeve—all admired his continuous efforts to make weather flying safer.

His safety record did win him the trust of his passengers. When these passengers were asked why they trusted him, they came out with vague answers such as, "He knows what he is doing. He's good, and so forth." Loftholm's answer came closer. He said, "Gillam had a quiet confidence in himself that others absorbed."

On the subject of passenger confidence in pilots, no one has made a better explanation than Anne Morrow Lindbergh, Charles Lindbergh's young wife. Immediately after their marriage, she flew with her husband constantly. She also acted as his Morse Code radio operator when they flew on worldwide exploratory trips searching for future Pan American air routes. Although she has written a number of books telling of flights with her husband, it was in her,

Hour of Gold—Hour of Lead, that she discussed directly why she trusted her husband as a weather pilot. Her remarks were put down just after weather-related crashes (in 1929, 1930) of two Transcontinental Air Transport planes. This fledgling airline was Charles Lindbergh's attempt to provide safe, scheduled air service from coast to coast, as Gillam had attempted to do on a lesser scale between Cordova and Fairbanks.

Anne Morrow Lindbergh states specific reasons for her confidence in her husband as weather pilot-relates to Gillam's attributes.
(United Press Int'l photo/ Courtesy Harcourt, Brace, Janovich)

The fact that these were large, tri-motor planes and there were no survivors in either crash made it a devastating blow for the safety-conscious Lindbergh. The blow was even more crushing, especially for young Anne, because many of the passengers had been personal friends. Both crashes, besides being weather related, involved pilot error stemming from an inability to maneuver the large, trimotor aircraft in conditions of limited visibility.

After receiving a briefing on the details of the tragedies, Anne Morrow Lindbergh described her feelings about flying through weather with her husband during their long exploratory flights. She stated,

I come out with two conclusions about Charles:

1) That he does know when to turn back. He does not rely on weather reports but uses his own judgements about what weather he can go through. He looks at it and knows. No one can be perfect, but he is very, very good and doesn't take that kind of chance, if he isn't sure.

2) He is one of those rare people who do their best in an emergency, instead of their worst, the way most people do.

The degree of trust established between Gillam and his passengers suggests that Anne Morrow Lindbergh's two conclusions would apply equally to him.

As a final statement on trust between Gillam and his passengers,

Rudy Billberg in his biography, *In the Shadow of Eagles*, spoke to a bond of trust between an entire community and its pilot.

> I spent much time (in the early 1950s) at the air crossroads village of McGrath on the lower Kuskokwim River, which was a main stopping point on the mail and passenger route that Gillam served in the late 1930s. Longtime residents spoke of Gillam almost reverently. They adored him.

Up to this point in the chapter attention has been given to comments by Gillam's fellow bush pilots who genuinely admired his ability to fly through difficult weather. Stress was also placed on the importance of an individual pilot's weather-making decisions along with a seeming unawareness of how to go about making them.

A detailed examination of the criticisms pertaining to Gillam as a pilot, especially his ability to fly weather, which arose after his final flight, needs to be made. Also needed are challenges to most of those criticisms. However, before doing so, it might be well to consider the whole matter of the trust relationship between Gillam and his passengers during that final flight. It ended in a crash which destroyed the plane, resulted in one indirect death, and injured the four others on board. Does this mean the trust relationship between Gillam and his passengers was unwarranted? A thoughtful rereading of chapter 22 will uncover not even the slightest suggestion of resentment toward Gillam; that he might have been responsible for their plight as survivors. On the contrary, right after the crash, they stood in unbelief that they were all still alive; that Gillam had brought the plane down as he had. Cutting, just before the crash, brace himself for the end. Then, moments later, he stood unharmed, not being able to believe the miracle that he and all the others had escaped death.

Another point needs to be made before going on to the criticisms of Gillam. If those survivor had not struggled so courageously to save themselves, the facts about what happened after the crash would never have become know to the outside world. As will be noted in a moment, the search was officially called off. It was two of the survivors who reached the Coast Guard vessel, were then rescued, and the story of their ordeal was told in the articles by Gebo and Cuttings. According to the survivor's own words, they could not have survived without being rescued, but the search for them and been called off. True, the red underwear and the boots Gillam had hung up on the tree before dying might have, as the seasons passed, been noticed by a passing boat. If that had happened, the search might have been renewed and now with the search area narrowed, the survivors would have finally been found, but not alive. So the story of what happened on the plane before the crash, during crash, and afterward would not be known. The people on Gillam's plane on that last flight would have been mourned and Gillam would have been blamed for their deaths. His critics would have been vindicated. His feelings of self-importance and invincibility had led him to challenge weather once too often, his luck ran out, and his passengers trust in him had been unwarranted.

The view of the critics was encapsulated in these words of Oscar Winchell, pilot and Gillam's former employee, as taken from his biography,

> ...news was out that Harold Gillam was missing out of Seattle. It had happened, Gillam had taken off into bad weather once too often. Oscar held a certain feeling that Gillam would never fly again. He seemed to sense that his old employer had foiled nature just to often, and this time he would not survive.

Fortunately, the survivors did persevere and did effect their own rescue and now it is time to examine, in detail, the criticism of Gillam as a pilot which surfaced after his last flight.

The negative attitude was basically aimed at Gillam's credibility as a weather pilot. It held that his supposed legendary status had its foundation in luck rather than in any special aptitudes or skills. The claim that *luck* was an essential ingredient in Gillam's success requires first that we define the term. Webster states, "to prosper or succeed especially by chance." In turn, Webster defines *chance* as "an assumed impersonal, purposeless determiner of accountable happenings." To better understand the concept of *luck* and *chance*, another related term, *fate*, needs to be considered. Webster's definition connects

Ernest K. Gann-Airline pilot and author who supported fate as an important factor in a pilot's longevity. *(Jim Morrow photo/ Courtesy Simon and Schuster)*

it to *luck* and *chance* by defining it as "a determining cause—why things happen."

It was Ernest K. Gann, a well-kown author and an airline pilot who accumulated thousands of hours in his log before retiring, who related the concept of fate to the world of flying. His meaning, as fully developed in his autobiography, *Fate as the Hunter,* saw fate as an unknowable force, predictable only to the extent that it opposes any human effort that insists on striving for progress. To obtain a complete understanding of Ernest K. Gann's meaning of fate, one would need to read his autobiography.

Now back to luck, the supposed force that determined Gillam's destiny as a pilot. Most people use the words *luck* and *lucky* too lightly and too often. How many times has one heard, "You must be pretty lucky" or "I wish I had your luck." However, in dealing with Gillam's critics and their references to luck, the word takes on a deeper meaning. In this deeper sense luck, chance, and fate are identified as unknowable, and mostly unpredictable, forces that influence "what happens" in the lives of human beings. No one will disagree that in the lives of all human beings unexplained things happen and are accepted. This is not the same as believing that life itself is controlled and determined by unknown and unpredictable forces. To accept this view would lead naturally to anxiety and possibly doubt as to whether an individual's efforts have any meaning when it comes to determining the direction of his or her life.

Glacier Pilot Reeve. *(Reeve photo/Courtesy Holt, Rinehart and Winston)*

A number of people in Alaska aviation, both pilots and nonpilots, have used the word *luck* with its deeper meaning in connection with Gillam's achievements. To be specific and yet brief, we have chosen one well-known bush pilot to tell his view on how luck operated in Gillam's life and flying achievements. At the same time he tells us how luck influenced his own life as a pilot. Bob Reeve was chosen because he believed in luck as a significant force operating in the lives of pilots. Also, he was a colleague of Gillam and had a genuine respect for him as a pilot. Most important, he was not afraid to voice his opinion on any subject. And in the way he expressed them, he made it clear they were opinions, not facts, and therefore open to challenge.

Bob Reeve's biography, *Glacier Pilot,* is filled with references to luck. For example, chapter 7 is titled, "I Was Pushing My Luck."

Chapter 9 is titled, "I Ran Out of Planes—and Luck." Then, after coming out of an unusual spin, alive, he responded with,

> I knew by all rights I should have been dead. To this day I don't know how that plane ever came out of the spin. It must have been luck. If it was—I'd used up all my luck for twenty years in advance.

Having established Reeve's firm conviction that luck was instrumental in keeping himself alive, he then gives his view on how luck functioned in Gillam's flying life? All his comments were taken from his biography.

Reeve focused on Gillam's final flight to explain how luck operated. He stated,

> "Gillam's death," says Bob soberly, "was no big news to any of the pilots who knew him. The kind of flying he'd done, he'd already run out of luck ten thousand years in advance! But it was none the less hard to believe. A fine instrument flyer, Gillam, Reeve feels, could have eventually found his way, if his engine hadn't quit…His luck ran out, that's all. In a critical time like that, when he most needed luck it went sour."

Note that in Reeve's statement about the role of luck, he also credited Gillam as being "a fine instrument pilot." In doing this he acknowledged that "luck" wasn't everything. To Reeve, although unknowable, luck was not a fatalistic force where events are fixed in advance and cannot be changed by human effort.

Now Reeve found himself in a bind. Gillam, with the continuous help of luck, had created a legend around his uncanny ability to fly successfully through extreme weather conditions. Yet, Reeve admitted that luck abandoned Gillam. But after so many years of helping, why this sudden abandonment? Reeve didn't have the answer. Unfortunately, he found one in the negative attitude that surfaced after the crash, among those who had become disenchanted with the Gillam legend. They felt Gillam had acquired a bad case of *hubris*, as the Greeks called it. That he had acquired an exaggerated sense of pride and self-confidence. The Greeks also claimed that this condition invariably resulted in retribution—some sort of punishment. The individuals who were disenchanted with the Gillam legend took this position and Reeve, never one to avoid giving his opinion, did just that. He said,

> "He got himself into a trap," comments Reeve. "He was a brilliant flyer, but he got a reputation built up that he couldn't live up to

without killing himself. Harold was a little guy, you know, and he loved to show up his contemporaries. He got so he couldn't turn down any job, or any risk. He had to live up to his reputation." (pp.261-62)

Others have made personal criticisms of Gillam, some long after the crash. Pat Wachel in her previously mentioned article (chapter 16) published in the June 1966 issue of *Alaska Northern Lights* made this statement,

Charles Harold Gillam, a man of small stature, challenged life as though he were invincible...He was an unusual bush pilot who flew without regard to his safety or that of his passengers. His flights were a desperate effort to prove he was just a little bit better than the other pilots of his time.

Reeve, on the other hand, knew Gillam personally, had flown with him, and had a high regard for his skills. It seems his response should not have included such an emotional judgement of Gillam's motives which, of course, could not be supported. Yet it is apparent that Reeve was stating his opinion and a response to that opinion is indeed in order.

Let's take the part where Reeve stated, "He got himself a reputation built up that he couldn't live up to without killing himself." Whether this statement was true of previous flights will not be questioned. With regard to this particular flight, though, the CAB report showed it to be a routine one, a flight which Gillam had made before and for which he had carefully prepared, especially with regard to the weather. The weather was basically VFR (visual flight rules) except for the last hour before landing. The landing at Annette Island would have been routine except for two occurrences. The first, relatively minor, was Gillam's failure to have with him in the cockpit a current chart. It was contained in the CAB report, though not as a cause but as a factor that may have had an effect. Since it was mentioned by the CAB, one can speculate how Gillam's failure to have a current chart showing the changed headings for an instrument approach, might have denied a safe landing at Annette Island. Had he used an up-to-date chart and followed the correct heading on the approach he would have saved time. This time was consumed following the wrong heading until he sensed something wrong and decided to change over to his radio direction finder for the approach. One can speculate further that, had he used the correct chart and saved these minutes, he might have been lined up for the final approach when the engine quit. If so, it would have been simple to let down for the landing on the remaining engine. This is pure speculation but needs to be mentioned.

The second occurrence, the engine failure, was cited by the CAB report as being the primary cause of the crash—not weather. The flight was routine except for the engine failure. Reeve, therefore, was not justified in stating, "Gillam felt obligated to maintain his reputation by taking on a flight which went beyond his piloting capabilities.

Note also Reeve's claim that the failed engine was a sign of luck abandoning Gillam. As it turned out, the engine failure was caused by a series of minor human errors, or at least bad judgements. The Lockheed factory installed the seriously underpowered 410 hp Wright engine in the Electra. This particular engine was also prone to failures and required much maintenance. The Army Air Corp used this model engine in its basic trainers, and replaced them because of their unreliability and high maintenance requirement. To support this criticism, the left engine on Gillam's Electra, the one that failed, had been removed for major maintenance only three months after it was put into service. Also, a major overhaul had been performed on that engine at the time Gillam purchased the plane. To go on, the factory did not equip the Electra with full-feathering props. Thus, prop windmilling caused considerable drag on the failed engine. Changes in the Electra were later made. The 450 hp Pratt Whitneys became standard, as did the full-feathering props. These facts establish that errors in human judgement played a greater part than did luck in this tragic happening.

At this point comment should be made concerning the sources of the information obtained concerning Gillam's final flight. All was obtained directly from individuals alive at the time. Some of it obtained directly from the survivors of his last flight where they stated what they did and how they felt. This involved no criticism of Gillam. The CAB's formal findings found the cause of the crash to be engine failure. Gillam was cited only for not having the most recent navigational chart in the cockpit. Reeve, a fellow pilot, indirectly faults Gillam by introducing the element of luck. Also Oscar Winchell, a fellow pilot, makes a critical statement regarding Gillam's weather flying in his biography. Last, the group most critical of Gillam as a weather pilot, those interviewed by Jean Potter concerning Gillam's last flight within a short time after that flight. The results of her interview were reported in her *The Flying North*. Hopefully, questioning the accuracy of responses to Potter's questions will give readers a sounder foundation from which to make their own judgements as to the validity of Gillam's supposed legendary status. It is possible that the facts and impressions of the individuals who lived through that time may have an element of dis-

tortion stemming from a personalized view. A recent report in the
science section of Newsweek magazine (July 16, 2001) confirmed this
possibility. It stated, "Memories can be illusions...Memory's 'sins of
commission' shape—and often distort—our view of reality."

The comment in Potter's book which was most damaging to Gillam's
credibility, and which was also untrue, stated, "The Civil Aeronautics
Board...officially designated the basic cause of the wreck as pilot error."

The CAB report actually stated, "...the stoppage of the left engine
from an undetermined cause in extremely rough weather over hazardous terrain undoubtedly was the primary cause of the accident...."
(see official CAB report end of this chapter).

Unfortunately, placing blame for the accident on pilot error, that is,
Gillam's error, was repeated in future writings on Gillam's life. For
example, Rudy Billberg, in his biography, in connection with the Gillam
crash, stated simply, "The CAA cited pilot error as cause of the crash."

The CAB did state two contributing factors, but these were not cited
as causes. The first was; Gillam's failure to equip himself with up-to-
date charts. This was true and no excuses should be made for his
failure to do so. Second, Gillam failed to use his available radio aids to
accurately establish the position of his flight while on instruments.
There seems to be some confusion here. He had been constantly aware
of his position by following the radio range legs. This was evidenced
by his timely approach to the Annette airport. It was only in the final
minutes of the flight that he became uncertain (because of the out-
dated chart) and then, as an emergency procedure, decided to use his
radio direction finder to make the approach for landing.

The following paragraph from Potter's book is repeated here because it not only states incorrect information but its rendition implies
that Gillam showed an arrogant attitude. It stated,

> Gillam was informed that a storm was moving toward the Alaska
> coast. Other northbound flights had been canceled that day, but
> he, after considerable argument with Boeing Field clearance of-
> ficers, loaded his ship and took off.

The implied arrogance or belligerency on Gillam's part is apparent
but untrue. The CAB reported an entirely different attitude during the
weather briefing. Gillam had always felt that studying weather would
help make him a better weather pilot. Appleton spoke of his constant buying and studying books on meteorology. According to the
CAB report, Gillam gave serious attention to the weather information
available. There was no argument. The last part of the above paragraph is also repeated for evaluation. It stated,

So sure was he of his time-tested ability that he carried no medical supplies and almost no emergency equipment and made not one radio report all the way north.

Again the tone suggests arrogance. The reference to his carrying almost no emergency equipment is untrue. The survivors referred to two week's supply of food and to the use of blankets and sleeping bags. No one mentioned lack of emergency supplies. Failure to make radio reports was true and will be discussed in connection with the search efforts.

Potter also included a remark about Gillam made by one of his colleagues. It openly stated Gillam's attitude of self-importance. "He (Gillam) got to the point where he almost acted like he was superhuman," says a colleague. "He was plain asking for it."

In referring to Jean Potter as the source of the criticism of Gillam, One must constantly keep in mind that she was reporting what she heard during her interviews.

The criticism that Gillam failed to make any contact during his four some hours in the air needs to be examined more fully because it implies that this made a search for the plane all but impossible. Potter made this statement,

When Gillam's plane was reported missing the CAA sent an inquiry to every telegraph station along his entire route. Forty planes, Army and civilian, searched the coastal mountains. Coast Guard boats scouted deep into bays and inlets. The searchers had few clues…The Electra could have crashed anywhere on the long route from the States to Alaska.

The above statement, if true, would dishearten even the most motivated and hopeful searcher. The CAB did confirm that Gillam failed to make any position reports and commented that this did make the unsuccessful search more difficult. Now add to this CAB statement the previous totally untrue reports of Gillam's attitude and actions. For example, his suggested arrogance in taking off into a gathering storm when all other flights were cancelled, his arguing with the clearance officers at Boeing Field, and finally, taking off without proper emergency gear on board. If you combined all these reports, what would you get? There is a good possibility that you would find individuals not enthusiastic about making a thorough search for Gillam.

True, Gillam was not prone to using the radio unless there was an urgent reason to. On this flight, though, he had the military on his side. At this point in the war, with Japan's invasion of Alaska, the army had issued strict orders that pilots in the Territory were not to use their voice radio unless absolutely necessary. This was aimed at keeping the Japanese military from gaining knowledge of United States military activity in Alaska. The order was difficult for civilian bush pilots in Alaska to obey because they disliked obeying any kind of order. It did not take them long, though, to realize that with a nation at war and with enemy soldiers occupying American soil, they must obey. As a result, bush pilots were especially zealous about obeying the army's order.

Gillam, in this instance, was navigating along the legs of the radio ranges which required no voice communication. Therefore he had no reason to use his radio to communicate until he reached Annette Island, when engine failure created an emergency. This emergency must have triggered in his mind an urgent need to make known his position. His report was probably a conditioned reaction nurtured by his many responses to the plight of other downed pilots.

Robert Gebo, one of the survivors, gave firsthand information on Gillam's response to this emergency. When the engine failed, Gebo in the copilot's seat, stated that Gillam responded immediately with a call to Ketchikan radio. Here is an example of how carefully Gillam prepared for unexpected events. Anticipating a possible need to contact the voice radio he was flying toward, he had preset his radio to that station's receiving frequency. Thus there was no need to take precious time twirling knobs before making his voice transmission to Ketchikan radio.

Also, when the plane entered a severe downdraft immediately following the engine failure, Gebo reported that Gillam let go of the mike and gave full attention to righting the plane's attitude—thus another example of Gillam's right response in an emergency.

His quick call to Ketchikan radio was an essential step to aid a rescue effort, should one be needed. It restricted any search effort to the area surrounding Annette Island.

Those setting up a search of course would not have had available the information which was later obtained from the survivors, especially that obtained from Gebo who was in the cockpit right up to the time of the crash.

Nevertheless, without this additional information, common sense could have put together what was available, especially Gillam's call to Ketchikan radio, and then restricted the search to the Annette Island area.

Examining the official CAA chart included here should help the reader understand why the search area could have been restricted from the very beginning.

What, then, was the available information? The Electra had been in the air some four hours, the time between takeoff and the call to Ketchikan radio. Gillam, a competent pilot, had filed an instrument flight plan to Annette Island. We can assume he stayed on course by flying the appropriate radio range legs. This assumption was proven as fact when, after those many hours in the air, Gillam made an emergency call to Ketchikan radio reporting an engine out (notice on the chart, Ketchikan Radio is nearest to Annette). His near-

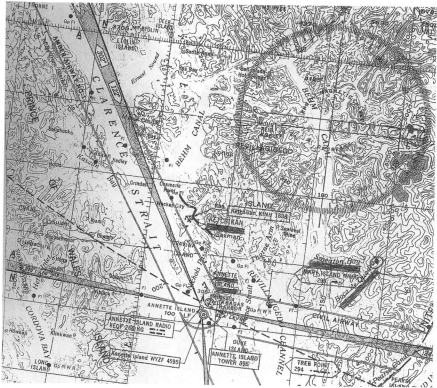

(CAA, Now FAA, Chart Service)

ness to Ketchikan and Annette Island was verified by the clear quality of his radio transmission. Gillam was where he was supposed to be after those hours of flight. This was a clear justification for restricting the search area.

Then an additional piece of information was provided. It located the downed plane even closer to the Annette Airport, its destination. The Annette tower also reported hearing Gillam's transmission. Because airport towers deal only with local traffic, they are extremely limited in the distance over which they can transmit or receive. This is especially true in mountainous terrain.

The search directors refused to believe the tower operator could have received the transmission and therefore refused to further restrict the search area. The matter was not settled until a Morrison-Knutsen plane flew in Thomas Donohoe, Gillam's friend, to investigate. The young tower operator was accused of seeking publicity but was vindicated. Receipt of Gillam's message by the Annette tower was officially noted in the CAB report. Unfortunately, the change to further restrict the search area came too late. By that time the search was in the process of being suspended.

What wrong-headedness, or at least lack of common sense, must have prevailed in the thinking of the search directors. Claiming that Gillam's failure to radio his position had made an effective search almost impossible was simply not true.

The fact that the survivors heard and saw two planes that first clear day after the crash and saw a single plane fly below them a day later suggests that local pilots, having heard informally about Gillam's radio transmission, got out immediately on that first clear day and nearly effected a rescue. Given a few more days, they probably would have succeeded.

However, after that first attempt right after the crash, the survivors neither saw nor heard another plane. This indeed does indicate that the search had broadened its focus to a larger area. This provided publicity but no results.

Dissatisfaction with the search itself and the directors' decision to call it off after two weeks, resulted in a deeply felt sentiment. This sentiment led to the following statement in Potter's book,

> It was believed that Gillam's ship had dropped into the ocean. One wonders what became of the dauntless tradition of northern rescue, which Gillam had honored so magnificently in behalf of others. The reason is hard to find and the fact disturbing to many today; the hunt, after only two weeks, was called off.

The unsatisfactory search response moved Bob Reeve to make an emotional criticism in his biography. He stated,

> In one of the shameful blots on aviation history, the search was called off before any trace of the crash had been found. It was a month before the survivors, in critical condition, were picked up by the Coast Guard.

True, there was a war to be won, thousands of men were dying, and so forth. Yet all this sounds like reasons for abandoning an effort which the leadership had never supported.

Returning once more to an evaluation of Gillam's possible legendary status, a conclusion must be drawn as to the validity of Bob

Reeve's claim that Gillam's exceptional ability to fly weather was to a considerable extent due to luck. Earlier definition of the term relates it to chance and fate. The definitions of all three terms included reference to a powerful but unpredictable force operating in all human lives, especially, though, in the lives of pilots who have chosen a vocation which challenges both gravity and nature's ever changing weather. In such a vocation it is only natural that chance, or unexplained events, will occur more often than in the lives of those who have chosen to become sales clerks. Also, in the case of pilots, these chance happenings can result in death.

In Reeve's thinking, this luck could work for or against human desires or destinies. In his biography he went to great lengths to examine the many life-or-death situations that had arisen in his life as a pilot. He then explained how this powerful force, luck, had favored him and allowed him to keep on living.

Reeve is not the only one who has explained the existence of this powerful force that can influence a pilot's destiny, one way or the other. Ernest K. Gann, mentioned earlier in this chapter, took pretty much the same position as Bob Reeve regarding this powerful force. In his autobiography, *Fate as the Hunter,* he referred to this force as "fate" then went on to describe it as all-powerful and unpredictable in the use of its power to determine human destiny. Like Reeve, he felt it was particularly active in the lives of pilots because that vocation provides so many opportunities for fate or chance to operate.

Ernest K. Gann flew as an airline pilot during the late 1920s, the 1930s, and during World War II. This was a time when well-financed airlines such as Lindbergh's Transcontinental Air Transport took on the challenging task of providing scheduled airline travel in large multi-engine aircraft. The toll in human lives during that period was unbelievable, and most crashes occurred because of weather.

At the beginning of his book he listed the names of 397 pilots who were colleagues during his flying career and who died in cockpits. Ernest K. Gann, like Reeve, escaped death until his retirement. Again like Reeve, he was moved by his escaping death in a cockpit and, after relating the episodes in the air where he should have met death but didn't, proceeded to present his concept of fate as a hunter.

Both pilots came to the same conclusion. Luck or fate is a fickle power that bestows, or withholds, favors depending on its mood.

To hold, or even consider, such a belief would surely be anxiety producing. In the past such anxiety led to superstition. In such a situation, individuals named this all-powerful, unpredictable and sometimes vindictive force "god". Individuals then tried to placate their gods with certain behaviors. Anxiety or outright fear was still present because this arbitrary god might, depending on its mood, move against a person for no perceived reason.

Naming the powerful, unpredictable force "god" was an unfortunate occurrence for the religions of the world. In early times superstition and religion were basically alike because their aim was to placate a powerful force. They differed in that religion had a fixed behavior by which humans could avoid the disfavor of their god.

It is interesting to note that in the advanced civilization of the Greeks, which became the foundation of our Western or European civilization, superstition was still the cornerstone of their religion. Individual Athenians lived in fear of their powerful but arbitrary and unpredictable gods. Western Civilization advanced when it retained Greek contribution in art, architecture and ideas but replaced its superstition-prone religion with the Judeo-Christian heritage and its value system.

The religious belief within the Judeo-Christian heritage was similar to the Greek and other primitive religions of the past in that it had as its foundation an all-powerful and unknowable force. In that sense it also agreed with Reeve's idea of luck and Ernest K. Gann's idea of fate. It differed significantly, though, in that its unknowable force—God—was neither unpredictable nor arbitrary.

By rejecting these two characteristics, it separated religion from superstition and went a long way toward removing anxiety and fear from human life.

The Judeo-Christian religion, which became the foundation of our Western Civilization, in return for God's written promise to act always in a consistent and benevolent manner toward all human beings, made but one demand. This demand, an ethical one, was also written down and would not change. The expectation had to do with how human beings should treat one another. His promise and expectation have been written down and examined in a basic document called the Bible. What He expects is perhaps most clearly and simply stated in the Hebrew *Old Testament*, the book of Micah, chapter 6, verse 8. It states,

> And what does the Lord require of you?
> But to do justly
> To love mercy
> And to walk humbly with your God.

Regardless of how the followers of the Judeo-Christian religion use and abuse this basic expectation by what they say or do, that basic expectation by which humans should live their lives does not change. Now one might ask, Did Gillam in his daily words and actions appear to live by this Judeo-Christian expectations rather than by luck or fate? Of course, at the end of his life some wanted to believe that his words and actions reflected the opposite. That he demonstrated excessive pride and overconfidence. There is no evidence to justify this position. For example, criticism of his words and actions before his final flight were proven to be untrue.

What has been shown to be true in the pages of this biography is his concern for others. This was demonstrated in his choice of goals. These goals were not easily achieved but working toward achieving them was a pleasure for Gillam because he was blessed with an intense love of flying.

This, in turn, led him to become involved with others by encouraging and helping them. Thus, he gladly counseled Mudhole Smith when Smith felt unsure. He responded to young Bud Seltenreich when young Bud hung around the Anderson garage in McCarthy, asking questions. He managed to give a young high school student in Cordova his first airplane ride. Then there were his mercy flights during those many years of flying. However, his concern for others was most dramatically shown in the final days of his life, which led to the following epitaph on his headstone in the Clay Street Cemetery, *Greater Love Hath No Man…*

And what about "walking humbly with his God?" To many people this means going to church on Sundays. There are no indications that he did much of that. "Walking humbly with your God" has deeper meaning. It requires walking humbly with those you come in contact with every day. Alaska Linck's account of an episode (chapter 18) gave a good example where Gillam did this. He had taken off from Fairbanks with a load of passengers who were planning to catch a steamer at Cordova. He encountered severe turbulence, but saw no reason to turn back. Then one or two of the passengers became upset. He tried to calm them by calling down from the cockpit but it had no effect. Finally these particular passengers panicked and started screaming. He had passengers on board intent on catching the steamer. And, yes, he had a reputation to uphold. However, he also had compassion for those individuals who were in misery. So he returned to Fairbanks. Alaska Linck was there when the passengers entered the waiting room. She remarked that those who had not panicked had nothing but praise for Gillam's flying skills and his compassion.

Did Gillam's composure and understanding of others in stressful situations in any way relate to his inner self? Evidence is found in the words of that beautiful and wise young woman, Kay Kennedy. After talking with him but for a short while, she said, "I began to realize that he was his own man—not cocky, but sure of himself in such a quiet way."

Others, such as Loftholm, mentioned Gillam's ability to remain calm in tense situations and how this led to a quiet assurance to those around him. Such serenity can only come from experience, from attention to learning, and from the absence of anxiety about one's rightful place in this mysterious universe. Again Kay Kennedy's words about Gillam seem to suggest that he knew, and was satisfied with, his rightful place when she said,

> Gillam was a lone eagle. He flew with supreme confidence in himself or whatever he believed in, right to the last. He seemed to be one with the storm and the weather.

He did appear to have a "supreme confidence in himself and in whatever he believed in." At one point a series of previous human errors, not his own except for an obsolete chart, found him on instruments with an engine out. With his radio on the Ketchikan frequency, he keyed his mike and reported. Seconds later, when a severe downdraft required his full attention he let go of the mike and with instruments alone, kept the plane in a flying attitude. Then when he dropped out of the clouds at 2,500 feet and saw the mountains in front of him, he used his exceptional eyesight to pick out a relatively cleared spot on the mountainside. Chopping power on the remaining engine, as if to make a spot landing, he maneuvered the plane without power and with its stall speed at more than 100 miles per hour, putting it down so the wings would impact the trees and cushion the forward speed rather than the fuselage. The G-pressures on the bodies in the aircraft, produced by the sudden stop, rendered everyone unconscious for a moment, but with all still alive.

In a situation that would make even the most experienced pilot cringe, he succeeded. It is just possible that the supreme power that Gillam believed in was not luck or fate. And that this power may have intervened in the matter of providing visibility at 2,500 feet and perhaps giving a tad of help and moral support while Gillam "did his best."

In a final attempt to discredit Bob Reeve's theory of how luck functions in pilots' lives, specifically Gillam's, a writer who interviewed Reeve for a short statement to be included in a 2001 calendar commemorating Alaska bush pilots and published by the First National Bank, stated,

> Reeve flew into and out of many areas previously considered inaccessible, and attributed much of his success to "fantastic luck." The truth was, however, that Bob Reeve was a superb flier who mastered glacier landings and takeoffs with uncommon courage

and an inventive nature that spurred him to devise new ways to stack the odds in his favor.

This same statement that credits Reeve's uncommon courage and skill over luck; many of us believe would also apply to Harold Gillam's achievements.

No one can know what view Gillam held with regard to forces in the universe that decide a pilot's destiny. We can, though, be somewhat more certain that he would agree with a statement published in the February 1994 issue of the FAA Alaskan Flyer regarding flying weather. It stated,

> Learning HOW to fly takes approximately 45 hours
> Learning WHEN to fly can take a lifetime

Finally, the judgement as to whether Gillam deserves legendary status as a weather pilot must be left to the individual reader. Below are included a few comments about flyers and flying which, hopefully, will prove inspirational, whether you are a pilot or just interested in flying.

Sir Gordon Taylor in his, *"The Sky Beyond"* gave a mystical, poetic description of his feelings after a twenty-five hour flight in a single-engine plane from Australia to Honolulu.

> A flight in darkness, leaving us alone but in harmony with the world of the aircraft. In that world there grew a sense of security: something that did not admit the possibility of an engine failure. (p. 43)

> I just sat there, filled with a curious sense of gratitude that we had been given the conditions to find these islands, that the engine had never shown a sign of failure in the 25 hours of flight; and the most wonderful sense of anticipation for arrival at Honolulu. (p. 59)

> All my senses were in harmony with the sound, the sight, and the touch of the aircraft and the air, and I sat there relaxed and happy, flying into the dawn. (p. 60).

Saint Exupery, in his *Wind, Sand, and Stars* paid tribute to a fellow pilot who was known for his pioneering mail routes for France,

> Pioneering thus, Mermoz cleared the desert, the mountains, the night, and the sea. He had been forced down more than once in desert, in mountains, in night, and in seas. And each time that he

got safely home, it was but to start out again. Finally, after a dozen years of service, having taken off from Dakar (Africa) bound for Natal (Brazil) he radioed briefly that he was cutting off his rear right-hand engine. Then silence. (p. 27)

Ernest K. Gann in *The High and the Mighty* spoke eloquently of an exceptional pilot's traits.

The plane in which they sat had been conceived by men whose passion was the conquest of gravity, clever, brilliant men who hammered their dreams into realistic machines of marvelous efficiency. And yet when their work was completed they were nearly helpless to insure the final results, for even their genius could not control the design of a pilot's mind. The burden in the end, fell upon men like Sullivan with his big sure hands...Their pride in their part of the endeavor, their total absorption in this little time before the takeoff was an unlikely mixture of emotion and cold concern with numerical facts. Hobie Wheeler (a new, inexperienced pilot) could not as yet fully appreciate either the pleasure or the seriousness of their mood. (pp.ss 49-50)

Chapter 24
AN UNFINISHED ENDING

To err is human, to forgive, divine.
(Alexander Pope)

Harold Gillam Sr.'s physical remains were laid to rest in the Clay Street Cemetery on March 5, 1943. The community of Fairbanks genuinely mourned his passing, as did other Alaskans. Gillam's children, except for Harold Gillam Jr., were too young to really understand. The three youngest were staying with their grandmother Gillam in Seattle and Don, the oldest, does remember his grandmother's grieving.

Among the adult members of the family it is difficult to say who suffered the most, the mother or the wife. Gillam's mother lost her only son. His wife, though, lost more than her husband. She must have realized, in the midst of her grief, that she had also lost the hoped-

Gillam's death caused more than just grieving. *(Author's photo)*

for reconciliation with her husband. Not only that, but the children were far from her and being cared for by her mother-in-law, who was totally opposed to Nell's, method of child-rearing. In addition, her sister-in-law, Elsie, agreed with her mother on the matter of bringing up children properly.

Then, mixed in with Nell's grief and loneliness for her children, may have been a measure of guilt. In spite of all that was happening around her, she could hardly put out of her mind the fact that her actions had caused her husband to erupt in anger, which in turn had resulted in a temporary disruption in their long standing, loving relationship. True, Elsie had been part of the problem with her open disapproval of Nell as a mother. She also conveyed that disapproval to her brother. Those thoughts, though, couldn't erase her feelings of guilt over what she had done to bring on her husband's anger.

What did happen after Gillam's body was laid to rest? Not just the family but also the management of Gillam Airlines had to work at picking up the pieces. As for Gillam Airlines, Tom Appleton was officially a mechanic. Over the years, though, he had taken over what might be called the management function. He had also become Gillam's friend. Long before his death, Gillam had provided Appleton with a general power of attorney. This was fortunate, for at Gillam's death, Appleton could continue carrying on the day-to-day operations while the court searched for an administrator of the estate. It did not take long for Appleton to be chosen. Thomas Donohoe was added as co-administrator.

Tom Appleton always there to "take care of things" even after Gillam's death. *(Pat Franklin photo/Courtesy of Tordoff)*

The major problem in settling the estate involved determining the value of Gillam Airlines. Those chosen to do the inventory were well-known to Gillam: Robert Gebo, head of M-K in Alaska; Merle (Mudhole) Smith, former Gillam pilot now flying for Cordova Airlines; and J. Gerald Williams, a lawyer. The value they finally assigned was $78,000 (a considerable amount at that time). The airline was sold in June 1945 for the inventoried value.

The major amount was paid for the Certificate of Convenience and Necessity issued to Gillam by the CAB in connection with his Kuskokwim mail contract. This certificate gave the buyers exclusive rights to scheduled Flights in the Kuskokwim River region. The buyers then joined together to form Northern Consolidated Airways, which later joined with Wien Airlines and became Wien Consolidated Airways. In this manner Gillam's dream of scheduled air transportation continued long after his death.

The value of the total estate, after expenses and taxes were paid, was divided equally among the four children and came to some $25,000 for each. Although Harold Gillam Jr.'s mother had remarried many years previously, his father had continued to pay child support until his death. This prompted the administrators to assume that Gillam would have wanted his oldest son to be provided for, especially his educational expenses. Nell Gillam was not provided for in the distribution.

Meanwhile, Nell Gillam's greatest fear was realized. Soon after

Gillam's death, his mother, grandmother Gillam, filed for legal custody of the three younger children. The petition was filed on May 28, 1943, in a superior court of Washington State.

Certain irregularities, if not violations of legal procedures, occurred in acting on this petition for legal custody. These irregularities or possible violations had the effect of making it more difficult for Nell Gillam to exercise her rights to continue as mother and guardian of her children.

The first seeming irregularity pertained to proper jurisdiction. The petition of Elsie B. Gillam (the grandmother) stated that both the mother and father were Alaska residents. This was certainly true. However, she then stated the three children to be "residents of the city of Seattle." It would seem that both parents agreeing for the grandmother to temporarily care for the children during the duration of the war, in order to insure their safety from possible dangers caused by the Japanese invasion of Alaska, did not make the children formal residents of any location except that of their parents. This being the case, the petition should have been filed with the court system within the Territory of Alaska. Having the hearing on the petition in Alaska would have made it much less difficult to protect Nell's rights as the mother of the children. This was particularly true where the nation was at war and civilian travel between Alaska and the lower forty-eight was extremely limited. There was no road between the two locations and the water connections between them using steamships were not available except to the military. This left only air travel and here priority was given to military-related movements.

Not knowing the details of the laws in force back then, one must concede this choice of jurisdictions was probably legal, although unjust and against Nell's interest in keeping her children.

The second abnormality in the process appears to be more of a direct violation of Nell's right to be notified of the date, place, and time of the hearing. An officially notarized document signed by the affiant—the server who is officially responsible for seeing that all individuals with a vested interest in the outcome of the petition are informed through a formal notification— showed that Mr. H.W. Haugland was the affiant in these particular proceedings. On the first of September, 1943, after the formal outcome of the petition had been announced, Mr., Haugland made his final notarized statement which included the following: On June 3, 1943, he served a copy of "petition for appointment of guardian" and "order fixing time of hearing petition" upon each of the following named persons (here he gave the names of Elsie B. Gillam—the grandmother—and the three younger Gillam children). He handed personally a copy of the documents to each of the named individuals.

On that same date, June 3, 1943, he mailed, by registered letter, to Mrs. Nell Gillam, at her last known address, a true and correct copy of the "said petition" and "order fixing time of hearing,"

We can assume Nell received the documents because she had used that address since her marriage to Harold Gillam Sr., more than five years previously. Notice, though, that the document "fixing the time of hearing" that Nell received did not state the place and date of the hearing. It was merely petitioning the court to set such a date and time. This information was to follow.

The only other serving Mr. Haugland carried out, according to his final notarized statement, was after Elsie B. Gillam died, which was on July 23, 1943.

Before the grandmother's death, Elsie Gillam Benson had come to care for her mother and the three children. After the grandmother's death, Mr. Haugland served "a true and correct copy of said petition and order fixing time of hearing" upon the said Elsie Gillam Benson by handing the same to her personally in Seattle, Washington on August 20, 1943 and did notify such person that the hearing would come on definitely for final determination on September 1, 1943.

Notice that Mr. Haugland did not, according to his own final notarized statement, serve notice on Nell Gillam as to the exact date, time, and place of the hearing. So, according to the formal court papers we see that Nell was sent a copy of Grandmother Gillam's petition asking for formal custody but was not served with the actual date, time, and place of the hearing. Nell's failure to be present at the hearing, although through no fault of her own, naturally prejudiced the case against her and assured the outcome would be in Aunt Elsie's favor.

A question could be raised as to how the petition presented by Grandmother Gillam could be used, after her death, as the basis for approving her daughter as guardian. To Nell this would have made little difference, since Aunt Elsie's reasons for rejecting Nell as a "fit mother" would have been basically the same as that set forth by her mother. From the standpoint of law, though, this seems most irregular.

What a shock it must have been to Nell, while waiting to hear when the hearing was to be held and while preparing to arrange the transportation to get to Seattle, to receive notice that Elsie had been given legal custody of her children. This notice more than likely came through Tom Appleton, since he would immediately have received a wire requesting that he change the child support payments from Grandmother Gillam to her daughter.

Suddenly Nell's whole world had changed. The law now said she could no longer have her children to love and to care for and that was to be forever. She knew the rigid beliefs of both Grandmother Gillam and Aunt Elsie on all matters, but especially on the matter of raising children. Not only were these beliefs directly opposed to those of Nell Gillam, the two also felt an urgent need to impose their beliefs on the children. To do this they would have to undermine the mother's position. This Nell resisted and in her loving letter to her mother in March 1941 she already expressed her resentment of Grandmother's "meddling." Even back then, Nell felt threatened, although she was at the time mother of a loving family in which she had the confidence of her husband. Aunt Elsie, when she married and built her house across the Chena River, evidently had "meddling "in mind. From there she could keep an eye on the day-to-day events at the Gillams'. Her intent was to undermine Nell's confidence in herself and her brother's confidence in his wife. Elsie was obviously not welcome in Nell's home and this was used to Elsie's advantage. She could now take on the role of offended family member. This also gave her justification to possibly exaggerate when commenting to her brother about how Nell raised the children. Gillam, with his strong feeling of loyalty to family, whether mother or sister, felt at least a need to listen to his sister. Was Elsie able to subconsciously undermine Gillam's confidence in his wife? There is some evidence that she planted seeds of doubt. Such seeds were possibly at work when Elsie reported to him the episode of Nell leaving the children alone. We don't know how long they had been left alone. The two older children remember being cold. They then picked up the baby, Winona, and all crawled into their parents' bed. They were huddled there for warmth when Elsie arrived.

It was indeed a serious matter with little or no justification. Yet Nell had the habit of leaving the children alone while they were asleep, at least for short periods. This is evidenced by her remark at the close of her March 18, 1941 letter to her mother where she stated, "The kids are asleep now so I guess I can go mail my letter." Of course this was a much more serious matter. The two older children remember the house being cold and their taking the baby and crawling into their parents' bed.

The question is, Did Elsie, with her justified concern, use the situation to put Nell in the worst possible light? Such a question is not based just on conjecture. The children themselves did report behavior on Aunt Elsie's part that gives credence to Winona's statement that "Aunt Elsie did seem to possess a mean streak." Gillam's violent reaction toward his wife over the episode, even if temporary, was certainly partly due to the groundwork laid by Elsie's previous criticisms of Nell.

And now with Aunt Elsie in total control of the three children, her behavior made it evident what she saw as the role and conduct of a proper mother. Her first step was to completely isolate the children from their former family. Her brother, no longer living, posed no problem. The mother, though, must be cut out. And she showed no compassion in doing this.

All three children were at various stages of grieving for their father, who had died only a few months back. Their grandmother had died the previous month. It was a difficult period. The two daughters missed their mother, especially Maurine, who was not quite six. She remembered going around whining, "I want my Momma." This moved Aunt Elsie to begin the task of cutting out their mother by telling all three that they would never see their mother again, that their mother was a famous newspaper reporter and had been killed in a plane crash. This came as another sudden shock in their young lives. Maurine remembered the sadness that came over her but admitted, "I stopped whining about wanting to see my mother."

Of course what Aunt Elsie had told them was absolutely false. She was willing to lie, though, if it kept the family together and limited it to five individuals—herself, her husband, Verner, and the three children. Winona remembered, when in junior high, hearing kids talking about "their cousins." She had never heard the word used at home so she asked Aunt Elsie, "Do I have any cousins?" The answer was an emphatic "no" and she left the room.

Aunt Elsie's strictness with the children was perhaps not too different from Grandmother Gillam's, except that Elsie lived under a fear of losing these children who were now hers. She had no children of her own and this fearfulness led to an element of unnecessary harshness. Winona still remembers when Donald did something that displeased Aunt Elsie and she yelled at him, "Your behaving like this made Grandmother so sad and that's the reason she died."

Aunt Elsie's harshness with the children was again demonstrated when Maurine was about eight. This was also an example of Aunt Elsie's commitment to her beliefs even at the expense of the children's well-being. What happened is still remembered by all three, now-adults. Maurine became sick with what was later diagnosed as appendicitis. The child became violently ill as time passed. Yet Elsie refused to allow her to be taken to a doctor. In addition, she also insisted that Maurine take her turn doing the dishes, although the girl was almost unable to move. Don, then about 11, finally confronted his Aunt Elsie and her husband, Verner, with the statement that his sister was going to die if they didn't do something. This led Verner to take Maurine to the hospital, where she survived.

How might things have changed if Nell had been informed of the hearing date and been there to testify? She would have undoubtedly responded to errors in the petition and have made a statement, based on deep maternal love, as to why the children should remain with her. She would also probably have explained why the children were temporarily sent to their grandmother, that there was an agreement between her and her husband to do so.

If there was still concern for the physical safety of the children by their being returned to Alaska in the midst of the war, Nell would now have had the option of moving with her family to her parents' ranch in nearby Oregon. After the war she could then decided whether to return to Fairbanks.

Of course, the situation would have changed drastically for the children, and for Nell, had they been returned to her. Mainly, the love which had enveloped the children during their formative years would have been restored and Nell would again have had a strong reason for living. Important also, if they had moved to Oregon, temporarily or permanently, the children would have come to know their mother's family—cousins, uncles, aunts, grandparents, and so forth.

The one person Aunt Elsie could not keep from appearing at her home was Harold Gillam Jr. He was the somewhat older half brother of the three other Gillams. He attended college in the Seattle area when the other three were still teenagers and insisted on keeping in touch. On weekends he would drive a considerable distance just to

With the recent death of Big Brother (Harold Jr.) and his wife, Janet, will some younger family member keep the Gillam name on this mailbox? (Author's photo)

329

spend time with them. Aunt Elsie didn't exactly make him feel welcome but didn't close the door in his face either. After all, he was a Gillam. The younger Gillams looked on him as "big brother." They kept in touch even after he married and, with his wife, Janet, moved into their old home in Fairbanks.

It was a sad day, filled with many memories when the three returned during the first days of May 1999 to attend the funeral of their beloved big brother. There, in that familiar house that had been their home during those first years of life, they spent hours sharing memories, both pleasant and sad.

Although, as Don explained, Aunt Elsie was incapable of love, raising that family must have been a troubling time for her also. The teenage years are usually stressful ones for all concerned. In Aunt Elsie's case, she also had to deal with the resentment the two girls felt because she withheld love of the kind that their mother had showered on them in their early years. This led Maurine and Winona to move in with a neighbor, at least for a time, while still in high school.

Yet, in spite of those troublesome years, all three younger Gillams grew into mature adults. Don, now retired, followed in his father's footsteps, but as a helicopter pilot. Both Maurine and Winona, although they worked outside the home, gave special attention and love to their families. Maurine, who had always looked after her "baby sister" Winona, must have taken special pride in how that baby sister turned out. At age 18 Winona was working and living alone in an apartment when her brother, Don, brought over a friend. Both boys were on motorcycles, and after introductions, the three went for a ride. In a few short weeks marriage followed. This was a good one as evidenced by a continuous commitment, which resulted in grown children and with grandchildren eventually appearing on the scene.

Maurine had a failed marriage but it did give her two sons, one of them a Delta Airlines pilot. She then met up with someone whom she knew back in 7th grade. They married and are now enjoying making this marriage a happy, lifetime affair.

Who knows why, after more than their share of difficult times, all three made a success of their lives. No one can be certain. However, some of us would like to believe that genes mixed in with special affection given to them in their beginning years, plus an unknown force, provided a certain strength which allowed them to overcome difficulties rather than being overcome by them.

What was happening to Nell at the time the registered letter containing her mother-in-law's petition arrived soon after June 3, 1943? News of the custody proceedings was undoubtedly a shock, although Nell probably had been thinking about getting the children back to Fairbanks. The threat from further invasion of Alaska by the Japanese was over. Wartime travel restrictions, though, were still in effect between Alaska and Seattle. Since Tom Appleton was now main administrator of the Gillam estate, perhaps he would have some ideas for getting the children back home.

Since Gillam's death, Tom had been sending support monies directly to Grandmother Gillam. Nell had asked for no money from the estate for her living expenses. Appleton's final report on the estate showed this. She was undoubtedly working and probably had been since the kids left for Grandmother Gillam's in September 1942. Since she was living in her home with no rent to pay, she probably did some saving for any possible future need. Not that she had any qualms about asking Appleton for money to cover the kids' travel expenses.

Any thoughts she may have had along these lines came to an end with receipt of the petition. Now all her efforts must have been on having money ready to get to the hearing. Because he was a family friend, she would have spoken to Tom Appleton. He would probably be able to get airline reservations as soon as the hearing date was sent. But no notification of the hearing date was sent to Nell. The next news came shortly after September 3, 1943, telling that Aunt Elsie had been granted custody. The news probably came from Appleton. As administrator of the estate he would have received a wire directing him to change the child support payments from Grandmother Gillam's name to Aunt Elsie's.

So it was final. Aunt Elsie had, by law, custody of Nell's three children. The blow can well be imagined but the resolve she expressed in her November 6, 1941 letter was still there. She went to Seattle and faced Elsie. Since no estate money was given for the travel she must have saved enough for the ticket. Appleton may still have helped get a reservation. He was known for his thoughtfulness and kindness, and must have known of the agony in Nell's heart. He probably admired her for not giving up.

An account of Nell's visit to Aunt Elsie is told from the viewpoint of the three children. Though now adults, they remembered much. For them the time was not clear except that it happened when Don and Maurine were in school. Winona was too young so she was at home the day their mother came to the house. It probably happened in the fall of 1943, right after Nell got the news of Aunt Elsie's appointment as guardian on September 3. It could have been the following spring of 1944 if Nell needed time to get her airfare together and to get the priority needed for wartime travel between Fairbanks and Seattle. Anyway, this is Winona's account.

Elsie was inside and Winona was in the yard entertaining herself when a taxi pulled up in front of the house and a lady got out.

Winona, curious, stood watching her walk into the yard. She stopped and looked down at Winona, who felt immediately that this was her mother. Winona was pretty young when the three kids were sent away to their grandmother's. Still, she felt sure.

About that time the door opened and Elsie appeared. Winona didn't remember any details except that the two women went inside and that Aunt Elsie was angry and upset. Still being curious, she came up to the closed door and listened. All she could hear was Elsie's angry voice almost shouting. She remembers Elsie's words, "You have no right to come here" and then something about leaving. To Winona, as young as she was, she knew Aunt Elsie was upset about the woman coming. She didn't remember any more exact words but knew Aunt Elsie didn't ever want her to come back.

The encounter was short. Soon Elsie opened the door to let the woman out, then quickly closed it again. Winona was still standing close by where she had been listening. As the woman came by she paused and looked down directly at Winona and their eyes met for a brief moment. Now she was even surer that this was her mother.

When the woman was gone, Winona went in and asked Aunt Elsie, "Was that my mother?" Aunt Elsie, still upset, answered, "I'm your mother."

Winona shared everything with Maurine when she came home from school. Maurine, being much older, knew what questions to ask. The two of them agreed that the woman was their mother. The questions Maurine asked and the answers Winona gave, helped fix the details of what happened in both their minds.

Maurine was also old enough to remember Aunt Elsie telling the children their mother was dead. This alone was enough to justify Aunt Elsie's unusual behavior.

As adults, when the three shared their ideas regarding the encounter, Don was willing to admit that Winona made an accurate report of the woman coming to the house and Elsie becoming angry, that Winona obviously heard the words, "You have no right to be here" spoken by Aunt Elsie while she was upset. Don, though, felt that the woman need not have been their mother. It could have been some other woman. The two adult Gillam sisters still steadfastly believed that the woman who paused to look into four year-old Winona's eyes was their mother, the mother who would never again be seen by any of the children. Given the background and the details of what happened, Don, who usually takes sound positions, is quite possibly wrong in this instance. Wouldn't the two sisters have logic as well as a love for their mother to support their position?

One might now ask, What was Nell's purpose in making the trip? She knew Aunt Elsie had legal custody. Was it for some sort of confrontation? Probably not. She probably hoped in her heart that Elsie would allow her to keep in touch with the children. Little did Nell know about Elsie's insecurities and motives. As it turned out, Nell was not even given an opportunity to make a formal, final good-bye to her children. Nor did Nell know that Elsie intended to separate her from any future contact, and that she would accomplish this by simply telling the children their mother had died.

Maurine was asked in a recent interview why her mother didn't just give up and return to her parents' home in Oregon and start a new life. After all, her husband was dead and she had lost her children. There wasn't anything holding her to Alaska.

Maurine's answer came quickly. "She was too proud to go home a failure."

In 65 years the neighborhood changed but not the Gillam house.
(Authors's photo)

Nell returned to Fairbanks. The estate report shows she moved out of the house her husband had built for her, the house in which she had enjoyed five years of rich family life. The report shows she left during the early part of 1944.

Nell apparently had kept her financial independence even before Gillam's death. She probably went to work in September 1942, when the children left. This sense of pride stayed with her to the very end.

In early 1945, when the estate was finally closed, she refused to make a claim against it. Such a claim would have been recognized since Tom Appleton, in his closing letter, acknowledged Nell as Gillam's legal second wife. Also, the Territory of Alaska recognized her as having given legitimate birth to her three children.

This refusal to make any monetary claim against the estate puzzled J. Gerald Williams, the Attorney General for the Territory of Alaska. In a letter to Rose Walsh, United States Commissioner, he included the following,

> My further recollection is that at the time we sold the Gillam Airlines, we served a notice on Nell McGee…At that time she was residing in Fairbanks and made no claim against the estate…It would seem that if Nell McGee Glasgow was legally married to Gillam at the time of his death that she would have come forward with a claim against the estate…

Tom Appleton 's statement as executor and the Territory of Alaska's recognition of the legitimate birth of Nell's three children, eliminated marriage as an issue. What the Attorney General failed to grasp were the emotions and the moral stance of Nell Gillam. Feeling that she had failed in her marriage and having lost what was most important to her—the children—she would not allow greed or revenge to claim what was not important to her.

The children had no knowledge of their mother after she left Seattle. This was Elsie's way of dealing with the children's mother and her family. It was not until August 1997 that the Gillam sisters again established contact with their mother's family in Oregon. This happened when the wife of one of their mother's cousins had a son in school who was assigned a project of uncovering family roots. Obtaining information on the mother's family, the McGees, was not a problem because it was part of the local community in Oregon. On the other hand, there was no information on the father's side.

Kathy Zehner, mother of the boy doing research for his school project, found that Nell McGee had married Harold Gillam and that they had lived in Fairbanks. She called all Gillams in the Fairbanks telephone directory and made contact with Harold Gillam Jr. He provided the names and addresses of the three younger Gillams. Kathy Zehner then contacted and invited the two sisters to a McGee family reunion in August of 1997. Here they were reunited with their mother's side of the family.

Meanwhile, Nell Gillam had stopped corresponding with her family after her husband died. This meant that Harold Gillam Sr.'s daughters still had no knowledge of their mother's whereabouts.

Winona, the youngest Gillam, in the late 1970s did make her own earnest effort to locate her mother. She obtained copies of court documents on the custody proceedings but these provided no information on her mother after September 3, 1943 when custody was awarded to

Aunt Elsie. After that, she was able to make contact with her father's old friend, Cecil Higgins, who was living in Anchorage, Alaska. He could only tell her that he remembered people talking about Gillam's second wife having disappeared in a plane that was lost while flying from Kodiak to Anchorage. This had happened many years in the past and when Higgins asked his old bush pilot friends about it, they could say no more than that it had happened many years back. The wreckage was never found and they weren't even sure about the passengers on board since no flight plan had been filed with the CAA. All this left Winona with no information about her mother other than the belief that she may have died in a plane crash many years back.

Cecil Higgins, mechanic, pilot, and Gillam's lifelong friend died in the 1990s at a ripe old age. (Alaska Aviation Heritage Museum photo/ courtesy Fairbanks Daily News Miner Aug 1991)

Research for this biography did provide additional knowledge about Nell Gillam, enough to bring satisfaction to the three adult Gillams. The first information came from Lois McGarvey's book *Along Alaska Trails*. In one section she mentioned various bush pilots she had flown with, including Gillam. In all instances she talked about the pilot only and might, at most, give the wife's name. In the case of Gillam, she spent almost two pages on Nell. They knew each other only briefly, shortly after Nell was going through the loss of her family. It was from Lois' book that we discover Nell had married a miner from the Forty-mile country, Paul Glasgow. He was remember as a person famous for his parties, where drinking was the main attraction. He was also remembered as a person who depended on others to support his extravagant lifestyle. Glasgow was so clever in getting this support that people didn't know whether to be angry or amused at being unwillingly drawn into his clever manipulations. Lois McGarvey, who ran a roominghouse, was one of the unhappy ones.

Her first encounter with Glasgow involved renting a room to him and his wife. He then failed to pay the rent. Glasgow took advantage of a long standing, but little known, Alaska law that would not permit eviction for nonpayment of rent at any time during the cold winter months. Knowing of this law, Glasgow refused to pay his rent and seemed to enjoy living in Lois McGarvey's place at her expense. Lois had many contacts with Nell that winter but was upset with her husband rather than with Nell

The following episode, taken from Lois' book, gives another example of Paul Glasgow's method of free-loading:

> In the spring, early, a friend telephoned that Paul was in jail for passing bad checks. He said, "I felt sorry for him and picked up all I had money for. There are a few more. If you will pick them up I'll pay you back when I can." So I gathered up Nell and made her go along. We had to walk clear over to Grail, and she got tired, but I made her walk anyway. When we got home in the afternoon, I found that I had paid out over nine hundred dollars. I was pretty mad at that Glasgow outfit. I gave Nell enough money to pay for a room for a month at the Lacey Street Hotel, and Frank (Lois' husband) helped her move across the way before Paul got home.

It appears that at this stage in Nell's life, she had suffered loss of her children and undoubtedly felt guilt over what she may have done, or may not have done, that caused it to happen. At this point she may have readily taken part in the drinking parties her husband arranged.

This next excerpt shows more clearly Lois McGarvey's empathy for Nell's sincerity and an appreciation for her attempt to make up for her husband's irresponsibility. Lois stated,

> A week or so later, Nell came over and told me that Paul had a swell electrical job at Kodiak, and they would leave any day. She said she would send the money she owed me, which was music to my ears.

> A short time later we took a trip to the States, but we heard the Glasgows had gone to Kodiak. Later we heard they were coming back to Fairbanks. That was the last news until we returned home. Then someone told us that the Glasgows were missing. They had gone down on the plane returning from Kodiak to Anchorage...

> Months later Ed Stroecker, the president of the bank, called and told me he had a package for me. He said, "Nell Glasgow left it; she said if anything ever happened to her, I should give you this." He handed me a small square package. It was Nell's diamond ring, the one Harold had given her so long ago. It is the only diamond ring I have. I still wear it and feel sorry that things are as they are sometimes. After all, Nell was a lady.

After hearing these few words expressing Nell's attitude of obligation to others and her actions to make sure she met those obligations, one cannot help but agree with Lois McGarvey's statement, "Nell was a lady."

Unfortunately, Lois McGarvey gave no dates during which she had that brief contact with Nell, thus no indication when the plane went down.

Additional information, which gives more specifics on the tragic events that took Nell Gillam's life, was found in J. Gerald Williams' previously mentioned letter to the United States Commissioner, Rose Walsh. Williams stated,

> Subsequent to that time she was reported to be in Kodiak, Alaska, and it is my understanding that she and her purported husband Glasgow, together with another man whose name I do not have, hired a pilot known as Speed Dryer to fly them from Kodiak to Anchorage. The ship disappeared on this flight and none of the parties have been heard of since. At the time of the flights disappearance, I was employed by the insurance company to investigate the loss. As a result of the investigation, I was convinced that Dryer's plane, together with the passengers, was lost at sea somewhere between Kodiak and the mainland.

Since this statement of facts and findings concerning the plane crash that took Nell's life came from an insurance adjuster assigned to investigate the claim it can be accepted by the family as a verification of death. This, of course, brings the Gillams a bit nearer closure concerning their mother's disappearance.

Unfortunately, Williams gave no date of the plane's disappearance. One can establish, though, that it happened before December 1, 1949. This is the date on the letter to the U.S. Commissioner in which he refers to Nell's disappearance. Also, her disappearance could not have occurred before March 10, 1945. On that date a U.S. marshall attested under oath that he personally delivered to Mrs. Nell Glasgow a citation for her to attend a hearing dealing with the disposal of the Gillam estate, should she have questions. A copy of this citation, with the marshall's sworn statement, were found in the Gillam estate files. This now left a four-and-one-half-year time span during which the plane could have disappeared into the waters off Kodiak Island.

Combing the newspapers over such a long span of time presented a formidable task. The work was expedited, though, by the assumption that the local paper, the *Kodiak Mirror,* would have considered the disappearance of a local plane and its pilot along with passengers, that it would have been of sufficient importance to give it space on the front page. The *Mirror* was published weekly rather than daily which further expedited the effort. The microfilm examination began with the March 1945 issue and with a scrutiny of the front page only. The *Kodiak Mirror* for July 26, 1946 carried on its front page, news of the plane's disappearance along with a list of the passengers, which included Nell and Paul Glasgow. The actual date of the flight was June 16, 1946. Delay of newspaper coverage was partly due to the paper being a weekly. More important, perhaps, was the pilot's (Speed Dryer) failure to file a flight plan. Without it, there was no clear indication that the plane was actually lost. A flight plan had been filed for the previous day, June 15, which showed a stop at Homer, but this one had been canceled. When a search was finally begun, the plane had not made its stop at Homer so the assumption was made it disappeared in the waters of the Gulf of Alaska between Kodiak and Homer. For two months following the plane's disappearance all pages of the *Kodiak Mirror* were scrutinized for any news of floating wreckage, nothing was reported.

Now, in closing, one final look at the personal life of Harold Gillam and his wife Nell. Harold's physical remains rest in the Clay Street

Flowers bloom perennially over Gillam's physical remains. *(Author's photo)*

Cemetery, just two blocks from the house on Clay Street which he built for his new bride, in 1937. As was mentioned before, it stayed in the family after Nell left it, when Harold Gillam's oldest son, Harold Gillam Jr. and his wife, Janet, lived in it during their long and happy married life, until their recent deaths.

Harold Senior's many recognitions relate naturally to his accomplishments as a pilot. Geographical landmarks and locations have been named in his honor: Gillam Falls, in the Tebay Lakes region south of the Chitina River; Gillam Glacier, in the Alaska Range, due east of Denali National Park, between Mt. Deborah and Mt. Hess; Gillam Lake, in the shadows of the Wrangell-St Elias Range, where Platinum Creek flows into the Nabesna River; and Gillam Way, a Fairbanks street which, when driving north passes directly to the left of where Gillam's hangar stood. The site is now occupied by the Boy Scouts of America building.

Gillam Falls, an official, enduring remembrance. *(Jack Wilson photo)*

Nell's physical remains lie somewhere under the waters of the Gulf of Alaska, between Kodiak and Homer. No one can stop by her gravesite to leave flowers as a remembrance. Yet her three grown children, now finally knowing what happened since they saw her last, can tell their children and

Week's field second runway is gone so is the Gillam hangar but "Gillam Way" is still there and its location is well marked by street signs. *(Author's photo)*

keep the memory of her alive. An even better way to give future generations an understanding of Nell Gillam as wife and mother would be to reproduce and frame the letter she wrote to her mother in March 1941 as reproduced in chapter 16.

An even more concrete recognition of Nell Gillam's contributions as a woman are the two grown daughters who have kept in their hearts a special place for the mother who taught them to love during their brief time together.

Bringing together the lives of Harold Gillam Sr. and his wife Nell, it is their joint effort as parents that has made the greatest contribution to our society and their heritage. Like all parents, they made mistakes but it can be said of them, "Their hearts were in the right place."

It has also been said, "Someone who is remembered, will never die." Two special human beings, Harold Gillam Sr. and Nell Gillam deserve to be kept in the hearts of us all.

Sadly, missing from the recent photos shown below are the two main characters of this biography.

The three younger Gillam Children. From the left Don, Maurine and Winona. (Family photo)

Harold Gillam Jr. and his wife Janet. (Family photo)

INDEX

50 Years Below Zero 249

A

Acord, Randy 4
ADF 79, 227, 277
Air Comrades 133
Air-to-ground radio 102, 233
Airmail 263
Airmail service 58, 63
Airport Gang 143
Aklavik ... 201, 237, 238, 250, 263
Alameda 144
Alaska Airmotive 255
Alaska Airways 93, 96, 97
Alaska Aviation Heritage Museum
132, 171, 187, 335
Alaska College 133
Alaska Hotel 71, 76
Alaska Journal .. 89, 120, 203, 296
Alaska Life 278, 282
Alaska Railroad 39, 41, 43, 246
Alaska Range 221, 301, 339
Alaska Road Commission 21-27,
29, 30, 32, 44, 45, 88, 95, 140, 142,
144, 147, 152, 170, 172, 180, 192, 193
Alaska Steamship Company
.... 22, 36, 39
Alaskan Sportsman 276, 282
Alatna 82, 237-242
Alert Bay 277
Aleutian Islands 211
Amarillo, Texas 187
American Airlines 93, 177, 186, 218

American Legion 21, 85, 86
American Smelting and Refining 42
Amphibian 142, 145, 146, 150,
151, 152, 158, 161, 162, 167, 168, 174,
.... 208, 213, 237, 264, 267, 269
Anchorage 39, 53, 70, 74, 89,
. 93, 106, 114, 132, 140, 153, 157,
158, 162, 166, 170, 174, 182, 183,
188, 189, 201, 202, 208, 210, 213,
. 214, 216, 237, 257-259, 261, 264,
.... 265, 269, 271, 272, 74-276,
.... 300, 301, 335-337
Anchorage Air Transport 89
Anchorage Grill 201
Anchorage Times 201
Anderson Garage 32, 35
Angellson, A.W. 292
Annette
274, 277, 310, 312, 314, 315, 316
Annette Island . 277, 310, 314, 315
Annette Range 277
Appendicitis 167, 328
Appleton, Thomas 24, 26, 199, 205,
.... 225, 231, 244, 245, 246, 250,
.... 324, 326, 331, 333, 334
Apprentice mechanic 88, 275
Arctic Prospecting and Develop-
ment Company 82
Arctic Prospector
.... 89, 91, 133, 136, 145, 158, 173
Arctic War Birds 213
Argentina 64
Armistead, Clyde 255

Army 25, 57, 73, 273, 311, 313
Automatic direction finder 227
Aviation Corporation 110, 114, 145
Aviation, Sikorsky Corporation 145

B

Bachelor 134
Bachner, Jess 4
Barnhill, Harvey 109, 114
Barr, Frank 10, 26, 91, 190, 253,
.... 257, 260, 261, 264, 265, 266,
.... 267, 268, 273, 297, 303, 304
Barrack, James 297
Barrow
.... 72, 73, 76, 77, 78, 79, 80, 101,
... 235-245, 247-249, 253, 263, 270
Batzar, Winch Susan   276, 278, 295
Batzar, Susan's death 284
Bennett-Rodebaugh Air Service . 54
Beech, Stagger-wing 208
Bennett, A.A. 136, 141, 221
Bering Strait
  102, 104, 106, 107, 109, 114, 116
Bernard, Claude 170
Berry, Bill 151, 152
Bettles 270
Big Brother 329
Billberg, Rudy . 243, 273, 306, 312
Bilstein, Roger 58, 69
Bissner, Bill 122
Black Wolf Squadron 73
Boeing Field 275, 312, 313
Bookwalter, Vernon 264
Borland 98,
107, 108, 112, 113, 130, 135, 196
BOWER, CHARLE 249
Boxing 17, 18, 50
Bremner Mining District
.... 140, 148, 151, 152, 171
Brenwick, Lucy 4, 95
Bride 144, 145, 196, 216, 338
Brisbane, Arthur 92
British aircraft industry 59

Brooks 81
Brooks Range 82, 137, 241
Bouker, Johanna Walatka 273
Brower, Charlie
.... 238, 239, 242, 243, 245
Brower, Sadie 238, 242
Brown bear hunt 180
Bruder, Gerry 295, 296
Buck, Robert 302
Bucyrus Erie 45
Bulldozers 44, 45
Burder, Gerry 296
Burnette, Walley 259
Burns, Robert 97

C

CAA
257, 258, 276, 312, 313, 314, 315, 335
CAB 311
CAB rep 257, 258,
  259, 265, 276, 310, 312, 313, 324
CAB report
  276, 277, 278, 310, 311, 312, 316
Cameron, Norman 180, 245
Camps 30, 43, 200, 228
Camus, Albert 85
Canadian Pacific Airline 95
Cannery 215, 289
Cap Lathrop 140, 172
Cape Halkett 239
Cape Serdte-Janeb 110
Carlson, Carl 166
Casa Blanca 64
Casket 86, 133
Cathcart, D.V. 245
Cathcart, Dan 243, 244
Certificate of Convenience 324
Cessna 195 91
Cessna AW 91
Chadron
12, 13, 14, 15, 16, 17, 19, 20, 21, 32, 36
Chamber of Commerce
.... 140, 153, 155, 221

Chance 40, 41
Chatanika 41, 43, 47
Chatanika River 81
Chena River 209, 232, 297, 327
Cheyenne 271
Chichichu Creek 37
Chicken 149
Chile 64
Chisana 33, 37, 136, 150, 179
Chisana mine 95
Chitina . 21, 23, 24, 26-28, 35, 36,
96, 136, 137, 142, 146, 147, 149, 151,
.154, 157, 159, 165-167, 180, 182,
........183, 213, 216, 217, 219, 339
Chitina River 141
Chitina Weekly Herald 166
Chitutu Creek 172
Christmas
48, 122, 189, 195, 213, 239, 240, 274, 276
Chuckchi 105
Clay Street Cemetery
.... 297, 319, 323, 338
Clayton, George 275
Cleary 41, 226
Clemons, R. 249
Clough, Dave 301
Coal Creek 231
Coast Guard ... 121, 124, 277, 284,
290, 291, 292, 293, 294, 295, 296, 306, 313, 316
Coastal route 168
Coffee 201, 242, 267, 302, 303
Cole, Dermot
4, 10, 253, 260, 261, 262, 267, 268
Commercial Hotel 147, 182
Compagnie Generale Aeropostale 64
Consolidated PBY 237
Cooley, Irene 229
Copper Center 95, 136,
.... 142-145, 148, 149, 151,
.... 155-160, 162-168, 172, 174,
..........175, 181, 182, 186, 197199,
............215, 219221, 228, 237, 252
Copper Center hangar 159, 169

Copper River 23, 28, 29, 39,
.........82, 138, 142, 143, 146, 147,
........156, 160, 181, 189, 191, 233
Copper River and Northwestern
Railroad... 23
Copper River Region..... 26, 27, 35,
... 37, 95, 103, 112, 133, 137, 138,
141, 142, 144, 154, 156, 157, 165,
.... 170-172, 174, 180, 181, 183,
.. 185, 196, 213, 219-221, 229, 252
Cordova 15, 22, 23,
.... 24, 26, 29, 33, 36, 41,
.... 136, 138, 139-146, 148-157,
.... 159, 161-168, 170-173, 175-189,
.. 191, 192, 194, 196, 199, 201-203,
........213, 214, 216-223, 226, 228, 229,
.... 237, 249-253, 257, 259,
.... 270, 305, 319, 324
Cordova Air Service
171, 172, 175, 178, 186, 251, 252
Cordova General 67
Cordova Times 24, 138, 143 145,
........151, 152, 155, 157, 161, 167,
.... 178, 179, 183, 185, 187, 188,
.........203, 216, 217, 221, 226, 229
Corvallis...................................... 176
Crawford, Cecil 82
Crawling tractor....... 12, 25, 26, 30,
32, 34, 37, 41, 43, 52, 90, 170, 192, 193
Creek, Slate................................ 168
Crichton, Clark 105
Crosson, Joe 11, 50, 51, 53, 55, 83,
87, 89, 104, 108, 109, 111, 114, 116,118,
119, 133, 135, 136, 144, 180, 184, 193, 194
Crosson, Lillian 4, 194, 200
Crosson, Marvel. 54, 68, 71, 92, 93
Croucher, Jeri 4
Curtis Robin 94
Curtis Wright engine 271
Curtiss JN-4D 57
Cushman Street 53
Cutting, Percy 28, 276,
.... 278, 282-294, 296, 297, 306

D

Dakar 64, 322
Dan Creek 30
Danforth, Danny . 75, 80, 83-85, 87
Dassow, Ethel............................. 276
Davidson Ditch
.... 41-44, 46, 47, 49, 51, 52
Davidson, J.M. 41
Dawes County-Chadron Museum
.... 12, 13, 14, 15
Dawson, Bucky 295
Day, Beth 203, 246, 265
DC-3 95
de Saint-Exupery, Antoine .. 61, 252
Deep sea diving 192
DeLong, Leon (Slim) 272
Destroyer 18
Detroit Arctic Expedition 73, 74
Detroiter, Stinson 114
Dieterle, Adolph . 146, 148, 151, 161
Dillingham 152
Dimond, Anthony 188, 217, 235, 256
Diomede 116
Doctor Shore 167
Dodson, James 297
Dodson, Millie 77
Dog teams
..... 35, 72, 78, 109, 129, 138, 239,
.... 240, 241, 249, 254, 267
Dolan, Anna May 140
Donohoe, Tom
.... 176, 178, 186-188, 258, 259
Dorbandt, Frank
..........93, 103, 104, 110, 114, 116
Driscoll, Tom 90
Dryer, Speed 337, 338
Duarat 64
Duarat, Didier 64
Dutch Harbor 211

E

Eagle Rock Aircraft Company .. 137
Eaglerock, Alexander 82

Eakstrom, Tim 4, 188
Earl 13
East Cape 130
Eckroth, Kathryn 282
Eckstrom, Tim 199
Eielson, Ben
.... 11, 12, 58, 73, 93, 96-98,
.... 100, 109, 135, 196, 200
Eielson-Borland search
9, 93, 112, 131, 184, 195, 196, 229, 230, 238
Eleanor Stoy Reed 131
Elliot, Grant 142, 198
Elliot's Chariot 142, 143
Elmendorf 214
Emmons, Don 273
Empress Theater 24
Endicott Mountains 240
England 8, 58
Eskimo 72, 74, 79, 102,
.... 122, 240-242, 245, 248
Estate
199, 226, 324, 331, 333, 334, 337
Executive, Spartan 273
Exposition Park 73

F

F.E. Company
38, 41, 42, 43, 45, 46, 47, 48, 221
FAA 214, 315, 321
FAA Alaskan Flyer 321
Fairbanks 8, 12, 25, 36-41, 43,
45-48, 50-57, 62, 67-69, 71-83, 85,
86, 89, 91-93, 97, 108-110, 112-114,
.121, 124, 126, 130, 131, 133-137,
.. 140-142, 144, 150, 153-157, 172,
.174, 182 185, 187, 192, 195, 196,
198, 200, 201, 203, 206, 208, 210, 211, 213,
.. 217-223, 225-232, 235, 237, 238,
240, 241, 242, 244, 245, 246, 247,
........248, 249, 250, 251, 252, 253,
... 254, 255, 257-267, 269-272, 297,
.... 298, 300-302, 305, 319, 323,
.... 329-331, 333-336, 339

Fairbanks, a Pictorial History 72
Fairbanks Airplane Company
.... 50, 54, 73, 81, 83
Fairbanks Airport 48, 226, 245
Fairbanks Daily News Miner
38, 222, 228, 232, 249, 253, 264, 335
Fairbanks Exploration Company
.... 38, 41, 47
Fairchild 71, 110, 121,
124, 125, 126, 127, 128, 129, 130, 131
Faith 41
Family crisis 270
Farewell dinner 134, 135
Fate 61, 106, 127,
..235, 266, 276, 307, 308, 317-320
Fate as the Hunter 308, 317
Fear of flying 178, 202, 236
Federal Highway Act of 1921 45
Final radio contact 235
Final Rites 133
Finley, J.D. 175
Fire extinguisher 169
Firepot
  105, 113, 122, 169, 182, 242, 260
Flight in America 58, 273
Flight school 68, 74, 81, 83, 87
Fluery, Amos 167
Flying weather 98, 99,
..131, 231, 244, 299, 301-304, 321
Fokker 60, 62, 74
Fokker, Anthony 59, 61
Fokker F VIII 62
Fokker FII 61
Fokker-the Man and the Aircraft
.... 61, 62
Ford, Henry 45
Ford Snowbird 166
Fort Yukon 112
Forty-mile country
.... 149, 156, 265, 335
Fox Film Corporation 73
Fox Film expedition 79
Fox Gulch 42

France 59, 60, 62, 63, 64, 321
Franklin, Pat 223, 245, 247, 324
Freighting 37-
40, 42, 48, 52, 114, 126, 197
French 59, 63, 64, 103, 167
Funeral flig 130

G

Gakona 82
Gann, Ernest K.
.... 307, 308, 317, 318, 322
Gatty, Harold 155, 156
Gebo, Robert ... 273, 276, 314, 324
Gentile, Don 116, 119
Geographic, National Society ... 250
Geographic orientation
..................................99, 193, 300
Gerard, Tom 89, 91, 93
Gill, Brendan 79
Gillam Airways 26, 33, 35, 69,
.... 133, 137, 141-144, 146-148,
.... 151-155, 157, 161, 165-168,
.... 171-176, 184, 186, 188,
.... 197, 199, 213, 218, 220,
.... 222, 225, 229, 231, 233,
.... 245, 247, 248, 252,
.... 253, 257, 259, 260, 264-266
Gillam, Baby...................... 204, 205
Gillam, Don . 204, 205, 207, 208, 210,
211, 267, 323, 328, 330, 331, 332, 340
Gillam, Elsie 326
Gillam estate 331, 337
Gillam Falls 339
Gillam Glacier 339
Gillam, Harold Jr.
........232, 323, 329, 334, 338, 340
Gillam Lake 339
Gillam, Maurine...... 204, 205, 206,
..208, 211, 249, 328, 330-333, 340
Gillam, Nell
.... 190, 202-212, 215, 228,
.... 266, 267, 269-271, 274, 323-340
Gillam Way 232, 339

Winona Gillam
.... 206-208, 210, 264, 327, 328,
.... 330-332, 334, 335, 340
Gillam-Danforth crash 87
Gillam's father 21
Gillam's mother135, 176, 177, 209, 323
Gilmore 41
Glacier Pilot 203, 246, 308
Glasgow, Paul 335, 338
Gleason, Bob
.... 104, 120, 122, 126, 184
Gleason, Robert 4
Godfrey, Sam 39
Gold mining 37
Gold ore concentrate 159
Goldstream 41
Goulet, Emil 22, 27, 133
Grandfather clause 258
Great Depression 143
Great Northern Airways.............. 95
Grief 323
Grumman Goose 274
Guard of honor 133
Guilt 9, 323, 324, 336
Gulf War 44

H

Hanna, Dallas G. 250
Hamilton . 102, 107, 111, 127, 128
Hamilton monoplane 102
Hanson, Bob 4
Harrais, Mrs. Martin.................... 141
Haugland, H.W. 325
Hazelton 168, 187
Hegener, Henri 61
Helen Van Campen 200, 204
Heroism 278
Higginbothem, Ed 294
Higgins, Cecil 10, 12, 13, 15,
.. 16, 19, 26, 32, 90, 93, 119, 163,
.... 193, 196, 209, 230, 304, 335
Hill, Fred 294
Hine, Stuart K. 224

Hines, Art 112
Hispano Suiza 74, 81, 83, 87
History of Aviation 57, 59, 60, 62, 63
Holt 12, 26, 30, 31, 32,
34, 35, 42, 44, 45, 47, 48, 51, 52, 308
Homer 338, 339
Homestead 33, 35
Honeymoon 216
Hook, Art 294
Hospital 76, 83, 84-86, 89, 150,
163, 164, 167, 173, 182, 184, 227,
238, 264, 267, 283, 292, 294, 296, 328
Houston 207, 265, 266, 269
Hubbard, Percy 112
Hubris 309
Hutchinson (Hutch), James
.... 4, 125, 129
Hutchinson, Palmer 74

I

Icebergs 214, 215
In The Shadow of Eagles 273
Iferiority complex...................... 201
Inner self 319
Inouye, Ron 4
Intermediate stops
.. 80, 219, 253, 255, 258, 264, 265
International Date Line 117
Ireland Neptune 145, 157

J

Jack Wade Creek 149, 260
Jacobs, Catherine 195
James, Reuben.................. 158, 173
James, Reuben, ... 173
Jefford, Jack 222, 247
Jeffords, Jack, ... 247
Jenny 57, 67-69,
.... 73, 75, 76, 83, 87, 89
Jessen's Weekly 297
Journal On Nature of Man-Pacific
Discoveries 235, 250
Judeo-Christian 318, 319

Judge Reed 197
Juneau
   168, 187, 222, 223, 259, 263, 274
Junker 62, 126, 127, 128, 129, 130
Junkers F-13 .... 110, 126, 129
Junkers, Hugo 62

K

Kangas, Hana 243
Kankakee 13
Kate Snow White 247
Katella 151, 219
Keiss, Marguerite 262
Kelly Bill 58
Kennecott Copper Company 23, 24
Kennecott Mine 28, 158
Kennedy, Kay
54, 200, 201, 202, 319, 320
Kennedy, Michael 223
Kennicott Glacier 28, 143
Kennicott River 31, 34
Ketchikan
168, 278, 284, 292, 296, 314, 315, 320
Ketchikan Historical Aircraft Society
Museum 296
Ketchikan Radio 277, 315
Keystone Leoning 167, 213
King, George 83, 128
Kirckhoff, M.J. 170, 216
Kirkpatrick, M.D. 166, 167, 168,
.... 169, 171, 172, 191, 219, 249
Klerekoper 240, 249
Knutson, Adena
4, 145, 147, 183, 196
Kodiak 335, 336, 337, 338, 339
Kodiak Mirror 337, 338
Koluchin Bay 117
Koyukuk 51
Krammer, Frank 273
Kuskokwim 38, 191, 250, 253, 254,
256-259, 262 267, 273, 300, 306, 324
Kuskokwim River
.... 191, 258, 267, 300, 306, 324

L

Lacey Street Hotel 336
Lake Eyak
139, 140, 151, 156, 161, 163, 179, 189
Lake Eyak Airport 161
landing lights 191, 302
Langewiesche, Wolfgang ... 50, 302
Larison, Herb 36
Last flight
.........88, 131, 262, 266, 307, 311
Latecoere Airplane Company 64
Latecoere, Pierre 64
Legend 8, 230,
.... 231, 243, 248, 256, 299-302,
.... 307, 309, 311, 316, 321
Legitimate birth 333, 334
Lein, Bert 225, 227, 231, 253
Leoning 167, 168, 174-177,
.... 184, 208, 213, 264, 267, 269
Lerdahl, Herman 272, 273
LeTourneau 45
Levanevsky, Sigismund 235
License 54, 56, 69, 72,
......82, 90, 91, 110, 113, 114, 141
Liebes, Arnold 241
Lindbergh Alone 79
Lindbergh, Anne Morrow
.... 178, 236, 304, 305
Lindbergh, Charles 58,
.... 57, 70, 74, 79, 174, 178, 174,
.... 202, 304, 305, 236, 305, 317
Lindbergh of Russia 235
Lockheed Aircraft 72
Lockheed Electra... 222, 271, 272, 278
Lockheed Vega 72, 73, 101, 247
Loftholm, Bill 4
Loftholm, William 273, 277
Lomen, Alfred 114
Los Angeles 19, 21, 73, 92, 187
Lower-48 .... 11, 24
Luck 15, 19, 72,
.... 255, 288, 291, 299-301,
.... 307, 308, 309, 311, 317-321

Lyle and Dorrance Air Service
.... 175, 215, 252

M

Ma Barnes
.... 95, 144, 155, 197, 199, 220
Mail delivery
58, 146, 148, 149, 253, 256, 259, 263
Mail, Star routes 146, 180
Mariechild, Diane 36
Martin, James 73
McCarthy 23, 24, 27-35, 95, 96,
.136, 137, 140-143, 146, 148, 149,
.152, 163, 164, 166, 170-172, 179,
187, 191, 215, 216, 219, 227, 229, 319
McCrary, John 163
McCrary, Nels 163, 164
McDermott, H.W. 188
McGarvey, Lois 335, 336, 337
McGee Airways
.... 166, 170, 174, 202
McGee, Linous 203
McGee, Nell 202, 215, 334
McGrath Roadhouse 301
McKaughan, Henretta 267
McManus 41
Meade River 241
Meals, Owen 82, 137, 152
Mean streak 210, 327
Mercy flights 199, 319
Merrill Field 157, 158, 162, 214
Merrill, Russ 76, 93
Metzdorf, Dewey 276, 282
Michner, James 190
Midnight sun flights 232
Migeo, Marcel 61
Mills, Stephen 213, 256
Minchumina 191, 192, 267
Mitchell, Billy 256
Model T Ford 166
Moller, Fred 150
Monetary claim 334
Moore, Johnny 173

Moose Hall Auditorium 133
Morgan, Len 120
Morgan, Stanley 239, 242, 244
Morris, Stuart 97
Morrison-Knudsen
.... 210, 273, 276, 292
Morse Code 217, 304
Moton, Jack 158
Mountainous terrain . 137, 138, 315
Move down the mountain 286
Move to Fairbanks 39, 68
Mt. Blackburn 28, 133, 149
Mt. Wrangell 28, 155, 181
Mudhole Smith, Alaska Flier 172

N

Nabesna Mine
146, 153, 156, 159, 160, 171, 182, 183
Nabesna River 150, 339
Naske and Rowinski 71, 72
National Transportation Safety
Board 86
Navigable rivers 137, 138
Navigational aids 58, 78
Navy ... 13, 16, 17, 19, 20, 69, 70
NC 711Y 270
NC 733N 270
NC 780E 109
Negative attitude 307, 309
Nell's diamond ring 336
Nestor, Thomas 188
New Miner 250
News Miner 38, 48, 52, 67, 71,
... 83-86, 90, 95-97, 112, 120, 133,
........135, 200, 204, 221, 222, 228,
. 232, 236, 238, 240, 242, 244-249,
.... 251, 253, 257, 262-265, 335
Newsweek 312
Nieminen, Matt 115, 125
Nizina bridge project 30
Nizina Mining District 28, 29
Nizina River 28, 29, 30, 31, 33
No Kill'em Gillam 89, 229

Nome 38, 40, 73, 80, 93, 103, 105, 109, 110, 114, 115, 125, 126, 130, 140, 153, 221, 247, 266, 270
North Cape 96, 97, 101-104, 106, 108, 117, 118, 120, 129, 195
Northern Consolidated Airways 300, 324
Northwestern and Copper River Railroad 39, 138, 156
Notarized statement 325, 326
Nud, Barbara 142
Nulato 114, 125

O

Off-airport landing 91, 141, 148, 161
O'Neil, Geraldine 187
Onman 117, 118
Open cockpits 118
Oregon............................ 167, 176, ... 208, 269, 329, 333, 334
Osborne, Lillian ... 55, 71, 193, 194
OX-5 .... 12, 67, 74, 83

P

P-47 119
PAA 222, 223, 259, 263
Pacific Alaska Airways 200, 217, 221, 222
Pall bearer 133
Pan American
93, 103, 200, 217, 222, 230, 236, 304
Pan American flight . 180, 200, 230
Pan American hangar 275
Panama Canal 45
Pardner Mining Company 172
Parmenter, E.E. .... 231-233, ... 236, 237, 241, 249, 253, 255
Passenger confidence 247, 304
Pasteur, Louis 40
Pastor Klerekoper 248, 249
Paul, St., Minnesota 271
Paxson 168, 169, 182

PBY 237
Pearl Harbor 208, 211, 212, 261, 270
Pelikii 117, 118
Permafrost 41, 43
Petersen, Ray 4, 263, 264, 300, 304
Physical safety 211, 329
Pilgrim ..... 168, 171, 177, 186-189, ... 213, 215-218, 220, 222, 223, ... 225, 226, 229, 230, 232, 233, ... 236, 238-241, 244, 248, 251, ... 253, 254, 260, 261, 264, 266, ... 267, 269, 270, 273, 300, 301, ... 302-304
Pilgrim # 739 216
Pilot error 87, 305, 312
Pioneer Air Museum ...... 8, 25, 45, .. 46, 154, 217, 218, 230, 264, 267
Pioneers of Alaska 135
Poker 181, 301, 302
Polar bear cubs 239, 245
Polar flight from Moscow 235
Pollack, Frank 225
Port of Valdez 72
Portland, Oregon 167
Post, Wiley ... 78, 79, 155, 180, 236
Potter, Jean 4, 40, 50, 51, 106, 113, 118, 149, 159, 160, 164, 244, 301, 311, 313
Power shovels 27, 44, 45
Pratt and Whitney 110, 188, 254, 271
Preflight 174, 175
Preparation for war 256
Primary cause 277, 311, 312
Prince George 168, 187
Prince Rupert 168
Prohibition amendment 24
Ptarmigan 149

R

Radio Range 277
Railroad speeder 156, 183
Rainy Pass 301

Reeve Aleutian Airways 261
Reeve, Bob 203, 246,
247, 297, 304, 308, 316, 317, 320
Reid, Pat 125, 130
Reid, Vernice 4, 195
Religion 318
Renshaw, Ray 293
Republic Pictures 232
Richardson Highway
..........72, 142, 158, 174, 220, 222
Rickerts Field 73
Robin Hood 8
Rodebaugh, James 51, 62
Rogers, Will 79, 93, 236
Romer Brothers 171, 172
Ross, Walter S. 80
Rosswog, John 167, 168
Rough, Howard 72
Ruby 130
Russian Siberia 96
Rust, Jessie 125
Ryan Aircraft Company 70

S

Safety record 74, 304
San Diego 20, 55, 56, 57,
.... 64, 67-71, 108, 145, 150, 194
San Diego Aerospace 67, 71
San Francisco 108, 235
Saunders, George 241
Scavenius, Jack 273
Scheduled airline 61, 317
Scheduled Flights
156, 219, 223, 252, 253, 257, 324
School, Spartan of Aeronautics 273
Seaberg, Custer 203
Seatbelts 61, 62, 175
Seattle 16, 19-22, 27, 33, 36, 39,
.....55, 69, 97, 121, 124, 135, 146,
. 153, 154, 159, 167, 175-177, 184,
.... 187, 195, 198, 211, 217, 218,
.... 220, 222, 230, 238, 259, 263,
... 264, 269, 274, 276, 277, 300, 307,

.........323, 325, 326, 329, 331, 334
Seltenreich, Bud 4, 32, 152, 170,
172, 179, 181, 185, 188, 199, 202, 214, 319
Seward 39, 72, 121, 124, 153,
.... 157, 188, 214, 217, 218, 300
Sharp eyes 149
Siberia 91, 96,
116, 118, 120, 121, 137, 195, 242
Siberian Arctic 9, 104, 126
Sikorsky 145
Siphons 42
Sir Gordon Taylor
............................269, 282, 299, 321
Skagway 168, 227, 229
Skookie 206, 207
Sleetmute 267
Slepnyov, Mavriki 129, 134
Smeaton Bay ... 286, 287, 293, 294
Smith, Clyde 297
Smith, Maury 244
Smith, Merle 172
Sourdough Sky 52, 78, 158,
.... 163, 177, 256, 269, 270, 274
South Atlantic 64
Spencer, T.M. 4, 93, 94, 112,
153, 157, 176, 179, 181, 257, 272
Spitsbergen 73, 101
SS Aleutian 222
SS Nanuk 96, 97,
.. 100, 102-110, 114, 115, 119-123,
.... 126, 127, 129-131, 135, 195
SS Northwestern 146
SS Tucson 292
SS Yukon 86, 136, 150, 221
St. Joseph's, Hospital 85
Standard, Stinson 110
Star Airlines 259, 263
Star Air Service 162
Starkey, Harold 4, 160
Stearman C-2B.............................. 82
Stearman Mail Winds 167, 213
Stevens, Robert W. (Bob) . 4, 12, 47,
......51, 52, 55, 77, 78, 81, 82, 84,

... 85, 87-89, 91, 92, 97, 100, 103, ... 105, 107, 109, 110, 113, 116, 122-125, 128-131, 133, 134, 137, 142, 143, 145, 165, 170, 198, 202, 240, 300
Stinson Detroiter ... 77, 102, 104, 114
Stinson Standard 110
Stock market crash 96
Stony River 267
Stroecker, Ed 336
Superstition 317, 318
Swallow 430N 166
Swallow Aircraft Company 167
Swallow biplane 89, ... 112
Swartman, Gifford 125
Swenson, Marion 122, 127
Swenson, Olaf 96, 100, 109, 122, 123, 135
Szent-Gyorgyi, Albert 40

T

Taylor and Munson 57, 59, 60, 62, 63
Telegraph Creek 168
Teller ..101-110, 112-116, 118, 121, ... 125, 126, 130, 131, 135, 195
Territorial Legislature 139
Territory of Alaska . 10, 135, 146, 271, 325, 333, 334
The Alaskan Miner 262
The Eighth Sea 87
The Flying North 40, 50, 106, 149, 159, 164, 244, 301, 311
The Last Hero 80
The Line 64
The Sky Beyond 269, 282, 321
Thomas, Sode 21, 26
Thompson, Charles 109
Thompson Pass 136, 173, 174
Tibbits, Joseph ...... 276, 283, 284, ... 286-288, 292-294, 296, 297
Tibbs family 189, 213
Time Magazine 44
Time-Life Publications 164

Tom Mix 24
Tondoff, Dirk 223
Tonsina Roadhouse 145
Toulouse 64
Toward .85, 107, 191, 290, 291, 295, 314
Town Lake . 26, 142, 147, 151, 182, 185, 196
Transcontinental Air . 178, 305, 317
Trapline 214
Travelaire 77, 78
Tri-motor 305
Tulsa, Oklahoma 177

U

U.S. Department of Commerce 72, 139, 141
Unalakeet 126
Uncle Willie 208

V

Valdez ...... 26, 82, 134, 136, ... 137, 140, 141, 144, 151-153, ... 157, 158, 161, 162, 173-175, ... 196, 198, 199, 213, 219-223, ... 232, 233, 247-249, 251
Valdez City Council 141
Valdez Museum . 30, 136, 155, 232
Valdez Trail 142
Valley, A.J. 150, 157, 161
Vanderpool, Bob 267
Varney Airlines 167
Vault Creek 42
VFR 310
Vultee 272, 273

W

Wachel, Pat 201, 204, 310
Waco ..... 0 , 51, 80, 109, 110, 114, ... 115, 116, 118, 119, 123, 130
Walker Lake 82, 92
Walsh, Rose 334, 337
Waltka, John 273

Warner-Scarab 112, 148
Warren, Jack 106, 118
Washburn, Bradford 250
Waugaman, Candy 38, 43, 46, 227
Weather decision
.... 136, 301, 302, 303, 304
Weeks Field 12, 50, 52, 53, 73,
83, 88, 91, 93, 125, 131, 133, 144,
182, 196, 227, 230, 254, 255, 261
Western Civilization 63, 318
Whalen 116
Wheeler, Hobie 322
White River hunt 144
Whitehorse 95, 223, 227
Whitham, Carl 146, 148, 182
Wien Alaska Airways ...73, 74, 249
Wien Consolidated Airlines 266
Wien, Noel..................... 11, 12, 53,
....73, 76, 80, 85, 89, 92, 93, 102,
.... 138, 202, 230, 297, 299, 300
Wien, Ralph 80, 92, 93
Wiley Post-Will Rogers 236
Wilkins, George Hubert
........72, 73, 86, 87, 101, 237, 239
Williams, J. Gerald 324, 334, 337
Winchell, Florence 204
Winchell, Oscar
149, 158, 159, 161, 199, 307, 311
Winging It 222, 247, 255
Wiseman 76, 77
Wissler, Eddie 239

Wold, Jo Anne 47, 89, 203, 2
Wolfe, Lucille 188
Wolfert, Ira 119
Wood, Earl 157, 158, 165, 170, 171
World War I..................... 25, 44, 45,
.............57, 58, 60, 63, 64, 70, 87,
.........116, 120, 187, 256, 271, 317
Wrangell Mountain Range
.... 23, 28, 140, 181
Wrangell-St Elias Range ... 179, 339
Wright brothers 57
Wright J4A 54
Wright, Wylie R. 141
WWI 59, 60, 63

Y
Yakataga 151, 180, 219
Yeager, Chuck 119
Yukon Club Flying 95
Yukon River............................... 112
Yukon Stove 301
Yukon Territory 223, 260
Young, Ed 83, 85, 89, 90,
..93, 109, 110, 114, 115, 130, 135

Z
Zehner, Kathy 334
Zenith 6, 109,
.... 140, 146, 147, 151-154,
.... 156-169, 172, 174, 182-186
Zenith Aircraft Corporation 145